THE CRUSADES

THE CRUSADES

BY

HANS EBERHARD MAYER

TRANSLATED BY

JOHN GILLINGHAM

OXFORD UNIVERSITY PRESS

Oxford University Press, Walton Street, Oxford OX2 6DP

Oxford New York Toronto
Delhi Bombay Calcutta Madras Karachi
Kuala Lumpur Singapore Hong Kong Tokyo
Nairobi Dar es Salaam Cape Town
Melbourne Auckland
and associated companies in
Beirut Berlin Ibadan Nicosia

ISBN 0 19 873016 0

The German edition was originally published in 1965
© 1965 W. Kohlhammer Gmbh, Stuttgart
This translation © Oxford University Press 1972

First published 1972
Reprinted 1976, 1978, 1981, 1984, 1985

Printed in Great Britain by
Richard Clay (The Chaucer Press) Ltd,
Bungay, Suffolk

TO
FRIEDRICH BAETHGEN
OCTOGENARIAN
PRESIDENT
of the
MONUMENTA GERMANIAE HISTORICA
(*1947–1958*)
under whom
I was privileged to serve

PREFACE

FOR every author there is a special pleasure in seeing his work translated into another language; the fact of translation gives him some confidence that he has written something of value. Naturally I hope that this is true of this book. But there were, in addition, some very practical and down-to-earth considerations which led to the English translation of my *Geschichte der Kreuzzüge* (first published as a paperback, Stuttgart 1965). The English-speaking reader is fortunate in having excellent—indeed the best—general books on the crusades at his disposal. He can choose between Sir Steven Runciman's three-volume *History of the Crusades*, a *tour de force* of English historical writing, and the important collective work, *History of the Crusades*, edited by Kenneth M. Setton (Institute for Advanced Study, Princeton) in which both American and European scholarship may be seen at their best. Both works are indispensable for anyone who wishes to study the crusades at all seriously. But what has hitherto been lacking is an account of the crusades which is brief as well as being based on modern scholarship. To find good, short histories in English we have to go back to W. B. Stevenson's book, *The Crusaders in the East* (1907), and to the masterly article by Ernest Barker in the 1911 edition of the *Encyclopaedia Britannica*. In their day these sketches were excellent examples of English historical scholarship, but inevitably the questions now asked by historians are often very different ones. So there is a gap which this book attempts to fill. I hope that it will be useful to university students as well as to those members of the general public who are interested in the crusades. To this end I have made some additions and alterations to the text in order to take account of the most recent research; but the essential character of the German edition remains, I hope, unchanged. In particular, the bibliographical notes have been brought up to date and I would like to take this opportunity to draw special attention to the important two-volume work by Joshua Prawer, *Histoire du royaume latin de Jérusalem*. The first volume was published in 1969. Since I have not been able to take account of works published after December 1970 I have not had the advantage of seeing the second volume which, although officially a 1970 publication, was not available until May 1971. And, of course, it still remains true that anyone who wishes to study the crusades in greater detail must turn to Runciman and Setton as well as to the specialist literature to which I refer in the notes.

Faced by the perennial problem of the transliteration of oriental place and personal names, the translator and I decided, in the interests of readability and a simpler type, to renounce all diacritical signs. In most cases we have deliberately adopted Runciman's system of transliteration in order to make things easier for anyone who wishes to go on to read Runciman's work.

I dedicate this book to the Nestor of German medieval historians, Friedrich Baethgen, in honour of his eightieth birthday. He was professor of history, first at Königsberg and then at Berlin, at that time outstanding among German universities. For the crucial decade after the Second World War he was President of one of the most distinguished of all research institutes for medieval history. This was the Monumenta Germaniae Historica which had owed its origin to the patriotic spirit which characterized the approach to history in the period of the Wars of Liberation against Napoleon. Later in the nineteenth century the Monumenta Germaniae set a new standard of scholarship in the quality of the editions of historical texts in medieval Latin which were produced under its auspices. For nine years Friedrich Baethgen was also President of the Bayerische Akademie der Wissenschaften. But it is, of course, his writings rather than his offices which made him well-known in the English-speaking academic world.

Friedrich Baethgen it was who gave me the chance to join the Monumenta Germaniae. It was the decisive moment of my career. For twelve years I served the Monumenta Germaniae and so it was that a close bond was created which no change in the external circumstances of my life has been able to alter. It was not just the length of time which created this bond. It was also the meticulous work which was expected of me by the members of the Institute, and especially by my immediate superior, Theodor Schieffer; it was being given the opportunity to learn much; above all, it was the consciousness of belonging to a living tradition, a tradition established by some of the greatest names in German historical learning—the scholars who had made the Monumenta Germaniae famous. Thus in dedicating this book in gratitude to Friedrich Baethgen who opened for me the doors of the Monumenta Germaniae, I would also like to express my thanks to the Monumenta Germaniae Historica for those twelve years when I enjoyed complete freedom to research.

I cannot conclude without first thanking others. During the preparation of this translation both my German publisher, W. Kohlhammer, and the Clarendon Press have always been most helpful. My good friend and eminent colleague, Karl Leyser, of Magdalen College, Oxford, constantly encouraged me to have the book translated. I was extremely fortunate to find in John Gillingham, of The London School of Economics, a translator who is also a medievalist. I would like to pay my particular thanks to him for the boundless patience with which he has answered my questions and accommodated my wishes. On questions of content I have had the benefit of his friendly criticism and wide historical knowledge. It has been a most enjoyable co-operative effort; I could not have wished for a better translator.

When I see this book in print I shall look back with nostalgia to the months when, among other things, I put the finishing touches to the English edition; to the untroubled months when I was a guest in the gracious atmosphere of a scholar's paradise—the villa of Dumbarton Oaks in Georgetown, Washington D.C.

Washington D.C.
January 1971.

CONTENTS

LIST OF MAPS

1· THE MEDITERRANEAN REGION
IN 1095

THE geography of the world as men pictured it in the late eleventh century differed hardly at all from the conceptions formulated in classical times. It is important to note this before taking a closer look at the history of the crusades for, when the crusades were over, this, together with much else, had changed. Although the teaching of Ptolemy of Alexandria was generally accepted in the early Middle Ages, his theory of the spherical shape of the earth—a Greek doctrine which was fiercely opposed by the Romans—had been almost completely forgotten owing to the great influence of the encyclopedist, Isidore of Seville. But by the end of the crusading period a growing acquaintance with Ptolemy's own writings had given a new lease of life to this theory. Above all, a very great deal had been learnt about the inhabited world which lay east of Europe. This was new knowledge, based on the descriptions of travellers, and not merely the revival of traditional learning. By contrast, in the earlier period between the heyday of the Roman Empire and the start of the crusades, the frontiers of the known world had remained relatively stable, although some advances had been made as a result of the spread of Christianity into Germany, Scandinavia, and some parts of the Byzantine Empire.

From a European point of view the centre of gravity of the world of 1095 still lay in the Mediterranean lands. It was here that the pope lived; here were the capitals of the eastern and western empires, Constantinople and Rome. The imperial crown of the West was worn, it is true, by the kings of Germany, but a king of Germany (or rather, to use his contemporary title, a king of the Romans) could obtain that crown only from the hand of the pope and at Rome. Moreover, with the exception of Spain, the Mediterranean Sea was the great dividing line between the two world-religions, Christianity and Islam. Broadly speaking, the north coast was Christian, the south coast Muslim. In places where the Muslims had advanced north of this line they had either already been forced to retreat, as in France (c. 973) and Sicily (1091), or they were now in the process of being pushed back.

It might have been expected that Europe would be united as it gathered its strength for a vigorous counter-attack on the Muslims whose invasions had caused so much misery during the eighth, ninth, and tenth centuries. But although the continent had recovered from the direct consequences of these invasions and those of the Vikings and Magyars, and was once again in the ascendant, there was still no question of there being anything remotely approaching a coherent European political structure such as had once been supplied by the Carolingian Empire. Indeed on the eve of the crusades Europe was caught up in fierce internecine struggles. In the Investiture Contest the papacy, reformed and strengthened during the course of the eleventh century, attempted to shake off the protecting hand of the secular power. The visible symbol of this power was the royal practice of installing bishops and abbots in their offices by investing them with ring and staff. By virtue of the so-called 'proprietary church law' (*Eigenkirchenrecht*), the king then claimed rights of lordship over them. In the nature of things the pope's most important opponent in this contest was the emperor. Henry IV (1056–1105) broke completely with the pope and recognized an anti-pope, Guibert of Ravenna, as Clement III (1080–1100). The climax of the Investiture Contest—Henry IV's penance at Canossa (1077) and then the collapse of the position of his papal opponent, Gregory VII (1073–85)—was, it is true, already past; none the less the emperor was still excommunicated and agreement a long way off. It did not come until the Concordat of Worms in 1122. At any rate when a pope planned a crusade he left the emperor out of his reckoning.

But neither could he count upon the kings of France and England. Philip I of France (1060–1108) had been excommunicated in 1094 for sending his wife Bertha packing. William Rufus of England (1087–1100), a son of William the Conqueror, was still preoccupied with the consolidation of Norman power in England. His policies, anyway, were usually extremely anti-clerical. North Italy was caught up in the imperial-papal struggle; South Italy had only recently been subjugated by the Normans who had driven out the Byzantines and Saracens. In the Iberian peninsula the kings of Asturia-Leon, Navarre, Aragon, and Portugal were all engaged in expelling the Muslims, though not until 1492 was complete success finally achieved.

Since 1054 not even the Christian Church had been at one. On the surface, the schism, still unhealed today, was the result firstly of an interpolation of the creed by the West which the Eastern Church was unable to accept, and secondly of the liturgical problem of whether leavened or unleavened bread should be used at communion. But just as important as the growing differences in theology and ritual were matters of politics—church politics like the question of the primacy of Rome and secular politics like the rivalry between the two 'Roman' empires of East and West. The cultural differences between the Greek-speaking East and the Latin West were too great for the unity of Christendom to survive for long.

Not that all relations between East and West had been broken off since 1054.[1] On the contrary, the wish for a union of the Churches permeated papal policy throughout the Middle Ages, and time and again it had an influence on the history of the crusades. In Rome it was recognized that the schism in no way freed the West from a responsibility towards their Christian brothers in the East. Even before the crusades in 1074 Gregory VII had wanted to organize an expedition to help the Eastern Empire against the invading Seldjuks—though presumably he hoped thereby to reap advantages of his own. Then in 1078 he completely reversed his policy when a marriage alliance which he had just helped to arrange between Robert Guiscard, the Norman ruler of south Italy, and a Byzantine princess, fell through as the result of a palace revolution in Constantinople. Pope Gregory excommunicated the new emperor and then the next one—Alexius Comnenus (1081–1118), who also obtained the imperial throne by means of a palace revolution. In him, after long years of internal dissension, Byzantium had again found an energetic ruler. In these circumstances there was no immediate chance of a union of the Churches.

In 1071 the Normans had captured Bari, the last Byzantine stronghold in Italy. Ten years later, just when Alexius Comnenus ascended the throne, they moved on to attack the empire itself at Epirus. With Venetian help Alexius was able to drive the Normans back; then Robert Guiscard had to return home to deal with unrest in south Italy, where he died in 1085. The Venetians came out of it best, for they obtained far-reaching commercial privileges in return for their help. These privileges undermined the traditional trading system of Byzantium, established the long-lasting political influence of Venice in the Adriatic and provided a spring-board for further expansion towards Constantinople, the Eastern Mediterranean, and the Levant.

For Byzantium, however, the Muslims presented a greater threat than the Normans. Very soon after Muhammad's death it had become clear that the new religion was possessed of an enormous political energy. Borne up by the idea of the jihad, the holy war, the Arabs forced their way east and west in a breathtaking expansion of power. (Whereas the Christian holy war was, in theory if not always in practice, a defensive undertaking, the jihad was right from the beginning a war of aggression.) In the second half of the seventh century they conquered the whole of North Africa. In 711 the Ommayad Tariq crossed the Straits of Gibraltar and destroyed the Visigothic kingdom of Spain. Not until 732, when the Carolingian Charles Martel won the Battle of Poitiers, was the Arab torrent dammed. But the Arab conquest was not confined to this part of Europe. In the East they posed a serious threat to Byzantium. In the West they overran Sicily in the ninth century and established themselves in South Italy, where, in 982, they decisively defeated the Roman Emperor Otto II. From bases on the coast of Provence they devastated South France and Switzerland. They controlled the Alpine passes, and it was on the Great St. Bernard that they captured Majolus, the universally venerated Abbot of Cluny in 972. This notorious ambush marked a turning point. Gradually energetic counter-attacks were organized and the Arabs were driven out of France and, by the Normans, out of Italy and Sicily. In Spain, however, they were more firmly established and here the *Reconquista* lasted until the end of the Middle Ages.

Islam too was torn by schism, between Sunnite and Shi'ite. The development of this split must be traced in rather more detail since it had considerable influence on Muslim history in the period of the crusades.[2] It went back to the situation at the death of Muhammad. One group recognized Abu Bakr, one of Muhammad's close associates, as caliph, i.e. as the prophet's representative. The other group believed that Ali—as Muhammad's cousin and son-in-law—had a better claim by virtue of his kinship. And in fact Ali did become the fourth caliph. Ali's supporters called themselves Shi'ites (Shi'atu Ali means Ali's party) and would recognize only his descendants as caliphs. The opposing party called themselves Sunnites because they believed that they had held fast to the correct tradition. (Sunna means the orally transmitted sayings of Muhammad.) The Abbasid caliphs of Baghdad were Sunnites since they had to be very orthodox in order to make up for being upstarts who had wiped out the legitimate Ommayad caliphs of Damascus.

On the other side because Ali had had several wives it was inevitable that the Shi'ites too would split up. They all agreed that the line of Imams (the successors of Ali) would have to come to an end at some time, because the last Imam would work on in concealment in order to reappear as the Mahdi, an eschatological saviour who would bring justice to the world and convert all men to the Shi'a. But they could not agree on which of the Imams was the last one. Depending on the number of Imams they recognized the different Shi'ite sects were known as the 'Fivers', the 'Seveners', and the 'Twelvers'. The last made up the moderate wing of the Shi'ites, while the 'Seveners' who regarded the seventh Imam, Ismail, as the Mahdi—and were therefore called the Ismailites—formed an extremist group. Thanks to their leaning towards social revolution and to their close links with the Muslim guilds they were able to increase their numbers and, in 909, to found the Fatimid caliphate of North Africa (after 973 at Cairo) as a rival to the Abbasids of Baghdad.

The Fatimid caliph was now looked upon as the Mahdi. Even so he soon became as dependent on the army and bureaucracy as was his rival in Baghdad. When, in 1094, al-Afdal the vizier of Egypt chose a pliable younger son, al-Mustali, as the new caliph, thus passing over Nizar, the eldest son of the previous ruler, the Fatimids lost the support of the Ismailites. Within the Ismailite movement the centre of gravity shifted to its extreme wing, the Nizarites, the Persian branch of which became famous as the Assassins. The name derived from a corrupt Latin form of hashish, the drug with which they were said to intoxicate themselves. Tightly organized under a kind of 'Grandmaster' they elevated murder to the level of a religious duty as well as a political weapon. Early in the twelfth century some of them settled in North Syria. Savagely persecuted by the Sunnites they became a source of insecurity and terror for Sunnite and Christian alike. The troubadours of the thirteenth century gave eloquent expression to the fear felt by the Christians. Above all the Assassins fought to prevent the creation of a united Sunnite front which would have been directed against them just as much as against the Christian states formed as a result of the First Crusade. In this way they gave indirect help to the crusading states.

The world of Islam which had once been a domain of the Arabs was given a new political structure by the arrival of Turks from Central Asia.[3] Originally shamanist in their beliefs the Turks became Sunnite Muslims during the tenth century. In a sense they saved Islam because they brought to it the warrior spirit of the nomad just at the time when the political drive of the Arabs was fading. Particularly important were the Seldjuks, Turkish tribesmen who within little more than fifty years built up an immense empire which stretched from Khorassan and Persia to the

Caucasus, from Mesopotamia to Syria and Palestine and as far as the Hijaz, the birthplace of Islam. The orthodox caliphs were freed from the Shi'ite overlordship of the Persian Buyids only to become tools in the hands of the Seldjuk sultans. Sultan Alp-Arslan (1063–73) pushed still further west and in 1071 defeated the Byzantine army at Manzikert in eastern Anatolia. From that date on Turks migrated almost imperceptibly into Anatolia and slowly but surely undermined the Byzantine provincial administration. The reign of Sultan Malik Shah (1077–92) witnessed the final expulsion of the Byzantines out of what was the real power house of their empire. This left the Greek Church of Anatolia in a difficult position and at the same time it added to the problems facing pilgrims on the land route to the Holy Land, though not so much as scholars once thought. But for Byzantium the loss of Anatolia remained a catastrophe[3a].

It cannot be proved that the Turks actually did oppress the Christians in the East, as western sources, among them the speech attributed to Urban II at Clermont, maintained. In the conquered districts the native Christians were treated just as they always had been by the Muslims—as a subject minority population who paid taxes but who enjoyed the protection of Islamic law and a certain measure of freedom of worship. What happened to them at the time of the conquest was the inevitable result of war and was felt by all sections of the population. In particular the non-Melkite Churches of the East, Jacobites and Nestorians who did not speak Greek and who had been oppressed by the Greek Orthodox Church on account of their leanings towards monophysitism and other heresies, had no reason at all to regret the change. Their writers sang the praises of Malik Shah, who after the disturbances of the conquest symbolized the restoration of order, just as loudly as did the Muslim chroniclers. Apart from the persecution under Caliph Hakim (1009), there is no evidence of anti-Christian pogroms in the eleventh century. The persecution unleashed in Jerusalem by the Turcoman Atsiz in 1078 was definitely anti-Fatimid in character and the Christians were probably spared. It is significant that no appeal for help was ever sent to the West by the eastern Christians. When Urban II and the propagandists for the crusade emphasized the persecution of the Eastern Christians it was either because they did not know the real situation or because they wanted to arouse a vague feeling of resentment in Europe.

In Europe too the Byzantine emperor had a Turkish problem to face. The Petchenegs, a tribe of Turkish origin now settled in the Danube valley, allied with the Seldjuks of Asia Minor, and in

1091–2 they attacked Byzantium on two fronts. But in April 1091 Alexius, with characteristic forcefulness, defeated the Petchenegs so decisively that they practically disappeared from history. In Asia Minor, however, the Seldjuks were too firmly established for Alexius to be able to strike as effectively against them. He had to be content with coming to terms (1092) with Sultan Kilij Arslan (1092–1107). When the great Seldjuk empire broke up on the death of Malik Shah in 1092, Kilij Arslan's share of the inheritance was a part of Anatolia out of which the Rum-Seldjuk sultanate of Iconium (Rum means [East-] Rome) was gradually built up. The treaty of 1092 gave Alexius a respite from Seldjuk attacks and allowed the sultan to consolidate his own position in Asia Minor.

In Syria, however, Malik Shah's death led to serious disintegration lasting for more than a decade, by the end of which there had emerged a system of Seldjuk emirates so delicately balanced that the least alteration in the political relations of one with another necessarily involved the reconstruction of the entire system. This explains the incessant variation in the complicated pattern of Syrian alliances in the first half of the twelfth century. The newly created crusading states immediately became extra pieces on the political board.

Meanwhile there had been changes in the West. Gregory VII had died in 1085 and after the brief pontificate of Victor III, Urban II (1088–99) had become pope. As a diplomat he was more flexible than Gregory and he tried to improve relations with Byzantium.[4] In 1089 he sent an embassy of reconciliation to Alexius and released him from the sentence of excommunication. Alexius too was conciliatory and so between emperor and pope friendly relations were established which neither side wished to endanger by undue emphasis on the theological disagreements. Alexius was ready to continue the old practice of inserting the pope's name into the patriarchal lists (the diptychs) if Urban would send a satisfactory statement of faith within a fixed period of time. Nothing came of it because Urban was not prepared to do this, but neither of them treated it as vital so no harmful consequences followed. Urban was quite content that Alexius, now that he was safe from the assaults of the Normans and on tolerably good terms with the pope, should break off the negotiations with the Emperor Henry IV which he had earlier keenly pursued.

For his part Alexius could now concentrate on re-organizing the Byzantine army which had been declining in standard ever since its overwhelming defeat at Manzikert. One way of doing this was by hiring western mercenaries. One of the reasons he entered into negotiations on Church unity with Urban II may have been his hope of obtaining such men. Western mercenaries were nothing new in Byzantium. In earlier centuries an élite of foreign troops had formed the Varangian Guard at Constantinople. Despite the traditional enmity between Normans and Greeks there had often been contingents of Norman soldiers in the ranks of the Byzantine army; their fighting spirit was well-known and much feared. Even though Byzantium enjoyed a respite from war after 1092 this did not mean that Alexius could afford to do without mercenaries. Thus when he met Count Robert of Flanders on a pilgrimage he asked the count if he could supply him with such troops. And when, in March 1095, Urban II held a council at Piacenza to deal generally with Church reform, it was not surprising that envoys from the Byzantine emperor were also present to let it be known how welcome western mercenaries would be. Clearly they exaggerated the dangers facing the empire and so in papal circles men came to hold the opinion that only drastic measures could save Byzantium—and at the same time the Christian Church in the East—measures which might then lead to a reunion of the Churches under the primacy of Rome. Our information on the Council of Piacenza comes from the chronicler Bernold of Constance, and it is today generally accepted as being trustworthy though there was once a good deal of doubt on the subject. The discovery, some twenty years ago, of a thirteenth-century Byzantine chronicle tended to confirm Bernold's account for although itself written much later, the chronicle appears to contain excerpts from reliable contemporary historians. It also tells us that when Alexius appealed for help at Piacenza he deliberately emphasized the idea of help for Jerusalem because he anticipated that this would prove an effective propaganda slogan in Europe. In reality, of course, his own aims were quite different. He hoped to reconquer Anatolia and a crusade was the last thing he wanted. He had expected some mercenaries, in contingents small enough to be easily controlled, not the huge armies of knights which in fact set out on the first crusade. If he could have foreseen what was about to hit him he would probably have been very reticent indeed. But the keyword, Jerusalem, had been spoken and events now took their course. Little more than six months after the appeal for help at Piacenza, Urban II, at Clermont, called for a crusade.

2 · THE ORIGINS OF THE CRUSADES

POPE URBAN II opened the Council of Clermont on 18 November 1095—the moment that has gone down in history as the starting point of the crusades.[5] Since the summer of that year he had been travelling through south and south-east France; at Le Puy on 15 August he issued the summons to the council. Although Urban had made careful preparations for a discussion of the question of a crusade by the Church assembly, there was at first nothing which gave any hint of the extraordinary events which were to follow. The council was attended mostly by French bishops and it dealt mostly with internal Church affairs which particularly concerned the French clergy; with general questions of reform, lay investiture, and simony; as well as with the adultery of the king of France. Also on the agenda was the peace of God, i.e. the prohibition of feuding on certain days and the immunity of certain people, places, and things. The pope's presence meant that the Peace of God movement which had hitherto been organized on a purely regional basis, was now recognized by the papacy and its application was extended to cover the whole Church. Only one of the decrees of the Council dealt with the crusade. It laid down the conditions under which a crusader qualified for a spiritual reward.

The moment which gave the council its special place in history came right at the end on 27 November. On this day the pope was due to make an important speech. So many clerks and laymen gathered to listen to him that the meeting had to be held in a field outside the town. We have four reports of Urban's speech. None of them is unquestionably authentic. Some were written after the turn of the century; and they all differ considerably from one another. None the less it is possible to reconstruct his speech in rough outline, though naturally the actual words are irrecoverable.[6] With Gallic eloquence Urban painted a vivid picture of the supposed oppression of the Christian Churches in the east. The Seldjuks had occupied Asia Minor; the churches and Holy Places had been destroyed and defiled by heathens. Now even Antioch, the city of St. Peter, had been taken. Here then was a noble task for the knights of Christendom whose other activities had been restricted by the Peace of God. In moving words the pope called upon both rich and poor to help their Christian brothers in the east. In this way peace might be restored to Christendom; there would be an end to the fratricidal wars in Europe, to the oppression of widows and orphans and to the threats made against churches and abbeys by a rapacious nobility. In denouncing what was, in effect, a state of civil war, the pope (according to Robert the Monk's version of his speech) explained it in terms of the widespread poverty and malnutrition which resulted from inadequate cultivation of the soil.

The success of this appeal was extraordinary. *Deus lo volt*—God wills it—was the cry which went up from the listening crowd. Bishop Adhemar of Le Puy, who had undoubtedly known of the pope's plans for some time, was the first to take the cross. Many of those present followed his example. Garments were cut up into the shape of crosses which each of them attached to his shoulder in imitation of Christ (Matthew 10: 38). On 1 December messengers came from the powerful count of Toulouse, Raymond IV of St. Gilles, announcing their lord's readiness to take part in the crusade. Since Raymond must have sent his messengers before he could have heard any news of Urban's speech, it is clear that he had advance knowledge of the pope's intentions. The enthusiasm spread far beyond Clermont. Urban remained in France for several months longer and continued to preach the crusade, at Limoges for example. He also sent out written appeals. Three of these, to the Flemings, the Bolognese, and the monks of Vallombrosa, are still extant today. The bishops played their part in the crusading movement and sent preachers out among the people. The response was enormous, especially in south France but also in the Mâconnais, in Lorraine, in the western parts of the Empire, in Champagne, Normandy, and Flanders. Everywhere warriors and men of peace alike were ready to go on the journey to Jerusalem, certainly in far greater numbers than Urban could possibly have foreseen.

The success of the Clermont appeal has still not been fully explained and probably never can be. Nor will any definitive interpretation be offered here; after all, the reasons for taking the cross varied considerably from one individual to another. All one can do is to examine a whole range of spiritual and worldly motives of different kinds which coalesced not only to produce the spark of that unique and spontaneous success at Clermont but also to light a fire which burned for two hundred years.

Originally the object of the crusade was to help the Christian

Churches in the East. However unnecessary such help may, in fact, have been, it was in these terms that Urban is supposed to have spoken at Clermont. But very soon men had a more definite object in mind: to free the Holy Land and, above all, Jerusalem, the Sepulchre of Christ, from the yoke of heathen dominion. It seems that Urban himself had not used the word Jerusalem at Clermont. At any rate it is not mentioned by Fulcher of Chartres whose report of the speech is the one closest to the event. Only in the later versions does Urban make an impassioned appeal for the liberation of Jerusalem. But there is still better evidence of this in the letters which Urban himself wrote. The accounts of the Clermont speech in the chronicles are too much coloured by the tendency of the authors to show off their own rhetorical skills. In the letter sent to the Flemings late in 1095 the pope still speaks mainly of the liberation of the Eastern Churches; Jerusalem is mentioned only in passing. In the letters sent to Bologna and to Vallombrosa in September and October 1096, however, Jerusalem has quite explicitly become the goal. On the other hand the second canon of the Council of Clermont had referred to the remission of penance which would be given for the 'march to Jerusalem to free the Church of Christ'. Erdmann hoped to resolve the difficulty by making a distinction between the object of the war, the liberation of the Eastern Churches, and the goal of the march, Jerusalem. It is, perhaps, an oversubtle interpretation. Jerusalem cannot have been used merely as a lure; the name was too potent and would inevitably have pulled the whole enterprise in this one direction. It is rather more likely in view of the evident lack of over-all planning that Urban had not in fact made much of Jerusalem while at Clermont but that during the course of the next year he gave in to public opinion which needed and created a concrete goal.

Even the mere sound of the name Jerusalem must have had a glittering and magical splendour for the men of the eleventh century which we are no longer capable of feeling.[7] It was a keyword which produced particular psychological reactions and conjured up particular eschatological notions. Men thought, of course, of the town in Palestine where Jesus Christ had suffered, died, been buried, and then had risen again. But, more than this, they saw in their minds' eye the heavenly city of Jerusalem with its gates of sapphire, its walls and squares bright with precious stones—as it had been described in the Book of Revelation (21: 10ff.) and Tobias (13: 21f.). It was the centre of a spiritual world just as the earthly Jerusalem was, in the words of Ezekiel (5: 5) 'in the midst of the nations and countries'. It was a meeting place for those who had been scattered, the goal of the great pilgrimage of peoples (Tobias 13: 14; Isaiah 2: 2), where God resides among his people; the place at the end of time to which the elect ascend; the resting place of the righteous; city of paradise and of the tree of life which heals all men.

Since a good proportion of the crusaders would not have been capable of distinguishing between the earthly and the heavenly Jerusalem such images must have had a powerful effect upon them. They believed that they were marching directly to the city of eternal bliss. Above all it was the *pauperes*, the landless poor, whose apocalyptic and eschatological piety was crystallized in the vision of Jerusalem. The increasingly millenarian outlook of the masses has recently been studied by Alphandéry who, in the course of his investigations, has contributed many original and note-worthy ideas to the problem of the origins of the crusades, though he was probably inclined to exaggerate the importance of such eschatological influences. These influences, discernible chiefly in the form of visions, were not equally present throughout the crusade. They appear both before and during the departure but not again in any significant number until after the capture of Antioch in 1098. Between 1096 and 1098 there are few traces of this kind of thing. This suggests that the masses came under the spell of eschatological ideas only in certain situations and not while the crusade was advancing smoothly. Some visions were clearly induced and exploited by the leaders in order to raise morale at critical moments. The most remarkable example of this is the discovery of the Holy Lance (see below p. 56). But there are also clear signs of an eschatological outlook right at the start, especially when the poor were beginning their march without waiting for the official crusade. The 'signs'—a plague of locusts, a rain of stars from heaven—are apocalyptic in character (cf. Revelation 9: 3; 6: 13). Baudri of Dol tells us that this apocalyptic atmosphere was not created by the official preaching organized by the bishops. In-stead it was spontaneously disseminated through a process of mutual, sermon-like exhortations to which the *pauperes* responded all the more readily since the bad harvests of the years before 1096 made it easy to leave home and fields in order to follow the path to salvation, the road to a better future—a future which the theologi-cally uneducated masses, filled with dim, vague, and incoherent eschatological dreams, probably pictured in an entirely material fashion. Some of the *pauperes* certainly believed that they were of the elect, believed that the words of Psalm 147 referred to them: 'The lord doth build up Jerusalem; he gathereth together the outcasts of Israel.' Believing this they had no hesitation about occasionally bringing pressure to bear on the commanders of the crusade; on the other hand leaders like Raymond of Toulouse reckoned with such feelings and turned them to their own purposes. But the effectiveness of eschatological ideas should not be overestimated. The evidence comes from chroniclers who were themselves actively creating a doctrine of the crusade and who were writing after the event, some of them a long time after. There is a good deal more to the crusade than this. After all, a great many pilgrimages to Jerusalem were made in the year 1033, the millennium of Christ's passion. According to Ralph Glaber's account they too were preceded by supernatural signs and were entirely eschatological in spirit, seeming to proclaim the coming of Antichrist which itself precedes the Parousia, the second coming of Christ (2 Thessalonians 2: 3–12). Yet these pilgrimages did not become a crusade. Above all there was nothing like the all-embracing mass movement of 1095–6. In the final analysis what was decisive was not millenarian thought but the arming of the pilgrimage and the idea of a reward which was latent in the crusading indulgence.

Counting for just as much as the images conjured up by a child-like, mystical faith was the long tradition of pilgrimage to Jerusalem.[8] As early as 333 a pilgrim from Bordeaux reached Palestine; and not much later a Gallic noblewoman named Egeria visited the Holy Places. In 386 Saint Jerome settled in Bethlehem; half a century later the Empress Eudocia went into retreat at Jerusalem. Monasteries and hospices were built to receive the travellers who, following the new fashion—as it can fairly be called—came to Palestine. The stream of pilgrims never dried up, not even after the Arab conquest of the Holy Land in the seventh century. The growing east–west trade in relics played some part in awakening and sustaining interest in the Holy Places, but more important was the gradual development of the penitential pilgrimage. This was imposed as a canonical punishment and for capital crimes like fratricide it could be for a period of up to seven years and to all the great centres: Rome, San Michele at Monte Gargano, Santiago di Compostella and, above all, Jerusalem and Bethlehem. With the belief that they were effective ways to salvation the popularity of pilgrimages grew rapidly from the tenth century onwards. Saint John of Parma journeyed no less than six times to the Holy Land—given the conditions of travel at the time an astonishing achievement. Men of violent passions like Fulk Nerra, Count of Anjou, or Robert the Devil, Count of Normandy, went on pilgrimages to Jerusalem when their consciences plagued them on account of the crimes they had committed against church and monastery, so sometimes they had to go more than once. The new Cluniac order, gaining all the time in prestige and influence, used its far-flung net of contacts and its genius for organization both to urge men to go on pilgrimages and to improve facilities for those who did. For many pilgrims in the eleventh century the journey to Jerusalem took on a still deeper religious meaning; according to Ralph Glaber, himself a Cluniac monk, it was looked upon as the climax of a man's religious life, as his final journey. Once he had reached the Holy Places he would remain there until he died.

It is clear that in the middle of the eleventh century the difficulties facing pilgrims began to increase. In part this was a result of the Seldjuk invasions which made things harder for travellers on the road through Anatolia—a popular route because it permitted a visit to Constantinople. But it was also a consequence of the growing number of pilgrims, for this worried the Muslim authorities in Asia Minor and Palestine, just as the Greeks in south Italy looked sceptically upon the groups of Norman 'pilgrims' who were all too easily persuaded to settle there for good. It has been suggested that the Muslims may have had a commercial interest in promoting pilgrimages but, except perhaps in Jerusalem itself, the income from this source cannot have been very significant— poverty was, after all, one of the ideals of the pilgrim. So there was little or no incentive for them to make the journey any easier. Conditions were, of course, nothing like as bad as they had been during the persecution of the Christians under the mad caliph, Hakim, who, in 1009, had had the Church of the Holy Sepulchre in Jerusalem destroyed; but neither were they as favourable as they had been during the great days of the Byzantine Empire or in the time of Charlemagne who had himself taken a keen interest in the pilgrimage to Palestine. Yet despite the occasional trouble the number of pilgrims grew steadily. In 1064–5 Bishop Gunther of Bamberg led a party over 7,000 strong into the Holy Land. Near Ramleh in Palestine they were suddenly attacked by Muslims and for several days they had to fight a defensive battle. It is not easy to explain how they managed this since pilgrims were always unarmed.

Here we have reached the critical point of difference between crusader and pilgrim. The crusader carried weapons. A crusade was a pilgrimage, but an armed pilgrimage which was granted special privileges by the Church and which was held to be specially meritorious. The crusade was a logical extension of the pilgrimage. It would never have occurred to anyone to march out to conquer the Holy Land if men had not made pilgrimages there for century after century. The constant stream of pilgrims inevitably nourished the idea that the Sepulchre of Christ ought to be in Christian hands, not in order to solve the practical difficulties which faced pilgrims, but because gradually the knowledge that the Holy Places, the patrimony of Christ, were possessed by heathens became more and more unbearable. If the link between pilgrimage and crusade is obvious, the credit for bringing it about belongs to Urban II. Although historians today are less inclined to argue that the crusades were caused by increasing difficulties in the way of pilgrims, it still remains true that pilgrimages were of decisive importance in the rise of the crusading movement. In Erdmann's words, Urban 'took the popular but, in practical terms, unfruitful idea of pilgrimage and used it to fertilize the holy war'. It is significant that contemporaries were at first unable to distinguish clearly between the two things. Not until the mid-thirteenth century was there a Latin word for 'crusade' and even then it was seldom used. (The English word crusade, like the German word *Kreuzzug*, was only invented in the eighteenth century.) In the Middle Ages men almost always used circumlocutions like *expeditio, iter in terram sanctam* (journey into the Holy Land) and—especially early in the crusading period—*peregrinatio*, the technical term for pilgrimage. The line between crusade and pilgrimage was obviously a blurred one.

Naturally the idea of an armed pilgrimage appealed above all to the knightly classes. As Erdmann has shown, thanks to the influence of the Cluniac reformers they had gradually been drawn to the idea of the holy war, the battle for the Church against the heathen. Faced by the problem of harmonizing an inevitable evil with the peaceful and non-violent teaching of Christ, the attitude of the Church to war was understandably a delicate one. In the Byzantine world theologians had unambiguously condemned war but in practice their condemnation had little effect. In the Latin West, men were not ready for so radical and ineffective a point of view. Throughout the Middle Ages, St. Augustine's doctrine of the just war, *bellum justum*, remained authoritative.[9] Only in a just cause was war permissible; only when fought to defend or to recover a rightful possession. Clearly the second of these justifications left plenty of room for a generous interpretation of political circumstances.

The unceasing onslaughts of the pagans on the whole of

Christian Europe in the ninth and tenth centuries gave obvious importance to the concept of a defensive war. Armies and raiding parties of Vikings, Magyars, and Arabs swept into Christian territory and under this pressure the population had to endure the hardest time of the Middle Ages in the years following the collapse of the Carolingian Empire. Since the wealth of churches and monasteries made them obvious targets for plunder-hungry invaders, it was only natural that the Church should support what was undoubtedly a clear-cut case of a war of defence. As all these invaders were heathens—for not until after 911 when they settled in Normandy and became a little less aggressive did the Vikings become Christians—this was to be an important stage in the develepment of crusading thought. The idea of the *bellum justum* became closely associated with war against the heathen. In the ninth century Popes Leo IV and John VIII promised eternal life to all those who fell in battle against either the Arabs or the Vikings. Later on, crusaders received the same assurance. None the less it would be a mistake to see these promises as early symptoms of the crusading ideal. The two popes had been influenced by a dictum of the famous sixth-century Spanish bishop, Isidore of Seville: 'men whose wisdom and courage make them worthy of heaven are called heroes.' The importance of these papal promises lies in their emphatic support for the war against the heathen. This war itself was a royal and, in particular, an imperial duty. It had always been the emperor's special task to preserve peace within the Church and to further the spread of Christianity abroad. In time men went over from defence to attack but nearly always they continued to look upon it as a just war in St. Augustine's sense, a war fought to recover what was rightfully theirs. It was always possible to throw the blame for war on the other side and build up a plausible *casus belli* for oneself. It is from this point of view that medieval chroniclers, popes, and preachers must be judged when, and especially after the third crusade, they time and again refer to the Holy Land as the 'patrimony' of the Lord, which belongs to Christendom and which must be defended or reconquered. For this phrase alone was enough to justify the crusades.

The Church's attitude to war was further influenced by the Peace of God movement. In its beginnings this movement had been essentially a self-defence mechanism on the part of the Church. The disintegration of the Carolingian Empire had brought with it a decline in the authority of the state and a general decline of public morals. Everywhere in the tenth century the warrior class, composed of men who were gradually coming to be called knights, was patently brutalized. Private property, especially Church property, was attacked just as greedily as it ever had been by Vikings or Magyars. The state could do very little about this unhappy state of affairs and it became increasingly difficult to see any sign whatsoever of public order or security. Though it was primarily concern for its own property which persuaded the Church to step in at this point, it is none the less impossible to overlook the beneficial consequences for the whole fabric of society. In the early regional peace agreements, for which there is a good deal of evidence from the end of the tenth century onwards, it was usual for the local nobility to swear to observe the immunity of the clergy, unarmed persons, and ecclesiastical property. Then, from about 1040, it became increasingly the practice to issue decrees prohibiting feuding on certain days; the final stage was to try to abolish the feud altogether and replace it with arbitration. Credit for promoting this movement belongs chiefly to men associated with Cluniac reform. At Cluny, not far from Mâcon in Burgundy, a monastery was founded in 910 which under some vigorous abbots rose to be one of the most important monastic communities in the West. From this centre radiated a reform movement with the primary purpose of achieving a stricter and more profound observance of the Benedictine Rule as well as a liberation of the monastery from external aristocratic influence. But at the same time the outside world was by no means ignored. Efforts were made to bring about a certain spiritualization, a deepening of the layman's religious life so that he was more closely bound to those forces in the Church which, as the reformers saw it, regulated the moral order. In particular these efforts were aimed at the much brutalized knightly classes, and the Peace of God was just one of the means used to get at this group. Yet all this meant that the Church had made a decisive move towards war, indeed towards active participation in war, because it was simply not enough to persuade the nobility to swear peace-oaths; some way of forcing men to keep the peace had to be devised and, if necessary, put into practice. So, in order to punish disturbers of the peace, the Church became involved in organizing and directing military campaigns.

Ecclesiastical wars of this kind—and later, in another context, they were to become more common—were considered to be 'holy wars' fought in the service of an approving Church. But on this question Augustine's teaching presented difficulties of interpretation and so the views of individual clerics differed considerably; by the end of the tenth century the whole doctrine was in a state

of flux. In the eleventh century support for this concept of holy
war came from the reformers, both those who were chiefly concerned for the monasteries and those who, under papal leadership,
were trying to improve the condition of the whole Church. In part
doubtless the reformers recognized that in the 'holy war' the
Church possessed a valuable political weapon. The same men that
played such a decisive part in the transformation of the warrior
class into a knightly order were also involved in taking the responsibility for holy war out of the hands of the king who previously
had been held to be alone responsible for war, and transferring it
on to the shoulders of the knightly class as a whole. This development was an essential precondition for the growth of the crusading
idea.

But it has been suggested that not only the reform papacy looked
favourably upon the idea of holy war. Two popes from the days
before the period of Church reform have even been credited with
plans for real crusades.[10] Among the letters of Gerbert of Aurillac,
later Pope Sylvester II (993–1003), there is one he wrote before
he became pope. Although there has been much argument about
the genuineness of this document, it is difficult to reject it altogether. In it some historians believed they could see Gerbert
calling for armed help for the Church of Jerusalem. But Erdmann
has shown that in fact Gerbert was only concerned to raise alms. It
is true that the thought of military intervention did cross his mind
but only to be dismissed at once as impracticable. An encyclical
published by Sergius IV (1009–12), however, seemed to be more
significant. In this the pope really did appear to be calling for
some kind of crusade. He had heard the news of the destruction of
the Church of the Holy Sepulchre in Jerusalem by Caliph Hakim
(1009) and he declared his intention of commanding a fleet which
would sail to Syria and there defeat the Muslims and rebuild the
Sepulchre. At the beginning of this encyclical he referred clearly
to the tradition of pilgrimage to Jerusalem. It would have been
hard to overestimate the importance of this document for the
growth of the crusading idea, had it not, some twenty years ago,
been proved to be a forgery. In a fine piece of research Gieysztor
demonstrated that it had been written in 1096, not long after the
Council of Clermont, at the monastery of St. Pierre de Moissac
near Toulouse. In other words this 'encyclical' belongs to the class
of documents known as *Excitatoria* of which several others, in
letter form, are still extant today. They were written simply as
propaganda to drum up support for the crusade.

In fact it was not until the period of reform in the second half

of the eleventh century that the papacy was anything like powerful
enough to think seriously of a military expedition to the East. The
more active policies of the popes of this period also involved them
in a new attitude to war. In 1053 Leo IX (1048–54) one of the first
reforming popes, took personal command of a campaign in south
Italy against the Normans who behaved in much the same way as
the heathens and were therefore treated in a similar fashion. To
the Germans who took part in the campaign the pope offered
exemption from punishment for their crimes and remission of
penance. This came nearer the promise of 1095 than those made by
Leo IV and John VIII. Then Pope Nicholas II (1058–61) tried to
solve the Norman problem by allying with their leaders, Richard
of Capua and Robert Guiscard, at Melfi in 1059. The two Norman
princes agreed to be enfeoffed with their possessions by the pope.
Thus they became vassals of the Church and as such, like all vassals, they had the duty of doing military service for their lord,
though in this case the duty was still limited to undertakings
which could be reconciled with the teachings of the Church. So
now the Church had a feudal military force available for the
defence of the papal states, a force which could be used for the
purposes of holy war. For their part the Normans recognized the
usefulness of a holy war just as much as the churchmen did. Robert
Guiscard carried out his conquest of northern Sicily (1061–72) very
much in the style of a religiously motivated holy war, a war against
the heathen. He had announced his intention of doing this in his
oath at Melfi in 1059 and had thus obtained the approval of the
Church for the enterprise. Erdmann believed that this war for the
conquest of Sicily had been a kind of crusade, but in fact one essential ingredient of a crusade was missing. There is no evidence for
active papal participation though it is difficult to believe that the
popes did not connive at it.

Even more than these Norman wars, the fight against the Muslims in Spain has often been described in terms appropriate to a
crusade.[11] In particular, the conquest of Barbastro in 1064, in
which many Frenchmen took part, has been elevated to the status
of a 'proto-crusade'. But here too the same essential element, active
papal co-operation, seems to be missing. Alexander II's approval
of, and support for this war was limited to granting a kind of indulgence to all participants. The mere fact that the war against
the Muslims in Spain was believed to be meritorious and thus
attracted a certain number of French knights does not make it a
crusade. War against the heathen was, in general, felt to be meritorious and the old Church doctrine that a soldier had to do

penance even when he killed during the course of a just war in the service of a just prince was fast disappearing. What happened in Spain was, in fact, a normal holy war entirely in the style advocated by the Cluniacs. It was, after all, precisely in Spain that the Cluniac order—an enthusiastic promoter of the pilgrimage to Santiago di Compostella—was most energetic in the fields of cultural activity and colonization. In Spain the war against the heathen fitted into a long tradition of resistance to Islam and as part of the European pattern of resistance it naturally played an important part in the origins of the crusades. It helped to keep the idea of fighting the heathen in the forefront of men's minds, above all in France, where the Spanish campaigns awoke a very strong response. Obviously there was a connection, however tenuous, between resistance to the Arabs on the one hand and the crusades on the other. Nevertheless the war in Spain was not a crusade. Later it became a substitute for a crusade; French knights, chary of the difficult journey to Jerusalem, could instead fight Islam in Spain. The popes promoted this, recognizing it as the equivalent of a crusade. But this cannot hide the fact that these Spanish 'proto-crusades' were actually just holy wars. And not until the pontificate of Urban II can we see the influence of Spain on the developing concept of the crusade.

When making his own crusading plans Urban could look back to his predecessor, Gregory VII, after whom this whole period has been called the Gregorian Age. Gregory was one of the most energetic and pugnacious men ever to sit on the throne of St. Peter. For him it was no longer just a question of the freedom of the Church from secular lordship. He proclaimed the overlordship of the pope. This policy led inevitably to the struggles of the Investiture Contest. Both sides used polemical writings as war propaganda and, given the bitterness with which they waged the struggle, it was pretty well inevitable that they would in some way or another become involved with the question of holy war—especially since Gregory VII paid a great deal of attention to the knightly classes and tried to win them over to fight in the service of the Church. To do this he used the old concept of a soldiery of Christ, *militia Christi*. Previously this had been taken to mean the clergy who fought with the weapons of peace. Under Gregory it became a 'new model army', the *militia sancti Petri*, the knights of St. Peter, and retained little of the old peaceful content. The knights of St. Peter were the armed soldiers of the church. One of the most convinced Gregorians, Bishop Bonizo of Sutri, was, in his book *De vita christiana* (c. 1090–95), the first writer to compile a cata-

logue of the duties of the Christian knight. With this work the
Church had finally arrived at a new attitude to war. The knights,
as a class, had acquired their own professional ethos—an ethos
firmly rooted in the Church's conception of the world—with its
visible liturgical expression in the ceremony of dubbing. It is important to realize that on the eve of the crusades there existed a
fully developed class of knights, sharing a moral code which trans-
cended political frontiers and which enabled them to undertake
common enterprises.

Bonizo, however, expressly disavowed the idea of fighting the
heathen. They no longer posed an immediate threat and in the
heat of the Investiture Contest it was common for other considerations to assume greater importance in the Church's theory of war.
Instead of war against the heathen men thought in terms—once
again they were essentially St. Augustine's terms—of war against
heretics and schismatics. Without going into details it is possible
to distinguish roughly between the Gregorians who were in favour
of an aggressive war against heretics and the supporters of the
emperor who opposed it.

Even so the idea of war against the heathen was still far from
being dead. Ivo of Chartres, a man who looked for a compromise
solution to the Investiture Contest, continued to propound it. And
during the whole of the year 1074 no less a person than Gregory
VII cherished the plan of an expedition to the East. He wanted to
lead it himself and in this way help to defend the Christian empire
of Byzantium against the advancing heathens. It is impossible to
say whether Gregory wanted to go to Jerusalem itself, but Our
Lord's Sepulchre was mentioned—the words which later were to be
so effective had been spoken. We know about the plan from the
references to it in Gregory's letters, but how he came to devise it
remains a mystery. Occasionally his intentions were clothed in
such adventurous and fantastic terms that it is difficult to see
clearly just what lay behind it all. Certainly the plight of the
Byzantine Empire was desperate enough to warrant such intervention. The Greek army had been annihilated by the Seldjuks at
the battle of Manzikert in 1071 and, as a result, Anatolia lay open
to the Turcoman attacks. At the same time the Petchenegs were
pressing forward in the Balkans; in south Italy Bari fell to the
Normans. Moreover Gregory VII, like Urban II and many later
popes, hoped to mend the schism of 1054 and it is quite possible
that some idea of reuniting the Churches lay behind the plan of
1074. In fact, his plan was quite impracticable. With the Investiture Contest breaking out the pope could not leave and there was

no hope of German co-operation. Besides this, the Normans were at odds with Byzantium and Gregory was urging the French nobility to take action against their king in support of the Church's policy. None the less Gregory's plan is important in as much as here, for the first time, we can see the idea of a papally directed military operation in the Middle East. In broad terms, what Urban II proposed at Clermont was very similar to what Gregory VII had intended, and since in much else Urban was to carry through to completion the plans which Gregory himself had been unable to accomplish, it may well be that the similarity was deliberate.

In the historical discussion about the origins of the crusades it seems probable that too much attention has been paid to eleventh-century developments in the Church's concept of a holy war. Erdmann, in particular, was inclined to give this overriding importance. But one thing at any rate his investigations have shown beyond all question: a crusade was possible only after the Church had prepared the ground for it by working out a theory of holy war and by creating a class of Christian knights.

Despite everything that has been said about pilgrimages and holy war, it would be wrong to hope to explain the big part played in the crusade by the knights only in terms of religion, group psychology, and a professional ethos. Dry economic and social factors were also significant, more so indeed than is commonly allowed today. In recent years specialists have tended to ignore this side of the problem, important though it clearly is. Instead a great deal has been said about the knight's love of adventure and his lust for booty. In the East he had the chance of making a quick fortune and of rising to a much higher position than he could ever have hoped for in his native country. The Norman Conquest of England had shown what could be done. Doubtless some of the leaders of the First Crusade thought in such terms, especially the Normans from south Italy, Tancred and Bohemund of Taranto, and perhaps Robert of Normandy as well. After all, at Clermont Urban himself had promised that all those who went on crusade would enjoy undisturbed possession of the lands they conquered.

Love of adventure, lust for booty—these are characteristics of individuals. But thanks to the work of Duby and Herlihy we know of economic and social problems which touched the knightly class as a whole and taught it to look upon the crusade as a way out.[12] Herlihy has argued that there was a crisis in the agrarian economy of south France and Italy beginning in about 850 and becoming steadily worse until its climax was reached at about 1000. For the years after 1000 we have vivid chronicle descriptions of recurring famines which can be explained in terms of the failure of agricultural production to keep pace with the rising population. The still prevalent Carolingian custom of dividing an inheritance between all the heirs tended to hinder efforts to increase production. After 1000 the position began to improve, slowly at first, but then with gathering momentum. This was achieved mainly by doing away with the custom of splitting up the land into ever smaller holdings. There was no relaxation of population pressure. The Church and the nobility began to buy out small landholders in order to build up efficient economic units. Care was taken to ensure that land, once gathered together, should not again be dispersed. The knightly classes—the crusading classes par excellence—did this in various ways. In north France they developed the system of primogeniture, the right of the eldest son to succeed to the inheritance. Younger sons had to look after themselves, whether by entering the Church or by going in for a military career. Obviously the crusade acted as a kind of safety valve for a knightly class which was constantly growing in numbers. It is within this context that we must see an individual's love of adventure or hunger for loot.

In Italy and in France south of the Loire, above all in Burgundy, fragmentation of land was avoided by various forms of shared possession. We are particularly well informed about conditions in the Mâconnais, where there was a very strong tie binding the individual to the family. Here allodial land i.e. land which was freely owned, was almost always held in common by the members of the family. This was a legal form known as *frérêche* (*fraternitia*). It usually remained effective up until the second generation and prevented the splitting up of allods. Control of an inheritance passed to the brothers in common, or sometimes it might be shared with uncles, nephews, and even legal persons. Even if the individual's stake in the whole was only a small one, the community remained rich enough to equip one or two mounted knights. In this way the family's social status was preserved and at the same time provision was made for the uninterrupted administration of the estate by those who stayed at home. But this was an institution which worked only when the individual submitted to a tight discipline—the control exercised by the head of the family, a control which seems to have been extraordinarily strict at the end of the eleventh century. This was particularly so in matters of marriage, since, for economic reasons, the success of the *frérêche* depended upon an upper limit to the number of share-holders being enforced. Against the tide of a generally rising population the number of children had to be kept roughly constant. At that time

there was only one really effective way of doing this: by a deliberate restriction of marriage. If, despite this, there were still too
many potential heirs, some of them would have to be provided for
in monasteries or in cathedral chapters. It is in fact possible to
trace the outlines of such policies being pursued by the families of
the Mâconnais.

Thus the maintenance of the family's economic and social position, in other words its standard of living, involved considerable
sacrifices on the part of the individual. Men of an independent outlook may well have been frustrated by such strict family authority;
not all were prepared to bow to the harsh requirements of the
community, to renounce marriage even. One way out was to enter
the Church but that was to exchange one community for another.
The other great safety valve of the twelfth century, the crusade,
offered a real chance of escaping from the tutelage of the *frérêche*,
a real chance for the individual to become independent. But if
there were some men who went on crusade in order to break away
from the forced community of the family and to make a freer life
for themselves, there were also others who chose to go in order to
serve the best interests of the family, particularly in a situation
where there were too many heirs and where fragmentation seemed
inevitable unless some of them left home. An example of this occurred in the Mâconnais family of La Hongre. In 1096 it consisted
of five men. Two of them were monks; two went to Jerusalem and
did not return. This left Humbert who remained behind as the
sole heir of their allodial possessions. In 1147 one of Humbert's
grandsons went on the Second Crusade, leaving the whole inheritance to his brother. Thus the La Hongre family was still
well-off at the beginning of the thirteenth century when others
of their class were already beginning to feel the pinch of new
economic developments. It is also worth noting that the early
legislation of the crusader kingdom of Jerusalem was clearly appropriate to the needs of men with strong family ties like those of
the *frérêche*. The estates held by the knightly families of Jerusalem
could be inherited not only by daughters but also by collateral
relatives. Not until *c.* 1150 was the right to succeed limited to
direct descendants. The earlier custom was clearly designed to
persuade knights to settle down in the Holy Land; thus it had to
accept the requirements of the *frérêche*. If the crusader died then
the family back home in Europe could choose another member to
take over the Palestinian inheritance, in this way further easing
conditions within the *frérêche* itself.

It is not accidental that the Mâconnais has bulked large in this discussion. In this region Urban II's appeal met with a notable response. We know the names of many crusaders who came from this part of Europe in the first half of the twelfth century. This is not just the result of chance survival of evidence. It reflects clearly the social and economic situation of a class which looked upon the crusade as a way of solving its material problems or—to say the very least—which was, owing to this situation, all the more ready to consider going on a crusade.

One more motive for taking the cross remains to be considered; and this one was to put all the others in the shade. It was the concept of a reward in the form of the crusading indulgence.[13] In modern Roman Catholic canon law the indulgence comes at the end of a clear process of remission of sins. First the penitent sinner must confess and receive absolution so that the guilt of the sin is remitted and instead of suffering eternal punishment he will have to suffer only the temporal penalties due to sin. (It is important to note that these penalties may take place either in this world or the next and will include purgatory.) Then in return for indulgence-earning works the Church may grant him remission of all or part of the penalty due to sin, depending on whether the indulgence is a plenary one or not. This is a judicial act of grace based on the authority of the Church's power of the keys and is entirely separate from the sacrament of penance. The indulgence would affect both the canonical punishment imposed by the Church—the penitential punishment—and the temporal punishment imposed by God, since the Church could offer God a substitute penance from the 'Treasury of Merits'—an inexhaustible reservoir of merits accumulated by Christ and added to by the saints on a scale far in excess of what they themselves needed. Undoubtedly then the indulgence has a transcendental effect before God (*in foro Dei*). Where the theologians disagree with one another is on the question of whether one can absolutely guarantee that this judicial act will have a positive result *in foro Dei* or whether it runs up against the problem of God's freedom. In this case the positive result is only indirectly and morally assured in as much as the Church guarantees that the offer of a substitute penance is sufficient to discharge the whole of the punishment due, i.e. the sinner could not have achieved any better result even if he had himself done full penance. But when considering early indulgences, especially the first crusading indulgences, it is vital to remember that this logical doctrine was a later construction designed to give theological authority to customs which, in practice, already existed.

Not until after the First Crusade did the theologians of the twelfth century, first among them Hugh of St. Victor, work out—in practical, if not yet in formal terms—the distinction between the guilt of sin and the punishment due to sin which is crucial to the theory of indulgences. And not until *c.* 1230 was the important doctrine of the 'Treasury of Merits', which provided the equivalent substitute necessary if punishment were to be remitted, formulated by Hugh of St. Cher. The detailed problems of the precise nature of an indulgence and the justification for it were hotly disputed in the twelfth and early thirteenth centuries. Where even theologians found much obscure, there was little chance of popular opinion being well-informed. Any discussion of the crusades must take this point more fully into consideration than has hitherto been customary. In assessing the effect of the crusading indulgence what matters is what people understood or believed they understood by it, not what it actually was. And it is worth noting that the debate about indulgences which started *c.* 1130 was sparked off by the fact they were being abused. As long as the abuses were not too blatant, people looked upon the indulgence as an acceptable innovation without bothering too much about the theology of the matter. We must always remember that the publicizing of the first crusading indulgence took place in an atmosphere which was free of the limitations imposed either by an official Church pronouncement or by a proper theological debate. The only way the new elements could be defined was by comparing them with earlier penitential practices.

The indulgence must, in fact, be seen as a development of the Church's earlier penitential discipline. This was originally divided into three stages: confession, satisfaction, and reconciliation (i.e. being readmitted to communion). Satisfaction was looked upon as the element which earned extinction of sins and thus made the reconciliation possible. At this time no distinction would have been made between remission of guilt and remission of punishment. In principle, the penance had to be equivalent to the sin committed. One had to pay, as it were, pound for pound. But obviously it was only a matter of chance whether or not a precisely equivalent penance was found; thus in addition there had to be the temporal penalties due to sin which, being imposed by God, could measure exactly any guilt that was still remaining. Since God's temporal punishment was feared far more than any earthly penance, a penitential system of draconic severity was developed on the theory that the harsher the penance in this world, the smaller would be the settlement in the next. The fact that up until the sixth century only serious offences were subject to the penance of the Church helped to establish the severity of penitential practice. Yet when, for reasons which cannot be gone into here, this changed so that penance had to be done for venial sins as well, the old system at first remained in force. But now harsh tasks and long penances during which the sinner remained excluded from the sacraments were no longer always appropriate, so inevitably there developed a trend towards a milder and a more differentiated system of punishment. At first this was done by the use of commutation and redemption, i.e. one form of punishment was exchanged for another which theoretically was still equivalent to the sin committed. Thus if it were shorter, it was also supposed to be harder; but in practice it tended to be more lenient. Lists of the penalties due to various sins were drawn up tariff-fashion in the 'Penitentials', together with the appropriate redemptions. In these redemptions we have one of the main roots of the crusading indulgence. In the eleventh century the system became still milder when it became customary to allow reconciliation to take place as soon as a man had begun his penance, though of course he still had to complete it. Thus long-term excommunication—one of the most feared consequences of sin—was in effect abolished. This change also meant the end of the old custom of total reconciliation. Its place was taken by an absolution granted immediately after confession. This involved reconciliation with God and the Church, i.e. forgiveness of the guilt of sin, but it did not mean full remission of the punishment due to sin. Nevertheless absolution went further than redemption and thus came closer to the indulgence in that the Church made a powerful plea for pardon; so a transcendental effect was at least intended. This was still not a judicial act, however, nor was it a remission of punishment granted independently of the sacrament of penance. But from here it was only a short step to the indulgence, i.e. to a more clearly defined and more certainly effective remission of the penance imposed by the Church. By an act of grace allowance was made for the transcendental effect *in foro Dei* of the Church's plea. This then made it possible to curtail the penance imposed by the Church. According to Poschmann, one of the leading Catholic experts on the subject, 'the indulgence was no longer just a part-payment on the time after death, it was also a most welcome relief during this earthly life'. The special feature of the indulgence was that the ideal of equivalence was no longer adhered to in practice. Later on the doctrine of the 'Treasury of Merits' was developed in order to justify this practice.

It is revealing that the idea of indulgence only became really effective when it was linked with the pilgrimage to Jerusalem. Papal pronouncements rather similar to indulgences were occasionally made before the crusades, but these were, in fact, usually absolutions. Alexander II, for example, promised a remission of penance to the soldiers who had joined the Barbastro expedition of 1063. In addition he also offered them the *remissio peccatorum*, the remission of the temporal penalties due to sin. It has been argued that the pope's letter is a forgery, but in fact it is a perfectly genuine plenary indulgence. Yet for various reasons it had very little effect. For one thing, it was addressed to a much smaller group than was the crusading indulgence of 1095. Alexander's offer applied only to those who had already decided to take part in the Spanish campaign; and he left it open whether he would extend the terms of the indulgence to include those who joined later. Furthermore normal penitential practice was adhered to in that a penance had first to be imposed, at least formally, before it could be considered as cancelled by the indulgence. Finally a campaign in Spain did not have the same mass-appeal as an expedition to the Holy Land. This example shows clearly why the full effects of the indulgence were felt only when it became linked with the pilgrimage to Jerusalem.

In this context it was important that the penitential journey to Jerusalem was thought to be especially meritorious and salutary. In theory the Church had always taken the view that movement from one place to another did not bring a man any nearer to God; but it was impossible to extinguish the popular belief in the value of a pilgrimage to Jerusalem. Its popularity was assured from the moment when the reconciliation with the Church was moved forward to the beginning of the work of penance, in this case the pilgrimage. This applied, of course, to any penitential pilgrimage; what gave Jerusalem its special significance was the tradition of the Holy Places. There is evidence from as early as the eighth century for the belief that remission of sins could be earned by a visit to the Church of the Holy Sepulchre. But those who shared this belief in the value of pilgrimages were denounced at the Council of Chalons in 813. The council was relying on the authority of Jerome who said that it was not seeing Jerusalem that was praiseworthy, but living a good life there. Indeed, in Jerome's eyes, even this had no special purifying value. He wrote that he had gone to Palestine in order to understand the Bible better, not to obtain spiritual advantages. But since the Council quoted only Jerome's first statement and not his commentary on it, it was

possible to believe that both Jerome and the Council were prepared to concede an indirect purifying value to the journey to
Jerusalem—i.e. when it led to a long period of residence there.
Later on the Church quite patently failed to combat the belief that
the pilgrimage to Jerusalem was worth an indulgence. Indeed it
formally granted partial indulgences for it, like the year's indulgence allowed by Alexander III. This was during the heyday of
the crusades, when the crusader was granted an unlimited plenary
indulgence; understandably the peaceful pilgrim obtained just a
partial indulgence.

There are some good reasons for assuming that in the pre-crusade
period pilgrimages to Jerusalem were valued more highly and
that those who undertook them received promises rather in the
style of indulgences. The first official pronouncement on this point
was made by Urban II. In 1089 he revived the archbishopric of
Tarragona and ordered the Catalan nobility and clergy to help
with the rebuilding of the town. He then added that those who, in
a spirit of piety and penitence, were intending to go to Jerusalem
should be advised to devote to the rebuilding of the church of
Tarragona the money they would have spent on a pilgrimage. In
this way the town would become celebrated as a bulwark of
Christendom against the Saracens. Everyone who followed this
advice should be granted the same indulgence as he would have
obtained had he gone to Jerusalem. (Then, as now, the word 'indulgence' could be used both in a precise, technical sense and also
with a much more general meaning.) The final sentence of the
bull used to be treated with a good deal of scepticism by students
of papal diplomatics, but more recently its genuineness has been
vindicated. It is no longer possible, however, to ascertain just how
comprehensive was the reward for those would-be pilgrims who
instead helped to rebuild Tarragona. Certainly there can be no
justification for calling it a plenary indulgence.

The importance of the Tarragona appeal for the origins of the
crusades is obvious—though only Erdmann has given it the attention it deserves. Here the Christian idea of pilgrimage is linked
together with a project intended to promote resistance to the Saracens. Fully six years before the Council of Clermont the pope had
already granted an indulgence, indeed a pilgrim's indulgence, for
the war against the heathen. It has been objected that whereas the
crusade was an offensive enterprise, the rebuilding of Tarragona
was defensive in character. But this objection cannot be sustained.
When Urban returned to the same theme at some date between
1096 and 1099 he suggested to some Catalan counts that they

should help with the work at Tarragona in order to obtain *remissio peccatorum* (remission of sins). He argued that since the knights of other lands had unanimously decided to help the Church in Asia and to free their brothers from the Saracen yoke, it was only right that they in their turn should help the Church in Catalonia against the attacks of the Saracens there. The pope then offered to all who fell in the defence of Tarragona the same indulgence that he had granted to the crusaders. It is true that in this letter we hear only of a reward for those who were killed, but Tarragona could not be rebuilt by candidates for martyrdom alone. The majority of those who were willing to fight wanted to obtain an indulgence and return home alive. It was this majority that Urban had to persuade to go to Tarragona. So clearly those who came through the defence of Tarragona must have been granted the same indulgence as those who survived a crusade. If this were not so it would have been irresponsible to prevent Spaniards from going on crusade to Jerusalem—as, for example, Urban did in 1099 when he sent the archbishop of Toledo back on the grounds that there were plenty of heathens for him to fight at home. In other words, Urban's attitude to the rebuilding of Tarragona had not changed. In 1089 he had seen it as the equivalent of a pilgrimage; later as the equivalent of a crusade. The fact that for one and the same task he at first promised a pilgrim's reward and then a crusader's indulgence tells us a good deal about his way of thinking. For him the crusade was an extension of the pilgrimage.

Erdmann approached these facts in a rather different way. He believed that the idea of a christian and knightly holy war was in the forefront of Urban's mind and that the pilgrimage was merely incidental. The reverse seems more likely to be true and to fit better into the logic of things. It is easy to arm a pilgrimage and pursue entirely new ends while preserving the old forms; but it is difficult to force a warrior into the peaceful form of the pilgrimage, no matter how holy the cause for which he fights. As Erdmann saw, from the Church's point of view the decisive event at Clermont was not the indulgence but the militarization of the pilgrimage and the ecclesiastical sanction given to this process. The crusader was a kind of superior pilgrim, a pilgrim with the honour of bearing arms. He stood one step higher than the peaceful pilgrim but the difference between them was only one of degree. This is how contemporaries looked at it. The crusader's sword was blessed, but so were his staff and his scrip—the traditional attributes of the pilgrim. A hundred years later Frederick Barbarossa and the kings of France and England received the staff and scrip before they set out on crusade. It is true, as Erdmann pointed out, that on crusade the expression 'soldier of Christ' came to mean 'crusader' while the word 'pilgrim' dropped into the background. This observation undoubtedly played a considerable part in Erdmann's thesis that the pilgrimage was a minor factor in the origins of the crusade. But here so much depends on what kind of source material is used. Erdmann relied on chronicles and crusaders' letters. The chronicles are, however, poor evidence. Most of them were written after the capture of Jerusalem by churchmen who were working on the development of a doctrine of the crusade. More valuable testimony is provided by the charters of men who borrowed money from the Church in order to cover their crusading expenses. When they say anything about the purpose of the crusades, it is in phrases taken almost entirely from the world of the pilgrim. Only rarely does the idea of fighting the heathen appear. The unknown author of the *Gesta Francorum* wrote of the people of Macedonia: 'They did not believe that we were pilgims but thought that we had come to devastate their land and kill them.' It was in the crusading army itself that the conceptual change from armed pilgrim to soldier for the faith took place. But in 1096 when the march began it seemed—apart from its eschatological aspects—to belong entirely to the traditional world of the pilgrimage to Jerusalem.

This is how Urban II must have seen it. The two Tarragona appeals show clearly that his idea of the crusade was based on the pilgrimage. It was in this way that the wars in Spain contributed to the origins of the crusades. Not that Spain had seen any striking success of the kind that might have been likely to persuade Urban to apply more widely the combination of pilgrimage and war against the heathen. Despite the papal promise of a spiritual reward and the financial contribution made by the count of Barcelona, the first Tarragona appeal of 1089 achieved little. This lack of success indeed only serves to show that a pilgrimage was more attractive than the war in Spain. But what had failed in Spain might work if the combination of war against the heathen with the idea of a reward were transferred to the Christian East, the main goal of pilgrims. It is clear that the idea of making a pilgrimage there was far more potent than the idea of fighting the heathens in Spain. This is demonstrated by the fact that the pope could not even persuade the count of Barcelona to stay in Spain though as the local lord he was more involved than anyone in the rebuilding of Tarragona. He died in 1096 in the Holy Land. A watchful observer can hardly have failed to see that the pilgrimage motif would be of great help in organizing a military expedition to the East.

Although Erdmann drew attention to the Tarragona appeals he also explicitly denied that Urban II had any interest in the idea of pilgrimage except as crusade propaganda. But in fact the pope's few crusade letters tell us nothing about his attitude to pilgrimages. Neither does his speech at Clermont; in none of the versions is there even a passing reference to pilgrimages though practically every possible motive, religious, economic, and social, is touched upon somewhere. This is all the more remarkable since at Clermont Urban must have used the arguments which he judged would have the greatest effect on his audience. Yet, if we can believe the chroniclers who unanimously omit any reference to the subject, the pilgrimage was not one of these arguments—and this despite the fact that Urban had already closely concerned himself with the problems of the pilgrimage when dealing with the Spanish campaigns. For him then it cannot have been a propaganda device. But it was one of the basic roots of his concept of the crusade. Later on indeed the idea of arming the pilgrim was permanently taken over by the crusade propagandists when it had become obvious just how effective an idea it was. The false crusading encyclical of Sergius IV which was fabricated at this time is clear proof of this.

Even more important in the eyes of the general public was the indulgence, especially once it had been linked with the enormously popular pilgrimage idea. Basically there was nothing new about the 'indulgence' of Clermont. What the council decreed was, of course, a judicial act, but it was something thoroughly traditional —not a plenary indulgence in the modern sense. It laid down, in precise and unambiguous words, that whoever took the cross for reasons of religion alone, would be freed from all penances imposed by the Church.* Exactly this is repeated in Urban's letter of August 1096 to Bologna. I cannot agree with the generally accepted view that this was a plenary indulgence since nowhere does the council even hint that its decree would have a transcendental effect. It granted nothing more than a redemption or absolution i.e. the remission of the canonical penances by means of a kind of redemption, that is to say by going on crusade, a penitential task which was the equivalent of a full remission. It is impossible to see how this can somehow be regarded as less of an absolution than the remission of sins granted in 1079 by Gregory VII to the

---

* Quicumque pro sola devotione, non pro honoris vel pecuniae adeptione, ad liberandam ecclesiam Dei Ierusalem profectus fuerit, iter illud pro omni poenitentia reputetur.

English. This is formulated very much more, indeed almost precisely, in the terms of an indulgence. Yet, despite the difficulties,
theologians regard this as an absolution. The fact is that interpretation of the Clermont decree has been too much influenced by
what developed later, and too little by the actual text. So far as I
know, Poschmann has been the only one to realize this when he
writes that at first indulgences were plenary only in the sense that
they meant the remission of the entire penance (*remissio iniunctae
poenitentiae*); they did not yet mean the full remission of all the
temporal penalties due to sin in the next world. But against this
interpretation there is the existence of the customary formula
remissio peccatorum which, although it does not appear in the
council's decree, had always been used to mean the remission of
temporal penalties including those of the next world. It really is
impossible to see why an expression more precise than *remissio
peccatorum* could not have been found if no more than the
remissio poenitentiae was intended. The formula itself does
date back to the time when the single process of canonical satisfaction redeemed simultaneously both guilt and punishment. But
it was not used in papal letters until the second half of the
eleventh century and it inevitably became more and more
ambiguous as the distinction between guilt and punishment was
developed. Poschmann's argument becomes circular when he tries
to solve the problem by making the unproven assertion that at
that time *remissio peccatorum* meant only the remission of
penance. There is, however, no need to see in this argument an
attempt to refute earlier Protestant polemic against indulgences,
some of it in a very coarse style, which had tended to concentrate
heavily on the *remissio peccatorum* formula. Poschmann is simply
trying to reconcile what is, for him, irreconcilable—the Council's
decree and the customary papal formula. But in fact they are
irreconcilable only in the context of a preconceived and generally
accepted opinion: that the Council of Clermont proclaimed a
genuine plenary indulgence.

At Clermont words were chosen with precision and all that
was actually offered was the full remission of the earthly penances
imposed by the Church. Preachers then went out and preached
something else, the *remissio peccatorum* which literally means the
remission of sins and in theology refers to the remission of the
temporal penalties due to sin, though not until the time of
Huguccio (d. 1210) was this definition clearly established.
Popular crusading propaganda at once went unhesitatingly far
beyond the more limited formula used at the Council. None of

the contemporary chroniclers reproduce the official doctrine in
their descriptions of the Council. Orderic Vitalis was the only
one to mention the remission of penance and, even in his view,
the remission of the penalties due to sin—never in fact referred
to at Clermont—was more important. Erdmann misses the heart
of the matter when he says that in the eyes of the world it was a
meaningless distinction and that here we see the effect of the
popular belief that to go on a crusade was to obtain forgiveness
of sins. But, in fact, the men who tell us about the remission of
the penalties due to sin were trained in theology and well able to
make the distinction. Yet none of them utters a word of criticism
or explanation. Clearly the Clermont decree had been pushed
into the background by the crusade propagandists. It looks very
much indeed as though the preachers explained the distinction—
and then pointed out the advantages of the remission of the
penalties due to sin (or perhaps simply the remission of sins, cf.
pp. 36f.) which was now supposed to have been granted at the
Council. From now on the dominant note in the crusade publicity was the idea of a reward—and moreover a special reward
which could be obtained only by taking the cross. Although there
is very little evidence for the First Crusade, here at any rate we
are entitled to draw on what we know of the later crusades.

Up to a point the extended meaning given to the Clermont
decree can be described as a misunderstanding. More was promised
than could, according to the strict doctrine of the Church, be
given. But it must be remembered that the preachers were working,
so to speak, in a vacuum. It would have been no use them looking
for guidance from the official teaching of the Church or from
theological literature because at that date there was still no theory
of indulgences. For this reason there is no force in the assertion
made by early Protestant critics of the system of indulgences, that
the popes had here created for themselves a superbly manipulated
'instrument for the production of unconditional devotion' (T.
Brieger, 1901). It is true that in the thirteenth century the
crusading indulgence was used for political purposes; none the
less it was not a papal invention. Yet there is no way of explaining
the success of the crusade propaganda in 1095–6 except as a
consequence of this extension of meaning to include a transcendental effect, for, after all, the substitute—the crusade—was in
many cases harder than the penance it replaced. It seems likely
then that the full crusading indulgence was produced neither by
the pope nor by the official Church; rather it was 'manufactured'
by preachers who expanded on the Clermont decree. In other

words it emerged in response to the needs of the people and the requirements of the crusade. This much seems clear from the biting criticism to which the indulgence became subjected from c. 1130. Peter Abelard was the first in the field. In his fierce attack he pointed out that the Church had always held firm to the theory of equivalent penance (indeed if this had been given up the development of the doctrine of the Treasury of Merits would have been pointless). But in an indulgence there could be no equivalence—not, at any rate, until men had learned of the existence of the Treasury of Merits. In Abelard's day the bishops who dispensed indulgences relied upon their power of the keys (John 20: 23), but the French theologian was entirely within the bounds of traditional learning when he dismissed this as insufficient (Poschmann). Until the Treasury of Merits had been defined, the Church was, strictly speaking, in no position to remit the temporal penalties due to sin because it was unable to preserve the equivalence of the penance. Yet it is indisputable that indulgences were dispensed. It seems clear that a practice which originated outside Rome had been brought within the Church, and only later was the theory of it all worked out. Public pressure in its favour meant that the practice could not be eradicated, but it was not easy to justify and there is an air of helplessness about the attempts to do so made by twelfth-century theologians. Even Peter Cantor (d. 1197), writing after indulgences had been dispensed and discussed for a hundred years, and the first theologian to try to see something of positive value in the indulgence, still looked upon it essentially in terms of the long-familiar redemption. Nor have modern theologians tried, even hypothetically, to work out a flawless justification for the system of indulgences which would have held good even at a time when the Treasury of Merits was still unknown. They cannot do it—even only hypothetically—without being forced either to label the Treasury of Merits as not absolutely necessary or to explain it as the (still unrecognized) basis of the Church's official intercession for the remission by God of the temporal penalties due to sin.

It seems then that right at the start of the crusading movement control had slipped out of the hands of the curia. We have already seen how men disregarded papal schemes and chose Jerusalem as their own goal; and we shall see how the pope's plans for organizing the campaign were, in part, overtaken by events. Something similar had happened in the case of the indulgence. Urban's expressions of opinion on this subject are ambiguous. In the letter to the Flemings written at the end of 1095 he himself spoke of *remissio peccatorum,* i.e. remission of the penalties due to sin. But in his letter to the Bolognese he used the more limited formula of the remission of penance. Of course the first letter was intended to recruit crusaders, while the second was meant to prevent ecclesiastics from going. At all events the curia did not hinder the popular interpretation of the Clermont decree. Indeed in later years it became necessary for popes to make this interpretation their own. This development begins with Eugenius III who, on his own admission, looked back to the chronicle accounts, not to Urban's privileges, when he proclaimed an indulgence at the start of the Second Crusade. Not surprisingly this brought the *remissio peccatorum* into prominence.

Some popes like Gregory VIII tried to put the clock back. They avoided the highly ambiguous expression *remissio peccatorum* and only offered a remission of penance, as the Council of Clermont had done. But the process had gone too far to be halted now and in the crusade decree of the Fourth Lateran Council of 1215 it reached its conclusion. From then on this decree formed the basis of the papal theory of the crusades. To all men who, in person and at their own expense, went on a crusade it promised full forgiveness of all those sins which, with a contrite heart, they had truly confessed. The confusion was now complete, for this seems to have meant a full remission of the sins themselves, a complete discharge obtained through the Church by means of an extra-sacramental work of penance. It cannot possibly be referring only to the penalties due to sin for only sins can be confessed, not penalties. This is where the doctrine formulated by Huguccio and finalized by Aquinas came in. According to this doctrine there were two senses in which sins could be forgiven. Firstly the guilt, through confession, and secondly the punishment. But how could the preachers of the crusade have explained this? They were 'fishers of men'—as one of them, referring to Matthew 4: 19, called himself—and they hoped to make a good catch from an audience which consisted largely of illiterates. It was not the place for subtle and still not definitively accepted distinctions. It was not the time to be more papal than the pope who, after all, had said remission of sins even though he may have meant no more than the remission of the penalties due to sin. In any event there is no evidence that the preachers tried to give special emphasis to the narrower concept. On the contrary when Abbot Martin of Pairis preached the Fourth Crusade at Basle at the beginning of the thirteenth century the concluding words of his sermon were as follows: 'But if you ask, what more certain reward from God may you hope for in

return for such efforts, then I promise categorically that each of
you who takes the cross and confesses truly will be entirely cleansed
of all his sins.' What listener, if he were not trained in theology,
could have heard this and not believed that he was meant to look
forward to a complete remission of sins, both the guilt and the
punishment?

Favoured by the extended interpretation of the Clermont decree,
the reward motif, along with some other themes, played an important propaganda role throughout the whole period of the crusades.
None of the preachers felt able to do without it. They used clearly
drawn images and had no hesitation in calling a spade a spade.
The believer was offered a spiritual bargain and he would have
been a fool to refuse. Particularly effective was the picture of the
'shrewd businessman' which was first drawn in a propaganda letter
written by St. Bernard of Clairvaux, in which the transcendental
effect of the indulgence was most strongly emphasized.

O mighty soldier, O man of war, you now have a cause for which you
can fight without endangering your soul; a cause in which to win is
glorious and for which to die is but gain. Or are you a shrewd businessman, a man quick to see the profits of this world? If you are, I can
offer you a splendid bargain. Do not miss this opportunity. Take the
sign of the cross. At once you will have indulgence for all the sins which
you confess with a contrite heart. It does not cost you much to buy and
if you wear it with humility you will find that it is worth the kingdom
of heaven.

It could hardly have been said more clearly than this and it
could not have failed to make an impact. The same metaphor
reappears in an early twelfth-century poem in the collection
known as the Carmina Burana:

> The clever merchant will be there
> Who wants to purchase life . . .
> The last will be first
> And the first last
> The summoning is different
> But the payment (*remuneratio*) the same
> For to all workers (i.e. crusaders)
> The penny of life will be given.

A French crusading song of the same period runs:

> I have heard it said by way of advice
> That it costs gold to clinch a good deal.
> The man is thoughtless
> Who sees the good and takes the bad.

> Do you know what God has promised them
> Who will take the Cross?
> By God! He has promised to reward them well
> Paradise for evermore.
> He who knows how to make a profit
> Is a fool if he waits till tomorrow.

In these lines not only can we hear the voice of the persuader; we can also sense the mood of the persuaded. Towards the end of the century the Provençal poet Aimeric de Belenoi wrote:

> For the march means hope
> For possessions and joy and thanks
> And for diligence and honour
> And for deliverance from sin.

At about the same time Heinrich von Rugge, referring to the crusade, wrote:

> All my thoughts are fixed on a better reward.

From the early thirteenth century there have survived the crusade sermons of James of Vitry. In one of them he tells a story which does not have to be true but which must have been possible otherwise he would not have used it. It illustrates the frame of mind of his audience. A wife kept her husband indoors so that he would not be able to listen to the preaching of a crusade. But through a window he managed to hear what was said. As soon as he learned that by taking the cross a man could gain as much remission as otherwise would require fasting and wearing a penitential belt for sixty years and that he would most certainly escape purgatory and hell, he immediately jumped clean through the window in order to take the cross himself.

It would, of course, be wrong to assert that the crusade propagandists avoided a more spiritual approach and worked only in such blatantly commercial terms. Nevertheless a great deal was done by such methods; we should remember that it was an age which witnessed a tremendous boom in long-distance trade. St. Bernard, though he used the vocabulary of merchants, did, of course, also say very different things (see pp. 99f.), but he too did not want to renounce this effective propaganda theme.

It is perhaps better to put aside the question of whether or not the Church gave the impression that a complete remission of sin, both guilt and punishment, was possible through the indulgence and therefore through a procedure outside the Church's sacrament of penance. It is certainly possible that sometimes contemporaries did so interpret the Church's ambiguous terminology. But in any case the difference between remission of penance and remission of the temporal punishment due to sin, a difference which existed in the Church's traditional doctrine of indulgences, was of itself quite enough to explain the success of Clermont. There had been nothing new about being able to obtain remission of penance by going to fight the heathen. But that the penalties due to sin could be remitted simply as a result of taking the cross—as the crusade propagandists suggested—this was an unheard of innovation. Previously both the reconciliation granted at the start of the penance and the redeeming commutation had affected only the penances and had had no transcendental effect upon the penalties due to sin. It was indeed hoped that absolution would have such an effect, but it could certainly not be guaranteed. The indulgence on the other hand availed before God in a certain and in a quantitatively measurable fashion so that both the temporal penalties due to sin and the earthly penances were remitted and, in the case of a plenary indulgence, fully cancelled. Only Alexander II had promised as much as this for the war against the heathen and his promise, being addressed only to a small group, had met with little response. It was when linked with the universally popular idea of pilgrimage to Jerusalem that the explosive force of the crusading indulgence was revealed. Ekkehard of Aura spoke of 'a new way of penance' now being opened up. Here lies the secret of the astonishing success of Urban's summons, a success which astonished the Church as much as anyone else. Imagine a knight in the south of France, living with his kinsmen in the socially and economically unsatisfactory institution of the *frérêche*. His feuds and the 'upper class' form of highway robbery which often enough went with them, were prohibited by the Peace of God. Suddenly he was offered the chance of going on a pilgrimage—in any event the wish of many men. This pilgrimage was supervised by the Church; it was moreover an armed pilgrimage during which he could fulfil his knightly function by taking part in battle. There would be opportunities for winning plunder. Above all there was the entirely new offer of a full remission of all the temporal penalties due to sin, especially of those to be suffered in purgatory. The absolution given in the sacrament of penance took from him the guilt; taking the cross meant the cancellation of all the punishment even before he set out to perform the task imposed. Not to accept such an offer, not—at the very least—to take it seriously, would indeed have been mad. The 'shrewd businessman' seized his chance. And who did not want to be numbered among the shrewd?

Taking the cross in these circumstances was, of course, an act of faith just as much as an act of naive trust in the promises made by Church publicists. Naturally not all crusaders were moved by piety. In the Middle Ages too there were sceptics and the motives for going on crusade were many, various, and tangled, often social and economic in character. But the offer of indulgence must have had an irresistible attraction for those who did not doubt the Church's teaching, who believed in the reality of the penalties due to sin, or at least accepted the possibility of their existence. Such believers must have made up a great part of those who went on the First Crusade—whatever proportion of the total population of Europe they may have been. And, of course, the crusaders of 1095 could not have guessed that the offer which they were accepting was in reality much more limited than the one promised them by the 'fishers of men'.

3 · THE FIRST CRUSADE, 1096–1099

THE preaching of the crusade was by no means finished when the promise of a spiritual reward was made.[14] It was still necessary to endow the enterprise with a legal form which was appropriate to the kind of participants whom it was intended to attract. That the kings of Europe would take part was entirely out of the question. So Urban thought in terms of an army of knights under the control of the Church, for there was no other higher authority which could have taken command. While still at Clermont he nominated Adhemar, Bishop of Le Puy, as his legate, and later he described him openly as the leader of the crusade. How far Urban had originally envisaged Adhemar as a political, as well as a religious leader, has been much debated, but the political side of his functions should not be exaggerated. The military commander was probably to be Count Raymond IV of Toulouse, with whom Urban had discussed the project even before the Council met at Clermont.

All knights who swore to go on crusade were admitted to the ranks of the crusaders in a symbolic ceremony. Referring to the words of St. Matthew's Gospel about those who would follow Christ (Matthew 16:24), Urban, at Clermont, distributed cloth crosses to all those who were prepared to go, and they then sewed them on to the shoulders of their surcoats. The cross was to be the badge of every crusader on every crusade. As a symbol it had a double significance. First, it was a sign of God's protection, a sign that the wearer belonged to a special community, the sign of a pilgrim with the privilege of bearing arms. Second, it was a legal symbol, vouching for worldly privileges, for the Church issued far-reaching ordinances in favour of the crusader. The Peace of God and the Church's protection were extended to cover his belongings. During the period of his absence on crusade his privileges went, in theory, still further. His possessions were released from the controlling authority of the state: no taxes could be collected.[15] He was normally granted a moratorium on his debts, especially since he might well have to meet considerable expenses in preparing for the journey and have to borrow either from his peers or from the Church. But, in return, anyone who broke the oath to take the cross was excommunicated. The distribution of a cloth cross by the clergy was probably also intended to prevent unwanted elements of no military value from joining the crusade. It looks as though Urban grew nervous of the explosive effect of the crusading ideal on the non-knightly classes. In 1096 he did his utmost to stop the old and the sick from going. Clerks and monks were to travel only with the permission of their superiors. Urban fixed the start for 15 August 1096. It was probably intended that the different contingents should assemble at Constantinople.

For eight months after the Council of Clermont the pope remained in France. He avoided the territory controlled by the Capetian kings of France, but elsewhere he preached the crusade: in Limoges and Angers, perhaps also in Tours and Nîmes. Otherwise he left the preaching to the bishops. This explains why there was little publicity in those areas which had not been represented at Clermont—England, Germany, and south Italy. Apparently men in Germany and south Italy did not hear of Urban's call until the crusaders themselves passed through these regions.

Though Urban himself stayed south of the Loire, the crusade was also preached to the north, and not only by the bishops. In Normandy, for example, the abbot of St. Bénigne in Dijon was active. But above all it was the popular evangelists, themselves closely connected with the poverty movement which affected the lower classes, who took over the preaching. Robert d' Arbrissel (c. 1055–1117), one of the intellectual leaders of this group, which sought to imitate Christ in a life of complete poverty, preached in the Loire valley. But even he was completely overshadowed by the figure of Peter the Hermit.[16] Peter came from Picardy and before the crusade he had probably been active as a preacher in Central France. He did not look very attractive, usually being caked with mud and dirt, as he rode about the countryside on a donkey. Yet he was a man of electrifying eloquence who radiated an unusual power. In the Middle Ages a whole cycle of legends became attached to his name until he was—quite erroneously— given most of the credit for starting the crusades. He is supposed to have carried a letter with him, a letter from heaven, containing the message that the Christians would, if only they dared try it, drive the heathens from the Holy Places. Copies of this letter were actually disseminated. Other reports tell of visions which came to him at the Sepulchre of Christ while he was staying in Jerusalem as a pilgrim. His reputation went before him and must have contributed a good deal to his success. He preached in Berry, in the Orleanais, in Champagne, and Lorraine before going on in April 1096 to Trier and Cologne *en route* for the East. He was followed by a huge army of poor, among whom a knight, Walter Sans-Avoir, became particularly famous. These 'crusaders' were either badly or not at all armed; above all they lacked the money that was needed for so long a journey. The ecclesiastical authorities proved incapable of stopping them from going, although they had certainly never dreamed of a contingent of crusaders looking like this. Here we can see the immense power which emanated from Urban II's combination of pilgrimage, war against the heathen, and a spiritual reward. The idea gripped men of all classes; it could not be restricted to the knights—as the authorities had doubtless hoped. But when such advantageous offers were made, humbler men had no wish to renounce them.

From the Rhineland these troops, mostly drawn from the lower-classes, marched eastwards in various contingents through Hungary and Bulgaria to Constantinople. The first to go was Walter Sans-Avoir whose followers were chiefly Frenchmen. Peter the Hermit meanwhile spent more time preaching the crusade in Cologne. Walter's section reached Byzantium without too much trouble in mid-July 1096. Peter arrived about two weeks later with Lorrainers, Rhinelanders, and South Germans as well as the rest of the Frenchmen. At Nish it became clear that Peter the Hermit was less suitable than the knight Walter as a leader of disorderly troops. Undisciplined behaviour by the crusaders led to sharp clashes with Petcheneg mercenaries in Byzantine service and Peter's men suffered heavy losses. Other contingents, German rather than French in composition, were led by a priest called Gottschalk, a man named Volkmar whose origin is unknown, and by Count Emicho of Leiningen and the viscount of Melun. None of these contingents ever reached Constantinople. Compared with the armies of Walter Sans-Avoir and Peter the Hermit, which had maintained relatively good order, those which followed behaved like hordes of barbarians; as a result they never even set foot on Byzantine territory. In Hungary they occupied themselves with ravaging and looting and there they were all slaughtered. But even before leaving Germany they had managed to acquire a melancholy notoriety. Inflamed by irresponsible preachers and attracted by the wealth of the important Jewish communities of the Rhineland, they had indulged themselves in pogroms on a scale hitherto unprecedented in the Middle Ages. Emicho of Leiningen and his men made a special name for themselves here. The emperor, Henry IV, following the long tradition of the German kings, had taken the Jews under his special protection. In addition they paid large sums of money to the duke of Lower Lorraine in return for his help against the murderous greed of the crusaders. But it was all in vain. Marching downstream (not exactly the most direct route to the East) they plundered and killed the Jews in one Rhineland town after another: Speyer, Worms, Mainz, Trier, and Cologne. Other groups attacked the Jews in Neuss, Xanten, and even Prague. The extant Jewish accounts of these events make grim reading. It was in vain that some of the bishops tried to save them from the bloodthirsty mobs. As in the persecutions of the later Middle Ages, the argument that the Jews, as the enemies of Christ, deserved to be punished was merely a feeble attempt to conceal the real motive: greed. It can be assumed that for many crusaders the loot taken from the Jews provided their only means of financing such a journey. But, as it turned out, their newly acquired wealth took them no further than Hungary for there they were all wiped out.

Meanwhile at Constantinople the armies led by Walter and Peter had set up camp outside the city. Peter was given an audience by the emperor, Alexius Comnenus, who gave him rich presents and good advice. He ought to wait for the arrival of other contingents before marching on into Asia Minor. Peter was ready to do this but his followers were impatient. They became more and more restless and began to plunder the suburbs until finally the Byzantines too advised him to cross the Bosporus. On 6 August 1096 they were taken across and then they marched through Nicomedia to Civetot where there was an army camp which had once been used for English mercenaries in Byzantine pay but which now lay empty. They had now reached the frontier of the region controlled by the Turks and could not resist making forays into it. A French raiding party carried off rich booty from the neighbourhood of Nicaea. Some Germans, in trying to follow this example, were trapped by the Turks at Xerigordon. When the main army set out to try to help them it was routed by the Turks on 21 October 1096. A bare handful of survivors managed to return to Constantinople where Peter the Hermit had been for some time, having left the camp earlier in order to negotiate with the emperor. This meant that he was later able to accompany the knightly armies. The People's Crusade was over. It had ended in disaster and had achieved nothing. Worse, it had made an unfavourable impression on the Byzantine people and authorities. From now on the Byzantines looked sceptically upon crusaders—

upon the allies whom they themselves had called for. The prospects
for co-operation between Byzantium and the crusaders had been
dimmed right at the start by the shadow of mutual distrust.

The only hope for a successful crusade lay with the knightly
armies. Their expedition will be described here in some detail in
order to illustrate the difficulties facing all crusades. One of the
first to depart was Godfrey de Bouillon (d. 1100). With a great
following of Lorrainers, north Frenchmen, and Germans, he set
out in mid-August 1096, at the time appointed. He was a member
of the family of the counts of Boulogne; in 1087 he had been
appointed duke of Lower Lorraine by Henry IV, but he was
unable to make much of this position and it is possible that he
saw the crusade as a chance of achieving higher things. Although
we know nothing for certain of the reasons which led him to take
the cross, the fact that he sold his lands—even his castle of
Bouillon—suggests that he had burned his boats and had no
intention of returning home. As first ruler of Jerusalem he was to
become the focal point of legends which turned him into the ideal
crusader. This process was begun soon after the First Crusade by
Albert of Aix who made Godfrey the hero of his chronicle. If
he were not quite so pure in heart and spirit as medieval legend
made him out to be, neither was he the thorough mediocrity
described by nineteenth-century historians. He was rich enough to
be accompanied by a considerable retinue of vassals and knights,
among whom the Lorrainers were the most influential both during
and after the crusade. His brother, Baldwin of Boulogne, and
another relative, Baldwin of Le Bourg, were the outstanding
members of this group. He marched through Hungary and
Bulgaria and on to Constantinople via Belgrade, Nish, Sofia,
Philippopolis, and Adrianople. Thanks to good discipline and to
a treaty with King Colman of Hungary, to whom he gave Baldwin
of Boulogne as a hostage, the journey passed off almost without
incident. On 23 December 1096 he reached Constantinople where
he found that Count Hugh of Vermandois had already arrived.
Count Hugh, the brother of the king of France, had set out at
about the same time as Godfrey but with his small contingent had
preferred to take the sea route.

The Normans of south Italy had never been reluctant to go
East. One of their greatest feudal lords was Bohemund of Taranto
(d. 1111), the eldest son of Robert Guiscard and now about forty
years of age. He was clearly out to obtain more power than he
enjoyed in Italy. Guiscard's younger son, Roger Borsa, had
succeeded to his father's Italian possessions, while land east of

the Adriatic had been assigned to Bohemund. Thus the setback suffered in the Norman–Byzantine War in 1085 had hit Bohemund hard. It was understandable that he should wish to recoup his losses elsewhere. Without doubt he was the most ambitious and most unscrupulous of the crusade leaders. Restless and greedy for power he was a true Norman rather than a true crusader. But he knew well how to use religious ideals for his own ends. When he decided to take the cross—he was besieging Amalfi at the time—he freely distributed cloth crosses to his companions with his own hands. His followers were fewer in number than Godfrey's. Outstanding among them was his young nephew Tancred. He was also accompanied by the unknown knight or cleric who wrote a valuable account of the crusade, the *Gesta Francorum*, which thoroughly idealizes Bohemund. The Normans took ship over the Adriatic and then marched by the land route along the old Via Egnatia to Constantinople. Bohemund maintained strict discipline since he was determined to make a good impression on the Byzantines who looked upon his coming with mixed feelings; they had not forgotten the war with the Normans. For this same reason the inhabitants of the districts through which he passed were not very keen to sell him provisions. Even so he advanced without too much plundering or friction with the Byzantines, though things became worse after Bohemund left the troops under Tancred's command in order to hurry on ahead to Constantinople where he arrived at the beginning of April 1097.

The largest army, made up chiefly of Provençals and Burgundians, assembled in the south of France. Its commander, Count Raymond of Toulouse, was by far the richest of all the crusaders. His vassals alone made up a fine troop. In his company there travelled the papal legate Adhemar of Le Puy. Raymond was a fifty-five-year-old man who, by a combination of great energy, boldness, and cunning, had made himself lord of thirteen counties in Provence and Languedoc. He left them to his son Bertrand, while he himself took his wife with him on the arduous journey during which she bore him a second son. It is impossible to be sure whether or not he swore an oath never to return but in fact he never did see his home again. Among the leaders he stands out as the one least open to imputations of material ambition as his motive for taking the cross,[17] but his character is far from being an open book. The evidence of his chaplain, the chronicler Raymond of Aguilers, has to be treated with caution. His main purpose seems to have been to show that the will of God was expressed in history and he handled his subject-matter accordingly. It is not known how

Raymond's army reached the Balkans, but once there the count followed the Albanian coast south to Dyrrhachium where he picked up the Via Egnatia. Because he had not set out until October the army had to suffer considerably from the severe Balkan winter; but by and large Raymond managed to keep good discipline. On reaching Byzantine territory they were provided with a Petcheneg escort. Occasionally trouble broke out between crusaders and escort. In one skirmish Legate Adhemar was badly wounded and for a while he had to remain behind at Thessalonika. The town of Roussa in Thrace was pillaged by the Provençals. Shortly afterwards Raymond left the army and hurried on to Constantinople. In his absence the army was very roughly handled by the Byzantines. It reached Constantinople on 27 April 1097, six days later than its commander.

The powerful Count Robert II of Flanders (1093–1111) had arrived a little earlier. He had set out with Duke Robert of Normandy (1093–1106) and Count Stephen of Blois (1089–1102). Duke Robert had found the problems of ruling Normandy too much for him and had happily pawned the duchy to his brother William Rufus of England for 10,000 marks of silver. Stephen of Blois, son-in-law of William the Conqueror, 'had as many castles as the year has days' and had little difficulty in financing his crusade. In his retinue rode Fulcher of Chartres, later chaplain to Baldwin of Boulogne, and one of the chroniclers of the crusade. Their army also set out in October. Having crossed the Alps they met Urban II at Lucca and the pope gave full authority and the *cura animarum* to Arnulf of Rohes and Alexander, chaplains to Robert of Normandy and Stephen. Arnulf in particular was destined to enjoy a successful career in the East. Only recently has it become known that Adhemar was not the only legate to be appointed.[18] The pope had probably thought in terms of just one army and here we have a further indication that the crusade did not quite follow the pattern envisaged by Urban. More princes were ready to take the cross than had been foreseen. They would not have submitted to one commander, and so the possibility of unified leadership, giving the impression that the whole enterprise was directed by the pope, vanished. Against his own preference Urban saw himself forced to assign a legate to each contingent. Although Adhemar's appointment as the one and only legate was never formally revoked and he continued to play a leading part, he none the less travelled with the Provençals and inevitably became looked upon as their legate. From Lucca the army marched to south Italy where Duke Robert and Count Stephen spent the winter months while Robert of Flanders hurried on to Constantinople. The two others sailed across the Adriatic in April 1097 and reached Constantinople in May without much trouble. The muster of the troops was now complete.

Alexius had not reckoned with armies of this size but all he could do now was to make the best of the situation. There could, of course, be no question of allowing the troops into the city itself. They were quartered in camps in the suburbs. Only the leaders with a few of their men were allowed to enter, to gaze upon the riches and relics which filled this great treasure-house of a city. When he received them, Alexius displayed all the splendour of the Byzantine court ceremonial. He heaped presents upon them and we know that Stephen of Blois, for one, was delighted. But none of this could conceal the fact that the arrival of the crusaders raised political problems. Alexius could use the fact that he alone controlled the shipping needed to transport the armies across the Bosporus in order to bring pressure to bear on the crusaders. On the other hand he could not leave this for too long otherwise the number of troops outside Constantinople would grow to dangerous proportions. Moreover he naturally wanted to reach an agreement on what was to be done with the lands which the crusaders would conquer. For Byzantium nothing else would do but that the lands which had once been hers should be restored to her allegiance. On this question Alexius was fortunate that the first contingent to arrive in Constantinople, led by Hugh of Vermandois, was a very small one. Discreetly but unmistakably Alexius restricted the Frenchman's freedom of movement until he was ready to swear that all territories which had belonged to Byzantium before the Turkish invasions would be restored. Moreover any conquests made to the east of this (undefined) line would be held as fiefs of Alexius.

Alexius's treatment of Hugh could not be hidden from the other crusaders. The next to arrive, Godfrey de Bouillon, declined several invitations to visit the city. He also refused to swear the oath. He wanted to wait for the other princes and he may well have had doubts about a feudal oath since, as duke of Lower Lorraine, he was already a vassal of the western emperor. Twice Alexius tried to put pressure on him by cutting off the army's food supply. The Lorrainers replied by pillaging the suburbs. On the second occasion, in January 1097, Godfrey even laid siege to the imperial palace of Blachernae. This was more than Alexius was prepared to take and anyway he wanted to see Godfrey in Asia Minor before any more crusaders arrived at Constantinople. So he gave his troops free rein and they soon proved themselves the superior soldiers. Godfrey was now ready, on 20 January, to take the required oath.[19] He and his men were at once shipped across the Bosporus. They marched along the coast of the Sea of Marmora to Pelecanum, a Byzantine army camp. Not much later Bohemund and the Normans reached Constantinople. He was determined to live down his reputation as an old enemy of Byzantium and to make a good impression on Alexius. By mid-April he had sworn the oath and had promised not to keep parts of the empire himself nor to permit others to do so. Possibly he hoped that Alexius would appoint him as commander-in-chief of the imperial troops in Asia. As such he would have been the most powerful of the leaders of the crusade but, in fact, Alexius still distrusted him far too much to agree to any such scheme. The emperor was, however, prepared to supply the crusaders with arms and food.[20]

Hardly had Bohemund's army reached Pelecanum when Raymond of Toulouse arrived at Constantinople. Of all the leaders of the crusade he was the most obstinate in resisting the oath. This was partly because, in Urban's scheme, the Count of Toulouse was to be the military commander of the crusade and Raymond, whose wealth, power, experience in war, and age equipped him to fill such a post, now saw his position threatened—especially if there was anything behind the rumours of Bohemund's demand to be given the post of commanding officer. He declared coolly that he had come east to serve only God. The other leaders, who did not want to see the crusade held up, tried in vain to bring Raymond round. In their talks Bohemund openly took the emperor's side. Finally a compromise was worked out, perhaps with the help of Legate Adhemar of Le Puy. On 26 April Raymond swore a modified oath by which he promised to respect the person and the possessions of the emperor. It probably took a form common in south France and therefore familiar to Raymond while at the same time avoiding any implication that he was Alexius's vassal. Strangely enough the only one to keep his oath was Raymond who had held out for so long. But perhaps this explains why the others swore so readily. From now on Raymond was on good terms with the emperor; they had their dislike of Bohemund in common. The other princes made no trouble about giving Alexius the promise he wanted and soon they had all reached Pelecanum.

By the end of April 1097 Godfrey and the Normans had already left the camp. Their first objective was Nicaea, the capital of the Seldjuk sultan, Kilij Arslan. This town, famous as the site of some councils of the early Church, controlled one of the main routes to

the east through Anatolia. It was built in a good strategic position
on the shore of a lake and was defended by over 200 towers.
Godfrey arrived there on 6 May and, although it took a further
four weeks before the whole army had assembled, the serious
business of the siege began as early as 14 May. Inside the town
lay the Seldjuk treasure and Kilij Arslan's family. The sultan
himself was away in the east fighting the Danishmends—a Turkish
dynasty from east Anatolia who claimed possession of Melitene, a
town which, for Kilij Arslan, was the vital gateway to the Seldjuk
hinterland in Iraq and Persia. After his experiences with Peter the
Hermit's followers he clearly saw no reason to take the crusaders
seriously. By the time that he realized the full extent of the danger
and hurried back, it was already too late. Unable to enter his own
city, he met the crusaders in pitched battle on 21 May. He was
defeated and forced to retreat. For the first time the crusaders had
proved that if they could catch the Moslems in a pitched battle the
tremendous impact of their heavily armed knights could give them
victory. But while the lake approaches to Nicaea remained open it
was still impossible to take the city. Alexius, who was at Pelecanum
organizing supplies, sent ships overland. They were then refloated
on the lake and the blockade was completed. Disheartened first by
their sultan's retreat and then by this manoeuvre, the garrison
surrendered to the Byzantine admiral Butumites. Nicaea was once
again part of the Byzantine empire. In view of their oaths the
crusaders ought to have expected nothing else. None the less they
were disappointed. They were forbidden to enter the city and
there could be no question of sacking it. The distrust of the
Byzantines grew although Alexius distributed rich presents in
order to compensate the crusaders for the plunder of which they
felt deprived. But at any rate one obstacle on the way had been
removed and this was something to be cheerful about. Stephen of
Blois wrote home to his wife Adelaide: 'unless Antioch proves a
stumbling block we hope to be in Jerusalem in five weeks' time.'
It was to take them two years.

Just to march through Anatolia to Antioch took four months.
They had to endure the heat of the summer and a shortage of food
and water. The Turks, before retreating to the mountains, had
devastated the countryside far and wide. The crusaders did not
know the terrain and did not altogther trust their guides. For the
first time the disadvantages of not having a single commander-in-
chief became clear. The council of princes which acted instead was
somewhat ponderous and by no means always unanimous. They
left Nicaea on 26 June and headed south-east towards Dorylaeum

at which point they would have to choose between several possible routes through Anatolia. They marched in two sections. The first consisted of the Normans of southern Italy and northern France, together with the Flemings and a Byzantine contingent under the command of Taticius; the second of the Provençals and Lorrainers with the troops of Hugh of Vermandois. On 29 June the leading section, in which Bohemund was the dominant personality, came into contact with the army of Kilij Arslan. At dawn on the next day battle was joined. The Turks attacked from all sides. Using their lighter equipment and greater mobility to good effect, they were able to keep out of the way of the ponderous phalanx of heavily armed knights. At the same time they poured in a ceaseless rain of arrows. But they were not strong enough to break into the crusaders' ranks held tightly together by Bohemund. The battle was decided when the Turks were taken by surprise by the arrival of the second section under Godfrey de Bouillon and Raymond of Toulouse, who had been informed of events by a messenger from Bohemund. Adhemar of Le Puy distinguished himself by leading a successful outflanking manoeuvre, although it is not clear whether this had any influence on the outcome of the battle. The sultan fled, followed by his panic-stricken army. The Turkish encampment with its magnificent tents and rich booty fell into the hands of the crusaders. The battle had opened the way to Anatolia.

The army, however, avoided the shorter, northern routes even though this meant renouncing well-built Byzantine roads, because to take them would have forced it to go through the central region of Turkish power. Instead the crusaders chose the detour through south-east Anatolia, marching to Philomelium and then along the foot of the Taurus mountains as far as Iconium (Konya). From there they went on to Tyana where the road forked again. It had been a most arduous march. They had enjoyed one short rest—a week at Iconium in mid-August—and then at Heraclea they had to fight their way through against the combined forces of the Danish-mends and the emir of Cappadocia. From Tyana the most direct road to Syria led through the Cilician Gates, a steep and narrow pass through the Taurus, then down to Tarsus in the Cilician plain and from there over the Amanus range into the valley of the Orontes in Syria. Tancred, Baldwin of Boulogne, and Baldwin of Le Bourg left the army at Tyana and set out along this route.

For the main army, however, the Cilician Gates posed too many problems. So the other princes decided to follow the road which first took them north-east to Caesarea, the chief city of the Danish-mends, and then turned sharply south-east to cross the Anti-Taurus on its way to Marash. One advantage of this route was that the crusaders could hope for support from the local Christian population, above all from the Armenians. In the mid-eleventh century these people had been driven from their home in Armenia by the Byzantines. They settled first in Cappadocia but were then forced by the pressure of the advancing Turks to retire southwards and they now lived in a wide area from Cilicia in the west to beyond the Euphrates in the east. West of the Cilician Gates they were ruled by the Hethoumian dynasty; to the east the Roupenians held sway. Further east there was a group of lesser Armenian princes who recognized Turkish suzerainty. The most important of these was Thoros of Edessa.

At the end of September the army entered Caesarea which the Danishmends had abandoned. From here they marched over the Anti-Taurus; it was a difficult journey made worse by the autumn rains. In mid-October they reached Marash where they were warmly welcomed by the Armenians and could rest for a few days. On 20 October 1097 they fought their way across the Iron Bridge over the Orontes and on 21 October they arrived before the walls of Antioch, the key to North Syria.

Meanwhile Tancred and Baldwin had advanced southwards against the Turkish settlements in the Cilician plain—Armenian control being limited to the mountains. The two of them were almost certainly seeking their own private gain; nevertheless their enterprise did help the crusade. Firstly it meant that the right flank of the main army marching to Antioch was protected. Secondly, the conquest of Cilicia meant that a wedge was driven between the Anatolian and the Syrian Seldjuks, preventing them from joining forces to relieve Antioch. Tancred, with a small party of knights, captured Tarsus but was forced to relinquish it to the very much larger forces of Baldwin. Bitterly disappointed Tancred moved off eastwards to Mamistra. Despite his oath Baldwin had no intention of handing over Tarsus to Alexius, especially since there was no Byzantine official anywhere near. He left a Christian garrison in charge and was able to reinforce it with the help of a rich pirate, Guynemer of Boulogne, whose fleet happened to be cruising in those waters. Baldwin then moved on to Mamistra where there was some skirmishing between his men and Tancred's; but they just managed to avert open war. Tancred went south and with help from Guynemer captured the port of Alexandretta. Then he rejoined the main army before Antioch. Baldwin had already met the army while it was still at Marash, but he stayed only long enough to confer with the other leaders before heading east again in order to make a more permanent entry into Armenian politics. First he captured the important fortresses of Ravendel and Turbessel which controlled the territory west of the Euphrates. Everywhere the Armenians under Turkish lordship greeted him as a liberator. East of the Euphrates the position of the Armenian Thoros of Edessa was shaky. He had once served the Byzantine Emperor and he was Greek Orthodox by religion. This made him unpopular with his own subjects who were Monophysites belonging to the Armenian Church. Hoping to free himself from Turkish overlordship he invited Baldwin to Edessa. Baldwin wintered west of the Euphrates, then, with a force of only eighty knights, entered Edessa in February 1098. Thoros adopted him as his son, using the Armenian ritual whereby both father and son shared the same gown. Baldwin was now heir and co-ruler. But in the next month a conspiracy against Thoros ended with the old ruler being lynched. Baldwin did nothing to help his adoptive father; in fact he probably gave the conspirators his approval. On 10 March he accepted an invitation to be sole ruler of Edessa. As at Tarsus he had no intention of restoring it to the Byzantine emperor. The first crusader state had been founded, the county of Edessa, controlling an area both east and west of the Euphrates, inhabited chiefly by Armenians. It was to act as a north-eastern buffer state protecting the other crusader states further to the south. The new count, his hands full here, thought no more about helping the main army.

During their march through Asia Minor and even more during the coming struggle in Syria and Palestine, the crusaders profited from the state of disarray in Islam. Since the Muslims were unable to grasp what was about to hit them, they saw no reason to abandon their own internal feuds. Medieval Arabic, like medieval Latin, developed no word for 'crusade'. The crusaders they called simply Franks (the First Crusade being predominantly French in character), and the crusader states were the Frankish territories in the Holy Land. That a religious war could serve any purpose other than that of spreading one's own religion was incomprehensible to the Muslims, whose own idea of holy war, Jihad, was entirely based on this conception. To the Seldjuks the crusade must have looked rather like another Byzantine military expedition, the kind of thing to which they were thoroughly accustomed.

Up to 1095 the dominant political figure in Syria had been Tutush, brother of the great Seldjuk sultan, Malik Shah. He had driven the Fatimids and the Turcomans out of Damascus, Jerusalem, and Acre. His state was a rival to the other Seldjuk powers as well as a useful buffer for them against the Fatimids. In 1086 Tutush added Aleppo to his Palestinian and south Syrian possessions and so Malik Shah judged that the time had come to intervene. He established his own nominees as rulers in Mosul, Aleppo, and Antioch. When Malik Shah died in 1092 the Seldjuk empire disintegrated. Tutush again tried to extend his dominions and although he was pushed back into Syria by his nephew Berkyaruk, he managed to keep his hold on Aleppo. When he died one of his sons, Ridwan (1095–1113), inherited Aleppo, and the other, Duqaq (1095–1104), obtained Damascus. South Palestine was recovered by the Fatimids who used the opportunity provided by Tutush's death to advance northwards from Egypt. In 1098 they drove the Ortoqids, who had held Jerusalem as a Seldjuk fief, out of the Holy Land. The Shi'ite Fatimids had not the least intention of helping the Sunnite Seldjuks against the crusaders. On the contrary they suggested—though in vain—the formation of an anti-Seldjuk alliance. The growing independence of the minor Armenian principalities added to the confusion. None of the Syrian states was alone powerful enough to stop the Christian army, and so thanks to the disintegration within the Islamic world the crusade was able to reach its goal. For the moment, however, it still stood outside Antioch.

Beautifully situated not far from the sea and on a slope leading down to the fertile valley of the Orontes, Antioch had once been the third city of the Roman Empire. It was no longer quite so splendid but its huge walls and the 400 towers built by Justinian made it practically impregnable. Since 1087 a Seldjuk emir, Yaghi-Siyan, with his Turkish garrison had ruled over a population consisting mainly of Greek and Armenian Christians. Naturally the emir had reason to doubt his subjects' loyalty. When the crusaders arrived at Antioch on 21 October 1097 they decided against trying to take the city by storm, the course advocated by Raymond of Toulouse and one which might have succeeded. Instead, despite the fact that they could not completely encircle Antioch, they decided in favour of a regular siege. This was what Bohemund advised. He hoped to keep Antioch for himself; perhaps Baldwin's success at Edessa strengthened Bohemund's ambition. But the Gate of St. George in the west wall of the city remained open and allowed both supplies to come in and the besieged to come out in sorties against the crusaders, though not in sufficient strength to deal them a decisive blow. Not until mid-November when a Genoese flotilla, bringing reinforcements, sailed into the harbour of St. Symeon, could the besiegers turn to build-

ing fortified camps and extend, though not complete, the encirclement of the city. With the winter came food shortage and bitterly
cold weather. Stephen of Blois wrote to his wife that he could not
understand why anyone in Syria should complain of too much sun.
The foraging expeditions were forced to strike further and further
afield. At the end of December Bohemund and Robert of Flanders
with a large part of the army left the city and advanced up the
Orontes valley as far as Shaizar in search of provisions. Here they
unexpectedly stumbled upon an army led by Duqaq of Damascus
who had at last made up his mind to relieve Antioch. The
crusaders won a convincing victory. Later a half-hearted attempt to
relieve the city was made by Ridwan of Aleppo and met a similar
end.

Meanwhile the famine in the army grew worse and some of the
poor even turned cannibal. Some wild Flemings who had followed
Peter the Hermit and were known as 'Tafurs' acquired a considerable reputation for this kind of thing. They always fought in the
front line and made the most of any Turks they killed.[21] The
Greek patriarch of Jerusalem who had retired to Cyprus was in
contact with Adhemar of Le Puy and did his best to help the
crusaders, but the supplies he sent were just a drop in the ocean.
In January 1098 men began to desert. Among them was Peter the
Hermit, but he was caught and brought back. In February
Taticius, the Byzantine general, left the camp. It is hard to know
why he did this; and his departure was, of course, exploited by
Bohemund in order to stir up anti-Greek resentment. But despite
all the difficulties it was at last possible, in March 1098, to complete the blockade. Then in May the situation changed again when
it became known that a great warrior, Kerbogha of Mosul (d. 1102),
was marching to relieve Antioch. He had obtained additional
troops from the Ortoqids who, having been thrown out of Jerusalem, were now ruling in Mesopotamia. The approach of this
army put the demoralized crusaders in a terrible position. If
Antioch did not fall before Kerbogha arrived the crusade would be
all over. It was Bohemund who saved the situation. He had already
threatened to leave the army if Antioch were not handed over to
him and he now repeated this demand openly. He had established
a connection with a captain inside Antioch named Firouz, who
was willing to sell the city. Despite the objections raised by Raymond who wanted to remain true to his oath, Bohemund was
promised Antioch—if he could take it and so long as the emperor
did not come in person to press his claim. Although the fall of the
city was now imminent, one of the leading crusaders, Stephen of

Blois, decided to leave for home on 2 June. He had probably been responsible for supplies and may well have felt that since Antioch's surrender was certain, his task was now completed. On the return journey through Anatolia he met the emperor Alexius who was preparing to advance into Syria in order to safeguard his rights there. In the meantime other deserters had joined up with Stephen and they gave a depressing account of the situation at Antioch with the city now held by the crusaders who were, in their turn, besieged by Kerbogha. They painted so black a picture that Alexius altered his plans and Bohemund's chances of retaining Antioch were thereby much improved. In Europe public opinion turned against Stephen of Blois, accusing him, a little unjustly, of cowardice and desertion. His wife's welcome home was anything but friendly.

On the evening of the day that Stephen left the camp, the crusaders also marched away from Antioch, only to return under cover of night. In the early hours of the morning of 3 June 1098 Firouz admitted Bohemund and his knights into the city. It was not long before the crusaders were in control and had killed all the Turks they could lay their hands on. Yaghi-Siyan was slain while trying to escape. His son managed to reach the citadel which still held out. But the arrival of Kerbogha meant that the crusaders had not gained very much. Once the besiegers they were now themselves besieged in a city suffering from shortage of food.

Fortunately Kerbogha had come too late. He had spent three weeks vainly besieging Edessa and so lost the chance of destroying the crusaders while they were still outside Antioch. On arrival he at once took command of the citadel on the mountain ridge behind the city and from here he constantly harassed the crusaders besides organizing a complete blockade. Under the pressure of hunger, morale in the Christian army sank rapidly and the number of desertions remained high. Something drastic had to be done if any way out was to be found.[22] Since it was, in any case, a situation which was ripe for religious hysteria and visions of all kinds, use was made of a visionary from Provence, a man of humble origins called Peter Bartholomew. This man informed Count Raymond that St. Andrew had appeared to him on several occasions and had told him that the Holy Lance—with which the Roman centurion had pierced the side of Christ—was buried in the cathedral of St. Peter. Adhemar of Le Puy had his doubts about the story—after all another such lance was in a Constantinople collection. But diggings in the cathedral took place several days later and Peter actually did find a lance on the evening of 14 June. Today it is considered certain that the whole affair was a pious fraud but it is not easy to be certain about the identity of the men behind it. Later on, when it had become common to look upon the lance with scepticism, the Normans blamed the Provençals, but in fact Peter Bartholomew was quite capable, in other circumstances, of having thoroughly pro-Norman visions—especially after it was clear that at least one man from south France, Adhemar of Le Puy, did not have a very high opinion of him. The Normans could just as well have been responsible as could some unidentifiable group of churchmen. In any event, the immediate effects of the discovery were enormous. The army's morale was raised and all were united in the urgent determination to break the blockade and destroy Kerbogha. By now indeed a successful sortie was the only chance. Bohemund—always the central figure in the struggle for Antioch —was particularly insistent about this now that rivalries had broken out in Kerbogha's army. The Damascus contingent were offended because Kerbogha had requested help from Aleppo as well. The decisive battle took place on 28 June. Kerbogha did not attack early enough and his attempt to outflank the crusaders was foiled by Bohemund's prudence. It ended when the Turks, led by the Damascus contingent, fled in panic. The plunder was immense and Bohemund was the man of the moment. The citadel too now surrendered to him.

The most urgent problem now was a political one: what should be done with Antioch? On this subject the Normans and Provençals disagreed completely. The crusade came to a halt; in an atmosphere of general distrust no one was prepared to leave the city. In its present state the army could not be expected to march during the heat of the summer, so the starting date was fixed for 1 November. Then an epidemic broke out and the princes scattered to escape it. Bohemund went to Cilicia, Godfrey to Turbessel, and Robert of Normandy to Lattakieh. But Adhemar of Le Puy was struck down by the disease and died on 1 August. He had not been able to play the dominating role originally envisaged by Urban, but among the quarrelling princes he had always stood for compromise and harmony. From now on the conflict between Normans and Provençals grew worse. In September the princes returned to Antioch and dispatched a letter to the pope, informing him of the legate's death and asking him to come to Antioch in person to put himself at the head of the crusade. It was a measure born of desperation, taken in the hope of gaining time when there seemed to be no immediate prospect of reaching an agreement about Antioch. Forays into Muslim territory kept the troops occupied. In October Raymond captured the town of al-Bara and here the first Latin bishop, Peter of Narbonne, was installed, though of course he had to be consecrated by the Greek patriarch of Antioch who had now been restored to his position.* On 5 November the council of princes met again in the cathedral. This time Bohemund was able, by and large, to get his way. He had long had the support of most of the princes and now Raymond too had to yield in face of the restless army's insistent demand that the march be continued. But Raymond had no intention of simply allowing his rival to take over Antioch at once and he agreed only on condition that Bohemund would go with them to Jerusalem. The departure was further delayed, however, by fighting to the south of Antioch and during this period tension between Provençals and Normans mounted. In December Raymond captured Maarat an-Numan, a fortress to the south-east of Antioch, perhaps hoping to use it as a counterweight to the Normans in Antioch. For his part Bohemund began a systematic campaign to discredit the Provençals, in particular by exploiting the doubts about the genuineness of the Holy Lance.

Some time around Christmas a large part of the army offered to recognize Raymond as commander-in-chief if he would lead them on to Jerusalem. Raymond accepted this offer and on 13 January 1099 the march began. Raymond who was now nearly sixty years old left Maarat at the head of his troops, walking barefoot and dressed as a pilgrim. By this finely calculated gesture he reminded his fellow-princes of their crusaders' oaths for it was clear to him that his contingent by itself could achieve little. He offered sums of money to the others to try to persuade them to accept him as their leader; in this way he hoped to strengthen his own position against Bohemund. Tancred and Robert of Normandy were persuaded, but Godfrey and Robert of Flanders would not agree to serve under him. In early January Bohemund had managed to drive the last of the Provençal troops out of Antioch, and despite his promise to join the march to Jerusalem he refused to leave the city. Raymond's army moved south along the eastern slopes of the Nosairi mountains. The advance was free of incident since the local emirs were much too weak to put up any serious resistance and most of them were prepared to pay to avoid being attacked. After the disaster at Antioch the rulers of Damascus, Aleppo, and Mosul preferred to remain passive observers. They certainly saw no reason to help the Fatimids who in 1098 had again advanced into Palestine; indeed the Syrian rulers, as Sun-

* This was the first step towards building up a Latin Church which threatened the established rights of the Greek Church.

nites, may well have enjoyed seeing Christians move against the Shi'ite Fatimids. North of Tripoli the crusaders returned to the coast, and some small detachments moved northwards capturing a few ports including Maraclea and Tortosa. (The cathedral at Tortosa is one of the finest buildings of the crusading period still standing today.) These successes persuaded Godfrey and Robert of Flanders to change their minds. Even Bohemund joined their march south, but only for form's sake, and after a short while he went back to Antioch where he now ruled unopposed. In the next few years he was able to build up an extensive principality.

Raymond meanwhile had settled down to besiege Arqa, a town to the north-east of Tripoli which he had already marked out as the centre of a Lebanese principality for himself. But despite the arrival of Godfrey and Robert of Flanders the siege proved fruitless and so the army continued its march south along the coast road. The emir of Tripoli bought immunity for himself and for his city. On 19 May the crusaders crossed the Dog River; they were now in Fatimid territory. All the Fatimids' attempts to reach a settlement had failed. Their last offer had been conditional on the crusaders not entering Palestine—it shows how little the Muslims were able to understand what the crusade was all about. The advance continued: Beirut, Sidon, Tyre, Acre, Haifa, and then on to Jaffa where they turned inland. At Ramleh, a Muslim town abandoned by its inhabitants, they installed a Latin bishop and this time, there being no Greek available, he was consecrated by a Latin. The new bishop was to become secular ruler over Ramleh and the nearby village of Lydda where, in fact, his cathedral church of St. George was situated. On 6 June Tancred occupied Bethlehem and hoisted his banner over the Church of the Nativity. Next day, 7 June, the crusaders' road led them to the summit of a hill from where they could see Jerusalem. Many of them had tears in their eyes for they had waited so long for this moment. They named the hill Montjoie. Three years had passed since the day when Godfrey de Bouillon had set out from Lorraine.

Jerusalem was a well fortified city and the lie of the land meant that it was vulnerable, if at all, only from the north and south-west. The Fatimid governor had taken adequate precautions. He had expelled the Christian inhabitants as being unreliable. He had sufficient food and water and had taken the trouble to make the springs outside the walls unusable. The crusaders, too few in number to be able to invest the city completely, concentrated on the weaker sectors. On 13 June they tried to take Jerusalem by storm but, being insufficiently supplied with scaling ladders and siege engines, they were driven back. Then, quite by chance, six Christian ships sailed into the deserted harbour at Jaffa, bringing urgently needed building materials. Wood was brought from Samaria. But the construction of the wooden castles set on wheels and fitted out with catapults was a slow business. The heat and the water shortage had a bad effect on morale which again sank to a dangerous level. Then it was learnt that the Egyptian army was on the way. Once more a vision came at the critical moment, this time to a priest called Peter Desiderius. He was told that if they held a fast and then a procession round the walls, the city would fall into their hands within nine days—as long as they performed these tasks with sufficient piety. A fast was observed and then, on 8 July, to the astonishment of the besieged, the crusade turned into a barefoot procession of pilgrims which solemnly wound its way round the city. The procession ended on the Mount of Olives where they all listened to the eloquent words of Peter the Hermit and other preachers. The army had recovered its fighting spirit. When three 'castles' were ready, they began the assault during the night of 13–14 July. On 14 July Raymond managed to bring his castle up against the wall in the south-west sector, but he could not capture the wall itself. Godfrey had more success when, on 15 July, he manoeuvred his castle close to the wall near the Gate of Flowers and then made a bridge from the castle to the top of the wall. Litold, a Flemish knight from Tournai, was the first crusader to set foot on the wall. He was followed by Godfrey and the Lorrainers and then Tancred and his men. At this spot a large stone cross was to stand for as long as Jerusalem was held by Christians in memory of the capture of the city by the crusaders. While the Lorrainers opened the gates to their comrades, Tancred rushed ahead into the Temple area, the heart of the city, and seized the Mosque of al-Aqsa. The Fatimid governor who had been directing the defence in the southern sector, now realized that all was lost and withdrew into the Tower of David, a massive citadel near the western Jaffa Gate. In return for being allowed to retire safely to Ascalon he surrendered this to Raymond who thus obtained a strategically important strongpoint. The governor and his retinue were the only Muslims to escape alive. The intoxication of victory, religious fanaticism, and the memory of hardships bottled up for three years exploded in a horrifying bloodbath in which the crusaders hacked down everyone, irrespective of race or religion, who was unfortunate enough to come within reach of their swords. They waded, ankle-deep in blood, through streets covered with bodies. The Lorrainers were relatively restrained; at least they refrained from raping Jewish women. When the frenzy of killing was over the first task was to dispose of the corpses. The precious Jewish library (eight Torah rolls and three hundred and thirty manuscripts) escaped destruction and was sold, at a high price, to the Jewish community at Ascalon. The Muslim world was profoundly shocked by this Christian barbarity; it was a long time before the memory of this massacre began to fade. The crusade, however, had reached its goal. The Sepulchre of Christ was again in Christian hands. But for how long? The Egyptian army was coming closer.

After the sanitary problem of the corpses had been dealt with, the leaders of the crusade, both clerics and laymen, met to decide what was to be done next. The curious fact now became clear that they had left Europe without any idea of what to do with Jerusalem once they had captured it. Nor, apparently, had anything been worked out during the long march. It was generally accepted, however, that an ecclesiastical and a secular system of government had to be devised if they wanted to keep what they had won. The churchmen, headed by Bishop Arnulf of Marturano, demanded that the first step, before going on to secular affairs, should be the election of a patriarch.[23] But this had to be postponed when it was found that the clergy from Lorraine and Provence would not accept the only candidate, Robert of Normandy's chaplain Arnulf of Rohes. (The claims of the Greek patriarch were ignored. The crusaders believed him to be in Cyprus though in fact he had died a few days before they entered Jerusalem.) There were only two serious candidates for the throne: Raymond of Toulouse and Godfrey de Bouillon. The other leaders either intended to return home or lacked the necessary authority. The crown was first offered to Raymond but he refused it with the words that he did not wish to be king in Christ's holy city. He realized that the offer had been made half-heartedly and he hoped, by this cunning reply, to prevent Godfrey from accepting it. Godfrey was popular with the whole army and had managed, on the whole, to keep out of the unedifying quarrels of the princes. On the other hand it was clear that he lacked the personality of a Bohemund or a Raymond. But he was clever enough—or perhaps his advisers were—to find a solution to the immediate problem. He outmanoeuvred Raymond by refusing to be king but agreeing to be ruler, taking the title of *Advocatus sancti Sepulchri*, Defender of the Holy Sepulchre. This also had the advantage of leaving open for the moment the critical question of the relationship between the lay ruler and the Church, so avoiding a clash with the clergy.[24] Godfrey then tricked Raymond into handing over the Tower of David, the military key to Jerusalem. In a rage, Raymond left the city and went on a pilgrimage to Jericho and the Jordan. His absence simplified the problem of choosing a patriarch. The Norman Arnulf was elected, despite the fact that he was illegitimate and not even a subdeacon and therefore, in canon law, not eligible. For this reason he was enthroned but not consecrated. During the siege of Arqa he had finally demolished all belief in the Holy Lance and he now strengthened his own position by looking for and finding the True Cross—a relic powerful enough to supplant the 'Provençal' lance.

Despite all this tension, both Raymond and Robert of Normandy, whom Godfrey had somehow managed to offend, responded loyally to the new ruler's request for help against the Egyptian army. On 12 August 1099 battle was joined on level ground near the Egyptian harbour-fortress of Ascalon. The Egyptians were taken by surprise while still in their camp and were completely defeated. Their commander, the vizier al-Afdal (1094–1121) fled back to Egypt. On 13 August the victorious army returned in triumph to Jerusalem. The success of the crusade was now assured. The regaining of the Holy Land was an astonishing achievement. The rejoicing in Christendom was fully justified.

4 · THE CRUSADER STATES, 1099–1146

THE Bible had promised a land flowing with milk and honey but the crusaders found that they had conquered an economically depressed area with a geographical structure that tended to force people to settle in isolated groups and to favour the development of small or very small states.[25] At the time of their greatest extent the crusader states stretched from the Gulf of Alexandretta to the Gulf of Akaba in the Red Sea. Excluding the eastern outpost at Edessa which by that time had been lost again, they covered an area about 500 miles long and anything up to 100 miles wide. Throughout the whole of this region the main geographical features are very similar. Going from west to east there is a coastal plain rising gradually up to a high range of limestone mountains; then a steep drop into a depression which in turn opens out into a fertile cultivated plateau, though in places a second mountain range, the Anti-Lebanon, has to be surmounted. This plateau then merges into a treeless steppe country. In the south the coastal plain is wider and separated from the sea by a belt of sand dunes. The principal mountain ranges are the Nosairi and Lebanon Mountains (up to 9,800 feet high) in the north; the Anti-Lebanon and Mount Hermon (up to 8,800 feet) in the centre; and the Palestinian highlands (Hebron is over 3,300 feet above sea-level) in the south. The depression is formed by the Syrian rift valley with the Orontes in the north; it continues as the Leontes valley running between the mountains of Lebanon and the Anti-Lebanon and then as the valley of the Jordan and the Dead Sea (355 square miles in area; in places more than 1,300 feet below sea-level; salt content up to 22 per cent). The three main crossing points on the Jordan were Jacob's Ford north of the Sea of Galilee and, to the south, the Pont de Senabra and the Pont de Judaire. South of the Dead Sea the hills merge into the gently undulating plateau of the inhospitable Negev Desert. Apart from the coastal plain the whole region is rather infertile and becomes increasingly so as one moves south from Galilee. The Palestinian highlands are particularly rocky and lacking in water. There are few good east–west routes. The only good road to the Jordan runs from the much fought-over plain of Acre. East of the Jordan the crusaders penetrated temporarily into the Terre de Suète, a fertile plain east of the Sea of Galilee, and into the volcanic hill region of Moab through which strategically and economically important lines of communication ran from south Syria to Egypt. The climate is characterized by very hot, dry summers and by abundant cool winter rain, with occasional snow falls even outside the high mountainous areas. The temperature figures for Jerusalem are as follows: in July and August an average temperature of *c.* 25 ° C. (77 ° F.) with daily maxima of *c.* 35 ° C. (95 ° F.), sometimes going up to 40 ° C. (104 ° F.) at midday; average temperatures in January and February 8 ° C. (46 ° F.), going down to −5 ° C. (23 ° F.) in the early hours of the morning. At Jericho summer temperatures can rise as high as 50 ° C. (122 ° F.). Additional hazards were earthquakes (in 1114, 1170, and 1185) and plagues of mice (1120–4, 1127) and of locusts (1114, 1117, 1120) which decimated the herds and destroyed the vegetation. So far as climate and the rural economy were concerned, both Provençals and south Italians had been better off at home.

Early in September 1099 most of the crusaders left Jerusalem. Robert of Flanders, Robert of Normandy, Baldwin of Le Bourg, and Raymond of Toulouse marched north with their troops; the two Roberts were on their way home. Only Godfrey de Bouillon and Tancred remained in Jerusalem. With them were only some 300 knights and 2,000 foot soldiers.[26] Originally Godfrey's lordship consisted of no more than Jerusalem, the port of Jaffa, and some towns, Lydda, Ramleh, Bethlehem, and St. Abraham (Hebron) which he fortified strongly. The countryside was inhabited by hostile Muslims who at first—while Frankish power still seemed precarious—refused to co-operate with their new lords. Even the population of Jerusalem felt insecure because the city walls were still badly damaged and only the offer of considerable material advantages persuaded them to stay. According to the *Assise de l'an et jour* anyone who left intending to come back later when and if things had settled down, would forfeit his possessions to the person who, in the meantime, had held them for a year and a day. Only gradually was Godfrey able to extend his influence over the plains of Judaea and Samaria. Tancred moved further north to Galilee and carved out a lordship for himself. It was originally made up of Tiberias, Nazareth, and Beisan; later Haifa and the Terre de Suète together with the area which lay between them were added. Tancred held this region, the lordship of Tiberias, as a fief of Godfrey;

gradually it evolved into the principality of Galilee. In time God-frey's territory developed into a compact Christian state separating the coastal region which was still controlled by the Fatimids from the Muslim interior of the Hauran and Transjordan. The geog-raphy of the region required that the crusaders should try to push back the Muslims in the south and east until the desert had been reached. This could then serve as a *cordon sanitaire* between the Christians and the Muslims, with the latter being confined to Egypt and Mesopotamia. In order to achieve this the crusaders had first of all to capture Aleppo and Damascus. But in fact they failed to do this and had to be satisfied with the creation of a no man's land in the Hauran, the income from which they shared with Damascus.

Raymond of Toulouse meanwhile, once Godfrey had prevented him from building up a lordship in south-west Palestine, had also gone north. He had found his old rival Bohemund engaged in be-sieging Lattakieh, a Byzantine port south of Antioch which Bohe-mund had feared might be used as a bridgehead if Alexius decided to invade Antioch. Raymond forced him to raise the siege. Bohemund had been receiving naval support from a Pisan fleet commanded by Daimbert, the archbishop of Pisa. It was a sign that a new force was entering the politics of Syria and Palestine. The two great sea powers in the eastern Mediterranean were Byzantium and Egypt. The crusader states never owned a fleet worth mention-ing. But without a fleet the Egyptians could not be driven out of the harbour towns and without the possession of the fertile coastal plain and the economically valuable ports, the Frankish states would never flourish. The Byzantines generally needed their fleet for their own affairs so the Italian maritime towns stepped into the breach. Being realists they had originally looked upon the crusade with great scepticism. Only when, against all their calculations, it succeeded did they come round to giving official support to the crusaders' cause. But in return for their help they always de-manded and received a high price. The privileges which they secured, often by pure blackmail, seriously impaired the legal integrity of the state and became a permanent burden on its finan-cial resources.

The Pisans were the first to sense that a great opportunity had come. They equipped a fleet which Archbishop Daimbert was then able to use to further his own private ends in Outremer. Like Bohemund he was suspicious of the Greeks so he and the prince of Antioch were natural allies. After the abandonment of the siege of Lattakieh they travelled to Jerusalem where they spent Christ-mas 1099 together with Baldwin of Edessa who had joined them on the way. Bohemund and Baldwin had at last fulfilled their vow to make a pilgrimage to Jerusalem. But they had political considerations in mind as well. Godfrey needed their knights just as urgently as he needed Daimbert's fleet, and was in no position to resist their demands. Patriarch Arnulf was deposed and Daimbert (1099–1102) elected in his place. Then Godfrey had to submit to being invested in his lordship by Daimbert. Bohemund in his turn was ready to hold Antioch as a fief of the patriarch. Baldwin of Edessa did not follow this example. For Bohemund such an investiture offered only advantages. While Daimbert remained in Jerusalem his de facto influence in Antioch was small, while Bohemund, as vassal of the Latin patriarch, could at last claim that he had some right to Antioch which previously he had held unlawfully and against the terms of the oath he had sworn to Alexius.

It was once generally accepted by historians that Daimbert's actions were an expression of the theocratic nature of the Church's claims in the East. But there is, in fact, very little to support this view (see p. 61f., n. 23). Almost certainly Daimbert did not come armed with the authority of a papal legate—though his expedition had the pope's blessing. It is most unlikely that his actions were in accordance with Urban's intentions. The pope would hardly have planned to deal with the question of the relationship between the Latin and Greek Churches in Daimbert's crass manner. The rights of the patriarch of Antioch had been infringed not only by the investiture of Bohemund but also by Daimbert's consecration of four Latin bishops and archbishops in Bohemund's principality: Tarsus, Artah, Mamistra, and Edessa. These infringements and Bohemund's hostile attitude forced Patriarch John of Antioch to take refuge in Constantinople. The result was a schism since Bohemund immediately installed a Latin patriarch, Bernard of Valence (1100–35). For a while Daimbert even refused to allow the Greeks to hold services in the Church of the Holy Sepulchre in Jerusalem. By investing Godfrey the patriarch was acting like a pope, like Gregory VII, for example, who had become feudal lord of Aragon, of the Normans in south Italy and of the Matildine lands in Tuscany. What Daimbert intended to create was not a theocratic constitution but a principality for himself. He was not satisfied with the quarter of Jerusalem which the patriarchs had held ever since the Fatimids, for security reasons, had restricted the Christian population of the city to one part of it. He used his wealth and power in a campaign of blackmail which forced Godfrey to concede first a quarter of Jaffa, then the citadel of Jerusalem, and finally the whole city and the rest of Jaffa, leaving

Godfrey with no more than a life interest in them. Prawer believes that Godfrey himself in no way recognized any theocratic claim made by the Church but thought only in terms of the establishment of a patriarchal barony within his kingdom.

This agreement at least had the advantage of giving Godfrey time to extend his rule over the coastal plain. Several minor emirs, as well as some of the Transjordan sheikhs, were in fact ready to pay him tribute. Daimbert's stranglehold was weakened when the Pisan fleet sailed for home after Easter 1100. Then in June a Venetian fleet arrived at Jaffa. Godfrey welcomed it warmly for he saw a chance of further loosening the patriarch's grip. While he was still negotiating with the Venetians he became seriously ill; none the less a treaty was arranged. The Venetians were to be allowed to trade freely throughout the state, to hold a market in every town and were to receive a third of every town they helped to capture. In return they would help him until 15 August. The colossal price which Godfrey was prepared to pay for some temporary assistance shows how anxious he was to create a counterweight to Daimbert. But he himself did not live to enjoy the changing situation. On 18 July he died. As the first Christian ruler of Jerusalem he was found a worthy resting place on the hill of Golgotha, the place of the crucifixion.

Daimbert made one fatal mistake. He left Jerusalem shortly before Godfrey died. Had he been there he would probably have been able to see that the terms of his agreement with Godfrey were carried out. In that event there might never have been a kingdom of Jerusalem. But in his absence a group of Lorrainers, Godfrey's household officials, seized control of the city. Acting in accordance with the customs of their homeland they summoned Godfrey's nearest relative, his brother Baldwin of Edessa, to take over the inheritance. There was, in other words, no question of a free election of a new ruler. Later the 'election' of Godfrey was to be used as a precedent to justify the development of a system of election by the barons, though in fact Godfrey had been chosen by his peers and battle-companions, not by the barons of Jerusalem. In the course of time two parallel constitutional procedures came to be evolved. One emphasized the electoral rights of the barons and looked back to Godfrey; the other emphasized hereditary rights and looked back to the succession of Baldwin.

Daimbert tried to block Baldwin's succession by writing to Bohemund and asking him to prevent Baldwin from reaching Jerusalem. The letter never reached the prince of Antioch.[27] In August 1100 Bohemund, still ignorant of events in Jerusalem, had marched north to consolidate his hold on his border regions. He had been ambushed and was now held prisoner by the Danishmend emir. Baldwin of Edessa intervened to save Antioch and then, in October, having left Edessa to be administered by his cousin Baldwin of Le Bourg (1100–18), he set out on an arduous march to Jerusalem where he arrived in November. Daimbert now recognized that there was no chance of his plans succeeding. The best he could hope for was to remain patriarch so towards Christmas he came to terms. On 25 December 1100 he crowned Baldwin king. The ceremony took place, not in the centre of the kingdom's religious life, the Church of the Holy Sepulchre, but in the Church of the Nativity at Bethlehem. In his coronation oath Baldwin promised to serve and defend the Holy Sepulchre and to rule the Church and people of Jerusalem justly and in peace. His successors were to swear to protect the patriarch—but this was not mentioned in Baldwin's oath. Instead of being vassals of the patriarch, the rulers of Jerusalem were once again the protectors and defenders of the Holy Sepulchre, the position claimed for them in the title which Godfrey had assumed: *Advocatus sancti Sepulchri*. Baldwin's insistence upon the royal title completed the process of freeing the newly created state from the overlordship of the patriarch.

Baldwin I had originally been destined for the Church and he was correspondingly well-educated. Moreover, as he had demonstrated when he founded the county of Edessa, he was made of sterner stuff than his brother. Once Daimbert had crowned him he had no further use for him. With the assistance of a new papal legate, Maurice of Porto, he had him banished. (Maurice had come to the Holy Land with a fleet from Genoa, the last of the three great maritime republics of Italy to extend its sphere of operations to Outremer.) For a short while in 1102 Daimbert was able to regain the patriarchal throne thanks to the support he received from Tancred who had exchanged the lordship of Tiberias for the regency of Antioch during the absence of the captive Bohemund. But then he was finally deposed and once again forced to go into exile in Antioch. He appealed to the pope on the grounds that he had been unlawfully expelled by Baldwin and was, in fact, able to convince Paschal II of the truth of this version although as far as canon law went he had been validly deposed, for serious offences, by two separate synods. Paschal ordered his reinstatement and a new conflict with the king was avoided only because Daimbert died before he could return. The pope's judgement must be seen in the light of the contemporary Gregorian demand for the *libertas ecclesiae*. He would not and could not allow the king to rule the

Church in so direct a fashion. But the fact that even the ambitious Daimbert had to appeal to the pope shows that an end had been set to all attempts to create a special position for the patriarchate. The Church of Jerusalem was clearly subject to papal authority and was firmly integrated into the Roman system. From now on the patriarch was nothing more than a metropolitan in a particularly venerable city with a particularly venerable title. The Latin patriarch of Antioch had never claimed this special position and the unhappy quarrel between him and the patriarch of Jerusalem over the distribution of suffragan bishoprics (see below p. 81) only served to confirm the pope in his role of lord and judge superior to the contending parties.

In the West the success of the First Crusade had been greeted with universal jubilation. The election of a new pope in 1099 in no way interrupted the work of preaching the crusade. This was directed particularly at those men who had abandoned the crusade before it captured Jerusalem and who therefore had failed to fulfil their vows. But many others stepped forward to take the cross for the first time, moved both by the news of victory and by the requests for reinforcements which came from Outremer.[28] The preaching had its biggest success in Lombardy where a large army mustered under the command of Archbishop Anselm of Milan. In the south of France the powerful duke of Aquitaine, William IX —one of the earliest troubadours—took the cross. In the north, Stephen of Blois and Hugh of Vermandois were ready to march for the second time; both submitted to growing public and private pressure that they should fulfil their vows. Count William II of Nevers and Auxerre, Duke Otto of Burgundy, and Count Stephen of Burgundy set out from eastern France. Among the clergy to take the cross were the bishops of Paris, Laon, and Soissons, and the archbishop of Besançon. In Germany crusading enthusiasm affected Bavaria and Austria in particular. Old Welf IV, duke of Bavaria, and many of his lords took the cross. He was accompanied by Ida, the widow of Margrave Luitpold II of Austria, and by Archbishop Thiemo of Salzburg, Bishop Ulrich of Passau, the abbot of Admont, and the chronicler Ekkehard of Aura.

The first to go were the Lombards. They set off in autumn 1100 and reached Constantinople early in the next year. During the course of the summer the other contingents arrived. But the Lombards pushed on without waiting for their fellow-crusaders. They crossed the Bosporus after Easter and marched to Nicomedia where Stephen of Blois and the Burgundians caught up with them. Here too they were joined by Raymond of Toulouse, recently arrived from Lattakieh. In vain the experienced crusaders tried to dissuade the Lombards from their plan of invading north Anatolia in order to rescue Bohemund from his prison at Niksar in Pontus. On the march through north Anatolia the army suffered badly from lack of provisions. Their route is difficult to reconstruct but it ended in mid-July near Mersivan east of the River Halys where the crusaders were met by a Turkish army composed of contingents sent by Sultan Kilij Arslan, the Danishmends, and Ridwan of Aleppo. The battle lasted several days and ended with the complete destruction of the Lombard army. Only a few survived to find their way back to Constantinople, among them the counts of Toulouse, Blois, and Burgundy and the archbishop of Milan.

The army led by Count William of Nevers had no better luck. It also marched towards north Anatolia but then turned south at Ankara, only to be destroyed at Heraclea. William himself managed to find his way to Antioch. The Aquitanians and the Bavarians meanwhile had fought their way through the Balkans to Constantinople. There they had to swear the same oath that the first crusaders had sworn; and from there they took the same road that the first crusaders had taken. At Heraclea they too met their fate. In September 1101 they fell into a Turkish ambush and were completely defeated. Ida of Austria and Thiemo of Salzburg were imprisoned or murdered. The legends which sprang up around them contain motifs which were to become commonplace in the romantic literature of the crusades. According to the legend Ida married a Saracen emir and became the mother of Zengi the great enemy of the Christians. While he was in prison Thiemo was supposed to have been put to work repairing a Muslim idol. Suddenly the idol began to speak in a blasphemous fashion and, as a result, Thiemo had to suffer a martyr's death. The dukes of Aquitaine and Bavaria with a few followers got through to Antioch where they were soon joined by those who had earlier escaped back to Constantinople. From Antioch this pitifully small band marched on to Jerusalem. The crusade had failed. For the moment the West was not ready to dispatch another big army. A penitential crusade by which the emperor, Henry IV, hoped to have his excommunication lifted and in preparation for which he issued the *Reichslandfriede* of 1103, never got beyond the planning stage as a result of the hard lines still being taken in the Investiture Contest and the rebellion of the emperor's own son.

Meanwhile in Antioch the warlike Tancred was trying to extend the frontiers of his state in all directions. In 1101 he reconquered Cilicia from the Byzantines; then he moved south to Lattakieh which finally capitulated in 1103 after a long siege. But despite all his efforts he could not prevent Raymond of Toulouse and his Provençal followers from occupying the port of Tortosa, south of Lattakieh, and then settling down to besiege Tripoli. Ever since the First Crusade Raymond had had his eyes on this city and now he intended not to rest until he had captured it and made it the centre of a principality of his own. This state would form a link between the Normans in Antioch to the north and the Lorrainers in Jerusalem to the south and was intended to ensure that Raymond had the power to cope with his Norman rivals. By building a massive castle on Mount Pilgrim Raymond was able to control the land approaches to Tripoli. He did not live to see the surrender of the city but a charter of 1103 in which he already took the title of count of Tripoli admits of no doubt about his plans.

In 1103, on payment of a large ransom, Bohemund of Antioch was freed. The money was raised by the efforts of Baldwin of Le Bourg who had gradually come to realize that Tancred was too powerful a neighbour for comfort. But even after Bohemund had once again taken the reins of government into his own hands Tancred remained in Antioch. He could have returned to his old lordship, Tiberias, but declined to do so, possibly remembering his old rivalry with King Baldwin I. Bohemund immediately launched an offensive against Ridwan of Aleppo. In this he was supported by Baldwin of Le Bourg and Joscelin of Courtenay. Joscelin had arrived in the Holy Land in 1101 and had been enfeoffed with Turbessel by Baldwin. This made him the most important vassal of the count of Edessa west of the Euphrates. In 1104 they planned to capture Harran, the great fortress south-east of Edessa. The idea was good. Harran was the gateway to Mosul where the death of the powerful Kerbogha (1102) had been followed by bitter quarrels between the new atabeg (i.e. regent) and his Muslim neighbours. The possession of Harran would have effectively thrust a wedge between the three Seldjuk centres, Anatolia, Iraq, and Syria. In particular, Aleppo and Damascus would have been cut off from their fellow-believers in central Asia. Even in these circumstances, however, the ruler of Damascus was not prepared to go to war against the Franks for, in his eyes, Antioch and Edessa were valuable buffer-states against Aleppo and Mosul. None the less, on the banks of the River Balikh not far from Harran, the Frankish army was cut to pieces (1104). Baldwin of Le Bourg and Joscelin of Courtenay were captured, leaving Tancred happily in possession of the regency of Edessa. The defeat had other far-reaching political consequences though the importance of

these was not immediately apparent. Together with the failure of
the crusade of 1101 it destroyed the legend of the invincibility of
the crusaders. The failure to split the Seldjuks meant that Edessa's
position as an eastern outpost of Christendom was increasingly
vulnerable. The newly founded county survived for as long as
forty years only because of the lack of unity among the Muslims.

Byzantium took advantage of the defeat at Harran to reconquer
Cilicia from Antioch and to reoccupy parts of Lattakieh—the harbour and the lower town. Bohemund, desperately concerned about
the future of his principality once again handed the regency over
to Tancred and returned to Europe. He went first to his own lands
in Apulia and then on to Rome and France where he used all the
means at his disposal—money and propaganda—to raise an army
to fight Byzantium. He enhanced the standing of his family by skilfully arranging advantageous marriages for himself and for his
nephew Tancred. In 1107 he sailed across the Adriatic and laid
siege to the great coastal fortress of Dyrrhachium.[28a] But it was a
hopeless enterprise. Bohemund had no fleet of his own and Byzantium was now stronger than at the time of the last Norman war.
A year later (1108) he had to submit to the terms dictated by his
old opponent, Alexius, in the Treaty of Devol. He promised to
hold the principality of Antioch (less Cicilia and Lattakieh) as a
fief of the emperor and to restore the Greek patriarch. As compensation Alexius would allow him to keep any lands he could
conquer from Aleppo. This treaty, if carried out, would have
meant the end of Tancred's power in Syria, so, not surprisingly,
Bohemund never dared to show his face in Outremer again. He
returned to Apulia where, in 1111, he died, a forgotten man. With
him there vanished the most restless, ambitious, and unscrupulous
—and also the cleverest—of the leaders of the First Crusade. In
1108 Tancred finally took over in Antioch, formally as regent for
Bohemund, in fact as an independent ruler. Naturally he had no
intention of executing the terms of the Treaty of Devol. Instead he
devoted the rest of his life to the extension of Antioch. In the north
he drove the Byzantines out of East Cilicia for good; in the south
he expelled them from Lattakieh and captured Jabala, Buluniyas,
and Marqab from the Muslims. Marqab (in Latin Margat) was to
become one of the great crusader castles. As regent of both Antioch
and Edessa, Tancred was the most powerful man in Syria and
Alexius Comnenus (d. 1118) was too busy fighting the Seldjuks of
Anatolia to try to enforce the Treaty of Devol.

When Baldwin of Le Bourg and Joscelin of Courtenay regained
their freedom in 1108 a quarrel at once broke out between them

and Tancred. Tancred was reluctant to hand back Edessa. For the last four years he had been regent there and had been able to appoint a relative, Richard of the Principate (1104–8), to rule it for him. At first he gave way to Baldwin's and Joscelin's remonstrances but then a series of armed clashes occurred as a result of which the first alliance between Franks and Syrians was formed. To the Muslims there was nothing peculiar about such an alliance because they did not yet look upon the crusaders as enemies in a holy war. But on the Christian side a true crusader must have been shocked, for there can hardly have been anything so opposed to crusading ideals as a civil war between Christians in which both sides called in Muslim allies. It is very evident that the Syrian barons had moved a long way from the spirit of the crusade. On one side was Tancred supported by Aleppo; on the other, Baldwin, Joscelin, and Mosul. In the end, although Tancred was victorious in battle, Baldwin kept Edessa. But for reasons which are now obscure he made radical changes in his internal policy. Previously he had shown favour to the Armenian inhabitants of Edessa; now he drove many of them out of the land. There might well have been further fighting between Tancred and Baldwin had not the attention of all the participants been drawn to the question of the succession to Tripoli.

The old count, Raymond of Toulouse, had died outside the walls of Tripoli on 28 February 1105. He had been one of the outstanding figures of the First Crusade, indeed the humbler folk, the *pauperes*, regarded him as its real leader. Certainly he was the only man with the personality to stand up to Bohemund. Contemporary chronicles, Norman propaganda, and modern histories have not always been fair to him. Only in recent years, thanks to the work of J. H. and L. L. Hill,[14] have his achievements been given their due. When contemporaries described him as the most illustrious prince of Christian chivalry they were hardly exaggerating.

What complicated the succession to Tripoli was the fact that Alfonso-Jordan, Raymond's only son in Outremer, was still a child. The Provençal soldiers therefore chose his cousin, William-Jordan, as their commander. Back in Toulouse the barons who, in Raymond's absence, had been ruled by his eldest son, Bertrand, now refused to recognize him as Raymond's heir and instead had young Alfonso-Jordan brought home from Syria. So Bertrand decided to seek his fortune in the East. In 1108 he arrived at Mount Pilgrim and at once he and William-Jordan became entangled in arguments about the inheritance. When William recognized Tancred of Antioch as his lord, Bertrand asked King Baldwin I to act as arbitrator. Baldwin I answered the appeal and in July 1109 he held a meeting of all the princes outside the walls of Tripoli. Tancred and William faced by a united front—Baldwin I, Baldwin of Le Bourg, Joscelin of Courtenay, and Bertrand—were forced to accept a compromise. Tancred had to renounce his claims to Edessa. By way of compensation he was to receive his Galilean lands back should Bohemund ever return to Antioch. This was most unlikely, however, so Tancred suffered no real loss of face. Raymond's lordship was divided between the two claimants, each of whom became the vassal of his chief ally. This agreement restored the harmony so essential to the Christians in Outremer, and at once the princes, with help from Genoese and Provençal fleets, settled down to besiege Tripoli in earnest. On 12 July 1109 the city capitulated. The last crusader-state was finally established. Its division into two was short-lived. Shortly after the capture of Tripoli William-Jordan died of an arrow wound. The whole county was taken over by Bertrand and became a fief of the kingdom of Jerusalem.[29]

The settlement made by the princes at Tripoli in 1109 was a climax in the career of King Baldwin I. It revealed him in a truly royal light, chief arbiter of all the Christian princes of Outremer, to whose judgement even the formally independent Tancred of Antioch had to submit. Baldwin had reached this position as a result of his energetic extension of the kingdom. In 1101 he had captured the coastal towns of Arsuf and Caesarea. But Ascalon remained in Egyptian hands, a serious thorn in his flesh. It was an ideal base for Fatimid expeditions into Palestine and was in fact used as such by big Egyptian armies in 1101, 1102, and 1105. Only after fierce fighting in the Ramleh area—in which the Franks by no means always had the best of it—were these invasions beaten back. In one of these battles that tireless crusader, Stephen of Blois, met his death. During these years Baldwin was fortunate not to be attacked from the rear as well, but Damascus feared Fatimid imperialism just as much as he did and so made no move against him. After 1105 the Fatimids made no more serious attempts to reconquer Palestine; Baldwin had forced them to recognize that the Christian kingdom would not vanish overnight. Nevertheless the latent threat from Ascalon still remained. Baldwin once again turned his attention to the coast. He had already, in May 1104, captured Acre with the help of a Genoese fleet. In return he had been compelled to grant them extensive privileges—freedom from taxation, their own quarters in some towns, money rents. The self-

confident Italians had these privileges carved in letters of gold in
the Church of the Holy Sepulchre. But at last the kingdom had the
use of a large, safe harbour and one which was relatively unaffected
by the weather; in all these respects Acre, which quickly became
the economic centre of the kingdom, was far superior to the open
roads of Jaffa. This, however, was a development Damascus, dependent on its trading connections with the Palestinian coast,
could not afford merely to sit and watch. It began to give indirect
help to the Egyptian governors of the coastal towns by involving
Baldwin in a series of minor engagements in the Hauran (south
Syria) and Galilee where the lord of Tiberias had built several
castles to control the caravan routes to and from Damascus. Not
until 1108 could Baldwin secure a truce in this region and even
then Damascus continued to support the Egyptians on the coast.
In that year an attempted siege of Sidon failed and in the next
(1109) Baldwin had to march north in order to restore peace between the quarrelling princes of Syria. Sidon and Beirut held out
until 1110, succumbing only when Baldwin received vigorous help
from a Norwegian fleet under the command of King Sigurd.

The Franks now controlled all the harbours on the coast of
Syria and Palestine with the exception of Ascalon and Tyre. This
meant that the balance of forces in this part of the world was upset
and Damascus felt seriously threatened. So its atabeg, Toghtekin
(1095–1128) allied with the new ruler of Mosul, Mawdud (1108–
13). Under the auspices of the Seldjuk sultan, Mohammad ibn
Malik-Shah, Mawdud was trying to organize a great Muslim coalition to sweep the Franks out of Asia. A penetrating analysis of the
situation by Prawer has shown that up until 1115, and indeed as
late as 1119, the sultan's support for this project was dominated by
a conflict of interests between two power blocs, the Arabo–Syrian
and the Turco–Seldjuk. The Seldjuk sultans themselves were more
interested in Persia than in the territories west of Mosul, but public
opinion, skilfully moulded by refugees from Syria and Palestine,
forced the sultan to intervene in order to avoid losing prestige with
the Muslims. In this pressure exerted by public opinion we can de-
tect the beginnings of a characteristic aspect of the struggle between
Franks and Muslims which was to become more marked in the
course of time and was to culminate in the holy war. Mawdud's first
campaigns in 1110 and 1111 were indecisive because the Franks
were united under Baldwin I while the Muslim league was not as
firm as it seemed. But no sooner had the threat receded for a
moment than the Franks split into two camps. Baldwin of Le
Bourg found that Joscelin of Courtenay had become more power-

ful than he altogether liked, so he took him prisoner and forced
him to hand over the lordship of Turbessel. Joscelin therefore entered the service of King Baldwin and was given Tiberias which no
longer had to be kept available for Tancred now that Bohemund
had died in Apulia in 1111, leaving a son who was still a minor and
in whose name Tancred could continue to rule Antioch. When
Tancred himself died in December 1112 the regency was taken over
by his nephew, Roger of the Principate (1112-19). Thanks to Tancred's indefatigable zest for war Antioch was now a strong state. It
was an extraordinary achievement for a man who, like Baldwin I,
had once been a penniless adventurer. Bertrand of Tripoli also
died in 1112 and was succeeded by his young son Pons (1112-37).
Pons finally broke with the traditional anti-Norman policy of the
Provençals. Symbolic of this change was his marriage to Tancred's
widow. Another marriage, between Roger of Antioch and Baldwin
of Le Bourg's sister, completed the process of reconciliation in the
Frankish north.

When, in 1113, Baldwin I broke the truce with Damascus, Mawdud took the opportunity to launch another assault. This time he
directed his forces not against Syria but, in alliance with Toghtekin
of Damascus, against Palestine. He beat Baldwin's army in a battle
fought to the west of the Sea of Galilee and occupied the surrounding countryside. But most of the towns held out against him and in
September the approach of another Christian army, strengthened
by contingents from the northern principalities, forced him to retreat to Damascus. Here, in October, this outstanding and energetic Muslim soldier was murdered by an Assassin—much to the
relief of the Franks and Toghtekin himself, who had learned to
fear Mawdud and had no wish to see Jerusalem completely ex-
tinguished. For this reason he was suspected by the sultan of
Baghdad of being responsible for Mawdud's murder and so in 1114
he judged it wise to patch up another truce with Baldwin. The
outlook for the Franks had been further improved by the anarchy
in Aleppo which followed the death of its ruler, Ridwan, in 1113.
But this did not prevent the Seldjuk sultan from continuing to
organize the war against the Franks, commissioning first Aqsonqor
il-Bursuqi, whom he appointed atabeg of Mosul (1113-26), and
then Bursuq ibn Bursuq (d. 1116) to carry out his policy. Bursuq
was an outsider, a Persian, and all the powers of Syria united
against him. The Franks allied with both Aleppo and Damascus
and in September 1115 they defeated Bursuq in a battle of Tel-
Danith, south-west of Aleppo. The Muslim-Frankish coalition soon
collapsed in its turn because it was now the Franks who seemed to

be too strong. None the less Tel-Danith had put an end to the efforts of the Seldjuk sultans to reconquer Syria.

Although from 1109 to 1115 Baldwin I had been almost continuously involved with affairs in north Syria, he was well aware of the need to secure his southern border. To this end he pushed forward into the Negev desert in 1115 and there, south of the Dead Sea where it could control the road to Akaba, he built the great castle of Montreal (Shobak in Arabic). In the following year he occupied Akaba (Aila). He now had a base on the Red Sea and he protected it by fortifying the off-shore island of Graye. His policy in the Transjordan was limited to a loose supervision of the Bedouin tribes there, backed up by occasional punitive expeditions. Also in 1116 the problem of the king's marriage was settled. He had rid himself of his second wife, an Armenian, in 1113 and had then married Adelaide, the widow of Roger of Sicily. To Baldwin she was desirable on account of her dowry which he badly needed and because she represented the Sicilian alliance which could bring him both a fleet and a political counter-weight to the Normans of north Syria. She was able to secure Baldwin's promise that if they had no children then the heir to Jerusalem would be her own son from her first marriage, Count Roger II of Sicily, for Baldwin himself was still childless. It was clearly an attempt to have the succession to the throne based on hereditary right. But the marriage did not last. In 1116 the king, who was now ill, dismissed Adelaide in response to the demands of his clergy and she went back to Sicily. Possibly the king's illness had given rise to the fear that Count Roger might indeed press his claim to the throne. The Sicilian court was deeply insulted and for a long time afterwards would do nothing to help the kingdom of Jerusalem.

In 1118 Baldwin invaded Egypt, leading his troops to the banks of the Nile. But there he became seriously ill. He turned for home and died on 2 April not far from Ascalon. He was buried by the side of his brother Godfrey. He had been a great conqueror and bequeathed to his successor a well-established kingdom and a fine reputation. He had ruled firmly and had made sure that the fiefs held of the crown had not become hereditary; after a vassal's death the king could dispose of them as he liked. Once he had rid himself of Daimbert of Pisa, he remained on good terms with the Church, especially after 1112 when Arnulf of Rohes (d. 1118) archdeacon of Jerusalem since 1099, eventually achieved his old ambition of being patriarch—though even now Arnulf was unable to enjoy undisputed possession of his office, being temporarily deposed in 1115. Godfrey had not had the time to do more than make a start. Baldwin had conquered the coast, halted the Egyptian and Seldjuk attacks, established a *modus vivendi* with Damascus and added to his territories in the south. He was undoubtedly the real founder of the kingdom of Jerusalem and there was little dispute about his position as the overlord of all the Frankish princes in Outremer.

On the question of who was to succeeed him opinions were divided. Some favoured his brother, Count Eustace of Boulogne; others, led by the patriarch and Joscelin of Courtenay, preferred Baldwin of Le Bourg who arrived in Jerusalem at the right moment and who had already made a good impression as count of Edessa. Baldwin was chosen. Once again the question had been settled by a combination of election and hereditary right. Eustace was the nearer relative but there was clearly a growing body of opinion that the nearest relative who actually lived in Outremer had a good claim to the throne, though of course this had to be confirmed by an election. On Easter Sunday 1118 Baldwin II (1118-31) was consecrated king, though it was not until Christmas 1119 that he was crowned at Bethlehem, after it had at last become known that the count of Boulogne had renounced all claim. Like his predecessor, Baldwin II was a fine soldier, but he was also prepared to give more attention to the internal affairs of the kingdom. He had more self-control than Baldwin I; he was happily married to an Armenian princess, Morphia, and he was extremely pious; indeed he prayed so much that his knees had developed a horny layer of skin. None the less he was a cunning intriguer and somewhat avaricious.

He rewarded Joscelin of Courtenay who had done so much to secure his election by investing him with the county of Edessa (1119-31). Thus Joscelin returned to the principality from which Baldwin had once expelled him. No sooner was this settled than business in north Syria required Baldwin's presence. Roger of Antioch had so much increased Frankish pressure on Aleppo that the citizens had been forced to seek help from the Ortoqid Ilghazi of Mardin. He assumed control of Aleppo (1118-22) and formed an aggressive alliance with Toghtekin of Damascus. Aleppo's central position made it the pivot of the Syrian balance of power system; as such it was the object of a fierce rivalry between the Franks, the Ortoqids, and the rulers of Mosul and Damascus. The scales would tip in favour of the man who controlled Aleppo, particularly after 1118 when Ilghazi took the city out of the Seldjuk empire, just as Toghtekin had made Damascus independent in 1109. In 1119 Ilghazi invaded Antioch. In spite of all the warnings he received, in spite of all the lessons of past experience, Roger decided not to wait for the arrival of reinforcements from Jerusalem and Tripoli. He advanced to meet Ilghazi west of Aleppo with 700 knights and 3,000 foot-soldiers. On 27 June the Franks were encircled and completely beaten. Only two men of baronial rank escaped. Roger himself fell fighting in the midst of his finest knights. Those who were taken prisoner were killed later. The consequences of this battle, known to the Franks as the *Ager Sanguinis*, the Field of Blood, were far-reaching. It marked the end of the important part played by the Normans of south Italy in the development of the crusader states; from now on they were everywhere overshadowed by the French. Moreover the battle proved that the Muslims could beat the Franks even without the support of the Seldjuk sultan. The local rulers could do it themselves so long as they remained united.

Luckily for the Franks Ilghazi did not immediately follow up his victory. This enabled Baldwin II, after he had taken over the regency of Antioch, to push him back. Bohemund's son was still only a boy in Apulia and so until 1126 the government of Antioch lay in the prudent hands of King Baldwin. He redistributed the vacant fiefs and married the widows off to suitable knights in order to create a new fighting force as quickly as possible. As feudal lord of Tripoli and Edessa and as regent of Antioch the king of Jerusalem now ruled the whole Latin East. In 1120 this extraordinary power enabled him to promulgate twenty-five decrees at what is called the Council of Nablus, though it was in fact more like a meeting of the privy council attended by the most important ecclesiastical and secular office-holders, than a general council. Here, for the first time, penalties for adultery, sodomy, bigamy, theft, and other breaches of the law were laid down. In the period of conquest under Baldwin I only the bare minimum of legislation had been issued (see p. 64). Most offences had been punished by each individual judge according to what he felt was appropriate and in line with the custom of his home country. The list drawn up at Nablus is evidence of considerable uncertainty about the law in the absence of any uniform standard; this was now to be dealt with. It is not really evidence of widespread immorality. At the same council the jurisdiction of the king's court was more precisely defined and the right of self-help was correspondingly limited. Another important law, the *Establissement dou Roi Bauduin* (see p. 155) was promulgated either by Baldwin II or by his grandson Baldwin III.

In fact owing to Baldwin II's energetic rule the Frankish pressure on Aleppo was unremitting. The Christians received help from an unexpected quarter. King David II of Georgia became involved in a war with Ilghazi and defeated him in a bloody battle in 1121. Ilghazi died the next year, his power broken. But Balak, his nephew and successor in Aleppo, continued the fight. He captured first Count Joscelin of Edessa and then, as Baldwin II was hurrying to Edessa to make arrangements for the government there, he captured the king himself in April 1123. It says much for Baldwin's powers of organization that no constitutional crisis broke out. In Antioch Patriarch Bernard took over the administration; in Jerusalem the barons chose Eustace Garnier, lord of Sidon and Caesarea, to act as *bailli* (i.e. regent).

Joscelin soon managed to contrive an adventurous escape, but Baldwin II remained in prison until after Balak's death, being released in the summer of 1124 in return for promises which he did not keep. While he was still in prison the most spectacular event of his reign took place: the capture of Tyre. Much earlier, in 1119, he had sent an appeal for help to Venice. In autumn 1122 a formidable fleet commanded by the doge set sail for the East. The doge had judged his moment well. Pisa and Genoa were at war with one another and unable to spare much time for Outremer. Venetian help was therefore very precious and they could demand a high price for it. In May 1123 they defeated an Egyptian fleet in a battle off the coast of Ascalon; and they were now ready to help capture a port. But only after a bitter debate was it finally decided to attack Tyre instead of Ascalon. The constable and the patriarch of Jerusalem, Gormund (1118–28), concluded a treaty with the Venetians in which the privileges of the republic were set out in great detail. They were exempted from paying all customs duties; they were allowed to trade freely, using their own weights and measures. The only tax which they would have to pay was the tax on pilgrims. They were to receive 300 besants a year and a third of Tyre. Cases between Venetians and cases in which Venetians were the defendants were to be heard only in their own court at Tyre. The legal integrity of the kingdom had only recently been demonstrated at Nablus. Already, as a result of this treaty, it had been breached and the competence of the king's court had been seriously undermined. This was particularly dangerous since inevitably the same privileges soon had to be granted to all the other maritime towns of Italy and south France.

Following this treaty—which Baldwin II later confirmed—the Franks began a long and determined siege of Tyre. It was a well-fortified city linked to the mainland only by the narrow causeway which Alexander the Great had built in 332 B.C. Not until 7 July 1124 when supplies had run out and their position had become hopeless did the garrison surrender on condition that they were allowed to leave the city in peace. The terms of the treaty with Venice were then put into effect. Although the fall of Tyre was a triumph for the Christian cause it was nevertheless to create problems of ecclesiastical organization.[30] Traditionally the archbishopric of Tyre belonged, with all its suffragans, to the patriarchate of Antioch. But at Clermont Urban II had ruled that in the Christian East ecclesiastical boundaries should follow political frontiers; for centuries this had been the practice in the West. Even before the capture of Tyre the position of its suffragan sees had been awkward. The southern sees, Beirut, Sidon, and Acre, lay in the kingdom of Jerusalem and came therefore, according to Urban's ruling, under the authority of the patriarch of Jerusalem. But Tripoli, Tortosa, and Jebail lay in the county of Tripoli which had two feudal overlords, the prince of Antioch and the king of Jerusalem. Antioch was certainly not prepared to renounce old rights and thus arose the long, fierce quarrel over the archbishopric of Tyre between the two patriarchs which was anything but helpful to the peaceful growth of the crusader states. In 1111 Paschal II had confirmed Urban's judgement, but later on he became less sure and rather inclined to restore the old boundaries. From then on the papacy remained permanently undecided and so both sides made do without bishops, preferring to keep the disputed sees *sede vacante*. But when, in 1122, it became clear that a serious attack on Tyre was a distinct possibility, the patriarch of Jerusalem unilaterally consecrated an archbishop who, however, died before the city was in fact taken. After the capture of Tyre the metropolitan see remained vacant for four years and not until 1128 was the first archbishop consecrated, an Englishman named William (d. *c.* 1134; not to be confused with the historian, Archbishop William II of Tyre 1175–86). He recognized the authority of Jerusalem and so in turn the patriarch of Antioch began to consecrate bishops for the northern sees. The papal curia was now forced to make up its mind. It decided the case in Jerusalem's favour,[31] and as a result bishops were for the first time ever—as we can see in the case of Acre—appointed to the three southern suffragan sees. Later quarrels between the patriarch of Jerusalem and the archbishop of Tyre led to another, and this time definitive judgement in favour of Jerusalem in 1139. None the less the Tripolitan sees remained subject to Antioch because although in theory the curia upheld the verdict of 1139 up until the thirteenth century, in practice no papal legate ever did anything to subordinate Tripoli to Tyre. The curia tolerated the division of the archbishopric because it was not prepared to risk the whole painfully achieved *modus vivendi* for the sake of the unity of one province. Tyre itself remained permanently attached to Jerusalem.

One of the most important events of Baldwin II's reign was the foundation of the Military Orders.[32] A knight from Champagne, Hugh of Payens (d. 1136) was apparently the first to have the idea that it might be pleasing to God if a monk's way of life was combined with fighting against the heathen so as to create a new knightly ideal. He and eight companions swore to Patriarch Gormund that they would be obedient, poor, and chaste; then they took an additional, fourth vow, to offer help and protection to pilgrims on the still dangerous road from Jaffa to Jerusalem. Baldwin II granted them rooms in the royal palace, the so-called *Templum Salomonis* (now the Mosque of al-Aqsa). Thus they became known as the Templars. At first they lived there in poverty like a community of regular canons. Then they aroused the interest of St. Bernard, the influential abbot of Clairvaux, and with his help a rule of their own was approved at the Council of Troyes in 1128. Additional constitutions issued in 1130 by Patriarch Stephen of Jerusalem (1128–30) gave the rule its final form. At about this time the Templars, probably modelling themselves on the Cistercians, began to wear a white tunic. During the pontificate of Eugenius III a red cross was added to make plain the difference between the two orders. A rapid stream of new recruits came in, many of them moved by the eloquence of St. Bernard who was full of praise for the ideal of an order of knighthood dedicated to serving God, an ideal which, in his treatise *In Praise of the New Chivalry* (1128) he contrasted strongly with the banditry of the worldly knight. The new order was tightly organized under the direction of a Master. It consisted of three classes, the knights, the sergeants who served them, and the chaplains. In the course of the twelfth century the Templars freed themselves from the authority of the patriarch; indeed they cut right through the Church's diocesan structure, for every bishop was bound to consecrate the chaplains without in any way being able to control their entry into the order. The pope moreover granted them the privilege of having to answer to no other court but his. The value of the Military Orders was immense for in practice they were the only authority in the Christian East to hold a standing army always in readiness. On the other hand their privileged position meant that they formed a state within a state—a state which often proved to be a troublesome rival to both king and Church. They pursued their own policies and their rights of exemption were such that they constantly threatened to undermine the customary structure of authority. Their special position in Outremer was enhanced by the fact that they received rich gifts of land in every part of Western Europe and on the basis of this wealth they soon developed into an international organization of great importance in the world of finance.

The Hospitallers also profited from the rise of the Templars. In about 1070 some merchants from Amalfi had founded a Christian hostel on the model of older establishments. It was situated near the Amalfitan Benedictine monastery of St. Maria Latina in Jerusalem and dedicated to St. John the Almsgiver, a seventh-century patriarch of Alexandria. After the First Crusade the hostel community gradually freed itself from the control of the monastery and the patriarch whose fierce resistance to this process was overruled by the pope. Thus the Hospitallers too came to be directly under the pope's authority. Originally their role had been a purely charitable one and indeed this side of their activities always remained important, but by 1137 they had already accepted some responsibility for frontier defence. By the statutes of 1182 they were bound to take an active part in war. By the end of the twelfth century, at the latest, the community founded by merchants had developed into a socially exclusive order of knights dedicated, like the Templars, to war against the heathen. *Circa* 1155 they had been reorganized on the basis of the rule of St. Augustine. As the Order rose in importance so John the Baptist gradually replaced John the Almsgiver as its patron saint. Their battle dress (a red tunic with a white, eight-pointed cross) was not finally settled until 1259. Inevitably the two Military Orders became, in the end, bitter rivals, but at first the advantages of their foundation far outweighed the disadvantages.

We must now return to the history of the crusader states. In 1124 Baldwin had been released from captivity and at once he carried the war to Aqsonqor il-Bursuqi who, in 1125, had taken over control in Aleppo in addition to Mosul. This had upset the balance of forces in Syria. Previously Damascus had been balanced by Jerusalem, Aleppo by Antioch, and the lesser emirates in the valley of the Upper Orontes by Tripoli. But now there had arisen a larger state with a centre at Aleppo which was relatively distant from the Seldjuk bases of power and which thus had a chance of developing into a principality independent of Baghdad. This inevitably meant a shift away from the previous distribution of forces and it was, in fact, only with reluctance that Aleppo had exchanged its former independence for the greater security contained in the union with Mosul.

In May 1125 Baldwin II inflicted a heavy defeat on the troops of il-Bursuqi at Azaz in north Syria. In the next year he was at last relieved of the responsibility for Antioch. Bohemund II (1126–30), the son of Antioch's founder, arrived from Apulia to take over his inheritance. It would be his task to conquer Aleppo, a task which seemed quite possible in view of the incredibly chaotic state of the emirate following the murder of the atabeg in November 1126. In fact it was to be the last chance of capturing Aleppo but Bohemund II let it slip. He was already involved in the customary civil war with the count of Edessa, Joscelin. During 1127 and 1128 Imad ad-Din Zengi (d. 1146) rose to be ruler of Mosul and Aleppo. From then on it was too late. In Zengi the Franks had met a most dangerous opponent.

In 1128 the powerful ruler of Damascus, Toghtekin, died. Baldwin II, hoping to exploit the situation, tried to capture Damascus but the attempt failed. Two years later Bohemund II fell in battle in Cilicia. His only child was a two-year-old daughter, Constance; once again the king was forced to assume the burden of government in Antioch, though not before his own daughter Alice, Bohemund's widow, had attempted to seize power for herself. Despite the disgraceful lengths to which she was prepared to go her coup failed. But the years and the effects of two periods of imprisonment had begun to leave their mark on Baldwin. On 21 August 1131 after a fairly long illness he died. On his deathbed he was received into the community of canons attached to the Church of the Holy Sepulchre where, in the Golgotha chapel, he found his last resting place. The count of Edessa, his comrade-in-arms for thirty years, died shortly afterwards. Owing to a serious injury he had been forced to entrust the defence of Edessa to his son Joscelin II (1131–50; d. 1159). But his son refused to accept the responsibility on the grounds that Edessa's army was too weak to stand against the invading Muslims. This made the old warrior so angry that he struggled out of bed once more and had himself carried in a litter to meet the enemy forces. When they heard that he was coming they dispersed. Content, but exhausted by the effort, Count Joscelin I, still in his litter, died by the roadside.

With the deaths of Baldwin of Le Bourg and Joscelin of Courtenay the last two members of the first generation of crusaders had gone. Imperceptibly but steadily a new community was emerging, composed of the younger generation and newly arrived settlers.

They looked upon Outremer as their home and developed their own sense of political identity. In 1127 the chronicler Fulcher of Chartres, now in Jerusalem, wrote the following famous words:

We who had been Occidentals have become Orientals; the man who had been a Roman or a Frank has here become a Galileean or a Palestinian; and the man who used to live in Reims or Chartres now finds himself a citizen of Tyre or Acre. We have already forgotten the places where we were born; already many of us know them not, or at any rate, no longer hear them spoken of. Some among us already possess in this country houses and servants which belong to them as of hereditary right. Another has married a wife who is not his compatriot—a Syrian or an Armenian woman perhaps, or even a Saracen who has received the grace of baptism.... He who was once a stranger here is now a native. Every day our dependents and our relatives follow us, leaving behind, unwillingly perhaps, all their belongings. For he who was poor there now finds that God has made him rich here. He who had little money now possesses countless besants [gold pieces]. He who did not hold even a village over there now enjoys a town which God had given him. Why should anyone return to the West who has found an Orient like this?

No word here of chivalry or the spirit of the crusader. At a time when Bernard of Clairvaux in his treatise in praise of the Templars added a new element to the knightly crusading ideal, Fulcher of Chartres was giving eloquent expression to the self-confidence of a 'middle class' community of settlers. It was not easy to unite the two worlds; indeed often enough they were to stand in opposition to one another.

The succession to Baldwin II had been arranged while he was still alive. At a council which met at the end of 1127 or early in 1128 his eldest daughter Melisende (d. 1161) was formally recognized as the heiress to the kingdom (*haeres regni*). Then ambassadors were sent to France where they negotiated Melisende's betrothal to the powerful count of Anjou, Fulk V. Fulk was explicitly promised that when the marriage was celebrated he also would become heir to the throne and would eventually rule as king, not merely as prince consort. This settlement meant that, in principle, there had been a change in the customs governing the succession; the principle of cognatic succession (i.e. allowing all blood relatives, including daughters, to inherit) had taken the place of the agnatic principle which restricted the succession to men who were related through the male line.[32a] It is, however, doubtful whether the settlement of 1127/8 was seen in this light

at the time since there was then no agnatic heir and therefore no
possibility of the succession being regulated according to the
agnatic principle. At that time the only alternative to accepting
the principle of cognatic succession was to have an election entirely untrammelled by the claims of blood. However that may be,
the decision of 1127/8 in fact created the precedent which was to
determine future practice.

In 1129 Fulk arrived in the Holy Land and the marriage was at
once celebrated. Baldwin II's overriding concern was to ensure the
continuity of his dynasty. This meant not only that he had to
accept the principle of cognatic succession but also that he had to
make sure that Fulk would not be able to arrange that he, in his
turn, would be succeeded by the children either of his first marriage or of a third, as yet unmade, marriage. In other words Fulk
had to be prevented from acting in the way his own father had
done for he had been married four or five times. (Indeed Baldwin
I of Jerusalem had behaved in a similar fashion, repudiating his
second wife and packing her off to a nunnery.) The kingdom of
Jerusalem was not to fall into the hands of outsiders but should
be inherited only by Fulk and Melisende and by the children of
their marriage, the descendants of Baldwin II. This involved
arranging for Fulk and Melisende to rule jointly and in this way
clear limits were set to Fulk's enjoyment of his royal rights. It is,
again, uncertain whether Fulk can have been informed of this
restriction as early as 1128 for this might have been to run the risk
of seeing the negotiations break down. But on his deathbed in
1131 Baldwin II made his intentions absolutely plain. He designated three persons as joint rulers after his death: Fulk, Melisende,
and his two-year-old grandson, Baldwin III. On 14 September 1131
Fulk and his consort were crowned, this time not in Bethlehem, but
in the Church of the Holy Sepulchre in Jerusalem where the tremendous building programme undertaken by the crusaders was
still under way. Fulk's reign was to witness its completion though
the church was not to be consecrated until 15 July 1149. All future
coronations up to 1186 were to take place here. The connection
with Fulk (1131–43) considerably enhanced the prestige of the
Jerusalem dynasty. Now about forty years of age, he enjoyed the
confidence of both the pope and the king of France, while his son,
Geoffrey Plantagenet, had married the Emperor Henry V's widow,
Matilda, the only daughter of Henry I of England, thus founding
the house of Plantagenet which was to rule an immense empire:
England, Normandy, and the Angevin family lands. With the
accession of Fulk to the throne of Jerusalem, England began at last

to show some real interest in the well-being of the crusader states.

Immediately after his coronation he had to go north, just as his predecessor had done, in order to deal with the affairs of Antioch. His sister-in-law, the dowager princess Alice, had again tried to seize power, this time supported by the counts of Tripoli and Edessa, both of whom hoped to throw off the overlordship of Jerusalem. This forced Fulk to take the sea route to Antioch. Once there he took over the regency. He then defeated the rebel count of Tripoli in battle at Chastel Rouge and brought about an enforced reconciliation.

During this same period the kingdom was, for the first time in its history, disturbed by internal revolt. Roman of Le Puy who had been granted a large fief in Oultrejourdain (Transjordan) by Baldwin II, quarrelled with King Fulk,[33] possibly because he had usurped port dues and the right to mint coin. His fief was confiscated and given to Pagan, the king's butler. It is just possible that this revolt should be dated to the latter part of the reign of Baldwin II (perhaps 1126 or 1128), but in that case Roman must have rebelled a second time for he was undoubtedly deeply involved in the very much more dangerous rebellion led by Hugh of Le Puiset, the powerful count of Jaffa. Hitherto Hugh's rebellion has been dated to 1132. This is certainly wrong. 1133 is the earliest possible date and the latter part of 1134 the most probable. Hugh was the confidant of Queen Melisende, whose kinsman he was. He and his father before him had owed their rise into the ranks of the king's greatest vassals to the favour of Baldwin II. Rumour spoke of an affair between Melisende and Hugh and explained the clash between the king and the count in terms of Fulk's jealousy. But William of Tyre, although he repeats these rumours, also says that he does not know what the true cause of the dispute was. Fulk tried to rid himself of Hugh by having him brought to trial before the Haute Cour, the king's feudal council. Hugh had been accused of high treason by his stepson, Walter of Caesarea, and a judicial duel was arranged. Hugh failed to turn up and, as a result, must have been sentenced to the normal punishment for felony—forfeiture of all his fiefs—since only a verdict as drastic as this can explain his despairing and foolish reaction. He retreated to his fortified town of Jaffa and went so far as to bring in Egyptian auxiliaries from Ascalon. Now he really had committed blatant treason and his own vassals turned against him. Caught in an untenable position he had no option but to make his submission. He was banished for three years with the assurance that, at the end of that time, he would recover his fiefs. But before he left the kingdom he was badly wounded when he was the victim of an assassination attempt for which public opinion held the king responsible. Hugh recovered from his wound only to die in exile.

Many aspects of this rebellion have been overlooked by previous historians. Clearly Hugh had enjoyed the support of a considerable section of the nobility. His vassals seem to have been convinced that his cause was just for they stood by him until he committed the fatal error of making an alliance with the Saracens. The final punishment was unusually lenient—certainly more lenient than the earlier sentence passed on him, even though, in the meantime, his offence had become more heinous. This leniency was the result of mediation by influential people who felt that the very existence of the kingdom was at stake and who cited Matthew 12:25 in support of their arguments: 'Every kingdom divided against itself is brought to desolation.' Although Hugh had obviously gone too far to escape punishment altogether he still had supporters among the clergy and nobility who were able to force Fulk to acquiesce in a sentence which was much less severe than the king would have liked. The attempt on Hugh's life led to unrest in Jerusalem where the populace took the count's side. It is plain that the rebellion had been bound up with the political interests of Queen Melisende since her anger remained unabated for many months after the rebellion itself had been put down. The fact that she could afford to remain angry suggests that it was not her alleged liaison with Count Hugh that was at the root of the trouble. Her continued anger reveals moreover that Fulk had been the victor in appearance only. The royal marriage now went through a period of serious crisis. The queen's anger was such that it was unsafe for those nobles who were close to the king to appear in public and even Fulk himself went in fear of his life. Once more mediation was called for and was, in fact, finally successful in assuaging the queen's anger. But William of Tyre says that from this time onwards Fulk—whom he portrays as an energetic warrior with an unusually bad memory—became so uxorious that even in trivial matters he did nothing without his wife's consent. It is here that we have the key to the whole affair—an affair which had obviously shaken the kingdom much more severely than is suggested in William of Tyre's account. It seems that Fulk had begun his reign by trying to act as sole ruler, thereby not only infringing Melisende's political interests but also antagonizing that section of the nobility which wished to ensure that Baldwin II's last wishes were respected. This group could not allow Fulk to rule alone for it might then have been possible for him to oust Baldwin II's dynasty and replace it with his own (see above pp. 85f.). In the final analysis it does not matter whether the constitutional restrictions on Fulk's position date from 1128 or from the designation of 1131, for even if he had been told the truth in 1128, we can be sure that after Baldwin II's death he would have argued that his own interpretation of the agreement of 1128 had been quite different, i.e. that his understanding had been that by marrying Melisende he would acquire all her rights of succession and so would become sole ruler. On this interpretation Baldwin's death-bed designation in 1131 had broken the agreement of 1128. This was a question which at one stroke split the kingdom into two camps, and un-avoidably so, since Fulk, presumably claiming that he had, in effect, been elected in 1128, had called into question not only Baldwin's last wishes but also the newly introduced principle of cognatic succession. None the less Fulk found supporters among the nobility and this suggests that although a decision in favour of cognatic succession had undoubtedly been made in 1127/8 it had not been unanimous and thus may well not have been regarded as a final decision on the question of principle involved. Probably this decision only later acquired the power to bind the future owing to the normative force of a successful precedent. It was certainly not just a matter of chance that in those years Fulk had himself referred to as *haeres regni* (a unique form) in a charter recently published by Rudolf Hiestand.[32a] The reasoning which lay behind this emphasis on his right is revealed in the succession dispute and the division of power which followed. Against Fulk there was ranged a very considerable party which, led by Hugh of Jaffa, stood for the execution of Baldwin II's testament, for the rights of Melisende, for the cognatic principle and, in general, for the rights of the legitimate dynasty. This party proved strong enough to force Fulk to accept joint rule with Melisende though in return they had to sacrifice the count of Jaffa—but Hugh's position had, in any event, become hopeless. This allowed Fulk to save face and appear before the world as the victor. But the real winners were the principle of cognatic succession and Melisende, a woman of extraordinary vigour and—like her sister Alice of Antioch—of driving ambition.

These profound disputes over the right form of government, disputes which must have troubled the kingdom for some time before the open outbreak of Hugh's rebellion, were not the only things which Fulk had to worry about. Once again he was forced to go north to meet a threatened Muslim invasion of Antioch. It

was high time that the principality had a prince of its own and in
1133 Fulk decided in favour of Raymond of Poitiers (1136–49), the
thirty-four-year-old son of Duke William IX of Aquitaine. But it
took Raymond three years to reach Antioch. King Roger II of
Sicily, being a kinsman of the Norman princes of Antioch, believed
that he had a claim on their inheritance, and this forced Raymond
to disguise himself in order to escape from Apulia. During these
years Fulk was fully occupied in the south so yet again the dowager
princess Alice tried to take advantage of the situation. In 1135
she left her own estates at Lattakieh and appeared in Antioch.
There she bolstered up her insecure rule by an alliance with the
uncanonically elected patriarch Radulph of Domfront (1135–40).
Just as, on an earlier occasion, she had flirted with the idea of
being protected by Zengi of Mosul, so now she had no hesitation
about offering the hand of her nine-year-old daughter Constance
to a Byzantine prince, Manuel Comnenus, though in fact she had
already been promised to Raymond of Poitiers. The plan implied
Byzantine overlordship and was impossible to carry out in face of
opposition from the barons and the patriarch who had no intention of yielding his place to a Greek Orthodox rival. Radulph went
over to Raymond's side and in 1136, soon after Raymond's arrival,
he married him to Constance. In return Raymond is supposed to
have recognized the patriarch as his feudal suzerain. Alice had
been outmanoeuvred by an elaborate trick—she had been persuaded that Radulph was going to marry her to Raymond—and in
resignation she withdrew to Lattakieh where she spent the rest of
her days. Raymond immediately became involved in a war with
the Armenians of Cilicia which dragged on until settled by the
intervention of Byzantium. As a consequence of Raymond's arrival
the Norman elements in Antioch were finally ousted by French
influence. One indication of this change is the fact that the
Chanson des Chétifs, an epic poem in Old French, was written at
Raymond's court shortly before 1149. It was based largely on
memories of the 1101 crusade, the crusade which failed. This
remains as the only surviving piece of evidence for the contribution to vernacular poetry which was made by the crusader
states.[34]

Zengi meanwhile had been assiduously preaching holy war ever
since his accession to power in Mosul and Aleppo. But the chief
object of his ambition was in fact a Muslim state, Damascus. Indeed Prawer believes that it was only the Mosul historians, writing
after Zengi's death, who retrospectively applied the concept of the
jihad to the period of the struggle for Aleppo. The Damascus

chroniclers were understandably more reserved and did not celebrate Zengi as the protagonist of the holy war until after he had
captured Edessa in 1144. Zengi's first attempts to conquer Damascus, in 1130 and 1135, failed; he was all too often caught up in
the long-lasting succession dispute in Iraq which followed the
death of Sultan Mahmud in 1131. In 1134 indeed Damascus was
able to launch an invasion of Galilee and King Fulk was hard
put to it to hold his own. Three years later the Damascenes
attacked the county of Tripoli. In the struggle which followed
Count Pons lost his life and was succeeded by his son Raymond II
(1137-52). This aggressive Damascene policy was not at all to
Zengi's liking so he moved from Iraq to Syria. A brief, if unsuccessful siege of Homs clearly warned Damascus that he meant
business, though he had to agree to a truce when a Frankish
army approached. Instead of Homs, he now besieged the Franks
in the castle of Montferrand (Barin) in the valley of the Upper
Orontes. Fulk led his army to the relief of Montferrand but was
defeated in battle and had to take refuge in the castle where he
himself became the besieged. In July 1137 he and Zengi came to
terms. Montferrand was surrendered to the Muslims and the
Franks were allowed to go free. In making these terms Fulk had
been unaware that the united contingents of Jerusalem, Edessa,
and Antioch were marching to his relief, while for his part Zengi
had known that the Byzantine Emperor John II Comnenus was
on his way to Syria and had feared that he might besiege Aleppo.
The Frankish intervention dealt with, Zengi once more turned
his attention to Homs. Here, in spring 1138, he was surprised by
the news of a Byzantine attack.

At the beginning of his reign Emperor John II (1118-43) had
been compelled to neglect Syrian affairs. He had other wars on his
hands: against Venice, the Petchenegs, and the Danishmends of
eastern Anatolia. Not until 1137 did he find time to intervene. His
main aim was to restore Byzantine authority over Antioch and
North Syria, but he also wished to help the Franks against the
menacing power of Zengi. The apparent contradiction of these
motives is explained by the fact that if Byzantium wanted to
realize its theoretical claims to North Syria it had to spread its
protective wings over all the crusader states. It could not afford
to destroy them; at most they could be reduced to the level of
vassal states. Moreover as head of the Orthodox Church the
emperor was duty bound to protect his fellow believers from the
perils of Muslim dominion—even though conditions for them were
in fact sometimes worse under the Latins than they had been

under the Muslims, when, as *dhimmis*, they had been permitted to enjoy the status of a protected minority. But in the eyes of the Orthodox Church rule by the Latins was unquestionably to be preferred to rule by the Muslims.

The emperor's march through Cilicia turned into a triumphal procession and by the end of August 1137 he stood before the walls of Antioch. A few days later the city capitulated. King Fulk had not been prepared to support Raymond of Antioch against Byzantium. Though the emperor's arrival created political problems for him too, Fulk was quick to see that here was help against Zengi. Thus he agreed to the terms which Raymond was forced to accept. The prince of Antioch did homage to the emperor and the imperial standard was hoisted over the citadel. In return John refrained, for the moment, from entering the city. Nevertheless Raymond had to promise that if John could conquer Aleppo, Shaizar, and Homs he would accept them as a new principality and hand back Antioch to the emperor. This agreement was based on the Treaty of Devol of 1108 (see above p. 72). John spent the following winter in Cilicia. Then in March 1138, with support from Antioch and Edessa, he launched an offensive against Zengi. But a surprise attack on Aleppo failed, and when John moved on to besiege Shaizar, the town which controlled the middle Orontes, the Franks refused to give him proper assistance. They feared that if Shaizar fell then they might have to think seriously about carrying out the terms of the treaty of the previous year. Angrily John returned to Antioch and this time he made a ceremonial entry into the city. But before the main imperial army had arrived back at Antioch, Joscelin II of Edessa ingeniously engineered a city riot which forced John to leave.

The emperor spent the next few years in Anatolia fully occupied with a war against the Danishmends. Raymond of Antioch spent the time intriguing, in the end successfully, to rid himself of the ambitious patriarch Radulph. Zengi meanwhile had returned to his unfinished business with Damascus. In 1139 he besieged the city so closely that the ruler of Damascus was forced to appeal for help to Jerusalem. Fulk and his barons had no hesitation in concluding an alliance. Indeed the alliance was popular even with the citizens of Damascus who had learned to fear Zengi as a ruthless and brutal conqueror and who saw that as a result of the alliance Frankish pressure on the Hauran, the agricultural hinterland of their city, would be eased. For this reason in 1139 Damascus even helped the Franks to recapture Banyas, a town which controlled the road from Galilee to Damascus and from which, if

he had held it, Zengi would have been able to threaten both
Jerusalem and Damascus. Zengi was forced to retreat and for the
next five years he had his hands full in Iraq. During this period
the alliance of Jerusalem and Damascus remained intact. Fulk used
all his diplomatic skill to prevent the escalation of local border
clashes. During this breathing space he gathered up again the
threads of the policy of strengthening the defences of the southern
frontier which had been begun by Baldwin I. Just as Baldwin had
built a *Gegenburg*, Scandelion, to blockade Tyre in 1117, so between 1136 and 1142, Fulk constructed a ring of fortresses around
Ascalon, at Ibelin, Blanchegarde, and Beth Gibelin. This made it
difficult for the Egyptians to raid the kingdom and at the same
time enabled the Franks to devastate the countryside around
Ascalon. Moreover the protection afforded by these castles permitted the cultivation of the land, the settlement of Frankish
farmers, and an altogether more intensive exploitation of the
region. The castles themselves were granted to the Hospitallers and
to loyal vassals. They became the centres of important lordships
and powerful dynasties, notably the Ibelins, one of the best-known
families of Outremer, whose rise to fame really began when Balian
the Old was appointed castellan of Ibelin. From now until the fall
of the kingdom, and then in Cyprus, the Ibelins—a family whose
origins are probably to be found in Italy rather than in France—
were always to be found near the centre of the stage. In the
Transjordan Pagan the Butler, with Fulk's approval, was pursuing
a similar policy. He encouraged agriculture and in 1142 he further
protected the trade route between the Dead Sea and the Red Sea
by building at Moab a great castle known as Kerak or *Petra
Deserti*, the Stone of the Desert. The lord of Transjordan now
controlled the Bedouin sheep farmers and the saltpans of the Dead
Sea. He had joined the ranks of the great barons. Further north the
castle of Belvoir (built 1140) protected the Jordan Valley road and
the Pont de Judaire; Safed (built 1102, restored *c.* 1140) controlled
the road between Acre and Damascus and Jacob's Ford over the
Jordan; Toron (*c.* 1105) and Subeibe (*c.* 1130) controlled the road
between Tyre and Damascus; Beaufort (occupied in 1139)
dominated the valley of the Leontes and the approaches to Sidon;
Krak des Chevaliers (1142), the mightiest fortress of the Hospitallers, guarded the north-east flank of Tripoli. While Fulk built
castles, his wife Melisende founded several religious houses, notably
the convent at Bethany which she lavishly endowed with Jericho
in order to provide, in extravagant fashion, for her sister Joveta.
Then in 1142 John II Comnenus once again marched through

Anatolia and Cilicia into Syria. This time Raymond of Antioch, taking shelter behind the very real hostility of his vassals to the claims of Byzantium, refused to repeat his submission of 1137. The season was too far advanced for war, so John returned to his winter quarters in Cilicia. There he made plans which imply that he was even intending to restore Byzantine authority over Palestine though this had been lost to the Arabs as long ago as 638. By skilful diplomatic manoeuvring Fulk was able to persuade John to postpone an armed 'pilgrimage' to Jerusalem. But Antioch was saved only by a hunting accident in which John received injuries from which he died in April 1143 just before the time arranged for another invasion of Syria. Some months later a second hunting accident caused the death of Fulk (10 November 1143). He had ruled by virtue of his marriage to Melisende and since their eldest son, Baldwin, was only thirteen years old, she now took over the government. For the first time we hear nothing of an election. As William of Tyre's explicit phrases make clear, she ruled by hereditary right. The barons felt uncomfortable about being governed by a woman and they were able to ensure that young Baldwin was crowned with her, but for the moment of course he had little or no influence.

With the emperor of Byzantium dead and neither Melisende nor her son in any position to intervene in the affairs of North Syria, Zengi had an opportunity which was far too good to miss. He invaded the county of Edessa. The city itself was inadequately defended and Joscelin II was unable to march to its relief. On Christmas Eve 1144, after a siege of four weeks, Zengi broke into the city As Prawer has rightly emphasized, it was not just on account of the feeble personality of its ruler that Edessa succumbed so easily. The demographic and economic conditions in the county were also significant. The high proportion of Syrians and Armenians in the population inevitably meant that these two elements were represented in the army. But the Syrians were poor soldiers and both groups, moreover, suffered from the decline in the economic situation which was caused by the frequent Turkish raids into this crusader outpost. Thus it is not hard to see why the city of Edessa failed to resist for long.

Joscelin, from a new capital at Turbessel, managed to hold the line of the Euphrates until 1150. But he was then captured and died in prison in 1159. His widow, recognizing the hopelessness of her position sold the six strongpoints she still held between the Orontes and the Euphrates to Byzantium, but even the empire could not hold them for as long as a year. The first crusader state to be founded was also the first to go. Antioch was now robbed of its outer defence works to the north-east. Zengi, however, did not live to witness these later triumphs. He was murdered in 1146. In Mosul he was succeeded by his eldest son, Saif ed-Din Ghazi; the second son, Nur ed-Din (1146–74) took over in Aleppo. He was to ensure that the death of Zengi brought no relief for the Franks.

5 · THE SECOND CRUSADE, 1145–1149

THE news of the fall of Edessa caused a considerable stir in the West, but though it saddened men it did not immediately spur them on to a spontaneous crusade.[35] A Frankish embassy led by Bishop Hugh of Jabala arrived at the papal curia at Viterbo shortly after Eugenius III (1145–53) had ascended the pontifical throne. A little later on an Armenian delegation appeared. Eugenius listened receptively to their pleas and on 1 December 1145 he issued the first crusading bull, known from its opening words as *Quantum praedecessores*. But at first it met with no response at all. Indeed although it was addressed to the king and nobility of France, there is no evidence to show that it was, as yet, promulgated there. Eugenius's plan, however, clashed with certain ideas which King Louis VII (1137–80) himself developed, though it is not clear whether or not he knew of the papal bull when he formulated them. They were in any case not acceptable to the Church. The king held court at Bourges at Christmas 1145 and there he declared that he was planning to lead an expedition to the East. Various motives were attributed to him by contemporaries. But Louis was probably thinking in terms of a purely French armed pilgrimage which might also be of some assistance to the Holy Land rather than a crusade in the style of 1095. Thus at Bourges, after describing the plight of the crusader states, Bishop Godfrey of Langres called upon the nobles to fight for God at the side of their king; no mention was made of the pope, of the indulgence, or even of the papal bull. The appeal met with a cold response; the nobles were just not interested. When even his own chief counsellor, Abbot Suger of St. Denis, spoke against the scheme, Louis VII had no choice but to postpone a decision until Easter 1146 and, meanwhile, to lay the whole matter before Abbot Bernard of Clairvaux.

Unquestionably Bernard, (1115–53) was at that time the most distinguished figure in the intellectual and political life of the West. It was he who had given impetus to the new Cistercian order

which aimed at achieving a stricter observance of the Benedictine
Rule. He had been one of the leading Church politicians ever
since his tireless struggle to end the schism of 1130 between Innocent II and Anacletus II. On the question of the crusade his advice
was sought as though he were a 'divine oracle' as one of the
chroniclers put it. Bernard was probably well aware that the
clash between the king's plan and the pope's wishes created a
delicate political problem—a problem which was to play a considerable role in the later history of the crusades. Even if Louis
VII had only planned an armed pilgrimage this inevitably came to
be looked upon as a crusade in the light of the pope's crusading
bull which had, after all, been issued earlier. Should the French
authorities have argued that the bull had not been discussed at
Bourges and that the king acted on his own initiative, this might
have given rise to the opinion that a king could summon and carry
through a crusade independently of the Church. For this reason
the question of how much influence the pope's bull had on the
assembly at Bourges was bitterly debated in the last century—and
all too often debated in the polemical and anachronistic terms
common to nineteenth-century nationalism or religious feeling.
The sources simply do not permit a definite answer, though it is
perhaps more probable than not that the bull was already known
to the king, or at least to Bernard of Clairvaux. The only certain
thing is that it was indeed issued on 1 December 1145. This was
proved by the researches of Erich Caspar after it had long been
obstinately denied by those who wished to give Louis VII the
credit for initiating the crusade.[36]

Understandably enough the abbot of Clairvaux was not at all
inclined to support an expedition which looked as though it might
have been instigated by the king. This would have meant that
control over the crusade had been taken out of the hands of the
Church. The papacy would have to face a considerable blow to
its prestige if it could not maintain its position as overlord of the
crusading movement. Bernard therefore tried to give the initiative
back to the pope. He declared that he could not consider so
important a question without first consulting the pope. The result,
early in 1146, was a round of negotiations between the papal and
French courts culminating in the reissue of *Quantum praedecessores* (with a slightly amended text) on 1 March 1146. This
version was, both in form and content, to be the pattern for all
later papal crusading bulls. It was divided into three parts: the
narrative, the exhortation, and the privileges (*narratio, exhortatio,
privilegia*). Right in the opening phrases the pope—and here

doubtless the influence of his teacher, Bernard of Clairvaux, can
be discerned—asserted his claim to direct the crusade. He
vigorously emphasized the tradition of the Church, appealing to
the precedents set by his predecessors and describing the part
played by Urban II in setting the First Crusade in motion. There
followed a short account of the First Crusade and a description
of the fall of Edessa which the pope explained as a punishment for
sin (*nostris peccatis exigentibus*). Here Eugenius had hit upon a
formula which was to appear time and time again in the writings
of preachers and chroniclers. In the *exhortatio* he called upon
nobles and magnates to defend, like good sons, the land which
their brave fathers had won. As Christians they were summoned
to fight for the Church in the East so that they would obtain
remission of sins, help to enhance the dignity of Christendom and
preserve unblemished their own knightly reputations. Then came
a list of privileges headed by the crusading indulgence which, in
conformity with the interpretation current as early as 1096, went
beyond what had been authorized by the decree at Clermont. At
this point Eugenius explicitly referred to the indulgence granted
by Urban II but since, as Eugenius himself wrote, he was relying
upon chronicle reports and not upon his predecessor's letters, this
does not in fact tell us much about Urban's own point of view.
The chroniclers had very early gone further than the Clermont
decree warranted. The Church's protection for the wives, children,
and possessions of the crusaders was then renewed. The extravagant dress which had been all too common on the First
Crusade was forbidden. Crusaders who had to borrow money were
exempted from paying interest on it. This, together with the
provision which regulated the pawning of land to the Church,
meant that the most urgent aspects of the problem of financing the
crusade had been dealt with.

Eugenius entrusted Bernard alone with the job of preaching the
crusade north of the Alps; in France the bull *Quantum praedecessores* was promulgated only in connection with his preaching.
Eugenius III himself did no more than issue a crusading bull in
Italy in October 1146. He was unable to leave Italy because of the
situation in Rome. He had been driven out of the city and a
republic had been set up by Arnold of Brescia. In the German
king, Conrad III (1138–52), Eugenius hoped to find an ally who
would both enable him to re-enter Rome and support him against
the ambitions of Roger II of Sicily who had had himself crowned
king (1130–54) after bringing all the Norman lands in Italy under
one rule. Thus Eugenius naturally wished to see the preaching of

the crusade limited to France and Italy, the countries which had taken part in the First Crusade. The original impulse for the Second Crusade had come from the pope, but it was entirely owing to the eloquence of the abbot of Clairvaux that anything came of that impulse.

At first Bernard adhered to the papal plan of keeping Germany out of the crusade. He began his preaching at the court at Vézelay on 31 March 1146 after the pope's March bull had been read out. The eloquence of the 'honey-tongued teacher' (*doctor mellifluus*) which can still move the modern reader of his literary works and which was acclaimed by all his contemporaries, had its expected effect. The king and a crowd of great nobles took the cross. They decided to allow a year in which to make their preparations. Louis VII used this time to negotiate with the countries through which he intended to march, particularly Germany and Byzantium. He may also have taken a forced loan from some of the churches of France in order to cover his expenses, though the evidence for this is by no means compelling. In any event this would have been something quite different from a crusading tax.

In the following months Bernard preached unceasingly. If he could not appear in person he would send envoys to read letters of exhortation, the essential points of which he wrote himself but which his chancery would alter slightly to suit local circumstances before distributing them. About a dozen of these letters are still extant. Very characteristic of Bernard's preaching style is the one which was sent to the people of England. There are no cloudy eschatological notions here. For Bernard the crusade was a work of penance. The indulgence, once a means to an end, had become an end in itself. The East, of course, had to be freed from the heathen, but so too the souls of the crusaders had to be freed from sin. For this reason he welcomed the threat to the crusader states as a sign that 'the accepted time, the day of salvation' (cf. 2 Corinthians 6:2) was at hand. From now on the *acceptabile tempus* motif was an inseparable part of the preaching of crusades. Bernard had a disquieting tendency to take it for granted that his contemporaries were evil-doers who needed to repent. Thus he, more than anyone, emphasized the idea of a spiritual reward.

But Bernard's own words speak more clearly than any analysis. Here therefore some typical passages from his letter to the English are quoted as being representative of all later crusading sermons.

Now is the accepted time, the day of abundant salvation. The earth has been shaken; it trembles because the Lord of heaven has begun to

lose his land—the land in which, for more than thirty years, he lived as
a man amongst men.... But now, on account of our sins, the sacri-
legious enemies of the cross have begun to show their faces even there;
their swords are wreaking havoc in the promised land.... What are
you doing, you mighty men of valour? What are you doing, you servants
of the cross? Will you throw to the dogs that which is most holy? Will
you cast pearls before swine? ... What are we thinking of, my brethren?
Is then the arm of the Lord grown so short that he himself has become
powerless to bring salvation and must needs summon us, poor earthly
worms that we are, to defend and restore to him his inheritance? Can
he not send more than twelve legions of angels ... and so free his land?
Of course there can be no doubt that, should he wish to, he can do
this.... But I say unto you, the Lord God is testing you. He is looking
down upon the sons of men to see if he can find anyone who understands
and grieves over what is now happening on earth.... See then with what
skill he plans your salvation and be amazed. Look, sinners, into the
depths of his pity and trust in him ... He is not trying to bring you
down but to raise you up. What is it but a unique and wonderful act of
divine generosity when the Almighty God treats murderers, thieves,
adulterers, perjurors, and criminals of all kinds as though they were
men of righteousness and worthy to be called to his service. Do not
hesitate. God is good. ... He pretends to be in debt so that he can
repay those who take up arms on his behalf with the forgiveness of sins
and with eternal glory ... I would call blessed that generation that has
the chance to obtain so rich an indulgence, blessed to be alive in this
year of jubilee, this year so pleasing to the Lord.... O mighty soldier, O
man of war, you now have a cause for which you can fight without endangering your soul; a cause in which to win is glorious and for which
to die is but gain....

Or are you a shrewd businessman, a man quick to see the profits of
this world? If you are, I can offer you a splendid bargain. Do not miss
this opportunity. Take the sign of the cross. At once you will have
indulgence for all the sins which you confess with a contrite heart. It
does not cost you much to buy and if you wear it with humility you will
find that it is the kingdom of heaven.

The letter closes with some words of warning. The Jews are not
to be persecuted. In other letters Bernard advised men not to leave
too soon as Peter the Hermit had done—with terrible consequences
for those who followed him. They should wait and then march
east in good order. The abbot was an advocate of good order in
the Church, of everything being in its proper place within the
system. His preaching differed from the preaching of the First
Crusade in that he addressed himself not to the whole population
but to the knightly classes alone. He relied on their energy and he

tried to awake in them the feeling that they had been specially chosen.

The unauthorized activity of a Cistercian monk, Rudolf, caused Bernard a good deal of anxiety. This monk wandered through north France and the Rhineland in the style of one of the popular millenarian preachers of the First Crusade. He had received no dispensation from the decree forbidding monks to preach so he was infringing the preaching monopoly of the secular clergy. Moreover he was damaging Bernard's prestige since the abbot's sermons contained no statements of an eschatological nature. Worst of all was the fact that the inhabitants of the Rhineland towns were once again being inspired to massacre the Jews. In order to bring Rudolf's activities under control, Bernard himself had to go to the Rhineland at the request of the archbishop of Mainz. He dealt severely with the monk and then stayed on in Germany. It was no longer possible to keep the Germans out of the crusade since Rudolf had already filled them with enthusiasm for it. Bernard also had gone further than Eugenius had originally envisaged as his letters to the English and the Spanish prove. But if a German crusade was to have any success the support of King Conrad III was needed. Bernard and the king met at an assembly at Frankfurt in November 1146. Conrad withstood Bernard's appeal but did agree to another meeting at Speyer at Christmas. Bernard felt that the king's resistance was weakening and inexorably increased the pressure on him. In a tremendous sermon which retained its power even through the words of an interpreter, Bernard brought Conrad to the point of imagining himself at the Last Judgement standing before Christ. Then Bernard, as Christ, asked the king, 'Man, what ought I have done for you that I have not done?' This assault on his feelings was too much for Conrad. He took the cross and his example was followed by countless nobles headed by his nephew, Duke Frederick of Swabia. Germany had been won over to the crusade. The king's decision had been made easier by the settlement of the long and destructive feud between the count of Namur and the archbishop of Trier. One of Bernard's aims in coming to Germany had been to end this feud. On Christmas Eve Conrad's old enemy, Duke Welf VI, had taken the cross though it is unlikely that there had been time for the king to hear of this before he made his own decision. Following the assembly at Speyer a crusading letter was sent to the Bavarians. At an assembly held at Regensburg in February 1147 many of them, including Bishop Otto of Freising, who was to be one of the chroniclers of the crusade, responded to this appeal.

Next month at another meeting of the imperial court at Frankfurt Conrad decided to take the land route through Byzantium and Asia Minor. This was the route hallowed by tradition because it had been taken by Godfrey de Bouillon. To Conrad it seemed particularly suitable because he had a firm alliance with Byzantium sealed by the marriage of his sister-in-law, Bertha of Sulzbach, to the emperor, Manuel I Comnenus (1143–80). Moreover Manuel had enjoyed considerable military success against the Seldjuks of Asia Minor and this suggested that there would be no repetition of the disasters of 1101. In the previous month (February 1147) the French too had decided in favour of the land-route despite the efforts made by their ally, Roger II of Sicily, to persuade them to travel by the sea route from Italy. Roger had suggested that he might then join them on crusade, but Louis realized that in fact the king of Sicily was hoping to secure French support for the anti-Byzantine policy which, in the best Norman tradition, he was pursuing. Even so Manuel had little enthusiasm for the course events had taken. From his point of view the alliance with Conrad had been intended mainly to keep Roger II at bay. This was now out of the question. Since the French were Roger's allies it seemed to the Greeks that the fact that the Germans and French were now taking the same line of march through the Balkans might mean that Conrad had changed sides. Nor, of course, was the pope over-joyed to learn of Conrad's decision. He had been counting on his help in Italy. But once the crusade had become a general European enterprise there was little that he could or would do to hinder it. None the less the inclusion of Germany meant that right from the start the crusade was saddled with problems which say little for the political insight of Bernard of Clairvaux.

At the Frankfurt assembly of March 1147 the German contingent was weakened when the Saxon princes announced their preference for a crusade of their own against the Wends—Slavs who lived beyond the north-eastern borders of the empire. Bernard and Eugenius gave their approval and the pope granted these crusaders the same spiritual and material privileges as were enjoyed by those who went to the Holy Land. It would have been difficult to reject the Saxon plan when, at roughly the same time, Eugenius was granting the status and privileges of a crusade to a campaign against the Saracens in Spain organized by Alfonso VII of Castile. Even so the Wendish Crusade was a dangerous precedent. In Spain there was at least a long tradition of war against the heathen going back to the days before the crusades. To this extent Spain was a special case. In Spain moreover the enemy was also Islam. But if the example of the Wendish crusade were to be followed then the Holy Land might lose much of the support it so desperately needed, for heathens could be fought in many parts of the world, not just in the Holy Land. And in fact the system of crusades against the Slavs did become increasingly well developed, particularly after the Teutonic Order settled in Prussia in the thirteenth century.

The prince of the Wendish Obotrites, Niklot, anticipating the crusade, launched an attack first. A large German army led by Henry the Lion, duke of Saxony, Conrad duke of Zähringen, Albert the Bear, margrave of Brandenburg, and the archbishops of Bremen and Magdeburg marched out to meet his invasion. But the fighting ended without any clear victory. Indeed only the fact that the Wends went through a mock baptismal service prevented the real failure of the campaign becoming obvious.[37]

The crusade itself started at Regensburg in May 1147. The French set out from Metz a few weeks later. The German march through Hungary went off without incident. But once in the Byzantine Empire the excesses of the German troops so badly damaged relations with Manuel Comnenus, that when Conrad III reached Constantinople in September the two rulers did not even meet each other. Manuel was furious because the arrival of the crusading armies deprived him of all mobility. He had to remain in the capital while Roger II of Sicily seized the opportunity to ravage Corfu and to destroy the centres of the Byzantine silk industry at Thebes and Corinth. Two years passed before Manuel, with Venetian help, was able to drive Roger off imperial territory. For his part Conrad felt somewhat put out because Manuel, like his grandfather, had required an oath from him promising to respect Byzantine claims over Syria and Palestine. It was the approach of the French army more than the pressure applied by Manuel which persuaded Conrad to take his troops across the Bosporus into Asia Minor. Then, instead of keeping to the original plan and waiting for the French to join them, they decided to push on immediately in the direction of Edessa.

At Nicaea Conrad divided his army into two sections. One contingent, under the command of Bishop Otto of Freising, was instructed to take the longer coast road. Conrad had intended that this contingent should include all the non-combatants, but in fact some hangers-on remained behind to hamper the main army. This made its first contact with the enemy near Dorylaeum at the end of October. The Seldjuks won a convincing victory. The German retreat to the coast began in good order but control was soon completely lost and, in consequence, casualties were heavy. Most of the survivors who struggled back to Nicaea early in November left the army in order to return home. Otto of Freising's contingent meanwhile had marched south along the Aegean coast. It then struck inland only to suffer a severe reverse at the hands of the Turks at Laodicea. What was left of the army just about managed to reach the coast of Pamphylia but was then cut to pieces in February 1148. The bishop and a few other survivors finished the journey to Syria by ship.

Meanwhile the French army had reached Constantinople on 4 October 1147. On the surface relations with Manuel were good and the emperor himself went to some lengths to win over Louis VII. Within the French army, however, there was a strong anti-Byzantine party led by Bishop Godfrey of Langres. He was an unpleasant trouble-maker who claimed to enjoy the rights of a legate. In fact it seems that the pope had conferred them upon him but had later replaced him by Guido of Florence, cardinal priest of San Crisogono. His party derived encouragement from the news of Roger II's success at Corfu and gained more support when it was learned that Manuel had made a truce with the Seldjuk sultan of Iconium. This shocked the Latins although it was precisely their approach which had helped persuade Manuel to come to terms. Thus even before they reached Constantinople the anti-Byzantine party was pressing for an attack on the city and for an alliance with King Roger in order to achieve this. They continued their agitation while the army was encamped outside the city but failed to convince the majority who, with the support of Guido of Florence and Louis VII himself, pointed out that the pope had not authorized an expedition against Constantinople. Nevertheless here was the first sign that men were prepared to misuse the crusading ideal to the extent of turning it against fellow Christians. The capture of Constantinople by the crusaders of 1204 was foreshadowed.[38]

The French constantly postponed crossing the Bosporus until finally Manuel spread rumours about a German victory in Asia Minor. Fearing that they might come too late to quench their (typically medieval) thirst for booty—which made up an important part of a knight's income—the French hurried over into Asia Minor where they were reinforced by a contingent from Savoy. Manuel, however, refused to supply them with guides or provisions while the question of their relations with the Byzantine Empire was still unclear. Finally the French barons had to resign themselves to paying homage and Louis himself promised that he would not deprive the emperor of any town that rightfully belonged to him. Manuel now provided guides but in view of his treaty with the sultan he could give the crusade no more than half-hearted help. This gave further stimulus to the anti-Greek mood in the French army. At Nicaea they joined up with Conrad III and the remnants of the German army. From here they marched to Smyrna and then on to Ephesus where Conrad became so ill (Christmas 1147) that he had to return to Constantinople. Manuel took care of him personally in order to breathe new life into their old alliance. Meanwhile the French army had met the same fate as the German. Early in the new year they suffered a heavy defeat at Laodicea. The surviving contingents fought their way to the coast at Attalia but this Byzantine town was neither able nor particularly willing to accommodate so many crusaders. The Byzantines were asked to provide ships but so few arrived that only the king, the clergy, and the barons were able to sail. Those who were left behind tried to make their way overland to Syria, but soon after leaving Attalia they were routed by the Seldjuks; Louis and his followers reached Antioch in safety.

The position in Syria was not at all good. Joscelin II of Edessa had taken advantage of the death of Zengi in 1146 to try to recapture his capital, but Nur ed-Din stepped in and. by massacring the Armenian and Jacobite population of Edessa, ensured that it was lost beyond recovery. After this there were no important clashes; both Muslims and Christians were waiting for the arrival of the crusaders. Raymond of Antioch wanted Louis to lead an expedition against Aleppo to relieve the pressure on his northern border where he had to face the Seldjuks of Asia Minor as well as Nur ed-Din. It was a sensible plan. Only in this way was there any hope at all of reconstructing the county of Edessa, some fragments of which still remained on the west bank of the Euphrates. Nur ed-Din moreover was to become a most dangerous enemy of the crusader states, though this was perhaps not entirely clear in 1148. Even so, it must have been obvious that a victory over him could hinder the union of Aleppo and Damascus. But on his own Louis was too weak to be able to help Raymond in the north and in addition the rumours of an affair between his wife, Eleanor, and Raymond made him feel that he had been badly treated. What was left of the crusading armies was little enough already and a division of forces seemed stupid. So Louis marched south to join Otto of Freising and Conrad III who, after his convalescence, had reached the Holy Land in April 1148. After visiting the Holy Places the kings of France and Germany met at Acre where Conrad meanwhile had been trying to raise a new army. Here Louis's forces were reinforced by some newly arrived Provençal crusaders.

At Acre on 24 June 1148 the High Court of Jerusalem met. The crusaders were admitted to the assembly as they were entitled to be according to a tradition of the court, though this is the first time that the historian can actually observe the tradition being followed. Besides Conrad III the Germans were represented by the bishops of Freising, Metz, and Toul, by the legate, the bishop of Porto, and by the duke of Swabia, Duke Welf VI and the margraves of Austria, Verona, and Montferrat. For the French there were Louis VII, the bishops of Langres and Lisieux, Cardinal Guido of Florence, the counts of Perche, Troyes, Flanders, and Soissons. The kingdom of Jerusalem was represented by Baldwin III, Queen Melisende, the patriarch of Jerusalem, the archbishops of Caesarea and Nazareth, the bishops of Sidon, Acre, Beirut, Banyas, and Bethlehem, the Masters of the Temple and the Hospital, and the lords of Nablus, Tiberias, Sidon, Caesarea, Oultrejourdain, Toron, and Beirut. North Syria was not represented. After some debate the assembly made the incredibly stupid decision to attack Damascus. After 1146 there could be no question of Edessa being a war objective and in view of the absence of the north Syrians the case for Aleppo rather went by default. But Damascus was the last place to attack. The existence of the kingdom depended on the continuation of the alliance made with Damascus against Aleppo in 1139. Its association with the apostle Paul made it a sacred city but the alliance with the atabeg of Damascus was a matter of life or death to Jerusalem and ought not to have been sacrificed for reasons of this kind, no matter how idealistic. It is commonly believed that it was the barons of Jerusalem who put forward and carried through this proposal. But there is no evidence in the sources to support this theory and later events suggest that it is very wide of the mark. A glance at the composition of the assembly will make it clear that the young king of Jerusalem and his mother had little chance of resisting the wishes of the kings of Germany and France. Only the crusaders, ignorant of local needs, could have put forward such an absurd scheme.

The plan was as ridiculous in execution as in conception. On 24 July they encamped among the orchards on the west side of the city. The approach of a relieving army under Nur ed-Din frightened the atabeg of Damascus just as much as it did the Palestinian barons. The latter, playing a dangerously devious game, persuaded the two kings that the orchards were adding to the difficulties of the siege and that it would be better to move the army to the south-east. But here the army was caught on a hot waterless plain; a prolonged stay was out of the question, so on the same day it was decided to raise the siege and withdraw. In his chronicle, William of Tyre, whose comments on the discussion at Acre had been very laconic, was later to try to put the blame on the count of Flanders or the influence of Raymond of Antioch. But contemporary public opinion in the West blamed, rightly, the barons of Palestine. They, of course, had been in a dilemma and had acted accordingly. On the one hand they had to keep in favour with the West for they needed men and money and there was no other source of supply. Thus, for good or ill, they had to march against Damascus. On the other hand they had to wreck the expedition for otherwise the vital alliance would be lost. It was a measure born of desperation and its consequences were bad. For one thing, public opinion in the West was shocked; for another, although the atabeg of Damacus still remained true to the alliance, the city population which had once accepted it also now distrusted the Franks and in 1154 opened the city gates to Nur ed-Din. The union of Aleppo and Damascus was helped rather than hindered by the campaign of 1148. On 8 September Conrad angrily left the Holy Land. Louis VII stayed on until Easter 1149 but achieved nothing of note. As William of Tyre observed: 'from this time on the position of the Latins in the East deteriorated visibly.'

Conrad III went to Thessalonika and there, probably in October 1148 before he returned to Germany, he made a treaty with Manuel Comnenus, renewing their old anti-Norman alliance from the days before the Second Crusade.[39] It was agreed that, with the support of Byzantine money and troops, Conrad would lead an expedition against Roger II next year. The European truce which Bernard of Clairvaux had brought about so that the crusade could go forward, was at an end. But Roger had made his preparations in good time. In 1148 he engineered a rebellion of the Welf family in Germany. This prevented Conrad III from entering Italy. In July 1149 when Louis VII visited the king of Sicily on his way back to France, Roger took the opportunity to strengthen their alliance. He advocated another crusade, again with the intention of turning it against the Greeks. He was helped by the fact that in France meanwhile Bernard of Clairvaux, Suger of St. Denis, and Peter the Venerable, abbot of Cluny, had also begun to preach a new crusade —a genuine one—which was intended to make amends for 1148. Bernard of Clairvaux might even have been chosen at Chartres to lead the expedition had not the plan collapsed because the French knights were unwilling to shoulder the burden of a new crusade so soon. The shock of the last failure was still too great; losses had been too heavy. But at least a great European war was narrowly

averted when the pope refused to join the coalition against Conrad and Manuel because he was afraid of being politically dominated by the Normans.

The one success of the whole crusade took place in the wings.
In 1147 a group of English, Flemish, and Frisian crusaders who
were taking the sea route to Palestine, sailed up the River Tagus
and, after a siege lasting several months, captured the city of
Lisbon from the Moors.[40] It was a pitifully small return for a
crusade which had begun in such an atmosphere of hope and enthusiasm and which had been organized on so large a scale. The
disappointment was, of course, correspondingly deep. This is clear
from the many attempts which were made to explain the failure.
Some, above all the French chronicler Odo of Deuil, preferred
rational explanations—the hostility of the Greeks and Turks, the
difficulties of the journey. Others, like the Cistercians Otto of
Freising and Bernard of Clairvaux, used metaphysical arguments
—the sins of men, the inscrutable judgement of God. Between
these extremes we find all manner of natural and supernatural
explanations. Gerhoh of Reichersberg and the Würzburg Annalist,
the two severest critics of the crusade, subsequently went so far as
to regard it as the work of the Devil and Antichrist. The most important target for critics was naturally the abbot of Clairvaux
who had done more than anyone else to set the crusade in motion,
and had so closely identified himself with it. By his treatment of
the crusade as a means by which a soul could find salvation he had
aroused hopes which were brutally dashed by its failure. It would
be a long time before the crusading ideal would recover from this.
Bernard replied to his critics in the second book of his De Consideratione. There is no doubt that he took the criticism seriously
and was hurt by it; he compared the judgement of God—and it
was in these terms that he saw the criticism—to a hell in which he
was now standing. It could not shake his faith but his writings
show clearly that he found the subject a painful one. He discussed
the actions for which he had been—or might possibly be—re-
proached but he was not prepared to admit that he was in any way
responsible for subsequent disappointments. It might, however, be
argued that he had added to the difficulties of the crusade by
widening its scope both internally and externally in a political
situation which was not at all favourable to such a process of
extension. Bernard's self-defence always ended with his taking
cover behind the commission to preach the crusade which he had
received from the pope. That he should try to evade responsibility
for the crusade after it had failed reveals a side of his character

which is not very attractive. To answer those critics who, rightly, would not accept this excuse, he constructed a second line of defence. He described himself as the shield of God, drawing upon himself the fire of the blasphemers, the critics, so that God would not be touched by their poisoned darts. For the critics, he argued, were really attacking God, not him.[41] The zeal with which the Cistercians, the monks of Bernard's own order, emphasized a metaphysical explanation of the fiasco, rather suggests that they wanted to cover up other reasons for the failure. But public opinion was not deceived. In future it was not going to be so easy to preach a crusade.

6 · THE CRUSADER STATES, 1149–1187

T H E division of Zengi's lands in 1146 whereby Saif ed-Din Ghazi obtained Mosul and Nur ed-Din (1146–74) Aleppo was unfortunate for the Franks. It meant that Nur ed-Din was freed from the responsibility for the disorders in the east which had weighed so heavily upon his father. He could concentrate on the struggle against Damascus and the Franks.⁴² His first success came when he beat off Joscelin II's vain attempt to recapture Edessa (see above p. 105). Then in 1147 and 1148 he attacked the principality of Antioch, occupying the best part of its territories east of the Orontes. But for the moment he made no decisive move. Indeed the Second Crusade forced him to go to the relief of Damascus. His own base Aleppo, however, remained out of danger since the crusaders proved incapable of making the decision to attack in north Syria. As soon as the crusade was over Nur ed-Din resumed his war against Antioch. In the summer of 1149 he appeared before the walls of Inab, a fortress belonging to Antioch. Raymond and his knights went to its relief but on 29 July they were routed and Raymond himself was killed. It was Nur ed-Din's finest victory against the Franks. His prestige throughout the Islamic world was enormously enhanced.

Sir Hamilton Gibb has pointed out that the victory at Inab had other, more far-reaching consequences. From now on Nur ed-Din saw himself as the champion of Islam, as a man with a historic mission to fulfil. His task was to unite the Muslims against the Franks. To understand him it is essential to see that he was also a religious zealot; political unity presupposed unity of belief. Thus he took tough measures against the Shi'ites and promoted every cause which could help to reawaken and deepen Orthodox faith. Schools and mosques were founded. Poets and preachers were called upon to support his political and religious aims. Using propaganda slogans they worked to awaken the religious fervour of the people. Above all they condemned the 'scandalous' alliance between Damascus and the Franks which Nur ed-Din was determined to destroy. From 1150 onwards he steadily increased the pressure on Damascus; on several occasions he set up camp before its walls. After the death of Unur in 1149 the government of Damascus remained weak and unable to take advantage of his periodic campaigns in the region of Edessa where the capture of Joscelin II had permitted him to consolidate his conquests. In 1154, after a minimum of resistance, the people of Damascus opened the gates of their city to him. His religious programme was at once extended to include the new state. Muslim Syria was now united and the gaining of Damascus brought Nur ed-Din a considerable addition to the strength of his army. Gibb has estimated the number of his troops at a maximum of 10,000–15,000 cavalry. Two thousand of these were his own household troops and the rest consisted of contingents under the command of men who were granted territorial fiefs (iqta) so that they could support the required number of soldiers. During this period there was a very noticeable influx of Kurdish soldiers into both the officer corps and the regular army.

Lack of leadership among the Franks made the rise of Nur ed-Din all the more menacing. Baldwin III, king of Jerusalem (1143–63) was still not grown up; Joscelin II of Edessa was a prisoner; the prince of Antioch had fallen in battle. After the battle at Inab and even before finally extinguishing the county of Edessa, Nur ed-Din dramatically demonstrated the extent of his power by taking a bath in the Mediterranean before the eyes of his soldiers. Antioch itself was saved by the efforts of the patriarch Aimery (1144–93). Unobtrusively controlled by him, the government of Antioch was formally in the hands of Raymond's widow, Constance, whose main concern was to preserve the principality for her children. The intervention of Baldwin III persuaded Nur ed-Din to withdraw from Antioch thus ensuring, for the moment, its continued existence. But Baldwin was not able to do the same for Edessa. Conditions in the kingdom of Jerusalem did not permit the ruler to stay away for long. The king was now twenty and disliked sharing the government with his mother Melisende as much as the majority of his barons disapproved of this arrangement; a woman did not seem to be equipped to meet the dangers pressing in from all sides. The quarrel between the young king and his mother was more serious than William of Tyre's account of it would suggest. Only an analysis of the royal charters of those years reveals just how deep the rift between them was. Melisende was by no means without allies among the nobility; above all she could rely upon the support of the Church. At the beginning of Baldwin

III's reign she had controlled Galilee, Samaria, and Judaea; the last two provinces remained under her control until her fall from power, indeed Samaria she kept until her death. Her political dominance rested in part upon the support of the higher nobility of these provinces: the prince of Galilee, Philip of Nablus in Samaria, and Rohard the Elder in Judaea. She could also count on the rapidly rising family of the Ibelins in the south-west. In part she was made powerful by the loyalty of the men who held the great crown offices, notably the constable, Manasses of Hierges, a nephew of Baldwin II, who had arrived in the Holy Land in 1140. Only very gradually was Baldwin III able to match this strength by building up a power base of his own in the crown estates in the north around Tyre and Acre. From 1149 onwards the relationship between mother and son was more than chilly. Systematically Melisende set about excluding Baldwin from the business of government. The king responded by intervening in north Syria; by decisive action there he hoped to build up a reputation for himself. For several years the chancery was in complete disarray, dissolving in fact into two competing *scriptoria*. The queen mother built up her household and treated the parts of the kingdom which she controlled as though they were independent territories. So far did this process go that in the summer of 1150 the nobles who supported her took the unprecedented step of ignoring the king's summons to join the army he was leading into Syria. Clearly they intended to weaken his position until it had become impossible for him to exercise the traditional protectorate of the kings of Jerusalem over the principalities of Syria. Their plan miscarried. Baldwin, although he had very few troops in his train, marched north and proved himself to be not only an energetic ruler but also a skilful diplomat, well able to hold his own in some delicate negotiations with Byzantium. By 1150 the *de facto* partition of the realm had gone so far that it had become impossible for Baldwin III to let things drift any longer if he was ever to have any hope of rescuing the kingdom as well as his own position. Fortunately for him it was at this point that Melisende made a decisive mistake. Probably in 1150, although possibly not until 1151, she allowed her favourite Manasses to marry Helvis of Ibelin. All modern historians, relying on a passage in William of Tyre, have stated that it was this marriage which formed the basis of Manasses's power by assuring him of the support of the Ibelins. But in fact exactly the opposite is true. Earlier, in about 1148, Helvis had inherited the important double lordship of Ramleh-Mirabel from her brother; it passed into the hands of her first husband, Balian 'the Old' of Ibelin. Balian's three sons could justifiably look forward to a rich inheritance, but their hopes were dashed by their mother's second marriage, for it can be shown that Ramleh-Mirabel was now taken over by Manasses. The marriage of Balian 'the Old' had been the first really good marriage made by the Ibelins since their arrival in Outremer and what the sons would inherit from their father's side of the family only would neither provide properly for three men nor make them sufficiently eligible to attract the really wealthy heiresses. Thus unless the three brothers managed to bring down Manasses and the regime to which he belonged before he had sons of his own from the marriage with Helvis, they would have to face the ruin of all their hopes. The Ibelins moreover were one of the 'old families'—that group of baronial landowners which was becoming increasingly exclusive in outlook. Naturally they resented it when Manasses, a *homo novus* who had been kept on the sidelines for ten years, finally succeeded in entering the group—and at their expense. Fortunately for them the Ibelins had influential kinsmen among the nobility. Only against this background can we understand the full significance of William of Tyre's explanation of the cause of the final break between Baldwin III and his mother: the dissatisfaction of the barons with the supposedly arrogant rule of Manasses. Undoubtedly the constable's marriage to Helvis added considerably to his power—and that, in fact, is all that William of Tyre tells us about it. He does not say, although these are the conclusions which modern historians have drawn, that the marriage formed the basis of his power or that it enabled him to count upon the support of the Ibelins. Manasses had been constable ever since 1143 but cannot have married Helvis until 1150 at the earliest. In 1152 he was brought down. For this reason alone it is clear that the marriage to Helvis came too late to have been the basis of his power. By early 1152 the opposition to Melisende and Manasses was sufficiently well organized for Baldwin III to make his move. On the advice of the barons who supported him—but without consulting Melisende—the young king planned a second coronation in order to strengthen his position. The patriarch of Jerusalem wanted to alter this to an Easter crown-wearing in the presence of the queen mother, but this would hardly have added anything to Baldwin's authority so he tricked the patriarch by appearing in public in full regalia before Easter and without his mother. None the less when, immediately after this, the Haute Cour met, Melisende was still strong enough to force Baldwin to accept a partition of the kingdom. She kept Jerusalem and Nablus while he received Tyre and Acre. The one who lost most was the unpopular Manasses who had to yield his office as constable to Humphrey II of Toron. It soon became clear that the partition was impossible to carry out. The result was open war between mother and son. He besieged her first at Nablus and then in the citadel of Jerusalem—the site of the royal palace since shortly before 1150. She was forced to surrender the city and was no longer allowed to take an active part in government. From now on she lived at Nablus (a crown fief), retaining only a certain influence over appointments to Church offices. Manasses was forced into exile. Baldwin III now ruled alone but the civil war was hardly a good omen for the future and cannot have helped to enhance the authority of the royal family.

Baldwin III was a tall young man with fair hair and a thick beard. He had an unusually quick intelligence and a remarkable eloquence. He had been carefully educated and was much praised for his good manners, for the courtesy which he showed to all, for his military prowess, his legal knowledge, his preference for historical reading, and his pleasure in discussion. He was clearly of no more than average piety and even a favourably disposed observer like William of Tyre could not overlook his passion for dice and other games of chance as well as a certain sexual licence up until the time of his marriage.

As so often, Baldwin III's first task after his second 'coronation' was to march north where he had to compose a quarrel between Raymond II of Tripoli and his wife Hodierna. But during the king's visit to Tripoli, Count Raymond was murdered by Assassins (1152). Baldwin persuaded the barons of Tripoli to do homage to the countess who would rule on behalf of her young son Raymond III (1152-87). He also tried to convince Princess Constance of Antioch that she ought to marry again. In fact the patriarch had already put forward several candidates for her hand in vain, and Baldwin himself was to have as little success as the emperor, Manuel Comnenus, had with his proposal of a Byzantine prince which, though it would have meant help in the war against Nur ed-Din, would also have involved an increase in the Byzantine presssure on Antioch. In the next year Constance took everyone by surprise when she decided to marry Reynald of Châtillon. He had not been one of the candidates and there were no political considerations to commend the match which was opposed by the patriarch. But Reynald was handsome and recklessly brave and by secretly marrying him Constance was following her own romantic inclination. Unfortunately his character was totally undisciplined; he had no means, no followers, and no political common sense. To the end of his days he remained a dare-devil adventurer never able to measure and take account of the significance or the consequences of his actions.[43] Baldwin III was badly advised when he gave his approval to the match. Very soon after the wedding Reynald revealed the brutal side of his nature when he arrested the patriarch and then had his face covered with honey before leaving him to the mercy of the Syrian sun and the flies. Baldwin's vigorous representations forced Reynald to restore the patriarch to his office but, not surprisingly, the latter decided that it was safer for him to live in Jerusalem.

In the south meanwhile Baldwin III had achieved a spectacular success. By 1150 he had built a castle over the ruins of the ancient town of Gaza, thus blocking the route between the Fatimid south and Ascalon and so completing the encirclement of this town, the 'bride of Syria', which had been begun by Fulk. In January 1153 he concentrated all available forces on a siege. The garrison resisted obstinately but despite some reverses he never relaxed his pressure and on 19 August the fortress surrendered on condition that the garrison had three days in which to leave in safety. The plunder was enormous. The king's brother Amalric, count of Jaffa, was made count of Ascalon as well. Although this 'double county' became one of the greatest crown fiefs it was not just for family reasons that Amalric was enfeoffed with Ascalon. Hugh II of Le Puiset, an earlier lord of Jaffa, had regarded Ascalon as his future fief and even before 1130 he had given the great mosque in Ascalon, an important Shi'ite shrine, to the abbey of St. Mary Josaphat. It now became the cathedral of St. Paul and a canon of the Church of the Holy Sepulchre was elected bishop. But soon afterwards the bishop of Bethlehem protested about this to the pope; the new bishop had to stand down and Ascalon became just a parish in the diocese of Bethlehem. This meant that the ecclesiastical order of the pre-crusade days, when Bethlehem had been the parish and Ascalon the episcopal city, had now been reversed.

The capture of Ascalon was undoubtedly a great achievement. The whole coast was now held by the Franks; the last Fatimid fortress in Palestine had fallen. It was easier now to forget about the difficulties in the north. But in a sense it was a Pyrrhic victory. Ever since Fulk's reign Ascalon had not represented a serious threat to Jerusalem. But once it had fallen the way seemed open for expansion to the south where Egypt, rich and with few fortified cities, was a tempting prospect for the would-be conqueror. The kings of Jerusalem yielded to this temptation. In doing so they not only drew valuable resources away from the defence of the north, they also provoked Nur ed-Din and, after him, Saladin to intervene in the affairs of Egypt. The end result was the fatal encirclement of Jerusalem by a united Islamic empire. Some of the other consequences very soon became clear. In equipping his army Baldwin III had incurred debts on a scale which diminished his freedom of political manoeuvre. Thus although both the treaty of 1139 and Frankish self-interest demanded that he should help Damascus against Nur ed-Din's final attack in 1154, he was in fact unable to do anything effective. He had to watch the creation of the menacing union between Damascus and Aleppo and was content when Nur ed-Din, in order to consolidate his gains, made a truce and ordered that the tribute formerly paid by Damascus should be continued. Even so, in the following years there were frequent clashes between the Franks and Nur ed-Din, especially in the region of Banyas in north Palestine east of the Jordan.

During this period Syrian affairs came to the forefront once again. Fortunately for both the Franks and the Byzantines Nur ed-Din fell dangerously ill in October 1157. He made arrangements for the succession but they were not sufficient to prevent a political crisis from developing, particularly in Aleppo where the Shi'ites rebelled against the Sunnite authorities. The revolt was quelled when the sick ruler intervened in person, but for a while there were signs that his army was breaking up. Nur ed-Din lived but his convalescence was a long one and afterwards he never again showed that warlike energy which had characterized the early part of his career. Reynald of Antioch took advantage of the situation and with support from Baldwin III and Count Thierry of Flanders who was on a visit to the Holy Land, he was able, in February 1158, to recapture the fortress of Harenc which protected Antiochene territory east of the Orontes.

Generally, however, it looked as though the prince of Antioch was doing everything he could to make himself disliked. In particular he had angered both the Byzantine emperor and King Baldwin by combining with the Armenian prince, Thoros, to attack the rich Byzantine island of Cyprus in 1156. For three weeks the troops of Antioch indulged in an orgy of destruction, murder, and rapine. This was the first occasion on which it became clear that, in Reynald's eyes, greed for plunder prevailed over every reasonable consideration. Reynald's behaviour persuaded the king of Jerusalem to seek an alliance with Byzantium. In 1157 he began the negotiations which ended, in September 1158, with the magnificent wedding between Baldwin and Manuel's young niece, Theodora, whose rich dowry gave the king temporary relief from his financial embarrassment. The terms of the alliance were that Baldwin would agree to the humbling of Reynald of Antioch in return for receiving Manuel's help against Nur ed-Din. In autumn 1158 the imperial army began its march. The Armenians of Cilicia were taken completely by surprise and Prince Thoros only just had time to flee to the mountains. Reynald did not wait for the arrival of the far superior Byzantine army. He went to meet Manuel at Mamistra in Lesser Armenia. Barefoot and bareheaded he threw himself at the emperor's feet, begging for mercy. He had to promise to instal a Greek patriarch and hand over the citadel of Antioch. Soon afterwards Manuel and Baldwin met for the first time and even the emperor was won over by the king's charm and diplomatic skill. He agreed to be reconciled with Thoros and to say nothing more about an Orthodox patriarch in Antioch. Then on 12 April 1159 Manuel made a triumphal entry into the city.

Prawer believes that Baldwin III was planning a 'Grand Alliance' of all the Christian powers of the Near East from Byzantium to Jerusalem, with the aim of eliminating Nur ed-Din and conquering Egypt. If such plans ever existed, and the evidence for them is rather tenuous, they were soon brought to nothing. A week after his triumph at Antioch Manuel marched out again, but only to conclude a truce with Nur ed-Din and not, as the Franks had hoped, to make war against Aleppo. The terms of the truce, however, speak volumes for Byzantine statesmanship. There were advantages for all the parties to it—even for the Franks who believed that they had been betrayed. Nur ed-Din was freed from the immediate threat of an attack by Manuel; Manuel won Nur ed-Din's support for a campaign against a far more dangerous enemy of the empire, the Seldjuks of Anatolia. Manuel moreover had achieved his aims in Cilicia and, although no Byzantine administration was set up in Antioch, he had established a preponderance in north Syria which was to last almost twenty years. But this discreet Byzantine influence would not have lasted long without Nur ed-Din's constant pressure on Antioch forcing the Franks to accept an imperial protectorate. Manuel had created a complicated balance of power system which would work just so long as Nur ed-Din did not destroy the crusader states. He had demonstrated that in an emergency he could intervene most effectively on the side of the Franks. The imperial campaign had been sufficient to convince Nur ed-Din of this fact and herein lay the advantage for the Franks. At very little cost in terms of human lives Manuel had brought about a new status quo in north Syria which was to last until 1176. The Franks understood the situation; when Nur ed-Din campaigned against the Seldjuks of Anatolia they kept their military operations on a small scale and made no serious attack on his Syrian bases so as not to disturb the Byzantine balance of power system. In one skirmish in 1160 Reynald of Antioch was captured. He remained a prisoner of the governor of Aleppo for the next sixteen years. No one exerted himself to raise the money for his ransom.

Once again arrangements had to be made for the government of Antioch and the barons turned, as they had become accustomed to do, to Jerusalem, not to their new overlord Manuel. Baldwin entrusted the government to the newly returned Patriarch Aimery, passing over the claims of Princess Constance. Obviously this settlement pleased neither Constance nor the Byzantine emperor. The latter was, at this time, negotiating a new marriage; his first wife, Bertha of Sulzbach, had died in 1159. Baldwin, not wishing to see a further increase in Byzantine influence in Antioch, proposed that the emperor should marry Melisende of Tripoli but, after hesitating for a year, Manuel decided in favour of Maria of Antioch, whose mother, Constance, had appealed to him against Baldwin's arrangement. Although, as a result, Baldwin III had to fear a strengthening of Byzantine claims on Antioch, he was in no position to oppose Manuel's choice; the alliance with Byzantium was now as vital to Jerusalem as that with Damascus had once been. But not until 1163 was the governmental crisis in Antioch finally settled. In that year the barons drove Constance out of the city and installed her son, Bohemund III (1163–1201).

By this time Baldwin III was already dead. He was taken ill during a visit to Tripoli in 1162. When he realized that he was unlikely to recover he moved on to Beirut in order to end his days in his own kingdom. On 10 February 1163 he died. The funeral cortège took a week to reach Jerusalem and even the non-Christian population is supposed to have mourned the dead king as his body passed slowly by. He was buried next to his forefathers in the Church of the Holy Sepulchre. For more than ten years he had steered his kingdom with great diplomatic skill between the Muslim enemy on the one side and the occasionally overbearing power of his Byzantine ally on the other. In September 1161 his mother Melisende had died after a long illness. Her name lived on in her religious foundations and in the magnificent Melisende Psalter in the British Museum. Its fine miniatures are a striking testimony to the artistic heights attained in the scriptorium at Jerusalem.

Baldwin died childless and was therefore succeeded by his younger brother, Amalric I, now twenty-seven years of age and formerly count of Jaffa and Ascalon. His claim was based on heredi-tary right but the clergy and barons were able to exercise some influence over the succession in as much as they accepted him only after his marriage to Agnes, the daughter of Joscelin II of Edessa, had been annulled on the grounds that they were related in the fourth degree. He was then anointed and crowned. In some ways there was a superficial resemblance between him and his elder brother. He had the same aquiline nose and blonde hair, though this was already beginning to recede. He too was extremely well-versed in law and enjoyed reading histories. Indeed he was the patron who persuaded William of Tyre to become court historian and to write his famous chronicle, and it was he who provided William with the works of Arab historians with the help of which the archbishop of Tyre wrote a chronicle—now unfortunately lost —of the Islamic states from the time of Muhammad. But otherwise the new king was very different from the old. He was of medium height and unusually fat—despite taking care not to eat or drink excessively. He was less well-educated than his brother, taciturn, introverted, unsociable, and troubled by a slight stammer. If he took little pleasure in gambling he made up for this by his taste for amorous adventures. William of Tyre accuses him of avarice and of oppressing the Church by his financial demands. Certainly he appreciated the need for a full treasury, but he was clearly not over-scrupulous in the methods he used to keep it well filled—as he once disarmingly remarked to William, the possessions of the subject were safe only when the ruler himself had enough. Money was vital if the strength of the kingdom was to be maintained; often enough already royal policies had been vitiated by its lack. Amalric had no intention of suffering in this way but occasionally —and unfortunately—he gave the acquisition of money an un-reasonably high place in the priorities of his foreign policy. He was pious in a formal sense of the word—he seldom missed mass —but he deeply shocked his chronicler by expressing serious doubts about the resurrection of the body and by demanding to see some concrete proof of it.

In the realm of domestic policy Amalric was an outstanding legislator. His introduction of special courts to handle cases of commercial and maritime law worked well. In the first year of his reign (1163) he promulgated the famous *Assise sur la ligece* which, by means of an oath, brought the sub-tenants to recognize the king as their liege-lord i.e. to recognize that the lord king's needs had priority over the needs of their own immediate lord. This assise was once thought to represent a vigorous attempt by the king to use the lesser vassals as a counterweight to the higher nobility, but today it is clear that it in fact marks the breakthrough of the higher nobility into fields formerly reserved to the authority of the crown (see below p. 156).

Amalric's foreign policy was dominated by the assault on Egypt.[44] This was a policy which offered not only distraction from the reverses in the north but also the chance to furnish the cash resources which were urgently required by a royal demesne which was already becoming impoverished. After the capture of Ascalon such opportunities no longer existed within Palestine. Baldwin III had already prepared the way for this policy when, in 1156, he and the Pisans agreed to place an embargo on the import of timber, iron, and pitch (all ship-building materials) into Egypt. The result, of course, was that smuggling took the place of legitimate trade and neither the threat of the death penalty (in the thirteenth-century legislation of Jerusalem) nor the constantly repeated papal prohibitions were able to put a stop to it.

As count of Jaffa and Ascalon Amalric's attention had naturally been drawn to Egypt. The inexhaustible wealth of its natural resources exerted a tremendous attraction. There was the highly developed agriculture of the Nile Valley. There were fisheries, indigo deposits, and alum mines which facilitated the dyeing processes of an efficient textile industry (silk, linen, and cotton). Like much else these mines were a state monopoly. Soap, ointments, and ivory were also produced. Even greater profits were to be had from the trade in Sudanese slaves and from the control exercised over the transit of goods between India on the one side and Byzantium and the West on the other. By way of contrast the Egyptian political scene was in a state of disarray. The Fatimid dynasty had long since suffered the fate of all caliph dynasties; it had become a degenerate plaything in the hands of powerful viziers, two of whom, Dhirgham and Shawar, were at this moment engaged in a fierce power struggle. The bureaucracy was unusually well-developed, the system of financial administration being so complicated that right up until the nineteenth century it could only be understood by Coptic officials who were looked upon as bloodsuckers by the fellahin and as swindlers by the rulers of Egypt. It was clear that Nur ed-Din could easily become Amalric's rival in this part of the world. After 1158 when Syria was neutralized, Egypt was bound to become the decisive arena in the struggle between Franks and Muslims. Thus in 1163 Shawar, after having been driven out of the country by Dhirgham, turned for help to Nur ed-Din. Nur ed-Din hesitated at first since he had problems enough in Syria, but finally decided to send an army under his Kurdish general Shirkuh into Egypt. Shawar was restored to power but immediately quarrelled with Shirkuh and had to seek a new ally, King Amalric I of Jerusalem. Amalric had already made a brief entry into Egypt in 1163 and now, in 1164, he besieged Shirkuh in Bilbeis in Lower Egypt. Shirkuh's position began to look perilous so Nur ed-Din, feeling that the equilibrium in the Near East had been disturbed, launched a big offensive against the Syrian crusader states. In August 1164 at Artah he decisively defeated a joint army from Antioch and Tripoli, capturing both Bohemund III of Antioch and Raymond of Tripoli. Bohemund was soon released but Raymond stayed in prison for about ten years while Amalric governed Tripoli as regent. The fortress of Harenc again fell to the Muslims and the frontier of Antioch was pushed back to the line of the Orontes, this time for good. But in order not to provoke Byzantium Nur ed-Din did not seize the opportunity to attack the city itself. His offensive achieved its purpose when Amalric and Shirkuh came to terms and withdrew from Egypt.

In the following years Nur ed-Din forced the remaining semi-independent petty princes of Muslim Syria to recognize his authority. Then in 1167 he gave Shirkuh permission to lead another expedition into Egypt. If Amalric was to maintain the balance of power he also had to advance into Egypt. The Haute Cour met at Nablus. It decided in favour of war and imposed a 10 per cent tax on movable property to pay for it. The Frankish army then marched to the Nile and Shawar gladly agreed to an alliance with the aim of destroying Shirkuh. In return he promised to pay Amalric 400,000 gold dinars. Hugh of Caesarea who negotiated this treaty on behalf of the Franks insisted that it should be ratified by the caliph. So the Frankish envoys were taken to the palace in Cairo where they were amazed by the magnificent courtyards with their fishponds and aviaries. It is an eloquent testimony to the presumptuous self-confidence of the Franks at this time that Hugh demanded that he and the caliph should seal the treaty by shaking hands. This was bad enough in the eyes of the Muslim courtiers but their indignation knew no bounds when Hugh expressed dissatisfaction with the unwillingly proffered gloved hand and insisted on the caliph removing his glove.

After suffering some initial setbacks in Upper Egypt the allies succeeded in besieging Shirkuh in Alexandria and forcing him to make peace. Shirkuh and Amalric again agreed to leave Egypt thus restoring the *status quo ante*. But the Franks had gained a good deal. The alliance with Shawar was kept in being in return for an annual tribute of 100,000 dinars. The royal standard flew from the lighthouse at Alexandria and a Frankish garrison remained in Cairo. Egypt had become a kind of Frankish protectorate.

It ought to have been possible to maintain this state of affairs for some time since, as long as Egypt was not annexed, it involved no real loss of face for Nur ed-Din. But immediately after his return from Egypt Amalric strengthened the alliance with Byzantium by marrying the emperor's great niece, Maria Comnena. After long negotiations this marriage and Maria's coronation were performed with undue haste in Tyre rather than in the capital for, in the short space of time between his return from Egypt and the marriage, Amalric had admitted the Byzantine adventurer—later Emperor—Andronicus Comnenus into the Latin Kingdom and had enfeoffed him Beirut. Andronicus had frequently given offence to the government in Constantinople and had embarrassed the Byzantine court with his many inopportune love affairs. Before fleeing from the wrath of the Emperor to Palestine he had embezzled the public funds of Cyprus and Byzantine Cilicia. This cannot have failed to attract the ever-greedy Amalric to him. On the other hand, he risked forfeiting his bride's very substantial dowry and, indeed, the whole marriage if news of his harbouring Andronicus leaked out before the wedding had taken place. Byzantium might at least have cut Maria's dowry by the sum of what Andronicus had embezzled elsewhere. That the whole arrangement was a delicate one is shown not only by the fact that the deal had been negotiated for two full years and was then concluded hastily in an inappropriate location, but also by the circumstance that, contrary to all custom, Maria was first crowned and then married to Amalric. It seems that the government in Constantinople insisted on this sequel of events to make sure that Maria would not remain uncrowned. Earlier, in 1165, Bohemund III of Antioch had married one of Manuel's nieces and had installed a Greek patriarch. The Latin patriarch was driven into exile and stayed there until the Greek was buried in the ruins of Antioch cathedral as the result of an earthquake in 1170. Amalric, his confidence bolstered by a formal treaty of alliance with Byzantium, believed that he could now conquer Egypt and so he embarked on a new adventure—no other description will fit the expedition of 1168. He did not bother to wait for the arrival of the Byzantine fleet which was essential if Egypt was to be blockaded from the sea. Instead he allowed himself to be persuaded by the militants among the members of the Haute Cour that the terms of 1167 had been too lenient to the Egyptians. Following their advice he launched a premature attack. William of Tyre returned from Constantinople, having successfully negotiated the treaty, only to find that the army had already left (October 1168). In their imaginations the Franks had already divided the spoils of Egypt. The Hospitallers, the leaders of the war-party, had promised themselves rich pickings, while the Templars had refused to take part—either out of loyalty to the treaty with Shawar or on account of their financial interests in Egypt. In desperation Shawar turned to Shirkuh for help and meanwhile employed a scorched earth policy to gain time. In November the Franks captured Bilbeis and then besieged Cairo. But they were unable to bring Shirkuh's relieving army to battle and so Amalric decided to call off his attack. He could not have annexed Egypt; there were just not enough Latins for it to be possible to rule Egypt as thoroughly as the crusader states. And while no decisive success could ever be achieved in Egypt, the expansionist policy in this direction meant that Amalric had turned his back on what Prawer has rightly called the 'Golden Rule' of Jerusalem's foreign policy. This was the policy of ensuring that the northern crusader states were kept in existence so that they could stand as bulwarks in defence of Jerusalem. In accordance with this principle, the kings of Jerusalem had, up until c. 1150, gone north time and again either at the head of an army or to supervise the arrangements for a regency. It is true that the neutralization of north Syria by Byzantium meant that significant alterations in the military and political structure of this region were now out of the question, none the less it should still have been possible for Jerusalem to provide the northern principalities with a certain amount of protection. But now, with so much effort being expended on the southern frontiers, the Golden Rule of yesterday was forgotten.

On 2 January 1169 Shirkuh marched into Cairo. At once he had his old enemy Shawar killed and took over the post of vizier himself. When he died two months later he was succeeded in that office by his nephew Saladin (Al-Malik al-Nasir Salah ed-Din Yusuf, 1169–93).[45] He was to be the most terrible opponent that the Franks had to face. In the thirteenth century Sultan Baibars was as fierce an enemy but he never enjoyed the same universal respect within Islam. Saladin was born into a Kurdish officer family. He grew up in Baalbek where his father Ayub—the dynasty became known as the Ayubids—was governor. At first there seemed nothing to suggest a career out of the ordinary. The young officer was distinguished chiefly by his skill at polo. From 1152 he served in the household of Nur ed-Din and then assisted his uncle Shirkuh in the latter's Egyptian campaigns. Only after his appointment as vizier did he reveal what was in him. He at once consolidated his power by destroying the Egyptian-Sudanese army and building up his own military organization. He had an impressive citadel built in Cairo to defend the city against a possible Frankish assault. In 1169 he beat off an attack on Damietta even though this time the Franks were supported by a Byzantine fleet. In 1170 he counter-attacked. He recaptured Gaza from the Latins and also Aila, their port on the Red Sea. He marched up the Nile and also into Arabia and the Yemen, thus securing Egypt's hegemony in the Red Sea area and over the trade routes to East Asia. After some initial hesitation he made an end of the Fatimid dynasty in September 1171 when he ordered that the Abbasid caliphs of Baghdad should be mentioned in the Friday prayers. Thus the unity of Sunnite orthodoxy was restored. The fact that there was no popular re-action to this order shows that Shi'ite doctrine had made little impression on the people of Egypt. Formally he still remained vizier, under the overlordship of Nur ed-Din, but in practice Saladin was sultan of Egypt. This inevitably led to tension with Nur ed-Din who, in 1170, had added Mosul and Mesopotamia to the territories under his sway. Each of them looked upon his own area of influence as the real centre of Islam. Saladin refused to allow Nur ed-Din to treat Egypt merely as a source of money with which to finance his Syrian wars. The question was still unsettled when fate decided it in Saladin's favour. On 15 May 1174 Nur ed-Din died in Damascus. He had lived in a simple style and as he grew older he spent more time on pious exercises. His countenance was severe and he rarely laughed. After a century in which Syria had been ruled by the nomadic Seldjuks he had done much to strengthen the economy of the country. But his great achievement was his political and religious revival of Islam and his application of the Jihad idea to the war against the Franks. Even the Latin historian, William of Tyre, had to respect him.

On 11 July 1174, two months after Nur ed-Din's death, King Amalric I died of dysentery. In 1171 he had enjoyed a splendid reception in Constantinople. Whether or not he recognized Manuel as some kind of feudal suzerain is unclear,[46] but undoubtedly Manuel was unusually active in Palestinian affairs at this time. He had the Church of the Holy Sepulchre repaired and he ordered new mosaics for the Church of the Nativity at Bethlehem. In 1173 an Orthodox archbishop suddenly appeared at Gaza and a community of Orthodox priests at the Holy Sepulchre. At about this time the ceremonial dress of the kings of Jerusalem was remodelled on the style of the court dress of the Byzantine emperor, so that Eustathius of Thessalonika criticized the king for improperly setting himself up as an emperor. (It is significant that this fashion was dropped after the fall of Constantinople in 1204.) Quite simply, Amalric was dependant upon Byzantium. As a ruler he had lacked any special gift of foresight but he had been an indefatigable fighter. In internal affairs he had ruled with as strong a hand as circumstances permitted. Since 1169 the Assassins of Syria had been led by an energetic sheikh, Rashid ed-Din Sinan (d. 1193), better known as 'The Old Man of the Mountains',[47] who had attempted to form an alliance with Amalric against the Sunnite Nur ed-Din. Negotiations had promised well. Then in 1173 some Templars murdered the Assassins' envoys while they were on their way home. Amalric had no hesitation in using force to arrest the murderer and he then had him punished although this was a breach of the Order's privilege which made its members justiciable only by the pope. Amalric is even supposed to have considered dissolving the Order. Nevertheless, taken all in all, his superficially brilliant reign carried within it the seeds of internal decay.

Amalric's heir was a thirteen-year-old boy who was already seriously ill. It did not augur well for Jerusalem's future. The Syrian north was still suffering from the effects of the terrible earthquake of 1170 which had reduced Antioch and Tripoli to rubble. Then, to cap it all, Byzantium met with a catastrophic reversal. In 1176 Manuel Comnenus was completely routed by the Anatolian Seldjuks at Myriocephalum in Phrygia. In the aftermath of defeat it soon became clear that only an overstrained economy had made Manuel's brilliant foreign policy possible. Without exaggeration it can be said that the Battle of Myriocephalum—comparable in its results to the Battle of Manzikert in 1071—decided the fate of Outremer. Anatolia was finally lost to the Seldjuks, the Byzantine position in Cilicia and Syria was thus completely undermined, the ingenious balance of power system was finished, and the Franks had lost their protector. There were no other allies to be had, especially since a joint Sicilian-Frankish expedition to Alexandria in 1174 had failed owing to Saladin's energy and inadequate Frankish support. Unless help came from the West, the crusader states now stood entirely alone. And the more Saladin consolidated his position the greater the danger to the existence of the Frankish states.

After Nur ed-Din's death the Zengid empire rapidly broke up.

A group of Nur ed-Din's officers became rivals, each struggling to be the guardian of his small son. In 1174 Saladin, who believed himself to be the true heir of Nur ed-Din's high-flying plans, occupied Damascus. Two years later he married Nur ed-Din's widow and was able to reach a settlement with the Zengids though this involved leaving Aleppo and Mosul in the hands of two members of that house. But the caliph now recognized Saladin as overlord of Egypt and Syria. The Frankish states were caught in a deadly encirclement and Saladin intended to take full advantage of his position to carry out the programme which Nur ed-Din had publicly proclaimed as early as 1169 when he commissioned a pulpit for the al-Aqsa mosque in Jerusalem. From then on Jerusalem's recapture was the overriding objective.

Saladin used the next few years to build up his strength. Campaigns against the Franks in 1177 and 1179 made it clear that he could not expect much help from the Zengids of Aleppo and Mosul. On the contrary they represented a permanent threat to his position. Saladin by no means gave up the fight against the Christians; none the less in the years 1179–85 he concentrated on his Muslim rivals. Until they had submitted there was no chance of a decisive war against the Franks. Against these rivals he used the same combination of diplomacy, propaganda, and armed demonstrations of his power that Nur ed-Din had used against Damascus. In 1180 he allied with the Anatolian Seldjuk sultan, Kilij Arslan II. This alliance was directed primarily against Mosul but was later to prove of great value in meeting the threat of the Third Crusade. In 1182 he prevented an imminent union of Aleppo and Mosul; in 1183 he brought Aleppo under his control. In 1185 he made a four years' truce with the Franks. This gave him the freedom of manoeuvre he needed to deal with Mosul. The opportunity was exploited at once. Mosul's firm adhesion to Saladin's system of alliances meant that the strength of his army was increased by about 6,000 men.

By 1187 he had an army of something like 12,000 cavalry of which an ever-increasing proportion was Kurdish. The quasi-feudal iqta system which was used to pay the troops created considerable problems for Saladin. Payment was made in kind as well as in cash and this meant that the payee had to remain on his estates to supervise the harvest. Thus it was very difficult to keep an army in the field for a long period of time. Overcoming this problem put a tremendous strain on Saladin's treasury and involved a highly complicated rota system between the Mesopotamian, Syrian, and Egyptian troops. Since Saladin was not, in any

event, a financial genius and was forced by his strict orthodoxy—
his greatest political asset—to abolish all unorthodox taxes, he was
almost permanently bankrupt. What he had or acquired he
distributed freely among his relatives and supporters. The Ayubid
state which he founded was a semi-feudal family structure in which
the sultan's chief vassals were the princes of the blood. Each of
them had independent control of his own province, but was
obliged to rule justly, to help finance the sultan's wars, and to
provide troops. Each prince had his own vassals, all enjoying a
limited amount of independence; below them were the iqta
holders. What Saladin ruled was nothing like a unitary state; only
the fact that a vizier was appointed to assist each prince enabled
some uniformity of policy to be achieved. In Egypt the three main
offices of the central government were the diwans for military,
financial, and chancery affairs. Saladin, however, was a poor administrator and normally he left these matters to his brother al-
Adil and to his secretary, the Qadi al-Fadil. As a general he was a
good tactician but a bad strategist. He was a politician through
and through; his manoeuvres were successful because they were
always carefully prepared and appropriate to the particular situation. He was borne up by the unshakeable conviction that he was
destined to unite Islam. According to Gibb, his ultimate goal was
not to drive the Christians out of the Holy Land but to re-establish
the old empire of the caliphs as an expression of the rule of the
revealed law. He wanted to see the end of the patent political
demoralization of Islam which had already lasted far too long. This
presented a moral problem as well as a political one and the
methods used to solve it had therefore also to be moral ones. In
his dealings with friend and foe Saladin showed himself to be
absolutely reliable. He hardly ever broke his word—by the standards of his own day this was an almost incredible attitude. He
saw—correctly—that whether or not he succeeded would depend
in large measure on the moral authority he possessed in the world
of Islam. Owing to his magnanimity he became a favourite figure
in the European romantic poetry of the late Middle Ages.

By 1185 the forces opposing the Franks were all in position. By
skilful diplomacy Saladin had tried to isolate his intended victims
from all potential allies. He built up the Egyptian fleet and at the
same time tried to persuade the Italian maritime cities to transfer
their trade to Egypt in order to deprive the Franks of support from
this quarter. He also made diplomatic contact with Byzantium.
After Manuel's death in 1180 his widow, Maria of Antioch, ruled
as regent. Her policies were even more favourable to the Latins

than Manuel's had been and in 1182 the tensions at Constantinople between Latins and Greeks flared up into a bloody massacre of western merchants. The Latin party was finished and a new emperor emerged, Andronicus Comnenus (1183–85), a vigorous man with an adventurous career behind him. He was, of course, hostile to the Latins and so he expected the chief threat to his position to come from Europe; not so much from the Germans because the quarrel with them over 'the problem of the two emperors' belonged essentially to the realm of ideas; much more real was the threat from the Normans. In 1184 the latter drew closer to the western emperor as a result of the marriage between the Norman princess, Constance, and Barbarossa's son, Henry VI. In 1185 they sacked Thessalonika. In these circumstances Andronicus felt compelled to come to terms with Saladin (1185). This completed the isolation of the crusader states. It says much for Saladin's political skill that he was able to retain both the Byzantines and the Seldjuks of Anatolia as his allies.

As Saladin's star rose so the Frankish one sank.[48] When Amalric I had his first marriage annulled he took care to ensure that the children of that marriage were declared legitimate. He had no more male children so he was succeeded by Baldwin IV (1174–85). William of Tyre, who was responsible for his education, gave him credit for no special qualities except perseverance, patience, and a talent for handling horses. In his childhood he became a victim of leprosy. This disease disfigured his appearance and led to an imperceptibly progressive paralysis of the limbs which eventually forced him to exchange horses for a litter. His succession to the throne marked a decisive victory for the notion of hereditary right. Politically as well as personally his fate was a tragic one. He made heroic efforts to save his kingdom and to prevent the disintegration of the country into two bitterly opposed factions. But his illness frequently compelled him to appoint a regent (bailli). The first regent—until he came of age c. 1176—was his nearest male relative, Count Raymond III of Tripoli. As husband of Eschiva, widow of the last prince of Galilee, Raymond was also lord of Tiberias and thus a vassal of the king of Jerusalem. With iron self-restraint the thirty-four-year-old Raymond pursued a discreet, defensive policy, always looking for a settlement with the Muslims whom he had come to know well during his long captivity. He was the leader of the faction which can loosely be termed the party of the old families. The other faction was made up of more varied elements. It was dominated by the recent arrivals, men of the first generation in the Holy Land, who were anxious to find excitement and to obtain possessions. One of their leaders was Reynald of Châtillon. In 1175 he had finally been released but was unable to return to Antioch. Instead he made an advantageous marriage and acquired the important lordship of Oultrejourdain with its centre at the great fortress of Kerak. He was joined by Guy and Amalric of Lusignan, and by Joscelin III of Courtenay, titular count of Edessa (1159-1200) but a count without a county. He rose to become a seneschal of Jerusalem and, through sheer greed, succeeded in building up the lordship known as the 'Seigneurie de Joscelin' in the region of Acre. There was also his sister, Agnes of Courtenay, who was the king's mother and exercised a particularly unfortunate influence over Baldwin which even William of Tyre was unable to offset. William (d. 1186) had become chancellor in 1174 and archbishop in the next year. Until 1180 he was the king's chief political adviser, working to uphold the alliance with Byzantium which he had advocated ever since Amalric I's reign. But this alliance collapsed as a result of the massacre of the Latins in 1182. After 1186 the Military Orders tended to support Reynald of Châtillon's faction because the Master of the Temple, Gerard of Ridfort, had a bitter personal grudge against Raymond III of Tripoli who had earlier—before Gerard's entry into the Order—refused to allow him to marry the rich heiress of one of his vassals. When, in 1180, the queen mother, Agnes, secured the appointment of the morally worthless Archbishop Heraclius of Caesarea (d. c. 1190-1) as patriarch of Jerusalem in an election contested by William of Tyre, the line-up of the parties was complete. More and more William was pushed out of politics. The greater part of the clergy took the side of the patriarch and the Lusignans, undoubtedly in part because the king had clashed with the bishops on account of his miserliness towards the Church. The contrast with the generosity of his predecessors could hardly be more strikingly illustrated than by the fact that he, the leper king, did not even make a gift to St. Lazarus, the Jerusalem convent for lepers. In 1180 Baldwin IV's sister, Sibylla, married Guy of Lusignan who thus became count of Jaffa and Ascalon and one of the king's most powerful vassals. Sibylla already had a son, the young Baldwin V, the child of her first husband, William Longsword, marquis of Montferrat. Taken together with the establishment of the Seigneurie de Joscelin, the granting out of the double county of Jaffa and Ascalon meant that the royal domain was being rapidly dissipated. It showed up the weakness of a king who ought to have been keeping a firm hand on what land and money he possessed.

In these circumstances it was not possible to put up an effective resistance to Saladin. It is true that Baldwin IV won a brilliant victory at Montgisard near Ramleh in 1177, but more important that he was unable to follow up his advantage. In 1179 he could do nothing to prevent Saladin from capturing the newly-built castle of Chastellet on the Jordan near Jacob's Ford. In 1180 a two years' truce was agreed. Saladin's successful advance against Aleppo in 1183 forced the Franks to take counter-measures. Again a special war-tax was imposed, but then the king's disease took a turn for the worse and forced him to nominate Guy as *bailli*. This led to disputes within the army which limited its operational effectiveness. The Franks had to be content with keeping Saladin at bay. In the same year Baldwin dismissed Guy for inefficiency and then, with the consent of his barons, had his five-year-old nephew, Baldwin V, crowned and anointed. In 1184 Raymond of Tripoli was again appointed bailli, to hold office until Baldwin V came of age. But Joscelin of Courtenay, the boy's nearest male relative and a member of the opposing faction, was made guardian of the young king. In 1185, when an armistice suited both sides, Raymond and Saladin agreed to a four years' truce.

In March 1185 the unfortunate Baldwin IV died. No effective opposition was raised when Baldwin V succeeded and Raymond took over the regency. But if Raymond's opponents hoped to make capital out of the guardianship of Baldwin V, these hopes were dashed when the child king died suddenly in the late summer of 1186. He was the last king of Jerusalem to be buried in the Church of the Holy Sepulchre. There was no male heir and according to the terms of Baldwin IV's will it was now up to the pope, the emperor, and the kings of France and England to arbitrate between the claims of Sibylla and Isabella (or their husbands or children), the daughters of Amalric I by his first and second marriages. But by a skilfully organized *coup d'état* Sibylla and her supporters outmanoeuvred Raymond of Tripoli in September 1186. She was crowned queen and then she herself crowned her husband. Raymond tried to persuade Isabella's husband to be an anti-king but he preferred to go over to King Guy (1186–90). The barons had to accept the *fait accompli*. Raymond withdrew in anger to Tiberias and it proved just possible to avert a civil war between him and Guy. But Guy and his supporters were unable to use wisely the power which they had seized so decisively.

Early in 1187 Reynald of Châtillon gave Saladin the *casus belli* he needed when, ignoring the truce, he ambushed a Muslim caravan travelling from Damascus to Egypt. Even before this he had angered Saladin by similar ill-considered actions—attacking, whether it was peacetime or not, pilgrims on the road to Mecca and, in a sensational raid, plundering the towns along the coast of the Red Sea. Saladin could not put up with these constant threats to the main route between Egypt and Syria and to Egypt's Red Sea link with India. After Reynald had refused to make any restitution, he declared war. The crown was too weak to force some sense into the head of the lord of Oultrejourdain. But Guy did succeed in bringing about a reconciliation with the count of Tripoli who had earlier made an alliance with Saladin. Raymond now broke off relations with Saladin and sided firmly with his fellow Franks. Near Nazareth, in preparation for a decisive battle, there assembled the largest army ever mustered by the Franks. It numbered around 18,000 men, of whom, however, only 1,200 were heavily armoured knights and another 4,000 light cavalry. It was a mark of the special emergency that all able-bodied men had been summoned to arms, not just those who owed feudal service. Saladin, with his 12,000 cavalry outnumbered the Franks but the heavy Christian knights could still launch a charge with tremendous impact if only they were given the opportunity. Their strategy, however, was not to risk battle but, while avoiding contact with Saladin's army, to stop him turning the campaign into a war of rapid movement until the time when his army was affected by the usual seasonal withdrawals and he was forced to retreat. Saladin countered this by attacking Tiberias. This manoeuvre brought the Franks out of their safe defensive position where they had been well supplied with water. Raymond of Tripoli argued forcefully against the move even though it was his own wife who was besieged in Tiberias. His arguments were approved by the barons but during the night the Master of the Temple persuaded Guy to change his mind. Next morning, in the fierce summer heat, the march through the Galileean hill country to Tiberias began. The army did not get through. On 3 July 1187 the first brushes with the Muslims occurred at Hattin, west of the Sea of Galilee. The Franks were forced to halt for the night here, in a waterless region. Thirsty and with eyes smarting from the smoke of the bush fires which the Muslims had lit, they spent a terrifying night. When dawn broke they found they were completely surrounded. After a heroic fight they suffered a defeat far worse than anything yet seen in the history of the crusader states. Only Raymond of Tripoli and a few of his friends managed to break out. Many knights were killed in the battle. The rest were captured, among them the king, the

Master of the Temple and Reynald of Châtillon. Reynald's head was struck off by Saladin himself. The Templars too were executed; only their Master was spared. The precious relic of the True Cross which had once fallen into the hands of the Sassanids but which the Emperor Heraclius, in the seventh century, had returned to Jerusalem, was lost again and this time for ever.

The immediate consequences of Hattin were catastrophic. The kingdom had lost practically all its fighting men. Only small garrisons in some towns and castles were left. In an unparalleled triumphal progress Saladin marched through Palestine and Syria. An Arab chronicler lists fifty-two towns and fortresses which he captured. Because the Franks knew that he would keep his word it was easier for them to agree on terms of surrender. On 10 July the important port of Acre fell; on 4 September Ascalon. Jerusalem was defended by Queen Sibylla, Patriarch Heraclius, and Balian of Ibelin, but it capitulated on 2 October after a fortnight's siege. Even the most extraordinary rituals of penance had been to no avail. It was in vain that ladies had shaven the heads of their daughters and made them undress to take cold baths in public on the hill of Calvary. What the city lacked was fighting men and the few defenders had reason to be grateful that they were at the mercy of a merciful enemy. By the terms of a tariff which varied according to age and sex and which Saladin interpreted generously, those who had some money could buy a safe passage to the coast. The al-Aqsa mosque was again handed over to Islam in a cere-monial service and Nur ed-Din's pulpit was installed. Christian crosses on the roofs of churches were taken down, but four Syrian priests were allowed to continue to hold services in the Church of the Holy Sepulchre. The capture of Jerusalem, a holy place for the Muslims as well as Christians, was a triumph which resounded round the Islamic world. Practically nothing remained to the Christians. In 1188 and 1189 the last strongholds of Moab, the supposedly impregnable castles of Kerak and Montreal, fell. The Christians held on to Beaufort, Chastel Blanc, Krak des Chevaliers, Margab, and Tortosa. They hung on grimly in three coastal towns which Saladin was unable to take: Tripoli and Antioch, which were saved by the opportune arrival of a Sicilian fleet, and Tyre which twice held out against Saladin's onslaught. Tyre was com-manded by Marquis Conrad of Montferrat who arrived there shortly after the disaster at Hattin. His stubborn and vigorous defence of the city made him famous far and wide in the West. As the man of the moment he saw that he was being offered the chance of a lifetime. Before the walls of Tyre he won a sea battle against the Egyptians. Saladin was then forced by his emirs to raise the siege on 1 January 1188. None the less it seemed impossible to save the Holy Land and Saladin is supposed to have announced his intention of sailing overseas and completely exterminating the infidels.

7 · THE THIRD CRUSADE, 1187–1192

AFTER the Second Crusade Europe had had enough of crusades for a while.[49] But from the late 1160s the growing number of appeals for help coming from the Holy Land began to have some effect on public opinion. As always these appeals were sent primarily to Western Europe. The kings of the West, like the emperor, looked favourably upon the idea of a crusade; they saw it as the crowning moment of their life, as the highest fulfilment of the royal dignity.[50] But the political situation was anything but favourable. The emperor, Frederick I Barbarossa (1152–90), was fully occupied in Italy where he was trying to recover imperial rights in execution of the decrees of Roncaglia which he had issued in 1158. This had led to his entanglement in a fierce struggle with the Lombard towns which lasted until peace was made at Constance in 1183. Between 1159 and 1177 he was also fighting against Alexander III whom he was eventually forced to recognize as pope. At home in Germany his hands were tied by the Welf opposition headed by Henry the Lion, duke of Saxony and Bavaria. Not until 1184 when, at the Whitsun court held at Mainz, Barbarossa displayed the brilliance and power of the Hohenstaufen dynasty before the eyes of the world, was there any chance that he would be able to leave the empire. But then his awareness of the imperial dignity and his political common sense attracted him to the idea of a crusade. He saw that it would only diminish his reputation if the crusade were left entirely in the hands of the rulers of Western Europe. And, at the time of the crusade, he was indeed recognized in the West as the supreme lord of Christendom. A letter forged in England which purported to be sent from him to Saladin, described the emperor as ruler of the world. The leadership of the crusade was accorded, more or less spontaneously, to him. An English chronicler, William of Newburgh, even referred to him as 'our emperor'.

France was no longer the only kingdom in Western Europe to which men in Jerusalem looked for help. Above all they counted on Henry II of England (1154–89). The house of Plantagenet was related to the Angevin royal family of Jerusalem. Moreover since the king of England now ruled the greater part of France, the king of France would need the co-operation of England if he were ever to go on crusade. As vassals of the French king, Henry II and his sons ruled the duchies of Normandy, Britanny, and Aquitaine and the counties of Maine, Anjou, La Marche, Poitou, and Auvergne. Plantagenet and Capetian regarded each other with ineradicable suspicion. Neither could afford to go on crusade alone. Each knew that the other was just lying in wait for such an opportunity to invade. Equally neither could permit the other to go alone because this would result in a loss of prestige for him and a gain in authority for his opponent. There was simply no way out of the situation. For the moment only financial help could be sent. Henry II was very active in this way, doubtless because of his kinship with the kings of Jerusalem. France seems to have done less though this impression may be no more than a consequence of the relative paucity of the sources for France. In 1166 Henry II levied a general tax on income and movables, to be paid by clergy as well as laity, the proceeds of which were to go to assist the Holy Land. This was the first clearly discernible crusading tax in the West. For the rest the years up to the late 1180s were taken up with an endless to and fro of diplomatic activity. In 1172 Henry II promised to take the cross but then did not. In the Treaty of Nonancourt of 1177 the two kings laid down rules which were to govern their behaviour towards each other in the event of one of them going on crusade or one of them dying. But the crusade remained just a project and the Treaty of Nonancourt reveals far more of the two kings' mutual distrust than of their enthusiasm for a good cause. When Philip II Augustus (1180–1223) succeeded to the throne of France he soon became involved in a wearisome quarrel with the count of Flanders; while it was as much as Henry II could do to cope with the rebellions of his wild and unruly sons.

In 1184–5 a special embassy was sent from Outremer to Europe to emphasize the gravity of the situation to the rulers of the West, to try to make them see that something decisive must be done if there were to be any chance of saving Jerusalem, ruled as it was by a leper-king, Baldwin IV, who would be succeeded by a child-king, Baldwin V. The embassy was led by Heraclius, the patriarch of Jerusalem, Arnold of Toroga, the Master of the Temple, and Roger of Les Moulins, the Master of the Hospital. In November 1184 they met the pope and the emperor at Verona. Barbarossa was inclined to promise a crusade for 1186. He was in the middle of negotiating with the curia a financial settlement of the tiresome question as to which of them was the rightful lord of the Matildine lands in Tuscany. At the same time he was revising his Italian policy and coming to terms with the Normans of the south. This was done by means of a betrothal between his son Henry VI and Constance, the daughter of Roger II and the aunt of the reigning Norman king William II (1166–89). He may have used the offer of a crusade in order to smooth the path of his negotiations with the curia but the project fell through when, in November 1185, Urban III was elected pope and at once raised new points of disagreement and incited some princely opposition to the emperor in Germany. When the envoys from Jerusalem reached Paris, the king of France took good care to push them on to England as soon as possible. Henry II too merely assured them of his good will and, like Philip Augustus, immediately gave back the key of Jerusalem which they offered him. Bitterly disappointed the envoys returned home. The embassy does, however, seem to have been the stimulus behind a new crusading tax imposed in England and France in 1185 (or 1184). There has been some debate as to whether or not the tax was actually levied since there is no record of any of the usual reactions to a tax. Nor is it known for certain whether the pope had agreed to the taxation of the clergy.[51]

A real change of heart came only after the catastrophic defeat at Hattin in the summer of 1187. Urban III died under the impact of the news. His successor, Gregory VIII, although he was pope for no more than two months, gave decisive momentum to the preaching of the crusade. His crusading encyclical, *Audita tremendi*, issued on 29 October 1187 is a moving document and a masterpiece of papal rhetoric though his proposal of a seven years' truce between the European powers was clearly unrealistic. The first ruler to respond was William II of Sicily. He sent a fleet of fifty galleys to the East and they played an important part in the relief of Tripoli. But any further help he might have given was brought to nothing by his death. The first to take the cross was Richard Coeur de Lion, count of Poitou, the most chivalrous of Henry II's sons, though in this—as in much else—he acted spontaneously and high-handedly, without his father's permission. But Richard was carried along on a tide of general sympathy and Henry II could do little about it. In all kinds of ways public opinion was stimulated and roused to a transport of enthusiasm. Poets composed crusading songs and elegies on the fall of Jerusalem both in Latin and the vernacular. According to the reports of

Arab chroniclers, the mood of the populace was much stirred by rousing pictures. From Tyre there came a steady stream of progress reports and appeals for help.

The preaching of the crusade north of the Alps was entrusted to Archbishop Joscius of Tyre and Cardinal Legate Henry of Albano, a Cistercian of great diplomatic skill. He was even able to arrange a settlement between England and France. Amid popular rejoicing the two kings and many of their magnates took the cross at Gisors in Normandy on 21 January 1188. They planned to leave at Easter 1189 and to take the land-route. To finance the crusade a general tax of 10 per cent on all income and movable property (the Saladin Tithe) was imposed. The clergy objected to it most since the secular barons could not only avoid the tax by taking the cross but they could also keep for themselves the contributions paid by their tenants. In Wales the Cistercian archbishop of Canterbury, Baldwin, preached the crusade with the energy and style of Bernard of Clairvaux. In Germany the preaching was taken more calmly.[52] A crusading tax was not needed but each participant was required to take a two years' supply of money with him; this helped to limit the numbers of unwanted hangers-on. The first to take the cross did so at an imperial diet at Strasbourg in December 1187. The emperor delayed until March 1188 when, at the diet at Mainz known as the *curia Jesu Christi*, his old opponent, Archbishop Philip of Cologne, submitted to him. Now Barbarossa too was ready to take the cross; in April 1189, at Hagenau, he received the pilgrim's staff and scrip. Owing to the shortage of ships he had no option but to take the land-route. A series of negotiations and treaties with Serbia, Hungary, Byzantium, and the Seldjuk sultan of Iconium prepared the way. He sent an ultimatum to Saladin which the latter rejected. But Barbarossa's negotiations with the Balkan states and his alliance with the Normans made the Byzantine emperor, Isaac II Angelus (1185–95) extremely suspicious and pushed him into the arms of Saladin. The two of them renewed their former alliance, this time with the express purpose of preventing Frederick from marching through Byzantium. The German envoys in Constantinople were thrown into prison.

On 11 May 1189 Barbarossa's army moved off from Regensburg. If the crusade succeeded it would unquestionably make the emperor, now in his mid sixties, the dominating figure on the European political scene. With him there went his son, Duke Frederick of Swabia, the archbishop of Tarentaise, the bishops of Liège, Würzburg, Passau, Regensburg, Basle, Meissen, Osnabrück, and Toul, three margraves, and twenty-nine counts from all parts of Germany. An Austrian clerk known, wrongly, as Ansbert was the chief historian of this crusade. The men from Cologne, the Frisians, the archbishop of Bremen, Landgrave Ludwig III of Thuringia, and, later, Duke Leopold V of Austria chose the sea-route. The contemporary figure of an army of 100,000 men was a wild overestimate; none the less it was undoubtedly one of the largest crusading armies ever to leave Europe. The march through Hungary went smoothly but as soon as they set foot on Byzantine territory their troubles began. It became impossible to pass through in peace as had been planned. Barbarossa occupied Philippopolis and threatened to take the capital and destroy the empire. He ordered his son Henry to rendezvous at Constantinople with an Italian fleet in March 1190; meanwhile he waited at winterquarters in Adrianople. In February 1190 the weak ruler of Byzantium gave in. At Easter the German army crossed over into Asia at Gallipoli thus keeping clear of the capital as had been agreed in the Treaty of Adrianople. The weakness of the Byzantine Empire now stood clearly revealed.

On 25 April 1190 the army moved into Seldjuk territory in Anatolia. It soon became obvious that the treaty with the sultan, Kilij Arslan II, was worthless. Despite the hostile accounts given in western sources this was not because of the sultan's attitude. He, in fact, was quite well-disposed to the crusaders, but it was now his eldest son, Qutb ad-Din Malik Shah, who held the reins of power, and as Saladin's son-in-law he had no intention of allowing the German army to march, unopposed, to Syria. Putting up with unimaginable hardships, badly affected by hunger and thirst, the unwieldy formations dragged themselves through Anatolia, suffering severe losses on the way. On 18 May 1190, near Iconium, they encountered Qutb ad-Din's army which had been reinforced by the Turcoman hordes which had been plundering in Asia Minor since 1185. The Germans won a brilliant victory. In their service of thanksgiving they recalled Paul's tribulations in Iconium (2 Timothy 3:11). The old sultan re-assumed control of affairs and came to terms with the emperor. After resting a few days the army marched on in peace into Christian territory—Lesser Armenia. They crossed the Taurus Mountains and were approaching the sea at Seleucia when, on 10 June 1190, Frederick Barbarossa was drowned in the River Saleph which he had impatiently tried to swim across while the troops were being held up. He had been the last ruler to take the cross and the first to set out. He was the only one of them to meet his death while on crusade. 'At this point,' lamented a chronicler from Cologne, 'and at this sad news our pen is stilled and our account is ended.'

The German crusade broke up in confusion as a result of the emperor's death. His son Frederick lacked the personality needed to hold the despairing army together. Most of the crusaders made for Cilician or Syrian ports and then sailed home. The rest, led by Duke Frederick, marched to Antioch where, as a result of an epidemic, they suffered further losses. Here, in the cathedral of St. Peter, the emperor's body was buried after his bones had been removed in the hope that they might find a worthy resting place in Jerusalem. In fact they finished up in the cathedral of Tyre. On 7 October the battered remnants of the once proud army reached Acre where they met those of their fellow countrymen who had chosen the sea route. But then the sudden departure of the landgrave of Thuringia again reduced the size of their contingent. The Germans played an insignificant part in the rest of the Third Crusade. Of great importance for the future, however, was the founding, near Acre, of a German hospital community by some citizens of Lübeck and Bremen in 1190. In 1196 their foundation was confirmed by the pope. In the Spring of 1198 the hospital, which should not be associated with an earlier institution at Jerusalem, was transformed into a purely national order of ecclesiastical knights belonging to the house of St. Maria of the Germans in Jerusalem: the Order of Teutonic Knights. This transformation was immediately approved by the pope. The knights lived according to the Templar rule until about 1245 when the Order received its own rule and took the white tunic and black cross as its uniform.[53]

The Christians in the Holy Land were given fresh heart by Marquis Conrad of Monferrat's vigorous defence of Tyre (1187) and by the news that preparations for a crusade were under way. In June 1188 King Guy was freed on condition that he left the country. He at once secured his release from the oath that he had sworn. One after the other his former battle companions were also freed. In Tripoli he collected a handful of knights together and marched to Tyre. But Conrad had no intention of handing over the city which he had defended; it was a crown possession but he no longer recognized Guy as king. The struggle for power which now broke out between Conrad and Guy and lasted until 1190 involved an unparalleled dissipation of the already much diminished royal demesne, from which the chief gainers were the Italian and French maritime towns. Guy had been encamped for several months before the walls of Tyre without making any pro-

gress when suddenly he showed that he had more in him than men
had previously suspected. He allied with a newly arrived Pisan
fleet and marched, to Saladin's great astonishment, straight to
Acre. From a fortified camp on the hill of Toron he began to lay
siege to the city on 28 August 1189.[54] It seemed to be an act of
incredible folly since Guy's forces were not even equal to the city
garrison and there was the added danger that Saladin might come
upon him from the rear and crush him between the relieving army
and the city. But Guy needed a base from which to reconquer his
kingdom and Acre had always been its strongest and richest city.
With unyielding obstinacy he pursued the goal he had set himself.
The possession of Acre became a question of prestige and it was
a severe blow for Saladin when the city fell after a two years' siege.
It was not Guy but Saladin who had committed the act of folly
when he rejected his emirs' advice to raze the city to the ground
after he had captured it in 1187. This decision reveals his inadequate grasp of strategy. Instead he improved the fortress and
harbour and placed all his military equipment from Egypt and
Syria in the city. Guy's attack on Acre—and indeed the whole
Third Crusade—took Saladin by surprise and found him insufficiently prepared. He now had to deal with a problem never before
faced by a Muslim ruler—how to keep a standing army together
for three years (1190-2). According to al-Fadil he had 'used the
revenues of Egypt to conquer Syria, the revenues of Syria to gain
control of Mesopotamia, the revenues of Mesopotamia to win
Palestine'. Now his financial reserves were running dry. The long
struggle for Acre prevented him from pursuing his real aim, the
propagation of Islamic Orthodoxy. Barbarossa's crusade had filled
him with apprehension and he had collected information about it
from every possible source. Before he knew that he had no more
to fear from this quarter he was forced to take action against Guy.

From September 1189 onwards a steady stream of soldiers came
by ship from Europe to reinforce the Franks besieging Acre.
Frisians and Scandinavians brought the ships which were urgently
needed to blockade Acre from the sea. Flemings, Frenchmen,
Englishmen, and Italians came; a contingent of Germans under
Landgrave Ludwig III of Thuringia arrived. Even Conrad of
Montferrat supported the venture in its early stages. On 4 October
the Franks risked a battle against Saladin but were heavily
defeated. Nevertheless the city had almost been starved into submission when, at Christmas, an Egyptian supply fleet managed to
break through the blockade. The early months of 1190 were
characterized by the changing fortunes of war. The Franks won a

sea battle but an attempt to take the city by storm on 5 May failed. Their siege machines went up in flames when the wooden towers were bombarded by the dreaded Greek Fire, a mixture with a naphtha base which only vinegar could extinguish. From 19 to 26 May Saladin again tried to drive the Franks off but could win no decisive victory. On the other hand the Franks too suffered a setback when on 25 July the foot-soldiers, against the wishes of their commanders, tried a surprise attack on Saladin's camp. But it became increasingly clear that Saladin would not be able to defeat the Franks while they were entrenched behind a secure system of defence works. His troops were simply not equipped to deal with this kind of warfare. Reinforcements for the Franks continued to pour in. The most important new arrival was Henry of Champagne, count palatine of Troyes. As nephew of the king of England and the king of France he was well placed to reconcile the differences which the English and French troops had brought with them from Europe and which were visibly expressed by the fact that it had been necessary to set up a dual command in the crusader camp. On his arrival Henry of Champagne was given overall command. Then on 7 October the duke of Swabia with the remnants of the German army reached Acre; a few days later Baldwin, archbishop of Canterbury, arrived. On 12 November the Franks succeeded in driving Saladin out of his hill-top camp but he merely retired to a stronger position not far off.

Meanwhile Conrad of Montferrat had broken off his support for Guy. In the autumn Queen Sibylla and both her daughters died. Since Guy had ruled as Sibylla's consort, Conrad now sought the crown for himself. Guy and Sibylla had had no children so another claimant was Isabella, the younger daughter of King Amalric I, and the wife of Humphrey IV of Toron. Conrad leaked the information that she had married before reaching the age of consent. With great skill he combined this legal argument with the political hostility of the barons to young Humphrey which had its roots in the latter's precipitate submission to Guy in 1186 (see above p. 130). In a judicial farce the marriage between Humphrey and Isabella was annulled and she was then (24 November 1190) wedded to Conrad although he was, in fact, already married. The archbishop of Canterbury had opposed the match and died of grief when it went through. The papal curia hesitated but eventually reconciled itself to this bigamous arrangement. That winter (1190-1) the besiegers suffered terribly from a food shortage for which they blamed the marquis of Montferrat who had retired to Tyre. An egg cost a silver penny; a sack of corn cost a hundred gold pieces. In front of the ovens men fought among themselves for a morsel of bread. The situation did not ease until spring came. Then there arrived not only supply ships but also the soldiers who had long been looked for: on 20 April 1191 Philip II Augustus of France landed at Acre, followed seven weeks later by Richard Coeur de Lion.

The Anglo-French crusade had been delayed by a new war between the two kingdoms (1188–9). To make matters worse Richard Coeur de Lion again rebelled against his father. This state of affairs was openly criticized by poets as well as by the pope, but to no avail. The writer who was most active in promoting the crusade was Peter of Blois, author of a tract *On the Speeding-up of the Crusade*. At about the same time he wrote the *Passio Reginaldi* glorifying the foolhardy Reynald of Châtillon and pouring a stream of almost pathological abuse over Saladin's head. The cool approach of an Englishman, Ralf Niger, who soberly pointed out all the problems in the way of the planned crusade, could make little headway against this kind of passion.[55]

Peace was restored only with great difficulty. Shortly afterwards Henry II died in July 1189. His son Richard succeeded him both as king (1189–99) and crusader. He was thirty-two years old, fair-haired, tall and strongly built, a matchless warrior, a capable general, a superb knightly figure; but also a man of marked psychological instability who veered between the extremes of generosity, cruelty, and abject remorse. In contrast to him the twenty-five year old king of France was not a very compelling personality. He possessed a dry wit but he was also a hypochondriac who often suffered badly from a fear of death. He was as little interested in art or learning as Richard but he was a statesman who possessed patience as well as energy and who, step by step, cautiously but successfully built up the strength of the French crown. He was poorer but cleverer than Richard. Richard had inherited a well-filled treasury from his father and by selling crown offices on a large scale he raised even more money for the crusade. In his ten-year reign he saw England for ten months only; his kingdom was, in his eyes, just a bank from which he could draw the money needed to indulge his insatiable lust for war.

At last, on 4 July 1190, both kings left Vézelay, the appointed place of muster. They had, after all, decided to go by sea and at Lyons they separated. Philip marched to Genoa. According to the terms of his agreement with the Genoese there was transport for 650 knights and 1,300 squires with their horses, provisions and fodder for eight months, wine for four months. For all this the

Genoese were to receive 5,850 silver marks. Richard marched down the Rhône to Marseilles where he awaited the English fleet of about a hundred supply ships and twenty men-of-war. In September the two fleets met at Messina and wintered there. Richard had a feud with the ruler of Sicily, Tancred of Lecce, over the hereditary claims of his sister Joanna, the widow of the previous king. However he found time for an interview with Joachim of Fiore, the Calabrian abbot of Corazzo who was well-known as a prophet and who foretold victory for Richard in the East.[56] The arrogant behaviour of the English quickly fanned into virulent life the smouldering hatred of the Sicilians for foreigners. In turn Richard was forced to seize the city of Messina which he did in a lightning strike lasting just five hours. The Anglo-Norman poet Ambroise, whose *Estoire de la Guerre Sainte* is an imperishable memorial both to Richard's heroic deeds and to the sufferings of the poorer crusaders, wrote that Richard had taken the city into his hands in less time than it takes a priest to sing matins. Philip and Richard had arranged to divide the plunder between them and the first of their many quarrels arose out of this. On 30 March 1191 an angry King Philip sailed alone out of Messina. On 10 April Richard followed him. *En route*, in a boldly executed campaign, he captured the island of Cyprus from the 'emperor' Isaac Comnenus (May 1191). On Cyprus he met Guy, and being feudal lord of the Lusignan family in Poitou, he at once took Guy's part; Conrad of Montferrat was supported by Philip Augustus and the duke of Austria, now the leader of the German crusaders. This split further intensified the Anglo-French hostility; and the Germans too found it difficult to get on with the Frenchmen and vice versa.

Despite these problems the siege of Acre was pressed more vigorously after Richard's arrival on 8 June; the big French siege machines were particularly helpful. Saladin's attacks on the crusaders' camp failed to achieve any result and on 12 July 1191— despite Saladin's objections—the dispirited garrison surrendered. They were to go free on condition that Saladin restore the True Cross, release 1,500 named Christian prisoners and pay a ransom of 200,000 bezants. At last, after a siege of two years, the standards of France and England waved over the city. The losses had been heavy. A semi-official list of the dead names Queen Sibylla, Patriarch Heraclius, five archbishops, six bishops, four abbots, a prior, an archdeacon, two dukes, a landgrave, ten counts, three viscounts, and thirty more great nobles. The losses among the lesser knights and the infantry were not counted. The list of the Saracen dead was considerably lengthened when, in a fit of anger, Richard had the 3,000 prisoners murdered because there had been difficulties with the payment of the first instalment of the ransom which was probably beyond Saladin's resources.

The problem of the kingship was settled by a compromise. Guy was confirmed as king; Conrad of Montferrat was made heir to the throne. But for the moment the real ruler of Outremer was Richard, especially after the end of July when King Philip went home. He had often been ill; he had the domestic question of the inheritance of the count of Flanders to worry about; and he would, if Richard remained away, have an opportunity to move against Normandy. From the French point of view his departure was well calculated, but the English chroniclers accused him of cowardice and oath-breaking. His army remained in the Holy Land, now under the command of the duke of Burgundy but the latter was so short of money that he could pay the troops only by borrowing from the English.

For a whole year Richard campaigned against Saladin whose reputation had suffered a good deal as a result of the fall of Acre. His army showed ominous signs of breaking up; only the troops from Egypt and Mosul were at all reliable. Even his relatives, headed by his nephew Taqi ad-Din, plotted mutinies and engaged in quarrels which prevented him from devoting all his energy to the war. His main aim was to hold on to Jerusalem and so he concentrated on threatening the crusaders' supply lines in the interior of the country. This tactic did in fact stop Richard from making any serious attempts to take Jerusalem. But as a general Richard was Saladin's superior and was not to be tempted into a trap. On 22 August he marched south from Acre for if he wanted Jerusalem, he first had to be able to use Jaffa, the port nearest to Jerusalem, as a base. The march was a model of crusade tactics. The army's right flank was protected by the sea and the fleet, and the speed of its advance was dictated by the speed of the ships. The three squadrons of knights were in the centre, with their left flank protected by tightly packed infantry formations. To prevent too much strain being imposed on these footmen, they alternated with other infantry sections who otherwise marched right by the seashore. On 7 September at Arsuf, north of Jaffa, Saladin tried to break the Christian army in one decisive battle. But Richard stuck firmly to his order of battle and the much-feared English archers held the enemy at bay until they began to show signs of exhaustion. Only then did the massed English cavalry charge. The Muslims could offer no resistance. On both sides losses were small but the Latins had won a moral victory in the first big battle since

Hattin. The legend of Saladin's superiority had been destroyed.

After taking Jaffa Richard allowed the army a rest. From now on he negotiated almost non-stop to end the war. Saladin was represented by his brother al-Adil, an exceptionally able diplomat who wore down the Franks by his delaying tactics. Moreover he split them into two camps by negotiating simultaneously with Richard and Conrad of Montferrat. The whole business was conducted in a most courteous fashion, revealing a political sense which was very far removed from the religious crusading spirit. At one stage even so recondite a project as a marriage between Richard's sister and Saladin's brother was said to have been discussed. The problem of keeping the crusader states in existence was, of course, a political problem which, despite the religious enthusiasm which was doubtless to be found in the ranks of the army, could only be solved by political means. Even a man as impulsive as Richard could not but realize this for, like revolutionary enthusiasm, the crusading spirit did not last for long. But there is no point in lamenting the decline of a noble idea when it is clear enough that what was urgently needed was pragmatic action.

An advance was made towards Jerusalem but in the New Year a halt had to be called at Bait Nuba about twelve miles short of the inadequately fortified city. Popular opinion in the army criticized this decision but in view of Saladin's tactics it was the right one. The French then returned to Acre while Richard kept the English busy rebuilding Ascalon.

In April news came that Richard's brother John Lackland had engaged in treasonable negotiations with the king of France. The situation was not immediately dangerous but Richard realized that he could not stay in Outremer for ever. The compromise settlement between Guy and Conrad had not worked for long. In response to pressure from the barons Richard dropped Guy and allowed the vigorous Conrad of Montferrat to be elected king; by the law of inheritance he now had the best claim. Richard compensated Guy for this loss by making him ruler over Cyprus though he had earlier sold the island to the Templars and Guy had to buy out their claim. But Conrad was never to wear the crown. According to the chronicler Ernoul, on the evening of 28 April 1192 Conrad went to dine with the bishop of Beauvais because dinner at home was late as a result of his wife Isabella staying too long in the bath. Unfortunately the bishop had already finished his meal so Conrad slowly walked back again to the palace at Tyre. As he turned a corner he was stabbed to death by two Assassins. It was the last deed of the 'Old Man of the Mountains' who died soon afterwards. Public opinion accused Richard of plotting Conrad's assassination and to clear their king English writers inserted into their chronicles a forged letter 'written' by the sheikh of the Assassins to Duke Leopold V of Austria who was now back in Germany. There is no way of telling who in fact was responsible. After a few days Conrad's widow married Count Henry of Champagne who was then acclaimed king by the people of Tyre. Somewhat reluctantly Henry agreed, on Richard's advice, to take over the kingdom but he never claimed the royal title, probably because he was never crowned.

In the summer of 1192 the Christians again advanced on Jerusalem and again called a halt at Bait Nuba. While the army withdrew to Acre, Saladin captured Jaffa. As soon as Richard heard of this he gathered a handful of knights together, and sailed to Jaffa. There he carried out one of his most famous exploits, wading, still not in full armour, through the shallow water to the beach and rapidly clearing the town of Muslims. On 5 August he beat off an attack launched by Saladin. Then, on 2 September, the two adversaries made a three years' truce, recognizing that neither could inflict a decisive defeat upon the other. The Christians had to accept that they could not recapture Jerusalem. By the terms of the truce the coast from Tyre to Jaffa was to remain in Christian hands. Ascalon, which had been the chief bone of contention during the negotiations, was handed back to Saladin, but only after its fortifications, together with those at Gaza and Darum, had been razed to the ground. Jerusalem was kept by the Muslims but they agreed to allow pilgrims to visit the city. Richard himself did not trouble to take advantage of this concession. In October Tripoli and Antioch were included in the truce although they had remained neutral throughout the war.

On 9 October 1192 Richard left the Holy Land. A shipwreck forced him to travel through Austria and he had to go in disguise because he had made an enemy of the duke of Austria when he tore down the Babenberg banner at Acre. This was, of course, not the arbitrary act that it was once thought to be. When Leopold raised his banner he was staking a claim to a share in the spoils, thus endangering the monopoly which Richard and Philip of France had arranged between them. But Richard was recognized in Vienna and the duke had him imprisoned in the castle of Dürnstein. Later he was handed over to the emperor, Henry VI, who finally released him in 1194 after an enormous ransom of 150,000 marks of silver had been paid and Richard had agreed to hold England as an imperial fief. In 1199 Richard died while still at loggerheads with Philip Augustus. Saladin had died earlier, in March 1193, aged fifty-five. With him there vanished one of the greatest personalities of medieval Islam, a man whose success was based almost entirely on the moral force of his ideas. As always in the Muslim world, his empire began to fall apart as soon as he was gone. This development effectively prolonged the truce and gave the crusader states half a century of peace before they had to face a decisive onslaught from the Ayubids. The greatest of the crusades was over. Its achievement was a modest one; most of Palestine was still in Muslim hands. The united forces of Outremer and the West had, it is true, ensured the existence of the crusader states for another hundred years, but the West was never again prepared to send help on this scale.

Even so a new crusade was soon planned. The new emperor, Henry VI (1190–7) had high-flying schemes and among them was a crusade—a crusade in which political considerations played a large part.[57] Owing to his marriage with Constance and to the fact that William II died without issue, he unexpectedly became heir to Sicily and south Italy though he had to conquer his inheritance before he could enter into it (1194). He was the heir not just to Norman lands but also to their policies, to their traditional plans for expansion into the eastern Mediterranean. In 1194 Leo II, prince of Lesser Armenia under whose rule Cilician Armenia had its greatest days, successfully sought enfeoffment by the emperor. He and his Roupenian forefathers, while fighting a perpetual war against the Byzantines and their allies the Hethoumians (see above p. 52), had built up a vigorous Christian state, economically founded on the Cilician plain and the cities of Tarsus and Seleucia and protected militarily and politically by the strong fortresses of the Roupenians high in the Cilician Mountains.

But Henry VI turned his attention chiefly to Byzantium. In 1194 his brother Philip was betrothed to Irene, daughter of the Byzantine emperor, Isaac Angelus. In 1197 the marriage took place; it was to have momentous consequences in the history of the crusades. In the meantime the alliance gave Henry a family interest in the Byzantine crown and when Isaac Angelus lost his throne to his still weaker brother Alexius III (1195–1203), it enabled him to clothe his political pressure on Byzantium in the guise of a right to an inheritance. Henry himself took the cross in 1195, partly in order to reach a settlement with the pope. He promised to supply and maintain at his own expense 1,500 knights and 1,500 squires quite apart from the normal crusading army. In the following years the crusade was preached in Germany, but for the moment nothing came of it. This was in part because the emperor's plan to make Germany and Sicily into a hereditary monarchy fell through as a result of opposition from the princes of north Germany and from the papal curia; in part because, despite their religious differences, Rome came out decisively in support of Byzantium and pressed for a crusade to the Holy Land, not one against Byzantium. If the empire in the East had been unified with the empire in the West the papacy would have had to face the prospect of complete political impotence. In addition, the Greeks bought themselves a temporary respite by paying a heavy and unpopular tribute to the Roman Emperor—sixteen hundredweight of gold a year—known as the Alamanikon.

Henry had to give up his plan to lead the crusade himself. Instead he appointed the imperial marshal, Henry of Kalden, and the imperial chancellor, Conrad of Querfurt, bishop of Hildesheim, to be its leaders. From March 1197 onwards the German troops embarked in south Italy. The main contingent left Messina at the beginning of September. They broke their journey to Acre in Cyprus where the chancellor crowned Amalric of Lusignan, Guy's brother and successor, as king—thus establishing a suzerainty of the empire over the island. In the Holy Land too, the Germans achieved a lasting success. Led by the duke of Brabant they were able to restore the land connection between the kingdom of Jerusalem and the county of Tripoli by capturing Sidon and Beirut (24 October 1197).

The sudden and unexpected death of Henry VI in Messina on 28 September 1197 plunged the medieval empire into one of its worst crises. Henry had had no time to consolidate his great achievements. His power had rested entirely on his own personal authority as emperor and his only son was just a child. In these circumstances the German crusade soon broke up. Only Leo II of Lesser Armenia derived further profit from it when, in January 1198, he received the long-desired royal crown from the hands of the archbishop of Mainz. But the union of the Armenian Church with Rome, part of the price to be paid for the title of king, was never to be anything more than a pure formality.

8 · THE INTERNAL DEVELOPMENT OF THE CRUSADER STATES IN THE TWELFTH AND THIRTEENTH CENTURIES

WHEN the Muslim traveller, Ibn Jubayr, journeyed through the Holy Land in 1184 he was astonished to find it economically and socially flourishing despite the increasingly unhealthy political situation.[58] Here and there Franks and Muslims tilled the fields together and shared common pastures for their cattle. The great caravans were able to travel in safety to Acre where they were dealt with by a smoothly functioning customs system staffed by Arabic-speaking Christians. But this description should not lead one to suppose either that the Franks were tolerant or that a process of mutual assimilation between Christian and Muslim had taken place. If the yoke of Frankish rule did not press too heavily on the Muslims this was only because a shortage of manpower was at all times the greatest problem of the crusader states. At the conquest many Muslims were killed and others emigrated. Few of the crusaders remained behind in the Holy Land. In 1100 Jerusalem had only a couple of hundred inhabitants. Even in the towns, let alone in the countryside, living conditions were insecure. Those who did remain tended to settle in groups according to their place of origin. The men from Lorraine and north France stayed within the kingdom of Jerusalem; the Provençals went to Tripoli; the Normans to Antioch, though this principality was later to fall under French domination.

If Outremer were to survive then men who were prepared both to fight and to settle had to be attracted from Europe.[59] It soon became clear that the towns were more easily populated than the countryside. The fiefs granted by Godfrey de Bouillon were almost always money fiefs from the municipal revenues—though in part this was also a consequence of the small size of his domain. Not until the reign of Baldwin I do we find fiefs of land. In addition, of course, there was the land which was simply seized at the time of the conquest, and as a result of this there were scattered estates which survived for a long while as allodial land i.e. land which was freely owned and not held of any human lord. Jean

Richard has shown the probability of a similar situation existing in Cyprus. Thus the process of feudalization was a slow one. In the legislation of Outremer there were special provisions designed to persuade knights to come and settle. Here, in contrast to the customs of inheritance prevailing in Europe, a knight's fee could be inherited by daughters or by collateral relatives. This meant that if the knight fell in battle his possessions were kept in the family even when he himself had no children; his kin in Europe could send another member of the family out to the East. Because new arrivals frequently found it difficult to find witnesses, the *Assise du coup apparent* was promulgated during Baldwin III's reign as a concession to lower-class immigrants. It exempted pilgrims and poor people from the requirement of the courts of law for proofs offered by witnesses.

Thanks to their economic situation it was fairly easy to find settlers who were prepared to live in the coastal towns. In Antioch too there were few difficulties; the city enjoyed the advantages of a pleasant climate and a fine situation between mountains and sea as well as the security guaranteed by the immense fortifications— four hundred towers—dating back to the period of Byzantine rule. Moreover in a country where the city had always played a central role and which had known the advantages of the way of life common to both Byzantine and Oriental civilization, living in the city offered a standard of comfort unknown in Europe. The houses usually looked plain from the outside; but inside they were often magnificent. In Antioch there was an artificial sewage system and the citizens had running water in their houses; in these respects they were better off than a king from Western Europe. Ironically, although the whole point of the First Crusade had been to capture Jerusalem, it proved difficult to persuade men to live there. The entire native population of Jerusalem had been massacred in 1099 and indeed not until the capture of Sidon (1110) did the crusaders manage to find a different method of dealing with urban populations. Jerusalem was, it is true, the capital city, the seat of both secular and ecclesiastical administration, but apart from the pilgrim traffic it had no economic stimulus, neither manufactures nor long-distance trade. The kings therefore had to take special measures to provide for its repopulation, notably the *Assise de l'an et jour* (see p. 64). In about 1115 Baldwin I established a colony of Christian Syrians from the Transjordan in what had been the Jewish quarter and gave them special privileges. In 1120, in response to a request from the patriarch, Baldwin II abolished all duties on imported foodstuffs, in particular on grain. This suited the patriarch's financial interest very well for he had a virtual monopoly of the Jerusalem bakeries.

Although Frankish society always remained essentially urban, it was clearly impossible to rule Outremer effectively without also bringing the countryside under the control of a system of colonization and administration. The extension of the area of cultivation often went hand in hand with the requirements of defence. Usually the king, but sometimes powerful household officials, began the process by building castles—purely for military reasons—whether in the south-west around Ascalon or in the Dead Sea region to the south-east. Naturally settlements and a church then clustered around these castles; a little further off villages grew up; the colonists farmed the soil more intensively and paid dues to the lords of the castles who guaranteed their safety and who held their castles as fiefs of the king. The extension of settlement and cultivation in the Gaza region can be closely observed. In 1149 a castle was built there within the ruins of the ancient town. After the fall of Ascalon in 1153 Gaza became less important militarily, but the settlement developed so rapidly that a new and bigger circuit of walls had to be built.

We are particularly well informed about the construction and function of Castle Safed. It controlled the road from Acre to Damascus and the most important crossing point on the Jordan, Jacob's Ford. In 1218 it was destroyed by the Saracens and then, in 1240, rebuilt at great expense by the Templars who made of it a strong and inaccessible fortress. In peacetime the castle held a garrison of 50 Templar knights, 30 serving brothers, 50 Turcopole cavalrymen, 300 archers and another 820 men and 400 slaves. In wartime Safed could hold 2,200 people so it provided a safe retreat for the local latin population. The arable farming, the cattle breeding, and fishing of the region were described in detail by a pilgrim. He mentions grain, figs, pomegranates, olives, grapes, and vegetables; he refers to the production of honey, to the excellent stone quarries which were being commercially exploited, and to the irrigation system which served the plantations. The castle's water supply was ensured by springs and cisterns within the walls. Grain delivered to the castle could be milled there by the castle's own mills, both wind and animal driven, and baked in the castle oven. It is probable indeed that the bread for the whole district had to be baked there. Mills, however, were to be found outside the castle. Twelve water-mills are mentioned though there is nothing to indicate whether or not they belonged to the lord. The population of the region was estimated at 10,000, living in 260 villages. At the foot of the castle there was a settlement, rather larger than the rest, and a market. The writer described the castle's function as a centre of defence and settlement when observing that it prevented the Saracens from crossing the Jordan to raid in the direction of Acre and thus permitted agriculture and colonization (*terre colonia*) to be carried on in safety.

Also well documented is the Hospitallers' scheme for colonization at Beth Gibelin near Ascalon in 1168. This was settled exclusively by Franks, thirty-two families in all. Six of these had lived in Palestine for some time already; the others were new arrivals from Auvergne, Gascony, Lombardy, Poitou, Catalonia, Burgundy, Flanders, and Carcassonne. They each received 62 hectares (150 acres) of land in *tenure en bourgeoisie*; they were personally free in the sense that they were free to move away if they wished; and they paid the *terraticum*, a payment in kind based on the harvest and assessed according to the customs of Ramleh-Lydda. (These customs seem to have been used as the customary model for agricultural organization which here, as usual in Outremer, was carried out on the European pattern.) They also had to hand over a proportion of the plunder they took from the Saracens, so presumably they must have had to go to war occasionally. As an additional attraction the Hospitallers' right of pre-emption was abolished and, in return for a moderate payment to the lord, the land could be freely alienated. By the end of the century the settlement had its own court (*Cour des bourgeois*) and thus enjoyed a certain amount of self-government. In the interior of the land the Church played a considerable part in the business of colonization. *Magna Mahumeria* near Jerusalem, for example, was a large settlement established by the canons of the Church of the Holy Sepulchre. Here the administration maintained a stricter control and occasionally a settler was forced out. The lord's agent, the *Dispensator*, kept a close watch on the quality of work. He could reprimand, impose fines, or confiscate land, though he had to act in co-operation with the local settlers' organization. The stringent terms of their contracts suggest that some of the settlers may have been pilgrims who ran out of money and could not afford to go home. But the picture drawn by Bernard of Clairvaux (*De laude novae militiae, c.* 5, § 10) of the Holy Land as a kind of colony of criminals does the settlers an injustice. *Magna Mahumeria*, like Beth Gibelin, was settled exclusively by Franks, some 140 families in all, whereas in the south-east some of the colonies were composed of Muslims. There the unit of assessment for taxation was the hearth. After the coast, the region around Jerusalem was clearly the most densely settled part of the kingdom, for when the Hospitallers received 10,000 bezants in 1168 in order to buy land on behalf of the heir to the throne of Hungary, they had to report that they had been unable to acquire any in the neighbourhood of the capital.

Thus a second class of free Franks developed beneath the aristocratic upper class. These were the *burgenses* or *bourgeois* (see below p. 170) whose numbers were kept up by a continual flow of immigrants. Presumably, except in those exceptional cases already mentioned, they came in order to better themselves socially, since a Frankish bourgeois was naturally the social superior of a Syrian landowner, no matter how rich the latter was. Most of the bourgeois lived in the towns—Jerusalem, Acre, Tyre, Tripoli, and Antioch—but the number who settled in the country should not be underestimated. Altogether the kingdom of Jerusalem probably contained about 100,000 Frankish inhabitants, nobles and bourgeois, in 1187. Fulcher of Chartres (above p. 85) bears witness to the fact that from around 1120 they had developed a sense of belonging to a state of their own. In the prologue to his chronicle (1184) William of Tyre gave eloquent expression to this same feeling. Not until the thirteenth century was it seriously undermined, when the growing power of the communities of Italian merchants living on the coast and the establishment of the Teutonic Order led to the development of narrowly nationalistic foreign corporations which were prepared to put other interests above those of the Holy Land. The Italians put the commercial interests of their home town first; the Teutonic Order served the requirements of Hohenstaufen policy. For these reasons Jean Richard has referred to a process of 'de-nationalization'.

Only the Frankish nobles and bourgeois, in their higher ranks a fairly pure-blooded group, had any political rights. Below them came a lower class made up of an exotic mixture of races. Politically, ethnically, and religiously it was kept apart from the ruling class. At this time the religious barrier was the decisive one. If it could be overcome then ethnic difference would not prevent a man from rising in society (see below p. 178). Ever since the time of the First Crusade there had also been half-castes, known as *poulains*, the children of Turkish–Greek or Frankish–Syrian marriages. Fulcher of Chartres even talks of occasional marriages between Frankish settlers and baptized Muslim women. But sexual intercourse with an infidel was naturally prohibited and the man who kept a Muslim woman as a concubine was, according to the draconian measures laid down by the Council of Nablus (1120), to be castrated and have his nose cut off. The greater part of the native population consisted of Christian Syrians, themselves divided into several religious groups: going very roughly, from south to north they were Orthodox, Monothelete Maronites in Lebanon, and Monophysite Jacobites. Their language was very largely Arabic; Old Syriac died out in the thirteenth century. Even under the rule of Arabs and Turks the Syrian Christians had been a tolerated people, craftsmen and farmers, and their lot was little different under the Franks. Besides them there were considerable numbers of Armenians and Greeks living in the coastal towns, chiefly within the principality of Antioch but also in Palestine. Some were merchants; others, in Orthodox monasteries, served their Church. Amalric I tried to bring about 30,000 Armenian settlers into the kingdom of Jerusalem. Financially they were to enjoy the same lenient terms as the Muslims but they were also to do military service. The attempt failed, however, because the Church demanded a special tithe from which the Muslims—of course—and also the rest of the subject population were generally exempt (see below p. 167). Where the numbers of Franks and Syrian Christians were insufficient to cultivate the land, men turned to Muslims, usually of Syrian origin, and only zealots like James of Vitry, bishop of Acre in the thirteenth century, would ever try to convert them. The number of Arabs and Turks tended to decrease but there were always the nomadic Bedouin tribesmen who, together with their flocks, were considered to belong to the royal fisc. In the coastal towns the Jews were of some importance. They had something like a monopoly of wool dyeing and glass manufacture. In Jerusalem itself, however, it was not until Saladin's reconquest in 1187 that the Jews were allowed to re-establish their religious community there. A few Jews still lived in the country, particularly in north Galilee. From the beginning of the thirteenth century there was a growing movement for the return of Jews, especially from France, to Palestine. A leading exponent of this movement was the Spanish rabbi Nachmanides who settled in the Holy Land in 1267 and, in his commentary on the Pentateuch, argued that the pious duty of a pilgrimage should be replaced by an obligation to live permanently in Palestine which he held to be especially reserved for the Jews. Finally there were some Georgians, Coptic Ethiopians, and a few Nestorian Christians from central Asia who lived in Jerusalem in order to fulfil religious functions.

At the head of the social structure stood the king or, in the north, the ruling prince. The king was elected but increasingly election did little more than confirm the hereditary right of the heir.[60] The view that the crusaders created an ideal feudal state with an all-powerful nobility and a feeble monarchy on the *tabula rasa* of a conquered land is false and—though it has been restated in recent years by some of the most famous legal historians—it is high time that it was discarded. This view is based on the legal theory and practice of the thirteenth century. In fact, the process of feudalization was a slow one and, in the early days, the king quite clearly held the upper hand. Naturally he was not an absolute monarch. This was out of the question in a country where, in the twelfth century, war was normal and peace the exception. (For thirteenth-century conditions see below p. 242.) In the course of time this state of affairs brought the king into a condition of increasing dependence on his vassals. But at first things were quite different. The king ruled directly through his viscounts on the royal domain with its centres at Jerusalem, Nablus, Tyre, and Acre. During the first three decades of the twelfth century an aristocratic class was gradually formed but the individual families remained unable to establish themselves in particular lordships. The king kept these firmly in his own hands transferring them often from one family to another. His legislation, which in accordance with medieval convention required the consent of those affected by it, applied uniformly throughout the whole land. Naturally the king also issued administrative ordinances on his own authority alone. Thus, in the thirteenth century, a royal ordinance on street cleaning in Jerusalem was held to be unconstitutional because it had been issued in the twelfth century without the consent of the inhabitants. The king alone had the right to make treaties with the Italian maritime towns or with Byzantium. He alone could mint coins and impose customs duties. In about 1150 he possessed certain judicial rights throughout the entire kingdom, jurisdiction over thieves who were minors for example. In about 1170 he still claimed the right to approve the resignation of the Master of the Hospital. Until the end of the century he continued to appoint the patriarch. This took place in an uncanonical procedure by which he chose one of the two candidates put forward by the canons of the Church of the Holy Sepulchre; but he was also entitled to reject both of them. According to a law issued either by Baldwin II or Baldwin III (*Establissement dou roi Bauduin*) in twelve precisely defined cases the king could confiscate a fief without process of law. This right contrasts strongly with practice in Europe but, in harmony with Roman law, it covered not only purely feudal offences but also crimes against the state as represented by the king (*crimina laesae majestatis*), especially those crimes which tended to deprive the king of revenue: counterfeiting or minting one's own coin, infringing his port and highway rights. The list also included such typical crimes against the state as high treason and apostasy.

During a period of transition, approximately 1130–60, the nobility was able to strengthen its position relative to the king. Some families obtained a firm hold on certain lordships. For the first time we hear of baronial rebellions. Within the knightly class a clear sense of caste developed. The nobility became more differentiated; a higher nobility of about ten families emerged, each of whom, in contrast to the earlier state of affairs, brought several fiefs together in one holding. The outstanding families were those which held the four great fiefs: the county of Jaffa–Ascalon, the principality of Galilee, the lordship of Sidon and Caesarea, and the lordship of Oultrejourdain with St. Abraham. Only by marriage was it possible to enter the ranks of this self-assured élite. Beneath them came the great mass of lesser knights, most of them holding a fief from which the service of just one knight was owed. Usually these were money fiefs which just sufficed to maintain their standard of living and which kept them very dependent on their feudal lord. Amalric I's *Assise sur la ligece* (above p. 119) marked the decisive breach made by the higher nobility in the stronghold of royal power. Formerly it was believed that by making rear-vassals recognize the king as their liege lord, Amalric had raised them to the level of peers of the baronage and had thus created a useful counterweight to the higher nobility. But Prawer has shown that appeals to the Assise were always made *against* the king, never in his interest. The rear-vassals became peers only in relation to the king; within the framework of the barony they remained subordinate to the baron. The Assise, in fact, was an instrument by which the nobility could collectively renounce their obedience to the king so long as they could find a legally valid reason for such a step. Prawer has also discovered that this Assise annulled the earlier *Establissement dou roi Bauduin*. As a result a fief could only be confiscated following a judgement by one's peers in the Haute Cour and naturally this meant that only in the most extreme cases was a sentence of forfeiture passed by a body so representative of class interests. The Haute Cour became increasingly important. In the twelfth century there had been a kind of royal privy council, but it vanished and by the thirteenth century the Haute Cour had developed into the highest court of law for the ruling class. It acted as a legislative body; it elected king or regent, at any rate to the extent of deciding between competing hereditary claims; and, as an extension of the vassal's duty to give advice (*consilium*), it laid down the guidelines of policy. But not until the Kingdom's last few years were the acts of the Haute Cour recorded in its own register. The court was dominated by the great barons. During the reign of Amalric I they successfully defended the right of collateral relatives to succeed to their fiefs, while on the other hand the lesser vassals had this privilege taken from them. This only serves to confirm the fact that Amalric's reign witnessed not a weakening but a strengthening of the position of the higher nobility. They developed their own baronial courts and in the thirteenth century Jean d'Ibelin counted twenty-two fiefs to which the right of minting coin was attached, though in fact only from four of these fiefs have coins survived to the present day. The greatest barons even had officials modelled on the pattern of the royal household.

Financial problems brought the kings into an ever more difficult situation. By Baldwin III's time the king was already deep in debt. Amalric I had to borrow money in order to pay his mercenaries. The royal domain shrank during Baldwin IV's reign and was then decimated by Saladin's conquests and by Guy of Lusignan's extravagant grants to those men who had supported his bid for the throne. In the thirteenth century Amalric II tried, without success, to reverse this process. The nobility became more and more powerful. In the second half of the thirteenth century the barons even made their own peace treaties with the Muslims, though at this date, of course, the king lived in Cyprus. In part this was the inevitable result of the fact that from 1225 onwards all the kings were outsiders who only occasionally came to the Holy Land and who generally ruled through *baillis* (regents).

Moreover during their struggle against Hohenstaufen centralization (see below pp. 246f.) the nobles closed their ranks and energetically defended their rights. As a result they wanted to see them codified. According to thirteenth-century tradition the kingdom had always possessed a written code of law. Immediately after the conquest Godfrey de Bouillon is said to have had a collection of laws compiled and deposited in the Church of the Holy Sepulchre. It is then supposed to have been added to by a continuous process of legislation. This collection, known as the *Lettres de Sépulcre*, was believed to have been destroyed by Saladin in 1187. There may be a grain of truth in the story, but it is a very controversial question and certainly unlikely that there was ever a real code of law. Amalric II (1197–1205) wished to have the lost *Lettres de Sépulcre* (not Godfrey de Bouillon's 'code' but a collection of separate legislative acts) reconstructed by Ralph of

Tiberias, a noble famous for his knowledge of the law, but Ralph excused himself from a task which was so incompatible with his own class interests. To some extent orally transmitted customary law helped to keep the tradition alive until it was written down in a partial codification, the *Livre au Roi* (drawn up at some date between 1196 and 1205), which still reflects something of the strong monarchy of the twelfth century. Entirely different in character is the codification known as the *Assises de Jérusalem*[61] which is extant today only because it was also valid for Cyprus and was copied there. As part of the reaction to the Hohenstaufen policy of centralization, it summed up the rights of the vassals and is generally looked upon as the clearest and most comprehensive presentation of the structure of a highly feudalized state. But to be clear is not necessarily to be progressive. In fact the crass advocacy of class interests in this code of law together with its rigid formalism effectively nipped in the bud any possibility of vigorous development, even though it did produce fertile ground for the kind of legal trickery which left its mark on several treatises written by barons who were also learned lawyers, men like Philippe de Novare, Jean d'Ibelin, count of Jaffa, and Geoffrey Le Tort. The most important of these treatises was the *Livre de Jean d'Ibelin* (c. 1265) a legal manual which left no room for unwritten customary law except in those cases where the code gave no answer. Naturally in this traditionalist age the formal character of the whole codification and, in particular, of the individual assises was one of an authentic interpretation of the 'good old custom' rather than the creation of new law. These collections described in detail an immensely complicated procedural law which, in various ways, ensured that the accused would have his rights, down to the right of all Franks to defend themselves in a judicial duel, but which also set such dangerous pitfalls in front of him that it became absolutely essential to have a lawyer in any case which was heard before the Haute Cour. Philippe de Novare in particular was an eminent authority on the art of procedural chicanery—those lawyer's tricks by which the hearing of a case could be accelerated or slowed down according to need. In contrast Jean d'Ibelin's view of the law was clearly shaped by a guiding principle. For him the law of Jerusalem was based on a kind of treaty which had come into being, after the common enterprise of the conquest, as a result of the election of Godfrey de Bouillon. By this treaty loyalty to the feudal lord was the vassal's duty only so long as the lord observed the precisely defined rights of the vassal—rights which had been much extended since the twelfth century. In such a system the king and his *bailli* were playthings in the hands of various interests or, at best, merely first among equals.

So it was that as a class the nobility steadily improved its social and legal position. This did not mean that individual families were immune to the vicissitudes of fortune—on the contrary, as the example of the Mazoirs shows.* In the 1130s Reynald I Mazoir rose to be constable of Antioch. In the 1160s and 1170s we find his son Reynald II, as a vassal of Antioch and brother-in-law of the count of Tripoli, established in the huge, almost impregnable fortress of Marqab not many miles distant from the sea. Reynald II had his own household, a castellan, six or seven vassals, a notary, a clerk with a master's degree, a few bourgeois, and a Syrian estate administrator. But his household expenses must have been burdensome, for from 1165 we can trace an accelerating process of sales and concessions to the Hospitallers. Here the Order of the Hospital created the nucleus of a new lordship which they rounded off in 1186, when Reynald's son Bertrand sold them the castle of Marqab, the town of Valania, three abbeys, and nineteen villages 'on account of the unbearable expenses and the all too close vicinity of the infidels', in return for an annual payment of 2,200 bezants. Bertrand then moved to Tripoli but by 1217 he was in Cyprus where he agreed to the payment being reduced to 2,000 bezants. His daughter married a wealthy Cypriot baron named Amalric Barlais who rose to be *bailli* but who later, being a sup- porter of Emperor Frederick II, suffered the forfeiture of his estates and had to go into exile. In 1226 his son Amalric cashed the annual payment for a lump sum of 14,400 bezants. Marqab, which had become the headquarters of the Syrian administration of the Hospitallers, capitulated to the Mameluks in 1285.

The life span of the nobles was usually short. King Fulk was fifty-three when he died, Baldwin III thirty-three, Amalric I thirty- eight, Baldwin IV twenty-three and Baldwin V seven. Leprosy seems to have been common enough to call for legislation on the subject. Within the ruling class marriage partners were chosen al- most exclusively from Frankish families, though two kings married Armenians and two others married Byzantine princesses. Concu- binage with Christian women occurred at all levels of society— including the clergy. Child marriages were by no means rare and thus the men, worn down by war and the climate, often left young widows who were obliged by law to find a new husband soon in order to maintain the military value of a fief even when

---

* The Mazoirs were, it is true, a family from the principality of Antioch, but conditions there were essentially the same as in the kingdom of Jerusalem.

it was inherited by a woman. (They had to select one of the three candidates chosen by the king.) A classic example of this is provided by the career of Isabella, the younger daughter of Amalric I. The hereditary rights of women meant that, through her, men could succeed to the throne. In 1183 at the age of eleven she married Humphrey IV of Toron. In 1190 this marriage was annulled for political reasons. Then to one husband after another she brought both the crown and misfortune. Conrad of Montferrat (1190–2) was murdered by the Assassins; Henry of Champagne (1192–7) fell backwards out of a window; Amalric II (1197–1205) died of a surfeit of fish. Thus by the time she was thirty-three Isabella had been divorced once and widowed three times. She herself died shortly after Amalric. Among the royal princesses of the twelfth century she is very much an exception in that she married a nobleman from within the kingdom, Humphrey IV of Toron. Otherwise, if we accept Prawer's attractive surmise, the convention was that they should marry either a prince of Antioch or a count of Tripoli—thus strengthening the influence of the court of Jerusalem over these principalities—or someone who was either an outsider or a new arrival (Fulk of Anjou, William Longsword of Montferrat, Guy of Lusignan, John of Brienne, Emperor Frederick II—not all of whom added to the prestige of the royal house of Jerusalem). The reluctance to make a marriage alliance with one of the old-established noble houses is probably to be explained in terms of doubts about the wisdom of adding to the hereditary claims of an already powerful family by a method which could only cause resentment among the other old families who were not so favoured. If this convention had been disregarded the result would probably have been dissension, for the barons, who had the right to give counsel on a matter of this kind, would have found it almost impossible to accept one of themselves as the husband of a king's daughter. It was much easier to agree if only outsiders were considered. If, in the case of Isabella I, the rule was broken, this was because she did not seem likely to succeed to the throne. When Amalric I had his first marriage annulled (see above p. 119), he ensured that the legitimacy of the children of this marriage was officially recognized, so that between Isabella and the throne there stood Baldwin IV, her elder half-sister Sibylla, and the descendants of both of them. It had been impossible to foresee that to be given Isabella's hand in marriage would be tantamount to being given the crown, but as soon as it did in fact come to this, her husbands were again chosen according to the old convention. Both Conrad of Montferrat and Henry of Champagne were out-

siders, while Amalric II belonged to the first generation of his
family to live in the Holy Land even though he was the brother
of King Guy of Jerusalem and was himself already king of Cyprus.
Before Isabella married Amalric the question had been discussed
in the Haute Cour and an alternative candidate had been
proposed: Ralph of Tiberias. Ralph, who was famous for his
knowledge of the law, belonged to the second generation of his
family to live in the Holy Land although ancestors of his had
been among the first crusaders. But if his candidature is said to
have failed owing to his poverty and to German pressure in favour
of the king of Cyprus, rather than for any other reason, this need
not be taken as an argument against Prawer's thesis that candidates
who belonged to the old families were at a disadvantage. In this
case all these factors coincided. In most respects the position of
other women was very similar to what it was in the West.[62] James
of Vitry, it is true, writes of them being shut away in harems, but
to Orientals, with their very different ideas on the subject, it
seemed as though they enjoyed far too much freedom. Women
could hold fiefs—here there was a fundamental contrast with the
position of noblewomen in Europe. So long as all their brothers, in
order of birth, were already provided for, they could also inherit
fiefs. This right they owed simply to the particular environment of
Outremer rather than to any special position midway between East
and West.

By comparison with Europe the central administration was
fairly rudimentary. The great crown offices developed out of the
Lorrainer household offices of the first kings. The most important
man was the constable who commanded the army, paid the mercenaries and exercised jurisdiction in military cases. His second-
in-command was the marshal who was in charge of the mercenaries
and was responsible for replacing horses which had been killed.
The importance of these military offices was a consequence of the
permanent danger of war. In contrast, the seneschal, so important
in Europe, was less influential here. He was the king's deputy in
the courts of justice, he administered the royal castles, and presided
over the *Secrète*, a loosely organized financial office. Though we
know next to nothing about the detail of the *Secrète*'s procedures,
it is at any rate clear that they were taken over from either the
Byzantines or the Fatimids. The *Secrète* probably also functioned
as a kind of land registry office. The chamberlain had certain
honorary duties as well as having to supervise the royal household.
A special fief was assigned to him *ex officio*. The duties of the
butler are unknown. The viscounts were royal officials, normally

but not always of noble birth, who were responsible for local law and order. They presided over the *Cours des bourgeois* and administered the royal domain. Those barons who possessed their own courts also had their own viscounts at the head of local administration. The king's chancellor was always a cleric though he was not always one of the king's chaplains. Some chancellors, like William of Tyre, had considerable influence over policy-making. Chancery procedures are shrouded in darkness. There is no evidence of a register of out-going charters. The chancery was, of course, a writing-office staffed by clerks who drew up charters, but bureaucratically it was still undeveloped. All its business, including the conclusion of treaties, was transacted in the form of the solemn diploma; the simple administrative writ was unknown.

On Cyprus, where there was a much longer period of constitutional development, the administration became more thoroughly organized. Here the chancery did make use of the writ; there are registers for both the *Secrète* and the Haute Cour as well as documents recording the income and estates of individual landowners (*Remembrances de la Secrète, Remembrances de la Haute Cour, Prahtico*). On Cyprus the *Secrète*, presided over by a high royal official (*Bailli de la Secrète*) was more influential than in Jerusalem; the registrar of the Haute Cour was accountable to it. In the fourteenth century a whole new set of royal officials appeared in Cyprus. The most important of these was the *Auditor* who had his own clerk and his own register. Originally he was probably an official of a court which supervised property transactions; later he became the attorney-general in the Haute Cour. The *Bailli de la Cour* was a steward of the household, while on the royal domain each of the ordinary *baillis* had a diocese, an administrative area in which he exercised jurisdiction in minor cases. In Nicosia the *bailli* was replaced by a royal viscount, the only official on the island to hold this title. The *Maîtres des enquêtes* represented the interests of the fisc when dealing with the estates of the deceased (*Inquisitio post mortem*). Military organization on Cyprus produced further officers, the Grand Turcopolier (originally the commander of lightly armed auxiliaries) and the Admiral. In the fifteenth century there is evidence of a council of state, an institution imported from Europe which foreshadowed the cabinet of modern times.

On the surface the institutions of Antioch, which we can study in a rather fragmentary fashion in an Armenian translation of the assizes of Antioch, resembled those of Jerusalem. But, following Norman custom, it was an hereditary principality right from the beginning with the electoral rights of the Haute Cour limited to the choice of a *bailli*. Here the money fief was more fully developed and the native element in the administration a more significant one. Indeed the whole administration was based on the Byzantine pattern as, for example, in the establishment of *duces* to supervise the administration of Antioch, Lattakieh, and Jabala. These *duces* were appointed and dismissed at the prince's pleasure.

The king had various sources of revenue. The viscounts rendered quarterly accounts of the income from the royal domain to the *Secrète* which kept a register of these accounts. The income was derived from feudal dues and taxes on both agricultural and urban production. Regalian rights like the right to mint coin also yielded profits. A special feature of the coinage were the rather poor imitations of Islamic gold dinars which were struck at the royal and Venetian mints at Acre. When Pope Innocent IV (1243–54) protested about this Christian inscriptions such as 'Minted at Acre in the year 1251. One Lord, one faith, one baptism' (cf. Ephesians 4:5) were added in Kufic script to these coins which were much used for trade with the Muslims. In addition the king possessed certain manufacturing monopolies which were farmed out for fixed sums to agent-generals who ran the risks involved in actually collecting the duties (soap production, dyeing, tanning, and sugar production). The Muslims paid a moderate poll tax, the Bedouins paid tribute; the right of wreck belonged to the king; the general taxes on property imposed in an emergency have already been mentioned (see above pp. 121 and 130). The most valuable sources of income were the customs and harbour dues of Acre and Tyre. The king very frequently made assignments on the harbour receipts of Acre though these were not always met. In the thirteenth century a customs duty varying from 4.16 to 11.2 per cent of the value had to be paid on imports from the East which were due for re-export. Higher duties, up to 25 per cent, were imposed on imports which were for domestic consumption. The preference rate given to the transit trade was designed to meet the competition from the Egyptian Nile Delta ports. In contrast to Fatimid Egypt a double system of graduated tariffs, taking into account the religion of the merchant as well as the kind of goods—with preferential treatment for co-religionists—did not exist in the Latin East. In fact Saladin decided to abolish this discriminatory system in order to compete with the Franks for the trade of Syria. In the *funda*, a cross between a bazaar and a warehouse, special market dues were levied by the market police. Foreign ships had to pay an anchorage fee of one mark of silver and the *terciaria* i.e. one third of the sum paid by voyagers for their passage. This tax on pilgrims seems to have been important because it was expressly reserved to the king when other very extensive privileges were granted to the Venetians in 1123. The pilgrims themselves paid a duty on the property they brought with them until about 1130 when they were granted exemption by Baldwin II. But at all times the kings found this financial system inadequate and thus compared with their cousins in the west they were rarely in a position to indulge in policies which were deliberately designed to stimulate trade. Even so, we have already noted the important privilege which granted exemption from all internal customs to Jerusalem (see above p. 150). The king of Cyprus was more fortunate in this respect and indeed in general he was able to maintain a preponderance of political power on the island. In 1367, according to Jean Richard, the royal domain in the diocese of Limassol was as large as the combined estates of the whole secular nobility. The king had a revenue of approximately 100,000 bezants, of which 86,500 derived from his lands; the rest came from various other rights. In addition he possessed the valuable salt monopoly. On Cyprus the revenues from the royal domain were usually farmed out.

The military system was based on the fief, above all on the money fief of 400–500 bezants a year for a knight.[63] Jean d'Ibelin preserved an (incomplete) list of knight's fees as they were *circa* 1180. This gives a total of 675 knights from the great and small crown fiefs to which, of course, we must add the knights belonging to the Military Orders. The Church and the urban bourgeoisie provided *sergeants* (foot-soldiers). The patriarch, the canons of the Church of the Holy Sepulchre, and the cities of Jerusalem and Acre each had to raise 500; the archbishops of Nazareth and Tyre, the bishop of Acre and the abbot of Mount Sion 150 each; the bourgeoisie of Tyre 100 etc., in total 5,025. In addition there was the light cavalry recruited from the native population. These troops were known as Turcopoles. They were mostly baptized Muslims, one of them in fact being named Geoffrey the Baptized. Among the highest officers of the Military Orders were the Turcopoliers who commanded these troops. Right from the beginning mercenaries were employed. In emergencies every able-bodied Frank could be called to arms; and every year there was the useful assistance of the crusaders who had come to the Holy Land for a season's fighting. In war the aim was almost always a localized conflict with a clearly defined geographical objective rather than the complete destruction of the enemy forces. As the Muslim armies grew stronger this concept of a limited war developed into a defensive war strategy, avoiding the risks involved in a pitched battle, intending only to contain the forces of the enemy until, as regularly happened, his army began to dissolve and he was forced to withdraw. Fortunately for the Franks military service in the Holy Land was for an unlimited period, whereas in Europe it was normally restricted to forty days in the year. After 1168 (*Assise de Bilbeis*), however, the knights were permitted to refuse to do service on foot during sieges—a clear indication that a noble caste was in the process of formation. Tactically the idea was to hold the troops together in tight battle formation in all circumstances; according to the Templar rule anyone who offended in this respect could expect to be punished severely. If this tight formation were lost then the speedier and more mobile Turkish cavalry soon gained the upper hand. The function of the infantry was to protect the heavily armoured knights both while on the march and in battle until the opportunity came for them to charge in a phalanx into the enemy. If properly delivered it was very seldom that the Muslims could stand up to the weight of such an attack. The castles were frequently sited so that it was possible to use lights to signal from one to another. The castle's offensive role as a *Gegenburg* has already been mentioned. But its chief function was, of course, an administrative and defensive one (see above pp. 93 and 151), not because they could prevent enemy troops from penetrating into the interior but because they provided a place for refuge for the population and a base for counter-attack. The idea that Frankish castle-building techniques, using Byzantine and Arab models, were more advanced than those in Europe has been made to look a good deal less convincing by R. C. Smail's investigations; and the same fate, at the same hands, has befallen the idea that the Holy Land was divided into one outer and two inner rings of fortresses. In places the crusaders did take over Byzantine fortresses, and later the Ayubids and Mameluks made further additions to them, above all to the mighty Krak des Chevaliers. The contributions actually made by the crusaders to these castles seem to have been technically very similar to work being done in Europe. Their most striking features were the strength and solidity of the walls and their advantageous sites.

After the collapse of Patriarch Daimbert's attempt to create his own great ecclesiastical lordship, the Palestinian Church remained firmly within the community of Rome.[64] The authority of the pope was exercised through legates and judges-delegate. At the head of the ecclesiastical organization stood the patriarchs of Jerusalem and Antioch; the ecclesiastical boundaries followed the political ones, as was shown by the dispute over Tyre between the two patriarchs (see above pp. 81f.). The archbishoprics of Tyre, Caesarea, Nazareth, and Petra belonged to the patriarchate of Jerusalem; so, therefore, did the bishoprics of Ramleh-Lydda, Bethlehem, Sebastea, Tiberias, Beirut, Acre, Sidon, Banyas, and St. Abraham (Hebron), where in 1119 the bones of the three patriarchs, Abraham, Isaac, and Jacob were found and which, from then on, became one of the most popular places of pilgrimage for Christians and Muslims alike. Of course not all of these bishoprics existed from the beginning of Frankish rule; some were not established until later. The cathedral church of the patriarch was the Church of the Holy Sepulchre, the greatest church in the land, possessing extensive estates in Europe (1128: sixty churches in eighteen European dioceses, mostly in Apulia) as well as in the Holy Land. A house of Austin canons under a prior functioned as the cathedral chapter of the Holy Sepulchre. Until 1114 this was a community of secular canons but in that year, despite their opposition, Patriarch Arnulf regularized them. Here (and certainly in other cathedral churches as well) the kings of Jerusalem held royal canonries i.e. they were canons of the Holy Sepulchre and could use the yield from their prehends to pay the salaries of court officials who belonged to the clergy. Other important religious institutions were the house of canons on the Mount of Olives, the abbey on Mount Sion, the Benedictine abbeys of St. Mary Latina and St. Mary Josaphat at Jerusalem and Bethany, and the monastery of Tabor where the Cluniacs had settled. The Premonstratensians had a small centre in St. Samuel on Montjoie near Jerusalem. The Cistercians had houses only in the county of Tripoli and the principality of Antioch. In the thirteenth century hermits living on Mount Carmel formed the nucleus of the Carmelite Order. The Mendicant Orders also set up houses in the Holy Land not long after they had been recognized by the pope. In the second half of the thirteenth century Dominicans were to fill many episcopal sees.

The natural centre of religious life was in Jerusalem and its environs. Christmas was celebrated at Bethlehem; Candlemas with the canons of the Temple of the Lord—for this is what the Dome of the Rock, the superb octagonal Omar mosque which is the oldest surviving example of Islamic architecture—was believed to be. Other festivals were celebrated in the places hallowed by tradition: Ascension on the Mount of Olives, Whitsun on Mount Sion, the Feast of the Assumption of the Virgin at St. Mary Josaphat. Good Friday was observed on the Hill of Calvary. Every year on Easter Saturday in the Church of the Holy Sepulchre there occurred the 'miracle of the Sacred Fire'—a piece of pyrotechnic nonsense which was finally forbidden by Pope Gregory IX in 1238. The lamps in the Sepulchre Chapel were supposed to be lit by heavenly fire; it was probably spontaneous ignition brought about by a mixture of Mecca balsam and oil of Jasmine. When, in 1101, the miracle for once failed to take place there was hopeless confusion in the crowd and some anxious hours for the clergy. Finally there was a special festival on 15 July to celebrate the capture of the city and the consecration of the Holy Sepulchre. For young clerks there were schools in the Holy Land, at the Holy Sepulchre for example, but those who showed real promise went to study in France and Italy—William of Tyre stayed away for nearly twenty years. The clergy had their own courts, firstly to deal with cases in which they themselves were involved and, secondly, to deal generally with certain offences: heresy, witchcraft, testamentary and marital matters, and sexual offences. The Church was permanently involved in disputes with the Military Orders which remained outside and independent of diocesan organization and jurisdiction while, willy-nilly, the bishops were forced to consecrate priests belonging to these Orders. The Hospitallers infuriated the patriarch of Jerusalem by rebuilding their Hospital on a scale far surpassing the Church of the Holy Sepulchre. Then, in 1153, his fury knew no bounds when the noise of their bells drowned his attempts to preach a sermon in the chapel on the Hill of Calvary. One day they even entered the chapel armed and turned it into a kind of archery range; the arrows which were collected together at the end of the day were long left to hang in bundles in the church as a reminder of the outrage. Tithes, an important source of revenue for the Church, were a perennial bone of contention with both the Military Orders and the secular nobility. This was because, in contrast to the arrangement in Europe, in the Holy Land and Cyprus it was the lord of the land (including the king) and not the subordinate tenant who paid the tithes. Moreover these did not go directly to the parish clergy but were paid into a central office at the cathedral and were then redistributed among the parishes. This arrangement ensured that the Latin Church received indirect financial support from the large group of non-Latin Christians and even from the Muslims since the income of the Frankish lords, on which the tithe assessments were made, included the dues paid to them by these groups whose wealth could not have been tapped by a tithe on the European model. But from the pontificate of Innocent II and much to the indignation of the bishops, the Military Orders could claim exemption from tithes on those lands which they farmed themselves. Even so the survival of a tithes list of 1193 from the Antiochene see of Valania shows just how wealthy even an ordinary diocesan bishop could be, though of course much of this income was required to support his parish clergy. In order to prevent the balance of wealth in a small kingdom being upset by the continued alienation of land to the Church, the *Livre au Roi* forbade the sale of fiefs to the Church. This prohibition was also designed to prevent the king losing the military service due from the fiefs. Here we come to one of the peculiarities of the Holy Land. Although the Church was one of the greatest landowners in the kingdom, there was no significant development of ecclesiastical lordships in the form of crown fiefs. There might have been some thought of creating a patriarchal crown fief in Godfrey de Bouillon's time (see above pp. 66f.). Possibly the patriarch's quarter in Jerusalem was the last surviving remnant of such an arrangement. Undoubtedly the bishop of Ramleh was a tenant-in-chief of the king, for even before the capture of Jerusalem he had been made secular as well as spiritual lord of Ramleh. The archbishop of Nazareth also rose into the ranks of the tenants-in-chief. According to Jean d'Ibelin the bishop of Ramleh owed the king the service of ten knights while the archbishop of Nazareth owed six knights. But these were the only two prelates who owed knight service. Even the patriarch only had to provide foot-soldiers for the king's army, an obligation which was laid upon the Church and the bourgeoisie on the basis of the property they held and not on the basis of a feudal relationship. Only fief holders owed knight service. The others provided the king with *serjeants* not on account of fiefs but on account of their other estates (*tenure en bourgeoisie*). But in fact the prohibition contained in the *Livre au Roi* could not prevent the Church acquiring more and more land; the practice of this prohibition was always less rigid than the theory.

The kings themselves endowed the Church richly, not only because by doing this they conformed to the ideal standards expected of a medieval king, but also because they needed the Church's financial support. William of Tyre complained bitterly of the way in which his patron Amalric I, for example, laid his hands on Church property in order to finance his policy. On the other hand it was largely the Church's financial contribution to Amalric's government that enabled it to exercise a significant influence over policy. No one embodied this better than William of Tyre himself. He championed the *libertas* of the Church against the king, but never for a moment considered that the clergy should abstain from politics. Episcopal elections required the king's confirmation; during vacancies the diocesan revenues were paid over to the king. Here, as in most matters of ecclesiastical organization, practice in Outremer was based on the custom in Europe. Inevitably then the question of the relationship between *sacerdotium* and *regnum* arose in the Latin East, but it was never disputed with the dogmatic bitterness that was characteristic of the West and particularly of the empire. The distressing conflict over investiture with ring and staff (see above p. 2) was not carried over to the Holy Land. In its political dealings with the crusader states the papacy always held firmly to the demand for *libertas*, but at the same time always recognized that only a strong secular power could defend these states against the heathen. Thus the papacy did not oppose the influence of the king over the Church, displayed most clearly when the patriarch was chosen (see above p. 155). Not until the pontificate of Celestine III (1191–8) was this royal prerogative reduced to the level of a mere right of confirmation. During the Alexandrine schism between Alexander III and a series of anti-popes (1159–77) the king at first tried to steer a cautiously neutral course; he wanted to allow Alexander's legate to enter the country only as an unofficial tourist. Finally, however, a majority of the episcopate forced him to align himself with the Alexandrine party. William of Tyre, who returned from his studies in France and Italy in 1165, seems to have been more inclined to support the imperial side, possibly under the influence of the Bolognese legists whose lectures he had attended. He complained of the financial burdens which Alexander's legate imposed upon the Palestinian Church. Relations with the other Christian Churches were tolerably good. Tension was greatest with the Greek Orthodox Church; only for a short while were they permitted to hold services in the Church of the Holy Sepulchre (see above p. 125). But they retained most of their monasteries and in Byzantium a shadow patriarchate of Jerusalem was maintained; indeed its authority was acknowledged by the abbot-archbishop of the monastery on Mount Sinai (1166). Apart from isolated incidents like the plundering of the monastery of Barsauma by Joscelin II of Edessa in 1148, relations with the Jacobites were good. Queen Melisende gave them endowments —as she also did for the Armenian and Orthodox Churches. In 1181 the Maronites entered into a permanent union with the

Latins though within the Maronite Church there always remained a party opposed to this and prepared to use the weapons of homicide and murder. After 1187 as the kingdom became progressively smaller, the bishops and monasteries were forced to congregate more and more in Acre. After 1225 when the kings became outsiders who did not reside in their kingdom, they also lost the right to confirm the results of ecclesiastical elections. During the same period the prestige of the patriarch, the kingdom's *Seignor espirituel*, grew. From about 1220 he was, in real and not just in formal terms, the pope's plenipotentiary, for he was the *legatus natus* and cardinal legates *a latere* were now rarely sent to Outremer.

Below the nobility there developed a further class of freemen, the bourgeoisie, whose existence can be documented from *circa* 1130. It should not be thought that they were anything like the bourgeoisie of today. Certainly there was, in the towns, a social class —a bourgeoisie in the modern sense—made up of Latin and Syrian Christians. But in the crusader states the term bourgeoisie meant something else: it meant the form of political organization common to the non-noble Franks. The fact that the indigenous population had long been organized into religious and ethnic groups stimulated the development of the Frankish bourgeoisie as also did the principle—so precious to the Middle Ages—that a man should be judged by his peers. The bourgeoisie was composed in part of the inhabitants of the small new settlements both in the interior and in the frontier regions (see p. 152) whose tenure of land was described expressly as *tenure en bourgeoisie,* and in part of the artisans and shopkeepers in Jerusalem and the coastal towns. It did not include the merchants from Italy and South France because they belonged to their own communities. The bourgeois were personally free but owed allegiance to the lord of the district or town. In Jerusalem their law is an obscure subject though it is clear that the economic solidarity of the family became less marked in the thirteenth century; the twelfth-century restrictions on the free alienation of family land have disappeared. In Antioch the marriage and property rights of the bourgeois remained firmly in the Norman mould. It is interesting to observe that in this respect the law of the first comers was preserved whereas the property law of the nobility, orginally also Norman, kept in step with political developments in Antioch and became French.

The bourgeoisie in Jerusalem acquired their own code of law in about 1240 with the *Livre des Assises des Bourgeois,* based on the Provencal (and thus Roman Law) collection *Lo Codi,* and carefully amended to fit circumstances in Palestine.[65] But the legal organization of the bourgeoisie was much older than this. From as early as the end of the twelfth century there is evidence of the *Cours des Bourgeois*, their own courts and institutions of self-government, corresponding to the Haute Cour of the nobility. In the thirteenth century there were four royal and thirty-three baronial courts of this kind, meeting three times a week under the presidency of the viscount who represented the local lord. Twelve jurors (*jurati*), exclusively Franks, declared the law in both civil and criminal cases involving the Frankish bourgeoisie. From these courts there was no possibility of an appeal. In the Haute Cour it was at least theoretically possible to escape the gallows by challenging the court to a duel and defeating all the judges within the space of one day. For non-noble Franks the judicial duel was permitted within the framework of the *Cour des Bourgeois*. But the bourgeois fought their duels against each other, not against the judges, and they used staves not swords. Syrians, Greeks, and Saracens were allowed to fight judicial duels before the *Cour des Bourgeois* only if they were accused of murder. In general the *Cour des Bourgeois* exercised blood justice over all non-Franks and acted as a register office for the records of property transactions; for this reason the court kept a register of its own from 1250. In addition it functioned as a court of appeal for the *Cour de la Fonde* and the *Cour de la Chaine*. The *Cour de la Fonde* dealt with commercial cases in the market towns and kept a register of business transactions not involving real estate. Since the parties in such disputes were often Christian non-Franks as well as Franks, the court was composed of two Franks and four Christian Syrians. However cases in which goods worth more than one mark of silver were in dispute automatically went before the *Cour des Bourgeois* which was composed exclusively of Franks. So too was the *Cour de la Chaine* (*Chaine* = the harbour chain) since it dealt only with questions of maritime and navigation law where disputes with the native population could hardly arise. In these special courts the judicial duel could not be used as a method of proof.

In the thirteenth century communes also developed, but in contrast to the situation in Europe they were few and far between.[66] Examples of this kind of political structure occur in Tyre (briefly from 1187), in Antioch (from 1194), in Acre (from 1231), and in Tripoli (from 1288). They never had an important part to play in the history of Outremer precisely because a great part of the Frankish bourgeoisie already belonged to a legal community. Moreover there were alien bodies in the towns in the shape of the powerful Italian communities who would never recognize a commune as their overlord. Thus the Palestinian communes did not survive for long, especially when the Church opposed them, as it did at Acre at the request of Emperor Frederick II and at Antioch in a kind of reflex reaction to the egalitarian outlook of the commune there which had planned to tax all its members, clergy as well as laymen. All the communes of Outremer came into being at times when the lord of the town had shown himself to be either unwilling or unable to defend the community. In Acre the commune was a product of anti-Hohenstaufen feeling. It was joined by the nobles, even of the highest rank, men like Jean d'Ibelin. In Antioch the numerous Greek inhabitants of the city joined the movement right from the start; in Acre, however, the commune was organized entirely by Franks. It originated in the religious fraternity of St. Andrew's church and then developed into a sworn community for urban government with the town itself as an abstract concept being looked upon as the town lord. It was organized along European lines. At the head of the commune were the consuls or syndics under the chairmanship of a mayor; it had its own bells, its own budget and the right to tax its members, judicial authority, and doubtless also a militia. Whereas the commune at Antioch seems to have fallen into decay gradually, the one at Acre was formally dissolved in 1241 after which it reverted to its former status as the *Frairie de Saint-André*.

The most striking feature of the towns was the presence of the Italian communities. This went back to the early twelfth century when they were granted privileges on an unparalleled scale (see above p. 80). The kingdom had no war fleet of its own and was therefore dependent on the maritime cities of Italy. They were needed to carry the kingdom's exports and imports; finally indeed it became necessary to try to stop them from sailing to Egyptian harbours. Time and again the strong monarchy of the twelfth century tried to cut back their privileges to a tolerable level. King Fulk refused to pay the doge of Venice the 300 bezants from the port treasury of Acre to which he was entitled each year according to the treaty of 1123. In 1164 the money was still owing. In 1167 Amalric I annulled the Genoese privileges which had been carved in golden letters in the Church of the Holy Sepulchre and was not to be persuaded to restore them. But in the confusion before and during the Third Crusade (see above p. 139) everything was renewed and extended. Their settlements also continued to grow and develop. At first the merchants had simply been grouped as a community around their own national Church and had set up a rudimentary kind of self-government. But soon the home towns took the matter in hand. In 1157 we hear of the first Pisan administrative official and soon each community had its own *bailli*, viscount, or consul who directed the administration of the colony as the representative responsible to the home republic. In addition Venice continued to make use of the ecclesiastical organization. Then in the thirteenth century a higher administrative structure was devised to which all the Syrian colonies of each republic were subordinate; this made for more consistent policy-making. The Venetians had their main settlement in Tyre where from 1200 to 1247 they quarrelled with the archbishop; both sides claimed jurisdiction over the Venetian church of St. Mark. The Genoese and the Pisans were based on Acre. Less important both politically and economically were the colonies of Amalfi, Marseilles, and Montpellier. But they all shared common characteristics: the merchants lived and traded in their own quarter which was well situated by the harbour; they had their own church, warehouse (*funda, fondaco*), bath, bakery, mill, slaughterhouse, etc. They contrived to be economically self-supporting and thus to escape the dues which they would have had to pay if they had used the town lord's (i.e. the king's) monopoly services. Minor cases, particularly commercial disputes, were dealt with by their own court if the accused were an Italian, while blood justice remained the responsibility of the viscount's *Cour des Bourgeois*. Throughout the land the Italians enjoyed far-reaching trading liberties; they were exempt from every kind of due, toll, anchorage fee, and from the obligation to use the royal weights and measures. In their own quarters, especially in the market, they maintained law and order themselves; elsewhere this was the viscount's job. The weaker the kingdom became, the stronger the Italian communes. They intervened, frequently with armed force, in the internal quarrels of the kingdom. If the different republics had not been so hopelessly at odds with one another the Holy Land would unquestionably have become an Italian protectorate in the second half of the thirteenth century.

The volume of trade in twelfth century Outremer was first overestimated by historians and then underestimated.[67] Originally the markets of Syria and Palestine were not much visited by Europeans; before the crusades only merchants from Amalfi and occasionally from Genoa went there. Evidence from Genoa shows that the Levant trade, going mostly through Alexandria, was still in the hands of Jews, Greeks, and Syrians. The important Genoese notarial registers seem at first sight to show that this Egyptian predominance lasted far into the twelfth century. The Genoese notary Giovanni Scriba had fifty-eight clients from Alexandria during the period 1158–64 and only thirty-four from Syria. But the picture changes as soon as one turns from the number of commercial contracts to the amount of capital invested. The fifty-eight Egyptian clients represent 9,031 *livres genois*; the thirty-four Syrian ones add up to 10,075. The average investment in Alexandria was 156 *livres genois*, in Syria 300. A further conclusion which had once been drawn from this material also turned out to be false. This was the notion that trade circulated in the direction Genoa–Syria–Alexandria–Genoa, i.e. that goods were exported to Syria, which enjoyed a flourishing trade with Egypt, and that other goods were imported into Genoa from Egypt. Behind this theory lay the fact that many imports from Egypt were mentioned but very few exports to that country. Yet the real reason for this was not the pattern of trade but the fact that Egypt's main imports (iron, timber, and pitch, i.e. shipbuilding materials) had been declared contraband by popes and councils and therefore could not be mentioned in the notarial registers.

The commercial framework was provided by two types of contract, both designed to spread the risk between the parties to the contract: the investor (*socius stans*) and the merchant himself (*socius tractans*). In what was known as the *societas* the merchant contributed one third of the capital and claimed one half of the profits (33 per cent from his own capital plus 25 per cent from that of the investor) while he would have to bear only one third of any loss. In allowing the merchant a higher percentage in profits than he would have to assume in losses, the investor provided the merchant with an additional incentive to aim for the maximum return on the capital of the investor, who had no control over how this money was employed while the merchant was overseas. The other type of contract, the *accomendatio*, became more common in the thirteenth century. Here the investor contributed the entire capital; the *tractator* would receive only 25 per cent of the profit but since he had risked no capital he could suffer no financial loss. In addition there was the sea-loan condemned by the Church because of the usury involved. Here the *tractator* raised capital at a fixed rate of interest of 35 per cent per annum—which presupposes a normal profit margin of at least 50 per cent if the business was to be at all worthwhile. A clear interplay of business and politics is revealed by an analysis of the investors whose names appear in the registers of Giovanni Scriba. Eighty per cent of the capital invested in the Syrian trade was put up by seven people; the remaining 20 per cent was shared between twenty other investors. During the same period about one hundred people had a share in the trade with Egypt. Of the seven leading investors in the Syrian trade one was a Jew, one a Christian Syrian; the five others all belonged to the political élite of Genoa, the group from which every year the consuls were chosen, indeed three of them were members of the Visconti family. This select and illustrious group monopolized the trade with Syria. In Syria itself their interests were supervised by trusted associates from the same class, families like the Embriaco who from 1109 held Jebail as a Genoese outpost and made of it an aristocratic lordship in the thirteenth century. Naturally the influential capitalists stayed at home in Genoa; they acted only as *socii stantes*. It is, of course, true that Giovanni Scriba, as the official city notary, had close connections with the ruling class and quite a different picture emerges from an analysis of the 1191 register of William Cassinese. Here the number of middling investors is very much higher. 1191, however, was in every way an unusual year. The Third Crusade was under way and so trade with Egypt was completely prohibited. There was, none the less, a boom stimulated by two wars: the crusade and Henry VI's attempt to conquer Sicily. Thus both the sum total invested and the number of Sicilian and Syrian contracts were much higher than usual. In 1191, moreover, the Ghibelline party in Genoa asserted itself for the first time. It ended the regime of consuls chosen from the old families and entrusted the city government to an outside *podestà*. It is clear that this went hand in hand with the breakdown of the old Visconti monopoly of the Syrian trade. A later increase in the trade with Syria which was observable in other cities besides Genoa resulted from the destruction of Byzantium (1204) and from the long pause in the struggle against the Muslims in Syria (1229–44). At the same time trade with Egypt suffered considerably as a result of the crusades which were directed against Egypt in the first half of the thirteenth century. The wars waged after 1250 by the Mameluk sultans of Egypt were to some extent trade wars fought in support of the ports of the Nile delta and the Karimi merchants of Egypt. These were the men who were to monopolize the fourteenth-century spice trade in Egypt after the destruction of the crusader states, though in the Mediterranean itself the carrying trade still remained firmly in the hands of the Italians.

Throughout the twelfth and thirteenth centuries Egypt controlled the transit trade with India and Arabia, though some Indian spice did go through Acre and Tyre as did the trade of

Persia, Syria, and Mesopotamia. The main exports to Europe were drugs and pharmaceutical goods including ginger, aloe, myrrh, camphor, senna leaves, bitter-wort, and the incense needed for liturgical purposes. There were spices like pepper, cinnamon, nutmeg, cloves, caedomom; fabrics and textiles like linen, silk, damask, muslin; dyes for use in European textile production, particularly alum (imported from Egypt), indigo, and brazilwood; fine wood (sandalwood); ivory, steel manufactures from Damascus, perfumes, pearls from the Orient, jewels, and porcelain. In addition there were the products of Outremer itself: castor sugar (produced mainly in Tyre and Acre), Jewish glassware, and Galileean wines. Exports to Egypt included salted fish, fruit (dates, oranges, and citrus fruit), olive oil, and oil of sesame. Grain, salt, pottery, and poultry were imported from Egypt for domestic consumption in Outremer. European goods which went through the Holy Land on their way to Islamic countries included textiles from France, Flanders, and England; metals like copper, mercury, lead, and iron; wood, pitch, saddles, almonds, and nuts. Salted pork for the Franks was exported from Europe since this meat was not available in the Islamic world. To complete the picture there was the slave trade and the pilgrim traffic (see below p. 220).

Agriculture was chiefly in the hands of the indigenous population, both Christian Syrians and Muslim Fellahin. Apart from the Muslim slaves, the lot of this class was not a bad one though of course they had no political rights. The Muslims now had to pay the poll tax which, in the old days, the Muslim rulers had imposed on the adherents of other religions. Otherwise the Frankish conquest made very little difference to the rural population, apart from the fact that the Syrian Christians and the Muslims were now placed into roughly the same legal category relative to the Frankish conquerors. If they lived in the country, Syrians and Muslims were both without rights. Only the Syrians who lived in towns, thanks to their personal freedom (*Stadtluft macht frei*), were legally better off than the rural *vilains*, as the peasants, both Syrian and Muslim, were called. In the country the village was a religious and an ethnic unit as well as being the smallest unit in the Latin feudal system. As Prawer has made clear, the rural population was segregated into separate villages, each village being exclusively settled either by Syrians or by Muslims or by Franks. There was no village where the different races lived side by side. Outside the towns the Franks lived in enclosed and fortified Latin settlements. There were, in fact, far fewer Latin settlements than an over-hasty estimate had suggested. According to Prawer's calculations in the whole of the kingdom out of a total of 1,200 centres of population there were only fifty or sixty Latin settlements. The land was governed by Latins, but it was by no means settled by them. Not only was the Latin population sparse; it was also very unevenly distributed. It was concentrated in the coastal towns and in Jerusalem, and in rural settlements along the fertile plain and in the valleys; in the highlands, on the other hand, there were almost no Latin settlements and there were very few where, militarily speaking, they would have been most useful—along the threatened frontiers. To say that the change of rulers made little difference to the rural population does not imply that the countryside witnessed no changes at all. On this point Prawer's conclusions are important. Naturally the old landowning class was completely replaced by Franks. Moreover the old Islamic *latifundia* which, in the pre-crusade period, had been owned by the state or by individual magnates or religious and charitable institutions, were broken up. Since the Franks did not take over the land all at once but in a gradual process which kept pace with the piecemeal conquest of the country, there could be no question of the old units being preserved. Thus in two ways there was a completely new redistribution of the land. Firstly the landowners changed—for only the Churches and monasteries were allowed to keep their old possessions and they were, in any case, mostly Latinized. Secondly there was a change in the size of the landholdings. Nevertheless these changes had only a minimal affect on the life of the rural population since recent research has shown that, on the eve of the crusades, Palestine was already caught up in a 'process of feudalization' (Prawer), i.e. the creation of big *latifundia* involving the depression of a once-free peasantry into a condition of servility or semi-servility. Even before the Frankish conquest the class of free peasants had almost disappeared. Perhaps this explains why Muslim rebellions were rare. Where conditions did become worse emigration seems to have been a more frequent course of action. When the Frankish lord of Mirabel imposed dues at a rate four times that sanctioned by custom and then stepped in to silence a Muslim preacher (ostensibly because the man, an expert in Islamic law, was urging the peasants not to work in the fields on Fridays, but probably because he was attacking this imposition) the population of eight Muslim villages emigrated *en masse* in 1156 and settled in a suburb of Damascus where they established a centre of counter-crusade propaganda which flourished right into the Mameluk period. It is not hard to trace their political commitment to the expulsion of the Franks from the Holy Land back to their position as refugees after 1156.[67a] But in general the Franks could not afford to press the Muslims too hard. They were, it is true, tied to the land but they enjoyed freedom of worship (though they were, as a rule, allowed neither mosque nor qadi). Besides the normal dues they paid a moderate poll tax and, like the Syrians, they had a court of their own, the *Cour du Rais*. Muslim slaves could obtain their freedom by being baptized. From the lord's point of view this meant that he lost a slave but gained a dependant tenant. Baldwin I even allowed a Saracen to become his chamberlain after he had had him baptized and given him his own name. In the early twelfth century able Syrian Christians even succeeded in becoming members of the Frankish knightly class, the family of Arrabit, for example, who from 1122 appear as vassals of the Ibelins. The Syrian *ra'is* were often wealthy land-owners; we should not under-estimate their position. The *ra'is* (latin: *regulus*) was a free man holding an office which was hereditary in his family. In the period of Turkish rule he had been a kind of chief of police; under the Franks he represented their authority over his own social class, presiding over the court named after him. He had jurisdiction in minor cases; serious offences were tried in the *Cour des Bourgeois*. Prawer's researches have shown that there were considerable differences between individual *ra'is*. As a rule the *ra'is* had authority over a single village but there were cases both of *ra'is* who presided, like sheikhs, over several villages, and of villages which contained as many as three *ra'is*— in these cases they were probably just the heads of the leading family in the village. We are less well informed about a second native official, the *Mathessep*, successor to the Islamic *muhtasib* whose job it had once been to supervise public morals and local trade. There is very little evidence for the office in Jerusalem but in Cyprus the *Mathessep* was clearly a subordinate of the viscount exercising a certain authority over artisans.

Rural economic and social conditions in the lordship of Tyre have been studied in detail by Prawer.[68] An area of 174 square miles was densely settled. There were about 120 villages (*Casalia*); of these the king had originally held two thirds and the Venetians one third. By 1243 this distribution had changed. The king now held 36 per cent, the Venetians 31 per cent, the Church 13 per cent (not a great deal but acquired at the king's expense), individual lords 12 per cent, while 8 per cent was in other hands. The *casalia* differed enormously in size. The area of farm land in each varied from 190 to 1,120 hectares (470 to 2,770 acres) expressed in terms of *carrucae* each of about thirty-five hectares (86.5 acres). The *carruca* was originally supposed to represent the amount of land needed to support one family but it soon became a purely fiscal unit of measurement. All the farm land was divided into *carrucae* once and for all and this arrangement was entered into the registers of the *Secrète*. Included among the farm land were the sugar-cane fields, olive groves, vineyards, and also the pasture land (*gastina*, literally wasteland). The populations of the *casalia* varied from three to thirty-six families according to the size of each *casale*. Farming was carried on in a complicated two-year rhythm in a two-field economy with one field always divided. Within this system the growing of winter wheat alternated with vegetables, summer crops, and fallow. A proportion of the harvest was paid to the lord as his due, but apart from that the farmer had to pay neither a formal rent to the landowner nor tithes to the Church. In contrast to Europe there was no demesne which the peasants were bound to work for the lord. This may be because the old pre-crusade system—which knew no such institution—was left unchanged, as in general there was a very high degree of continuity in the rural economy. Or it may be that peasant labour in the Holy Land was too valuable to be used in a way which was acknowledged to be uneconomic. The second hypothesis is supported by the fact that even the Military Orders held little demesne despite being exempted from having to pay Church tithes on it and on produce which was destined for their own consumption. A further reason for the absence of demesne land in Outremer is, of course, the fact that the landlords lived in towns, not on their estates. As Prawer has made clear, to them their villages were nothing more than revenue-producing units. For this reason not only was there no demesne land but also there was nothing of that patriarchal relationship which existed between the European landlord and the dependant peasantry who could look to their lord for protection. The landlord in Outremer felt no such responsibility. This emerges very clearly from those cases where a village was owned jointly by several lords. Prawer's analysis of charters which laid down the terms on which villages were divided up shows that it was rarely the village population which was shared out and even more infrequently was it the land. The lords divided the income between them; they had no interest in either the land or its inhabitants. The individual lord laid no claim to a share of the estates or to some of the *vilains*, but only to the income that could be derived from them. On Cyprus where the *casalia* were further divided into separate hamlets (*presteries*) about one seventh of the arable land of a *casale* was held in demesne. Here the peasants had to do labour services and thus each *casale* possessed a well-developed administration to supervise the apportionment of the various tasks.

Culturally Frankish society in the East remained basically provincial and thoroughly dependent on Europe.[69] The Islamic influence which was so fruitful in Spain and Sicily was rigidly excluded in Outremer. The Franks coexisted with the Muslims but there was no symbiosis. The number of those from the upper ranks of society who bothered to learn Arabic was tiny. Their everyday language was French; Cyprus developed its own *lingua franca* out of French, Italian, and Greek. Only in superficial matters, dress, medicine, and domestic comforts was there any willingness to learn from Islam. Apart from the chronicle of William of Tyre and the thirteenth-century legal treatises, the Franks contributed little or nothing to the advancement of science and learning in the Middle Ages. This does not mean that the Franks achieved nothing of importance, merely that they hardly developed anything of their own. They were vigorous builders, as we can see not just from the great castles but also from the important additions to the Church of the Holy Sepulchre, from the beautiful Gothic church of St. Andrew in Acre—now to be seen only in a sketch done in 1681—and from the marvellous cathedral of Tortosa which still stands today. French and Venetian builders worked on the cathedral at Tyre; indeed in general it is probable that the artists who worked in the Holy Land were not born there but came from Europe or Byzantium. Five Romanesque capitals in Nazareth which can be dated to the years shortly before 1187 are Burgundian in style; they use scenes from the lives of the apostles to demonstrate the Church's victory over the forces of Satan. An exception to the otherwise purely western architecture was the palace of the Ibelins in Beirut. From the description written in 1213 by an astounded Willibrand of Oldenburg it is clear that it was strongly influenced by Byzantine styles. The front of the palace looked out over the sea; at the back there were orchards. The mosaic floor was ingeniously designed to look like the surface of water lightly rippled by the wind. In the middle of the palace there was a fountain, faced with marble and surmounted by a dragon; its high jet of crystal-clear water helped to keep the rooms cool and moist. It is possible that Frankish architects took over the pointed arch from their Muslim colleagues. The great cistern of Ramleh of 789 was already constructed with a full set of pointed arches and the crusaders must have seen it. Essentially however this question of the borrowing of an architectonic element depends upon the dating of the earliest examples of the pointed arch in the

West—and it is not entirely clear whether these belong to the period before or after the First Crusade. A few years ago the splendid refectory of the Hospitallers at Acre was excavated; it may be that here is one of the very earliest of the known Gothic structures. The coins of Outremer were generally of poor quality; the seals were rather better. There are very few products of Frankish craftsmen still extant; and what does survive may well have been imported from France. None the less in the Dome of the Rock the crusaders have left behind eight wrought iron grilles which are among the finest medieval examples of a smith's work.

The Franks made only a small contribution to literature. At the time of the conquest they destroyed the great Arab library at Tripoli and sold the Jewish library of Jerusalem. But later they did include Arab works in the fine cathedral library built up at Tyre (and certainly also at Jerusalem). William of Tyre, who was born in Palestine, became one of the outstanding historians of the twelfth century; he mentions the kings' interest in reading history. Yet although the crusades added richly to poetry in Europe (*Chanson d'Antioche, Chanson de Jérusalem*), only one such work was actually written in Outremer, the *Chanson des Chétifs*, a product of the court of Antioch at some date before 1149 which celebrated in verse the events of the crusade of 1101.

Book illumination, however, reached an exceedingly high standard in the scriptorium of the Church of the Holy Sepulchre. The liturgical books used by the royal family were produced here—superb luxury editions based on older Byzantine models and influenced by English and Italian styles. In a country as cosmopolitan as Outremer the development of a style was very much a matter of chance and could be independent of the otherwise predominantly French way of life. Even in the Jerusalem of the thirteenth century manuscripts could be illuminated in a truly royal fashion with Byzantine and Latin elements fusing to form a genuinely original style. But after 1244 the only centre for book illumination was Acre; the Arsenal Bible produced there under St. Louis shows that they were still capable of first-class work. After this, however, the art of book illustration becomes ever more provincial and second-rate, though the town nobility were still interested in French historical works and had them illuminated. Also under the nobility's patronage was a dramatic performance in 1286 of scenes from the legend of King Arthur and the Round Table. There were several studios in Acre which produced a large number of icons in the Byzantine fashion. Most of these did not survive the disaster of 1291 but enough were taken by pilgrims to the isolated monastery of St. Catherine in the Sinai for Kurt Weitzmann to be able to trace the existence of this Frankish school of icon painting. From fourteenth-century Cyprus there survive two manuals devoted to the training and veterinary care of falcons—a subject dear to King Fulk in the twelfth century—he had even promulgated a special law to protect these birds.

9 · THE FOURTH CRUSADE (1198–1204) AND FRANKISH GREECE (1204–1311)

THE collapse of the German crusade organized by Emperor Henry VI coincided with an important change on the papal throne. In 1198 Innocent III (d. 1216) was elected pope. He had been carefully educated in theology and canon law. He believed that the papacy should be set above the secular powers and that the pope should be a kind of priest-king. By a vigorous exploitation of the power vacuum created by the death of Henry VI he set out to turn theory into fact. In Innocent III's conception of the world there was no room for crusades directed by kings in which the pope's role was limited to his undisputed right of issuing the summons to a crusade. In his view the whole thing should be under the pope's control. But quite apart from this political objective, Innocent was deeply concerned to re-build the old Latin kingdom of Jerusalem which had been destroyed in 1187 and only very imperfectly restored in 1192. These two themes ran right through his pontificate, but, in pursuing them, Innocent III overlooked the fact that it was no longer possible to finance and lead an army to the East except with the active co-operation of the rulers. The reality of the situation may have been veiled by the fact that the only successful crusade so far had been the First Crusade in which kings had had no share. None the less as a result of the advances made in state organization in the West since 1095 there was now a new reality which ought to have been taken into account. In Innocent III's strivings for a crusade there was this tragic element: that the ecclesiastical form of crusade organization which he established, particularly in the crusading decree of the Fourth Lateran Council, was not in fact an adequate substitute for the power of the state. So Innocent III's crusades either failed or achieved only an apparent success.

In August 1198, soon after he had ascended the papal throne, Innocent proclaimed a new crusade.[70] He concentrated his attention on France, writing to the higher ranks of the clergy and nobility, and on the Italian maritime cities whose fleets were indispensable. The kings were supposed to make peace with one another so that their quarrels would not disturb the preparations for the crusade, but they received no call to take part. Not that Innocent would have tried to prevent them from going on crusade if they had wished, but in fact they were much too absorbed in their own affairs. England and France had their old quarrel, while Germany was divided by the conflicting claims of two rivals for the crown, Philip of Swabia and Otto IV. But in any case the pope was not anxious to see kings taking part and in his proclamation he emphasized the failure of the nationally organized crusades.

In France the crusade was preached with great success up until 1203 by Cardinal-legate Peter Capuano and a parish priest, Fulk of Neuilly (d. 1202). Since 1195 and with ever-growing success Fulk had been active as a preacher. He was a fine figure of a man whose great rhetorical gifts were combined with a well-groomed appearance which made a favourable contrast with some of the unkempt popular preachers of earlier crusades. The content of his sermons was very different too. He was a product of the Paris schools and had begun his preaching career as an advocate of moral reform, fiercely denouncing usury, extravagance, and prostitution. The eschatological motif—with its hope that the end of time was at hand—which had played such a big part in the First Crusade, was pushed into the background and its place was taken by the preaching of a practical code of morals with the accent on a purifying act of penance here and now. Fulk was aided by the movement for apostolic poverty which had grown in strength during the course of the twelfth century and which Innocent III helped to bring within the framework of the Church. Earlier Peter of Blois had, in his disappointment over the delays to the Third Crusade, touched upon themes which were now to be heard more frequently. The rich, headed naturally by the kings, are unworthy of the true atonement and of the Holy Land, their crusades have failed; the true chosen ones are the poor. The idea that everyone is called to the crusade is rejected. Here we can see the effect of the christology of the poverty movement which had been taught by—among others —Peter Cantor, Fulk of Neuilly's old teacher. By the side of St. Paul's very spiritual Christ it set the humble, impoverished, and suffering Christ as the pattern of human behaviour; in place of the anointed Christ it emphasized the naked and defenceless Christ crucified. Like many other ideas for improving the world, the idea that the poor and the pure in spirit were called to free the Holy Land was ethically unobjectionable but completely out of touch with the real world. Less than ever was it now possible to renounce the help of princes. During the period of recruitment for the crusade it became clear that the machinery of the feudal system was needed if a sufficient number of knights were to follow the example of their lords and take the cross. The fact that this crusade was to be diverted from its original goal was in the last resort a consequence of that shortage of money which only the kings could have remedied. And in its noblest and purest form the idea of the poor crusaders led ultimately to the ill-fated children's crusade of 1212.

In 1199, after the first date set for the mustering of an army had come and gone with nothing achieved, the pope, while still continuing with his unremitting preaching of the crusade, tried to help the cause by decreeing a crusading tax of one fortieth on clerical incomes. Although on this occasion he promised that this would not be taken as a precedent for regular papal taxation of clerical incomes, in 1215 he found that he had to resort to this measure again since he had no other means of financing the crusade at his disposal. The Cistercians—the great advocates of the Second Crusade—now refused to pay the tax of 1199. Indeed they accused the pope of persecuting their order and despite the severest pressure, Innocent could do no more than obtain a voluntary contribution from them in return for confirming the principle that they were exempt from such taxation. None the less success now attended his efforts. In November 1199 the first contingents gathered at a tournament in Champagne. Contrary to a widely held opinion there is no evidence for the presence of Fulk of Neuilly at the tournament. Count Theobald of Champagne and Louis of Blois took the cross as also did the marshal of Champagne, Geoffrey de Villehardouin (d. 1213) who became the semi-official historian of the crusade. Equally interesting is the account written by the Picard, Robert de Clari (d. after 1216). He consciously described himself as *pauvre chevalier*—poor knight—thus documenting his adherence to the ideal of poverty. Soon afterwards Count Baldwin of Flanders and Hainault took the crusader's vow. Many nobles of north France followed the example of their lords. The three counts then sent six envoys to Italy to negotiate a treaty about the transport of an army with one of the maritime cities. The negotiations became a milestone in the history of diplomacy. For the first time we hear of plenipotentiaries with complete freedom of action. The envoys had been provided with blank charters sealed in advance by their lords in readiness for the treaty. Even the decision to negotiate with Venice was made by the envoys. The treaty which they then concluded with Doge Enrico Dandolo

(1192–1205) laid down that Venice would provide transport and victuals for a year for 4,500 knights, 9,000 squires and 20,000 foot-soldiers; in addition the city was to take an active part in the crusade by supplying 50 warships. The price for this was fixed at 85,000 marks of silver payable in four instalments. The size of the army was based on estimates made by the envoys—estimates which later proved to be much too high. In a secret clause in the treaty it was decided that the expedition should be directed against Egypt, but both sides agreed that for the moment it would be wiser to allow the crusaders to think that they were going to the Holy Land; difficulties would certainly arise if the truth were known. Yet in fact Egypt was the only sensible target since effective help could not be given to Jerusalem until the centre of Ayubid power in Egypt had been decisively weakened.

Hardly had the envoys returned home with their treaty when Count Theobald of Champagne died. At a meeting at Soissons (June 1201), the barons chose Marquis Boniface of Montferrat as their new leader. The choice of an Italian seems a surprising one even though it was supported by the French king. But for genera-tions the Montferrats had maintained contacts in the East, with both Byzantium and the Holy Land. Unquestionably the family had an 'Oriental tradition'. Whether or not Boniface at this stage voiced his claims to Thessalonika and already intended to fight on Greek soil is uncertain.

In April 1202 the date fixed for the army's departure passed by unheeded. The Burgundians and the men from Provence decided to sail from Marseilles because it was closer and by so doing they weakened the main army. Only the men from north France and a small German contingent led by a Cistercian abbot from Alsace, Martin of Pairis, made their way to Venice. Here they found them-selves in an acutely embarrassing financial position. No more than about 10,000 men had assembled and the Venetians refused to lower their price even though it had been calculated on the basis of an army of 33,500. Despite all their efforts they remained 34,000 marks in debt. At this point the doge suggested a moratorium on their payments if they were prepared to recapture Zara, a city on the Dalmatian coast which the king of Hungary had taken from the Venetians in 1186. The leaders of the crusade had little choice but to comply with this suggestion for otherwise the Venetians would have pressed for immediate payment of the arrears. In the army there were some who protested at what they felt was an unparalleled sin, the attack of a crusading army on a Christian city. But this opposition was overruled and in October 1202 the fleet set sail from Venice. On 24 November Zara was captured, though not before opposition to this turn of events had broken out afresh, led by the Cistercians, under the abbot of Les-Vaux-de-Cernay, and a group of northern French barons under Simon de Montfort. They obtained the pope's support but his intervention proved ineffective. As a result the entire army was excommunicated and only with some difficulty were the French and Germans able to persuade Innocent to lift the sentence on them at least. The Venetians remained excommunicated but the pope omitted to prohibit all human and political contact with them. He still hoped to save his crusade and so he sacrificed principles which ought not to have been given up. The attack on a city of Christian Hungary, whose king was himself preparing to go on crusade, was a most dangerous precedent. Now, as later, the pope's attitude to the Fourth Crusade remained ambiguous. Reluctantly Innocent was forced to reconcile himself to the twists and turns of a crusade which he looked upon as his own. He tried to make the best of every situation and by so doing he had only himself to blame when it became clear that he had laid himself open to the charge that his was the guiding hand behind the diversions of the crusade.

It was now too late in the year to do anything but spend the winter at Zara. The crisis of the crusade came at the turn of the year 1202-3. There arrived some unexpected envoys sent by the German king, Philip of Swabia (1198-1208) and by the pretender to the throne of Byzantium, Alexius IV Angelus. Alexius was the son of that Isaac II Angelus who had been blinded and driven off the throne by his own brother Alexius III. His sister, Irene, was the wife of Philip of Swabia. In 1201 the young Alexius IV managed to escape from a Byzantine prison but Pope Innocent III refused to aid his cause so he naturally turned to his brother-in-law. Philip could not give him any active support; he had just suffered a severe setback in his struggle to win the German crown in the shape of the pope's decision in favour of Otto IV (1198-1218). At this stage someone remembered the crusading army which Alexius had in fact already seen while it was mustering at Venice. So envoys were sent to Zara with the proposal that the army should restore the rightful ruler, Isaac Angelus, to the throne. In return Alexius, with the easy generosity of a pretender, promised the earth: reunion of the Orthodox Church with Rome, huge sums of money for the Venetians and the crusaders and support for the crusade in the shape of 10,000 Byzantine soldiers as soon as he was restored to power. The doge liked the idea and the most powerful leaders of the French signed the treaty—but only twelve barons in all. As an open supporter of the Hohenstaufen cause Boniface of Montferrat was also in favour of accepting the plan. But there was fierce opposition led once again by Simon de Montfort and the abbot of Les-Vaux-de-Cernay who in the course of this winter made the bitter decision to return home. Finally, however, even the bishops were persuaded to agree to the project. In their advocacy of the plan the leading barons made much of the legal argument in favour of a legitimate dynasty, an argument which made a considerable impression on the knights. In suppressing the opposition the ties of feudalism proved to be as effective as the fact that to leave in winter involved great risks. For the mass of the crusaders, as Frolow has rightly observed, there was sufficient bait in the descriptions of the unbelievable quantity of relics which were to be found in Constantinople. This argument appealed not only to the medieval soldier's notorious greed for booty; it also fitted in with the hatred of the Greeks which had been steadily growing in intensity ever since the schism of 1054: the schismatic Byzantines, so it was asserted, were no longer worthy to be custodians of the richest treasure of relics in the world. The work in which Gunther of Pairis describes the journey of Abbot Martin provides ample evidence of this point of view. The opposition was all the more easily overborne because the pope, though he had known of Alexius IV's intentions as early as November 1202, did not protest to the crusaders about the change in their plans until June 1203. By then it was already too late. In April, soon after the arrival of the Byzantine pretender from Germany, the fleet had left Zara. On Corfu half of the army again rebelled against this most unchristian turn of events and Boniface and the Venetians had a great deal of difficulty in preventing the dispersal of the troops. But on 24 June 1203 the fleet dropped anchor at Chalcedon, opposite Constantinople.

An enormous amount of ink has been expended by scholars discussing the diversion of the Fourth Crusade. The question is basically an unfruitful one and will probably never be settled, yet even today there is no sign that the flood of literature on the subject will dry up.[11] The positions taken up by the two sides in the controversy can roughly be characterized as the 'chance theory' (i.e. that it was the result of a series of accidents) and the 'intrigue theory' (i.e. that it was the result of a skilful plot, long prepared). The chance theory is based essentially on Villehardouin's account. Those who hold the intrigue theory—and in the nineteenth century some of them were by no means free of national prejudice—are sceptical of Villehardouin and look for a scapegoat. The debate was opened by Louis de Mas-Latrie in 1861. He accused the Venetians of treachery on the grounds that they had concluded a commercial treaty with Egypt just before the army left Venice. One of the terms of the treaty was supposed to be that they would ensure that the crusade was diverted against Byzantium. This was what was reported by the Cypriot chronicler Ernoul who was writing in the first quarter of the thirteenth century. Ernoul reflected the opinion of the French in Cyprus who were anxious to clear their fellow countrymen from any blame for such a scandalous undertaking. And indeed it is true that the diversion of the crusade fitted in well with the political schemes of the old doge, Enrico Dandolo, a statesman of real stature whose cool assessment of *Realpolitik* meant that he was indifferent to the emotion engendered by the crusading ideal. He was determined to ensure the perpetual dominance of Venice in the Eastern Mediterranean. Although Venice had enjoyed an immensely privileged position within the Byzantine Empire since 1082, her merchants had suffered time and again from violent anti-Latin pogroms, most recently in 1182. Moreover the Byzantine government had tried to free itself from Venetian pressure by granting commercial privileges to her great rivals, Pisa and Genoa. But what cannot be proved is that in the camp at Zara the doge plotted the complete destruction of the Byzantine Empire. In 1867 the anti-Venetian theory gained impressively in weight when no less an authority than Karl Hopf produced details of the negotiations between Egypt and Venice, giving both the names of the envoys and the content of the treaty of 13 May 1202. He did not supply any evidence, however, and a painful shock was to come in 1877 when Hanotaux and Streit, working independently, proved that Hopf's treaty had never existed and that, at best, Hopf had been looking at a treaty which had long been known but which was concluded in 1208, not 1202. This discovery seemed to acquit the Venetians at the right moment, for Count Riant, writing in 1875, had just introduced a new culprit. This time the conspirators were Philip of Swabia and his Ghibelline kinsman, Boniface of Montferrat. It had undoubtedly been Philip who had recommended his brother-in-law, Alexius IV, to the crusaders in the camp at Zara. Clearly then he had something to do with the change of direction but it is very unlikely that there was any skilful and long-prepared plot. Philip was, it is true, the political heir of the old Norman and Hohenstaufen schemes against Byzantium; his own marriage to Irene added to his interest in Byzantine affairs and the family alliance made it likely that he would support the pretender. But it must not be forgotten that at this time Philip was caught up in a life-and-death struggle with Otto IV and Innocent III and that he hardly had time to intervene actively and decisively in the Byzantine question. Indeed he may well have sent his brother-in-law to Zara simply because he could not help him and it was a convenient way of ridding himself of an additional problem—though this, of course, would not exclude the possibility that Philip hoped to gain something later should the expedition succeed.

So far as it is still held today the intrigue theory on the whole tends to hold Philip responsible. The theory, however, depends very much on the question of the date of Alexius IV's arrival—a question which is by no means easy to answer. The Byzantine historian Nicetas reports that Alexius escaped in 1201. Villehardouin appears to date his arrival in Europe to 1202 though recently Jaroslav Folda has observed that Villehardouin does not expressly say that Alexius escaped in 1202, but merely refers to Alexius's flight to Europe during his account of the year 1202 because it was then that the pretender opened negotiations with the crusaders. The other western sources are equally ambiguous. In November 1202 Innocent III wrote that Alexius IV visited him *olim* (i.e. once). H. Gregoire believed that this must have meant 1201, not 1202 at all events, but the argument is over-subtle and presses the source too hard. *Olim* can mean anything from the distant past to the distant future. If Alexius did not reach Italy until 1202 then there is no time for a carefully planned Hohenstaufen conspiracy; if he arrived in 1201 then such a conspiracy is at least possible, though there still remains the need for a satisfactory explanation of Philip's intentions.

Soon after their arrival the crusaders launched an attack on Constantinople. They seized the suburb of Galata and broke the chain which protected the entrance to the harbour of the Golden Horn. On 17 July they attacked Constantinople from both sea and land. The city was saved by the courage of the English and Danish Varangian Guard. But Alexius III lost his head and fled. So now Isaac II Angelus and his son Alexius IV came to the throne as co-emperors. In fact their government was entirely in the hands of the crusaders encamped outside the city. Soon enough it became clear that Alexius did not have a hope of fulfilling the financial obligations incurred in the Treaty of Zara. Since, on the other hand, he was hated by the anti-Latin population of Constantinople his political position rapidly deteriorated. A revolt in January 1204 swept him and his father off their throne. They were both murdered. The new emperor was Alexius V Ducas Murzuphlus

but the crusaders had no intention of putting up with his openly
anti-Latin attitude. They decided to make an end of the venerable
empire of East Rome in deliberate revenge for the Byzantine anti-
Latin pogrom of 1182. In March 1204 they laid the foundation
stone of the new state which was to replace the old empire by
drawing up a treaty in which they made detailed provision for its
constitution.

This time the city was stormed with more success. On 12 April
1204 the crusaders won control of the walls; on 13 April it was all
over. For three indescribable days Constantinople was given over
to killing and looting. Countless irreplaceable works of art were
destroyed by a barbaric mob of soldiers. The most splendid article
of plunder was the famous sixth century Quadriga which the
Venetians took home with them and which today still adorns the
facade of St. Mark's. For the relic hunter it was the chance of a
lifetime. Gunther of Pairis, with naive openness, describes how
Abbot Martin threatened to kill a Greek priest from the Church
of the Pantocrator until he was shown a hoard of relics which
impressed him more deeply than all the treasures of Greece.
'Quickly and greedily he plunged both hands in and, girding up
his loins, he filled the folds of his gown with the holy booty of the
Church which, laughing happily, he then carried back to the ship.'
Gunther's list of these relics suggests that Abbot Martin must
have been a very powerfully-built man for his loot included a
trace of the blood of the Lord, a piece of the True Cross, quite a
considerable part of St. John, an arm of St. James, a foot of St.
Cosmas, a tooth of St. Laurence, relics of a further twenty-eight
male and eight female saints, not to mention fragments, mostly of
stone, from sixteen holy places. Many relics now to be found in
France were also taken from Constantinople in 1204.[72] While
Villehardouin boasted that never before was so rich a haul taken
from a single city, another eyewitness, the Byzantine chronicler
Nicetas, his own life saved by the kindness of a friend, a Venetian
merchant, penned a moving lament on the fall of Constantinople,
a document of helplessness and impotent rage, a rhetorical masterpiece richly studded with quotations from the Book of Job and the
Lamentations of Jeremiah. In the conquest of Constantinople the
Latin hatred of the Greeks which had been growing steadily ever
since the First Crusade, celebrated its greatest and most disgraceful
triumph.

In accordance with the terms of the treaty of March 1204 the
Byzantine Empire was dismembered methodically and in cold
blood; here the calculating hand of Venetian policy is evident.[73]

Those Venetian claims on the crusaders which were still outstanding were met by a grant of three quarters of the plunder.
Then, as was laid down, an electoral council of six Venetians and
six Frenchmen met to choose a new emperor. The united Venetian
front had no difficulty in blocking the candidature of Boniface of
Montferrat and obtaining instead the election of the weaker Baldwin of Flanders (1204-5). On 16 May Baldwin was crowned in the
Hagia Sofia as first emperor of Romania, the Latin Empire of
Constantinople. The coronation service, though Byzantine in its
magnificence, was celebrated according to the Latin rites; afterwards, following Byzantine custom, the emperor signed his charters
in red ink. He was to enjoy, however, only a shadow of the full-
ness of power once possessed by his Byzantine predecessors. Right
at the outset the terms of the treaty of 1204 deprived him of any
real power by excluding him from the distribution of the six
hundred or so fiefs and thus preventing him from building up any
dynastic wealth. The distribution was carried out by a commission composed equally of Venetians and Frenchmen. In accordance with the terms of the treaty the emperor received the
palaces of Blachernae and Bucoleon in Constantinople as well as
a quarter of the empire: Thrace and north-west Asia Minor,
Lesbos, Chios, and Samos. Boniface of Montferrat had originally
laid claim to Asia Minor but instead he went on to found, despite
many difficulties, the kingdom of Thessalonika, consisting of
Macedonia and Thessaly; here most of the new ruling class were
Lombards. The Venetians were realistic enough to take only as
much of their share as they reckoned they could hold. Thus they
renounced Epirus and Morea (the Peloponnese) but took the
Adriatic coast, some ports on the west coast of the Peloponnese,
the Ionian Isles, and bases on the Archipelago. Here in 1207
Marco Sanudo was to found a duchy of the Archipelago with Naxos
and Andros as its centres and with suzerainty over the Cyclades.
Euboea became a Venetian protectorate where the *baillis* of Negroponte exercised authority over their Lombard vassals in the name
of Venice. Venice bought out Boniface's claims to Crete which, as
Candia, was to remain a Venetian outpost in the eastern Mediterranean until 1669. The most important harbours on the Hellespont
and the Sea of Marmora also went to the Venetians; so did three-
eighths of the city of Constantinople including St. Sophia in a new
division of the empire drawn up in October 1204. The Venetians
now had absolute control of the sea route between Venice and
Byzantium. A Venetian colonial empire had been created which
was to last until it was overrun by the expanding might of the

Ottomans in the sixteenth century. This empire was ruled by a Venetian *podestà* assisted by a council; after some early difficulties it remained firmly under the control of the republic of San Marco. In October 1205 a third treaty laid down the amount of military service which the Venetians owed to the empire and set up a kind of council of state composed of both Frenchmen and Venetians under the presidency of the emperor. The three treaties of March and October 1204 and October 1205 remained the backbone of the constitution; before he was crowned each new emperor had to swear to observe them. According to the *Assises de Romanie*, the law of Jerusalem was adopted by the Latin Empire but in fact this is only a later legend. It seems probable that unwritten customary law prevailed through the empire. In fact the interests of the emperor, the powerful feudal nobility, and Venice were so much at variance that the constitution only served to hasten the steady decline of the state.

The 'crusade' was at an end; no one spoke of sending help to the Holy Land. The conquerors settled down to life in their new land. The pope and the West were at first delighted by the news of the fall of Constantinople, the *civitas diu profana*. But when the pope heard of the atrocities of the sack he was deeply shocked. Even so, he was able to reconcile himself to the *fait accompli*. He was enough of an optimist to hope that a strong Frankish state in Greece would be of great assistance to the *terra sancta*. Moreover he could look forward to the long desired union of the Greek Orthodox Church with Rome. But it was entirely contrary to canon law when the cathedral chapter of St. Sophia was filled with Venetians—in accordance with the treaty of March 1204 which gave this privilege to Venice if the new emperor was chosen from among the Franks. Despite all papal efforts, the office of the Latin patriarch of Constantinople was from now on a benefice securely in the hands of the Venetians. In formal terms the union was achieved but it was always a hated union imposed by force. The Greeks remained intransigent in faith and ritual; they were merely made to accept a jurisdictional subordination. Most of the Greek prelates were replaced by Latins and the traditional hierarchy was drastically altered, generally for financial reasons, when bishoprics were changed, re-sited or newly founded. Later the Cistercians and the new Franciscan Order established houses in Greece. The most difficult question was the problem of the Church estates. The treaty of 1204 assigned the Church barely enough to exist; everything else was declared to be plunder. Outside Constantinople the Church had originally been granted one fifteenth of the land in the empire; finally in 1219 after various compromises it was fixed at one eleventh. Similar agreements had already been reached in north and central Greece (1210); in 1223 a settlement was reached in south Greece. The Latin inhabitants had to pay tithes; the Greeks were allowed to pay only one thirtieth in the hope of making the union more acceptable to them.

Thanks to the vigour and energy of the new king of Thessalonika (though this was a title which he never used officially), new Frankish principalities, loosely subordinate to the feudal authority of the emperor, rose in central and southern Greece. In Attica there was the duchy of Athens (the ducal title was official after 1280) under the Burgundian Otto de la Roche; on the peninsula of Morea there was the very French principality of Achaia under first William de Champlitte and then the house of Villehardouin. The surviving Byzantines grouped themselves in three centres where the traditions of the ruined empire were kept alive. Relatively insignificant was the empire of Trebizond on the Black Sea, ruled by Comneni until it was absorbed by the empire of Nicaea. Nicaea, with its centre of power in Bithynia, was governed by the Lascarid dynasty. In north Greece there was the despotate of Epirus under the Angeloi. The Franks now had to face these three states as well as the Bulgars, the old enemies of Byzantium. Their first clash with the Bulgars ended in disaster at the Battle of Adrianople in 1205. The emperor was captured and never seen again. Soon afterwards Doge Enrico Dandolo died and was buried in St. Sophia. Baldwin's brother Henry became regent and then emperor (1206–16). He was the only effective ruler in the history of Romania. He saw rightly that his own power would be secure only if he was able to destroy the empire of Nicaea in Asia Minor. But at first he was himself almost completely driven out of Asia Minor and not until 1211 could he defeat the Lascarid emperor. Then, in the peace of 1214, he was at least able to restore the *status quo* of 1204 which left the north-western corner of Asia Minor in the hands of the Latins. Earlier he had been distracted by clashes with the Lombard barons of Thessalonika but by about 1210 he managed to settle things satisfactorily. His policy towards the Greeks was one of reconciliation.

Under his weak successors the Latin Empire went inexorably downhill. The vassal states became, to all intents and purposes, independent and the empire was thrown back on its own resources. Henry's successor, Peter of Courtenay, count of Auxerre (1216–19), did not even enter his dominions, being captured while he was still on his way to Constantinople. After a brief period of rule by his wife Yolande, the crown passed to his second son Robert. During Robert's reign the kingdom of Thessalonika was lost. Boniface of Montferrat had fallen in battle in 1207 and his young son Demetrius was unable to defend his realm against the violent assaults launched by the ruler of Epirus, Theodore Angelus Ducas Comnenus (1224–30) whose three imperial names were programmatic. In 1224, after the loss of his capital, Demetrius fled to Italy.

In Nicaea the fight against the Latins was taken up by Emperor John III Vatatzes (1222–54), a most able and economical ruler. In the peace of 1225 he forced the Latins to evacuate almost the whole of Asia Minor. His armies marched to Thrace and Adrianople. He was threatening to take Constantinople when his advance was halted by the ruler of Epirus who had ambitions of his own in Thrace and who drove back the Nicaean army at Adrianople. The Latin Empire was saved by John II Asen, King of the Bulgars, when he broke the power of Epirus once and for all in 1230. From then on the empire was at his mercy. Robert de Courtenay was succeeded by his eleven-year-old brother, Baldwin II (1228–61; after 1261 he was emperor in name only until his death in 1273). Baldwin II was the only Latin emperor to be born in Constantinople and for this reason he assumed the old Byzantine title *Porphyrogenitus* (born in the purple). In 1231, in an attempt to gain some relief from the pressure exerted by the Bulgars, the barons chose as co-emperor the titular king of Jerusalem, John of Brienne, who had earlier lost his kingdom in the Holy Land to the Emperor Frederick II. In 1236 John put up a stout defence against a menacing Bulgarian-Nicaean coalition but in the end it was only the disunity of the allies which saved the situation. When John died in 1237 the empire was completely surrounded by Nicaean territory and consisted of little more than Constantinople itself. After the death of John Asen II in 1241 the emperor of Nicaea was left as the only serious contender for mastery over the Byzantine Empire which John Vatatzes and his successors laboured to revive. Thus Nicaea also became the seat of the exiled Greek Church. The position of the Latin Empire became ever more hopeless. No help from the West was forthcoming even though Gregory IX (1227–41) was prepared to accept participation in the struggle in Greece as a satisfactory fulfilment of crusading vows. The ruler of Constantinople lived in abject poverty. Probably there was no emperor or king who was ever so short of money. For years he travelled the world from England to the Nile in order to raise cash by selling both his European estates and precious relics from Constantinople. Even the Crown of Thorns was pawned to the

Venetians to be redeemed in 1238 by Saint Louis of France and taken to the Sainte Chapelle in Paris. When all the relics had gone and the lead from the roof of the imperial palace had been sold, the emperor even pawned his son Philip for an advance of about 400,000 marks. This debt was redeemed by King Alfonso X of Castile. But Baldwin II was never able to organize the crusade he hoped for. Politically he remained utterly dependent on financial and moral support from France. Ethnically Romania was very much a French empire; as early as 1224 Pope Honorius III had called it *Nova Francia*. Baldwin received little or no help from the German Emperor whose quarrel with the pope led him to keep on good terms with the emperor of Nicaea. Even Pope Innocent IV (1243-54) was no longer prepared to back Constantinople; on the question of Church union he negotiated directly with Nicaea. It is one of the ironies of history that it took the fall of the Latin Empire to open the way to union. This was finally accomplished under Pope Gregory X in 1274 when Charles of Anjou was threatening to establish a new Latin Empire in Byzantium. It lasted only until 1282 however and was as ineffective in practice as the union of 1439 which was worked out at the Council of Ferrara-Florence in response to Turkish pressure.

The end of Latin rule in Constantinople came suddenly. One of the Nicaean commanders while marching past the city on his way to Thrace discovered that the Latins were relying on a truce and were in no state to defend themselves. Without hesitation on 25 July 1261 he took the city. On 15 August Michael VIII Palaeologus (1259-82), the first of a dynasty which was to rule Byzantium until 1453, made his entrance into Constantinople. Baldwin II fled to Europe. Earlier in 1261, on 13 March, Michael had concluded the Treaty of Nymphaeum with the Genoese, giving them privileges as valuable as those enjoyed by Venice. The Venetian monopoly position in the eastern Mediterranean collapsed together with the Latin Empire. The Treaty of Nymphaeum proved to be the foundation-stone of a Genoese colonial empire with its chief bases at Pera (on the Golden Horn) and at Caffa on the Black Sea and Asov on the Sea of Asov. For this reason the treaty led to a series of wars with Venice which lasted for more than a hundred years until, in 1381, Genoa conceded defeat at the Peace of Turin. Even so, by the middle of the fourteenth century the Ligurian republic had been able to extend its rule over the Byzantine islands of Chios, Lesbos, and Samos.

In the end it was the Peloponnese principality of Achaia which proved to be the most important Frankish state founded in

Greece.[74] It was not until after the death of Prince Geoffrey I Villehardouin (1209–?29)—a nephew of the historian—that this became really clear as a result of the fall of the kingdom of Thessalonika in 1224. The rule of Geoffrey II (1229?–46) was marked by internal development and good government. His revenues enabled him to give forceful support to the Latin emperor during the wars of 1236 and 1238 against John III Vatatzes of Nicaea. The island county of Cephalonia, previously in the Venetian sphere of influence, now became a fief of Achaia. A knightly tour to Morea became fashionable for the young gentlemen of France who wished to learn the chivalric virtues for it was believed that nowhere could this be done better than at the prince's court of Andravida in western Elis. The highpoint of Achaian history came during the reign of Prince William II Villehardouin (1246–78). He conquered the rest of the peninsula of Morea, built one of the strongest fortresses in the land at Mistra, near the ancient Sparta, and accompanied Louis IX of France on his first crusade to the Holy Land. From Louis he received licence to mint money on the pattern of the French royal coins. The duchy of the Archipelago, the duchy of Athens, and the lordship of Negroponte were brought to recognize the feudal suzerainty of Achaia.

Achaia was now the centre of Frankish Greece. As a result of its geographical isolation the interior of the state became steadily feudalized. It was ruled by customary law which remained uncodified until the *Assises de Romanie* (*c.* 1320). This law did not, despite the assurances of the author of the *Assises*, come to Achaia from Jerusalem by way of the Latin Empire. Jerusalem lent no more than the lustre of its name and a few formulae. The importance of the principality can be judged from the fact that in its heyday Achaia and the states under its lordship contained about 1,000 knight's fees. In Achaia itself there were about 600 fees. At the apex of the feudal pyramid stood the prince, bound to observe feudal custom and dependent on his vassals on matters of taxation and procedural law. But the moral authority and thus the real power of the dynasty was far greater than in Jerusalem. The bulk of the prince's estates lay in the west of Morea together with his capital and the economic centre of Glarentza. His household was controlled by the constable and the marshal (both hereditary offices), by the logothete (chancellor), the treasurer, and the protovestiarios (chamberlain) who farmed out the prince's revenues to tax collectors and kept the register of fiefs for which there is evidence from 1209 onwards. Despite the fact that some of the titles were Greek the structure of the state was thoroughly western.

Four castellans administered the prince's family land and special officials (*enquêteurs*) supervised the administration of the barons (*bers de terre*). The dozen or so barons were ranked as peers and exercised blood justice. Their baronies varied in size between four and twenty-four knight's fees, of which about one third were subinfeudated while the rest formed the baronial demesne from which the baron met his own obligation to provide military service. Below the barons came the mass of liege vassals who only possessed jurisdiction over minor criminal offences. The service they owed was strenuous: four months service in the field and four months garrison duty; only for the remaining four months of the year could these knights stay at home on their own estates. Below them came the ordinary fief holders who enjoyed no more than civil jurisdiction over their own peasants. In arranging the marriages of their daughters they were subject to the consent of their lord and they were obliged to pay a special tax (*collecte*) in order to meet the cost of the prince's ransom or the dowry of his daughter. The amount of military service which they owed was in each case laid down in the charter of enfeoffment. Socially inferior to the ordinary fief holders, but in material terms more or less their equals were the *Archontes*, the old Byzantine magnates and pronoiars who were especially numerous in the mountainous interior and who had resisted until they themselves were incorporated into the western feudal system. Finally there were the non-noble Frankish sergeants who held only half a knight's fee. The custom of primogeniture applied to all fiefs, with both female and collateral heirs enjoying the right to inherit, preference going to the nearest relative even if his claim was through the female line. In contrast to Jerusalem, widows here could choose their own husbands. Agriculture was chiefly in the hands of *vilains*, a term which conceals the fact that they were the descendants of the Byzantine *paroikos*. They were tied to the land, *stasis* as it was called, and they owed their lord fixed dues as well as labour services on his demesne. In return for this they could not be dispossessed of their *stasis*.

The period of peace which had been enjoyed by Achaia came to an end about 1255. William II broke with Venice over a dispute about the inheritance to a Euboean fief and the whole of Frankish Greece became involved in the war which followed. (It was known as the *Guerre des tierciers de l'Eubée* because the lords of Euboea called themselves the *terzieri* in consequence of the island being divided into three large fiefs.) In the end William won this war. But then, in 1259, while fighting together with his allies Manfred of Sicily and Michael II of Epirus against Michael VIII Palaeologus, he was taken prisoner when the forces of Epirus changed sides during the decisive battle. He was not freed until 1262 after the restoration of the Byzantine Empire; in return he had to cede Monembasia and Mistra to Byzantium and acknowledge Greek overlordship. Not long after his return home he took up the fight again. This time he looked for help from Charles of Anjou who became lord of South Italy and Sicily as a result of his victory over Manfred at the Battle of Benevento in 1266. By the Treaty of Viterbo William granted Achaia and its dependencies to Charles while reserving the usufruct to himself for life. He was then to be succeeded by Charles's son Philip who married William's daughter Isabella. From now on Achaia was just an Angevin dependency, occasionally left to its own devices when the Angevins had more important matters to think about. It was largely thanks to the aid provided by Angevin money and troops, however, that Achaia held out against Michael VIII Palaeologus. The days of Frankish independence were gone. In this way Achaia was able to buy a period of peace for its most important northern and western parts, but it could not prevent the Byzantines driving a deep wedge in the south as far as Laconia and Arcadia. Since Philip of Anjou died in 1277, one year before William II, the next prince of Achaia was Charles of Anjou. But in 1282 his ambitious eastern plans were brought to nothing by the Sicilian Vespers, the revolt of the Italians against the hated French rule. Charles (d. 1285) managed to hold on to Naples but Sicily fell to Peter III of Aragon. Charles's son, Charles II of Anjou, was kept fully occupied by the struggle against Aragon and he was, in any event, a weak ruler. In 1289 he granted Achaia as an Angevin fief to William's daughter, Isabella. She married Florence of Hainault (1289-97). Nominally Achaia was independent again but the frequent interventions of Charles II show that Angevin predominance was still very much a reality. Thanks to his sensible policy towards Byzantium Florence enjoyed a peaceful reign in which some of the chivalrous splendour of earlier years was revived. Isabella's next husband, however, Philip of Savoy (1301-6), was an overbearing man who earned the dislike of both the native aristocracy and Charles II of Anjou. In 1306 Charles deposed him for a felony (breach of faith) and granted Achaia to his own son Philip of Taranto, the 'Despot of Romania'. The disaster which befell Athens in 1311 (see below) also had an effect on Achaia. The French ruling class was almost completely replaced by Italians; Italian became the language of the country. The principality went down amidst the growing complexity of the tangled Balkan policies of Venice, Byzantium, and the Ottomans. It became smaller and smaller in size until in 1432 it succumbed to the Greek despot of Morea; soon afterwards it was taken over by the Turks.

In Athens the last duke from the Burgundian house of de la Roche died in 1308. He was succeeded by Walter of Brienne, count of Lecce, who then lost his duchy to one of the most adventurous bands of brigands ever to plague Europe. A former Templar named Roger Flor (d. 1305) had founded the Catalan Company, a kind of itinerant republic, out of Catalan, Aragonese, and Navarrese mercenaries. For many years the company fought in South Italy in the service of Aragon against the Angevins of Naples.[75] When it became redundant as a result of the Peace of Caltabellotta (1302), Roger and his 6,500 men took up an offer of employment made by the Byzantine emperor, Andronicus II Palaeologus (1282–1328) who could see no other way of defending himself against the Turks in Asia Minor who, in their turn, were retreating before the western advance of the Mongols. But the Catalans themselves soon proved to be a menace to an empire which was badly shaken by both internal and external pressures. In 1305 they began to make war on Byzantium from their base at Gallipoli. First they plundered Thrace. Then in 1309 they turned their attention to Thessaly. In 1311, when this province too had been reduced to poverty, they overran the duchy of Athens. Catalan took the place of French as the vernacular; the *Assises de Romanie* gave way to the customary law of Barcelona. From their base at Thebes a band of Catalan brigands now ruled a considerable part of southern Greece. The allegiance which they owed to the kings of Aragon and Sicily who appointed a non-resident duke from 1312 onwards, was purely nominal. Even after Thebes itself fell to a Navarrese Company in 1379, they still remained in control of Athens with its mighty fortress on the Acropolis where the Propylaeum served as a palace and the Parthenon as the Church of St. Mary. In 1388 the Florentine banking house of the Acciajuoli came to power in Athens and ruled as dukes, sometimes subject to the Turks, sometimes to Byzantium, until 1456 when the Ottomans took over for good.

Most of the islands held out longer against the Turks. Negroponte became Venetian in 1366 and remained so until 1477. The Sanudo and then the Crispo families ruled Naxos until 1539 and Andros until 1566. In 1304 a Genoese dynasty established itself on Chios and in 1366 the island became a Genoese dependency, remaining so until 1566. Its economic importance was assured by the mastic monopoly held by the Giustiniani family. Lesbos was a Genoese duchy from 1355 to 1462; Rhodes was held by the Hospitallers from 1309 to 1522. The last of the islands to fall to the Ottomans was Crete in 1669.

10 · THE CHILDREN'S CRUSADE OF 1212 AND THE CRUSADE AGAINST DAMIETTA (1217–1221)

ALTHOUGH the outcome of the Fourth Crusade might have been expected to produce a cooling-off in enthusiasm for the crusade in Europe during the period of the establishment of the Frankish states in Greece, no such development in fact occurred. On the contrary the precedent of a crusade against Christians was followed by a period of considerable crusading activity within Europe itself. In 1212 the kings of Castile, Aragon, and Navarre defeated the Muslim Almohads in the Battle of Las Navas de Tolosa. It was the greatest victory so far in the *Reconquista* and was won with the assistance of an officially approved crusade. More important were the Albigensian Crusades 1209–29.[76] During the course of the twelfth century the Albigensians, heretics who had taken up the dualist doctrine of the Cathars, had made an increasing number of converts in Western Languedoc. Innocent III hesitated at first but then ordered the preaching of a crusade against their protector, Raymond VI of Toulouse. Owing to the fanaticism of the papal legate and the military commander, Simon de Montfort, the crusade degenerated into a humiliating scandal, all the more disgraceful in that it was precisely the Second Crusade which had encouraged the spread of this heresy outside the Balkans. The Albigensian Crusade became a power struggle for control of a Pyrenean kingdom consisting of Catalonia and south France. In the Peace of Paris (1229) the Capetian monarchy emerged as the real victor and began at once with the work of assimilating Languedoc into the French kingdom. The Albigensian heresy, though not entirely eradicated, was reduced to insignificance and the Church of Rome's hold on south France was assured. It is impossible to escape the fact that the original crusading ideal had been perverted by being used to justify war against Christians even if they were heretics. The canonical justification for this extension of the crusade which was later worked out by the canonist Hostiensis did not alter the situation. The same applies to the whole series of political crusades launched by the thirteenth-century papacy against its Hohenstaufen enemies in south Italy. Here it was not even heretics who were preached against but orthodox Christians. What was right for the head of the Church was just for its members. Thus the archbishop of Bremen had the Stedinger peasants branded as heretics in order to be able to launch a crusade which quite clearly served no purpose except the political aims of Bremen and which finally sealed the fate of peasant freedom in the Weser marshland as a result of the defeat of the Stedinger in the battle of Altenesch in 1234. The secular arm also played a part in these events since it was the recently tightened up heresy legislation of Frederick II which provided the legal basis for the dispossession of the Stedinger which was then carried through on a massive scale. But lack of space means that none of these expeditions can be examined at all closely; this applies equally to the 'crusades' against the Slavs mounted by the Teutonic Order in Prussia after 1226 in a style similar to that already used for the conquest of Livonia after 1184 by the north-German crusaders known as the Brethren of the Sword.

The children's crusade of 1212, however, cannot be passed over.[77] Probably it began in the Rhineland and Lower Lorraine. In the spring of that year large crowds of ten- to eighteen-year-old children gathered together with a sprinkling of adults and a few clerics. Their leader was a boy from Cologne called Nicholas whom they venerated and whose promises they believed. Asked where they were marching to, they replied 'To God'. Their goal was clear. They intended to capture the Holy Sepulchre and thus accomplish the task which had proved too much for the mighty of this world. Only to the rationalist is it inconceivable that they should fall victim to the erroneous notion that they could achieve this unarmed and deficient in both money and organization. The children themselves were absolutely confident. The year 1212 was a time when religious enthusiasm was at a height, whipped up everywhere by the encouragement to fanaticism which was contained in the preaching against the Albigensians. In addition there were more profound psychological causes. Children's 'crusades' were not entirely unprecedented. In earlier years there had been penitential movements which had seen the path to salvation in the work of helping to build a great cathedral like Chartres. Among these movements there had been groups made up entirely of children under the leadership of youthful miracle-workers. In north France and elsewhere at this date there was a deeply felt reverence for the Innocents, the children of Bethlehem murdered on Herod's orders, who were represented on this earth by the youngest members of the Church, the children. On Innocents' Day (28 December) the children were accustomed to choose and consecrate their own child-bishop. In the idea that the innocent children were specially chosen we can see one of the roots of the naive believe that they, the poorest and the purest, would be able—though unarmed—to recapture Jerusalem. The children's crusade marked both the triumph and the failure of the ideal of poverty.

Neither the ecclesiastical nor the secular authorities took sufficient trouble to disperse the children. Only the French king seems to have persuaded a large group of children to go home. This French group was led by Stephen, a boy from the Vendômois, to whom Christ was said to have appeared in a vision in the guise of a poor pilgrim bearing one of those highly popular letters from heaven. Fired with enthusiasm the children marched to St. Denis; whether or not they intended to go on to Jerusalem is uncertain. On the whole it is true that the comments of the ecclesiastical chroniclers on the children's crusade were acid; the majority of educated adults can have been under no illusions about its chance of success. But no effective steps were taken to prevent the departure of the unfortunate children. Where the clergy did oppose it they were held back by an over-enthusiastic laity. None the less the enterprise never enjoyed the official blessing of the Church so it was not, technically, a crusade.

Early in July the main body of children set out and, led by Nicholas, marched up the Rhine and then over the Alps to Italy. On 25 August they reached Genoa. Despite their losses *en route* they were still said to number 7,000. But at Genoa there were disappointments. The expected miracle failed to materialize; God did not allow them to walk across the sea. The Lombards, who had followed the march with much greater scepticism than the Germans, refused to supply them with ships. What happened next is unknown. According to one report, some of the children sailed in two ships from Pisa and were never heard of again. Others are supposed to have gone to Rome to seek the pope's release from the vows in which—even though this was not an official crusade—they were caught. But even the pope could only free those who, in any case, were not yet old enough to swear valid oaths. A few are said to have got as far as Brindisi, but the rest marched back over the Alps in November and, exhausted and disappointed, made their way home, now mocked by the very same people who had greeted them with such joy on the way out. Alberic of Troisfontaines mentions another group who left the main body and made their way down the Rhône valley to Marseilles, but confuses them with the group led by Stephen. His account is full of legends and is based entirely on a story allegedly told by a man who returned home after eighteen years as a slave in the East. But it contains some facts which can be confirmed from other sources and thus at least a grain of truth. According to Alberic two Marseilles merchants provided seven ships for the children. Two of the ships were wrecked off Sardinia, while the passengers on the other five were sold in the slave markets of North Africa and Egypt. After the miserable failure of an enterprise begun with so much fervour the chroniclers had little trouble in pointing to the absence of any help from God in order to brand the whole crusade as the work of the Devil. Behind this explanation there are clear signs of an uneasy conscience.

But the papacy too was preparing for a new crusade. Innocent III must have been hit hard by the way in which the Fourth Crusade had so completely slipped from out of his control for since the time of Urban II there had been no pope who had fought more keenly to make the crusade an ecclesiastical and specifically a papal enterprise. Besides he was genuinely determined to help the Holy Land and had hoped that the elimination of the Byzantine Empire would bring about this result as well as a union of the Churches. Instead, knightly families emigrated from Palestine and Syria and settled in the newly founded Frankish states in Greece —states which were at a safe distance from the forces of Islam. Inevitably Innocent became convinced that when secular powers like Venice or the Hohenstaufen exercised considerable influence over the course of a crusade there was little chance that it would be of any help to the Holy Land, to the crusading ideal, or to the political objectives of the papacy. From this point of view alone more vigorous papal leadership of future crusades was clearly called for. Moreover the children's crusade had shown that there was still an untapped reservoir of popular support for a war for the faith which, if it were possible, under papal leadership, to guide into the right channels, might well be used to the advantage of the Holy Land and the Church. Nor should it be overlooked that to Innocent a crusade was an essential means of realizing his hierarchical ideas. Like Frederick II after him he saw that high reputation and the support of public opinion—and thus political leadership—would belong to the man who could both make himself champion of the crusading ideal and bring such an enterprise to a triumphant conclusion.

After the bitter lessons of the early period of his pontificate, in his later years Innocent pursued his goal unwaveringly. In 1213, with the bull *Quia maior*, he opened a vigorous campaign for a new crusade.[78] The incident which gave him his opportunity, the fortification of Mount Tabor in Galilee by the Ayubids, was not in itself important; it carried no special threat to the crusader states. But the European political situation was favourable to the pope's aims. The kings of England and France were caught up in a murderous war, on the outcome of which depended the existence of the French monarchy and the Angevin continental possessions. This was decided at the Battle of Bouvines in 1214. Closely tied up with the Anglo–French conflict was the equally momentous struggle for the German crown between Frederick II and the Welf, Otto IV. Thus there could be no question of the kings taking part in the projected crusade. This was just as Innocent wanted it; his summons was sent to all the peoples of Christendom. *Quia maior* calls for the participation of all Christians irrespective of rank or ability; in Alphandéry's phrase, the bull authorized a kind of *levée en masse*. Spiritual as well as material weapons were to be used. The pope ordered that processions should be held monthly in order to intercede for the deliverance of the Holy Land. In this way even the poorest and weakest were given a part to play in the war against Islam. Innocent can have had few doubts about the successful outcome of his plan; he was filled with the quiet certainty that, as was promised in the Book of Revelation, the days of Islam were numbered. (Revelation 13:18: the number of the Beast is 666, i.e. Islam would last at most 666 years and, reckoning from its inception in A.D. 622, that meant that its end would come in 1288 at the latest.)

In order to make provision for the organization of the crusade, the pope called a council for 1215. But the preachers were at work as early as 1213. In France the outstanding preacher was the legate, Robert of Courçon. He and the pope had been fellow-students. His actions made crystal clear the intention behind *Quia maior*. He distributed the cross to all—to children, to old men and women, to the blind and the leprous. Despite the success of his preaching there was some opposition from the clergy, whom he wished to reform, and from the feudal nobility, whose jurisdiction he wished to limit in the interest of the Church. Even the pope had to disavow some of his actions. Nor could the king afford to keep silent. In evident rejection of the one-sided claims to leadership made by the Church, a royal decree of March 1215 regulated the legal standing of crusaders. In north-west Germany, Flanders, and Holland the preaching of Oliver, the master of the cathedral

school of Cologne, met with a great response. But together with
the success went an increasing amount of criticism. This is suggested by the fact that it was found advisable to supervise the
preaching more strictly. A kind of propaganda office was envisaged
for each diocese; from here the preachers were provided with collections of papal and other letters which gave them the arguments
they needed to make their work effective; the collection known as
the Rommersdorf Letterbook was one of these.[79] Soon overall
control of crusade propaganda was made the responsibility of a
newly established department of the curia, the penitentiary, which
had already been assigned the job of dealing with the steadily
growing volume of business concerning dispensations. The connection between the crusades and the penitential system could
hardly be made clearer.

The pope saw that a new organization was needed if the kings—
together with their financial resources—were to be excluded from
the crusading movement. It was to meet this need that he called
the Fourth Lateran Council. In November 1215 1,300 prelates
assembled at Rome; as a muster of the *ecclesia militans* it was most
impressive. They debated the problem of heresy, settled the fate of
the county of Toulouse which had been conquered during the
Albigensian Crusade, formulated the doctrine of transubstan-
tiation, and set limits to the translation of the Bible into the vernacular. But Innocent's chief concern was the crusade. A special
decree was issued in which every aspect of the crusade was dealt
with. The development of the papal doctrine of the crusade had
now reached its climax. Later (*c.* 1250) this doctrine was fully
interpreted and given a thorough legal underpinning by the
famous canonist Hostiensis, first of all in his *Summa aurea* and
then in his main work, the *Lectura*.[80] It was intended that the
crusaders would muster in June 1217 in the south-Italian ports of
Brindisi and Messina, where the pope himself wished to bless the
fleets. Clerks who accompanied the crusade were to be released
from their residential obligations i.e. they could continue to enjoy
their revenues even while they were away on crusade. All prelates
were to see that crusading vows were properly kept; if necessary
they were to enforce them by use of the weapons of excommunication or even interdict. A man who did not go himself was at least
to equip others for three years. Because the sea-route was now
regarded as the only possible way to transport large armies to the
East, shipbuilders were given special privileges. The curia promised to contribute 30,000 pounds of silver to the crusade itself
and it imposed a three-year tax of one twentieth of their income

on the whole clergy with the cardinals having to pay as much as one tenth. Those who sold strategic material to the Saracens were threatened with excommunication; confiscation of their property and enslavement was laid down for those who entered the service of Islam as freebooters. For the next four years the entire Levant trade was prohibited in order to ensure that there would be enough transport ships available when needed. All crusaders were exempted from taxes and tolls and were placed under the protection of the Apostolic See until their return or until the arrival of reliable news of their death. There was to be a moratorium on their debts. Christendom was bidden to remain at peace for the next four years.

Particularly momentous was the decree, now approved for the first time by a council, though it had been proclaimed by the pope as early as 1198, that a man who equipped another man should receive the same plenary indulgence as a genuine crusader. In the interests of sound finance this decree was probably as unavoidable as the taxation of the clergy; nevertheless it was a distortion of the original crusading ideal. From here it was but a short step to the commutation of crusading vows in return for a straight money payment. Taken together with a development which was, in itself, admirable—the organization of the Apostolic Chamber and the collectorates into a model of bureaucratic efficiency—this meant that the door was wide open for all kinds of abuses in the financial administration of the curia and the Church—the abuses which were to culminate in the intolerable pre-Reformation traffic in indulgences. Indeed as early as the thirteenth century the popes, often with the thinnest of arguments, were to elevate their Italian wars against the Hohenstaufen to the status of crusades in order to be able to use crusading taxes to meet the costs of their campaigns. But secular rulers also took advantage of the system. By taking the cross, but without ever actually fulfilling their vow, they could time and again have the income from crusading taxes assigned to them. Haakon V of Norway did this three times. Finally Boniface VIII was forced to recognize the right of kings to tax the clergy of their lands for their own secular political ends. Innocent III could not have foreseen consequences as far-reaching as this but even during his lifetime his policy was subjected to biting criticism from poets like Walther von der Vogelweide. The extension of the indulgence to cover those who made no more than a financial contribution to the crusade, however, was not just an economic necessity. It was also the only way to involve the entire population in the papal enterprise. He who wished to lead a crusade had to finance it and Innocent saw himself as sole leader of the movement. For this reason he was most unpleasantly surprised when the young Hohenstaufen, Frederick II (1215–50), suddenly took the cross in 1215. In part Frederick was undoubtedly fired by genuine zeal—he was under the influence of some Augustinian canons who were crusade enthusiasts—but in part he was persuaded by political considerations, and to this extent Innocent was justified in fearing that Frederick wanted to follow in the footsteps of Henry VI and challenge the papal position. The danger of this happening had been increased by Innocent himself. The extension of the crusading indulgence to cover paying non-combatants had its positive side; it meant that this instrument of salvation now became something more than just one of the class privileges of the knightly order and was restored to the common people who had played such a large part in the First Crusade. But the greater the number of those who could enjoy this privilege, the more likely it was that the leadership of the crusades would become a political bone of contention between Church and state, between pope and emperor or king, as is amply demonstrated by the later history of Frederick II.

In the midst of his preparations for the crusade Innocent III died at Perugia on 16 July 1216. His successor, Honorius III (1216–27) was as dedicated to the cause of the crusade as Innocent had been but he was a lesser man, lacking the political strength and energy of his great predecessor. It now became clear that not many crusaders could be looked for from France where the Albigensian wars still kept men busy. But there was great enthusiasm in Austria and Hungary; the king of Hungary had taken the cross as long ago as 1196. In return for the final cession of Zara the Venetians agreed to transport the Hungarian army. In August 1217 the Austrians and Hungarians assembled at Spalato. Leopold VI of Austria sailed at once and Andrew of Hungary left soon afterwards. Apart from a few French troops who embarked at Brindisi the ports originally designated by Innocent III were hardly used. At Acre the crusaders were joined by the prince of Antioch and King Hugh of Cyprus. But neither a single high command nor a clear-cut war aim emerged from the discussions which they held with the king of Jerusalem, John of Brienne, with the Masters of the Military Orders, and with the Frankish barons. Finally, with only lukewarm support from the king of Hungary, they undertook three expeditions against the Saracens during the late autumn and early winter of 1217. But since the Saracens were not prepared to give battle nothing decisive was achieved. In vexation King Andrew left to march home through Anatolia in January 1218. With him went Hugh of Cyprus, who died on the way, and Bohemund IV of Antioch. The remaining crusaders were too few to undertake military operations and so they spent the time helping to rebuild Caesarea and enlarging the Templar Castle of the Pilgrims' (Athlit) until it was an almost impregnable fortress overlooking the sea and guarding the pass on the road from Carmel to the south. Not until April and May 1218 when the crusaders from Frisia and the Lower Rhine under the command of Oliver of Cologne arrived at Acre after an adventurous journey lasting a year and including some fighting in Portugal, was it at last possible to think again of taking the war to the enemy. A council of war decided to attack the town of Damietta in the Nile delta, thus reviving the old plan of destroying the Muslim centre of power in Egypt as a prelude to the reconquest of Jerusalem. The bishop of Acre, James of Vitry, undertook the task of informing the pope of the decision and his letters constitute an important source for the history of the crusade.

At his death Saladin had divided the Ayubid empire between his sons and his brother and spiritual heir, al-Adil. The latter was able to out-manoeuvre his nephews and from 1200 to 1218 he was generally recognized as the overlord of the whole Ayubid state. He had no fixed residence and governed from wherever his presence was most needed. With the exception of Egypt, the Ayubid empire was in no sense a centralized state; within it there existed a whole range of centrifugal forces which it required great diplomatic skill to hold in check. It was largely owing to these difficulties that the Franks on the Palestinian coast enjoyed a period of peace during the days of al-Adil. Unlike Saladin moreover al-Adil was unable to count on the alliances either with the Seldjuks or, after 1204, with the Byzantines. Al-Adil's sons ruled the separate parts of the empire under their father's suzerainty. Al-Kamil, who was designated to succeed al-Adil, held Egypt, the heartland of the empire; al-Mu'azzam ruled Syria and Palestine; al-Ashraf governed al-Gazira, Upper Mesopotamia. In Syria and Mesopotamia there were a number of subordinate city states ruled by collateral branches of the Ayubid family or by dynasties of the second rank (Ortoqid, Zengid).

As has recently been shown by Gottschalk the Franks had given diplomatic backing to their Damietta project by accepting the offer of an alliance made by the Seldjuk sultan of Rum (Anatolia), Kaikhaus (1210–19). Kaikhaus had ambitions of his own in the direction of Aleppo and Mesopotamia; so he supported the

Frankish plan of a crusade against Egypt in the hope that this would tie the main Ayubid forces down in Egypt, leaving him with a fairly free hand in the north. The pincer attack began simultaneously on both fronts. At the end of May the crusaders arrived before Damietta, a strong fortress and the second most important port in Egypt; they pitched camp on the west bank of the Nile opposite the town. In June Kaikhaus attacked Aleppo but by August his campaign had already broken down in the face of al-Ashraf's determined resistance. It ended too quickly to give the Franks the flank support they had hoped for.

The key to the defences of Damietta was the Tower of Chains built on an island in the Nile. (The tower took its name from a chain which was stretched across the river from the tower to the east bank on which the town lay.) The channel to the west of the tower was apparently unnavigable so in effect it controlled the entire breadth of the river. The crusaders made this tower their main objective. Al-Kamil, who had been taken completely by surprise by the Frankish attack, hurriedly set up camp some distance south of the town on the east bank. His tactical aim was to prevent the Franks from crossing the river and completely encircling Damietta from the land. Using ships and fire-ships the crusaders launched several attacks on the tower but although they were supported by a ceaseless barrage from eight stone-throwing 'engines' they were beaten off each time. At this point the cathedral schoolmaster, Oliver, whose *Historia Damiatina* provides a valuable account of the crusade, took a hand in events. He had a special kind of siege-engine constructed and paid for with German money. Two cogs were lashed together and four masts erected; at masttop a wooden fort was built, and lower down draw-bridges controlled by a pulley system were constructed. On 24 August 1218, despite the fierce resistance put up by the defenders who almost managed to destroy the 'engine' with Greek fire, the Franks succeeded in lowering the bridges on to the battlements and in occupying the upper floors of the tower. The next day the garrison surrendered. The crusaders cut the chain, destroyed the bridge of boats which connected the island to the town and built instead their own bridge to their camp on the west bank. This success made a great impression on the Muslims. Sultan al-Adil died of grief. From now on it was always possible that the latent tensions in the Ayubid empire would come to the surface for neither al-Mu'azzam nor al-Ashraf had any intention of remaining permanently subordinate to their brother al-Kamil (1218-38).

For the moment, however, they were united in their opposition to the Franks.

From September 1218 onwards the crusaders received a steady flow of reinforcements from Europe: Italians, Frenchmen, Englishmen, and Spaniards. Unfortunately from early 1219 onwards the arrival of new soldiers was offset by a thin but continuous stream of men returning home—despite the promise made by the leading churchmen with the army that, if they would stay, their families too would be covered by their plenary indulgence. Despite the capture of the Tower of Chains they were still unable to gain a foothold on the east bank of the Nile. They suffered from the usual camp diseases. A great part of the army succumbed to dysentery and only a religious fanatic like James of Vitry could believe that the victims of the epidemic had greeted their illness joyfully as 'an invitation to a heavenly banquet' and had died almost painlessly. There has never been a time in history when the interested parties have not found some means or other of glorifying death in war.

Among the new arrivals of autumn 1218 were two cardinal legates sent by the pope. One of them, Robert of Courçon, soon died; to the other, the Portugese cardinal, Pelagius of Albano, fell the task of putting into practice Innocent III's conception of a crusade run by the Church. This was a task requiring great diplomatic skill, for although John of Brienne was supposed to be military commander there was in fact no unity of opinion in the army. Pelagius had been granted the plenipotentiary authority to enable him to carry out this task but he lacked the necessary personal qualities. He was a man of driving energy but hopelessly shortsighted, autocratic, self-satisfied, and uncommonly pig-headed. Robert of Courçon's death had deprived him of the influence of a colleague who might have been able to hold him in check. Once already as legate in the Latin Empire of Constantinople he had distinguished himself by his intransigence. Now he looked for support from the new arrivals, the Military Orders and the Italian merchants of Palestine; relying on them he could outmanoeuvre King John, the Frankish barons of the crusader states, and the Frisians and Rhinelanders led by Oliver. Before long the army was split into two hostile camps. Untroubled by the prohibitions of canon law, Pelagius intervened actively in military matters. None the less events went well for the crusaders. An attack on their camp launched by al-Kamil on 9 October was beaten back thanks to the watchfulness of John of Brienne. During the winter the crusaders made some rather hesitant attacks and in

February the energetic Pelagius took command. Now and later he demonstrated that once he had decided on a tactical plan he was not to be put off by early lack of success. This time he was assisted by the collapse of al-Kamil's position. The sultan's demands for troops together with the heavy taxes unremittingly imposed by him on the Coptic Christians and on the urban population led to a conspiracy among the Egyptian emirs. Al-Kamil fled followed by the rest of his panic-stricken army. So, on 5 February 1219, the crusaders were able to occupy al-Kamil's camp on the east bank, making a rich haul of booty. All supplies to Damietta were now cut off; the blockade was complete. Al-Kamil was thinking of fleeing to Yemen when his brother al-Mu'azzam arrived from Syria and took vigorous action. The leading plotters were transported to Syria and the conspiracy collapsed. This restored al-Kamil's confidence. But the threat to Damietta had now become serious enough for him to proclaim a holy war in March 1219. Previously had tried, unsuccessfully, to come to terms with the crusaders. In return for a thirty years' truce and the evacuation of Egypt by the crusaders he had offered to return the whole former kingdom of Jerusalem with the exception of the Transjordan for which he was prepared to offer 30,000 bezants compensation. The legate would not allow this offer of peace to be accepted. Once again the sultan resumed the struggle but his attack on the Christian camp was thwarted by its good defence works and the two pontoon bridges (one of them consisting of as many as thirty-eight boats) which the crusaders had built. Al-Kamil also tried to barricade the Damietta branch of the Nile and to divert the full flow of the river through the Rosetta branch but the attempt failed when the dams burst. In May 1219 the gallant Leopold VI of Austria returned home despite Pelagius's efforts to persuade him to stay. In July and August the legate organized a series of attempts to take the town by storm. They did not succeed but at least they kept the Muslims in a state of uncertainty. Not until 29 August was al-Kamil able to win any real success in battle. He then took advantage of his improved position to make another peace offer. This time he was even prepared to return the True Cross and to rebuild, at his own expense, the castles and walls of Jerusalem which he had carefully had dismantled in the previous March. Al-Kamil's overriding concern was to protect the Ayubid heartland, Egypt. Despite his military success at the end of August his overall position had deteriorated owing to the fact that the Nile floods had not come and the land was threatened by a harvest failure.

In Damietta itself conditions were almost impossible. The population was starving. A hen cost 30 dinars, a cow 800; grains of sugar were as rare as precious stones. Even so the capture of Damietta was by no means the same thing as the conquest of Egypt and al-Kamil's offer was extremely generous. John of Brienne spoke in favour of accepting these terms; over and above the immediate campaign in Egypt it was, after all, Jerusalem that they were fighting for. But again Pelagius turned it down. The Masters of the Military Orders believed that without the Transjordan it was impossible to defend Jerusalem and, as for the True Cross, Saladin had not been able to find it after the fall of Acre. The Italians were most anxious to set up a trading colony in Damietta. Thus it was that the chance to bring the crusade to a successful conclusion was allowed to slip by.

Staying in the crusaders' camp at about this time was St. Francis of Assisi who was to help bring about the triumph of the movement for apostolic poverty by his foundation of the Franciscan Order and through the example of his own purity. He hoped to succeed by preaching where the sword had failed. After some hesitation the legate allowed him to visit al-Kamil. The latter listened to him with the attention that was appropriate to a period of negotiations but never for a moment considered being converted. The political significance of this attempt was ephemeral but it did mark the beginning of a lasting Franciscan interest in the Holy Land and in the Christian mission to the heathens of Asia which the Franciscans initiated and to which they devoted themselves with great zeal if with relatively little success. From the thirteenth century onwards the curia showed a special preference for Franciscans when choosing embassies to the Near, Middle, and Far East, though the new Dominican Order of Preachers was also active in this field.[81]

By the autumn of 1219 it had become impossible to hold Damietta. On 5 November the crusaders found several sections of the wall undefended and there was practically no resistance when they occupied the town. Damietta fell so easily not because of treachery within the walls but simply because the townspeople were worn out by hunger and disease. The children were rescued by James of Vitry who had them baptized; all the other survivors were either dispersed or enslaved. The fall of Damietta made a devastating impression on the Islamic world. Al-Kamil did what he could. He withdrew up the Nile to Mansourah (i.e. the victorious) and there built a camp which blocked the road to Cairo and was to have a famous place in the history of the crusades. He sent al-Mu'azzam back to Palestine in order to keep the Franks there fully occupied. Otherwise his main aim was to gain time, for only with the united forces of all the Ayubids was a counter-attack possible and throughout the years 1218–20 his brother al-Ashraf had his hands full, initially with the Seldjuk invasion and then with a disputed succession in Mosul where a pretender was threatening to take the city state out of the Ayubid empire.

The crusaders settled down in Damietta but internal dissensions meant that the whole of 1220 was lost and not until the summer of 1221 was decisive action again a possibility. John of Brienne claimed the town for himself and had coins minted on which he was given the title of king of Damietta. Against him Pelagius declared that the town belonged to the community of all crusaders whom only the Church could properly represent. Early in 1220 John sailed back to Acre angry because the legate had made his provisional acceptance of John's lordship dependent on the decision of the pope and there could be little doubt what the outcome of this would be. Moreover the king had run out of money and in Palestine al-Mu'azzam had been operating very successfully; not much more than Acre and the half-deserted Tyre were left in the hands of the Franks. John's departure left Pelagius as the only possible commander but he was no more than partially successful in controlling the jealousies of the different national groups which sometimes resulted in armed clashes. The best that could be done was to assign them separate quarters of the town. Only the Italians continued to support the legate and then only after he had ordered a redistribution of the booty in their favour.

In order to spur the crusaders into action Pelagius had some Arabic prophecies translated into French and preached to the troops; he also had copies dispatched for circulation in the West.[82] The most important of these prophecies, the *Prophetie de Hannan, fils d'Isaac,* was supposed to have been written by a ninth-century Persian doctor and translator who was a Nestorian Christian. In fact it was put together by the Nestorians during the winter of 1219–20 and so, not altogether surprisingly, it accurately 'prophesied' the history of the crusade up to the fall of Damietta. In the figure of the tall and emaciated leader of the Christians Pelagius had no trouble in recognizing himself. According to the prophecy the Christians would conquer the whole of Egypt as far as Aswan on the border with Christian Nubia. Then two kings would appear. The first, probably to be identified with Frederick II, would conquer Syria; the second, clearly meant to be the Coptic Negus of Ethiopia, would destroy Mecca and exterminate Islam. This would be followed by the arrival of Antichrist and then, four years and four months later, by the Last Judgement. At least two other similar prophecies are known to have circulated during 1220 and early 1221. Common elements in both were the references to an early victory, to the promise of help from an eastern and a western ruler, to the conquest of Egypt and the meeting of the two kings in Jerusalem in 1222, followed by the end of the world. One of these was the translation of an Arabic version of the *Liber Clementis*, an apocryphal document supposed to have been published by Pope Clement I and to contain disclosures made by the Prince of the Apostles, Saint Peter. The second was a report mentioning a King David who was expected to give help now that the Negus had not come. Formerly this King David had been identified with David II of Georgia (1089–1125) whose task it was to guard the peoples of Gog and Magog whom God had, at the request of Alexander the Great, held imprisoned for a thousand years behind the Caucasus. But at the coming of Antichrist they were to be freed and for a short while they would devastate the earth (Revelation 20: 7–8). Quite independently meanwhile other reports reaching Europe from the East had, by the middle of the twelfth century, resulted in the growth of the notion of a legendary Priest-King, Prester John, also to be identified with the Coptic Negus whose title Zan sounded very like the French Jean. He was expected to come to the aid of the hard-pressed Christians of the East. The historical background to this figure was the victory of a Mongolian people, the Kara Khitai, over the Seldjuk sultan, Sanjar, in 1141; since this victory was in fact won in Central Asia it was occasionally supposed that Prester John's kingdom lay in India. Who the King David of 1221 was, is impossible to say—perhaps a Turkish conqueror in Inner Asia or even Genghis Khan, the Great Khan of all the Mongols, who in 1220 had just completed the destruction of the Khwarismian Empire in Western Turkestan. In any event the figure of David had become fused in the strangest and most involved fashion with the old David legend of Gog and Magog and with Prester John who was now identified either as David himself or as David's father. Everyone in Damietta placed his hopes not so much on the promised crusade of Frederick II as on the legendary Oriental ruler who was supposed to be a Nestorian. Pelagius himself was firmly convinced of the truth of these prophecies. For him they were very much more than mere instruments of propaganda and his apparently irrational refusal to have anything to do with al-Kamil's offer of peace only becomes comprehensible on the assumption that he was completely under the spell of these writings. Victory therefore was inevitable. Already King David stood no more than ten days march from Baghdad—or so Pelagius had reported to the pope.

Things did not turn out quite as Pelagius had expected. To begin with, Frederick II did not come although at his imperial coronation in 1220 he had once again taken the crusader's vow. He did, however, send about 500 knights under Duke Louis of Bavaria who, in defiance of the emperor's express command, supported the legate's demands for a war of conquest in Egypt. It was in vain that John of Brienne who had arrived back in Damietta on 7 July 1221 in response to the pope's reproaches, opposed so rash an enterprise. Al-Kamil offered peace once again but talks broke down when the Franks demanded Transjordan as well. This region served as a bridge between Syria and Egypt and from the Ayubid point of view it was indispensable. On 17 July the crusaders marched out to conquer Egypt, moving up the east bank of the Nile until 24 July when they took up a defensive position before Mansourah. Their camp lay in the angle formed by the Nile and one of its tributaries and only ignorance of the hydrography of Egypt could have made the crusaders believe that this was a good defensive position.

Meanwhile the situation in the Ayubid empire had altered. In early 1221 al-Ashraf had concluded the third Mosul war and had prevented the secession of a part of Mesopotamia. He was now able to comply with al-Kamil's ever more urgent appeals for help, although this meant that he had to refuse to go to the assistance of the Georgians against the Mongols. Like almost all the princes of Islam he underestimated the Mongol danger. By early August the troops of the three Ayubid brothers were united in Egypt. Manoeuvring skilfully they circled round the Frankish army and on 10 August cut its land and river communications with Damietta. Neither provisions nor a relieving army could reach the crusaders because al-Kamil had opened the sluice-gates and, it being high water on the Nile at this time of year, this meant that the surrounding countryside was completely flooded. On 26 August the crusaders tried desperately to cut their way through on the one road to Damietta that was still open, though well guarded by al-Kamil. But the sultan now gave instructions for this road to be flooded as well so after advancing a few miles they became bogged down in the morass. Pelagius was forced to sue for peace and on the following day an eight years' truce was made. The Christians were free to leave but they had to leave Egypt altogether. The crusade which might have witnessed the recovery of Jerusalem instead ended dismally owing to the legate's pigheadedness. On 8 September 1221 al-Kamil entered Damietta in triumph. Shortly afterwards in victory celebrations at Mansourah the unity of the Ayubid empire was once again demonstrated. Women sang: 'Most unjustly did the pharaoh of Acre come to Egypt to plague the land, but Moses came to help us with a rod in his hand and he drowned them, one by one, in the sea.' It was not in fact the pharaoh of Acre (John of Brienne) who was responsible. Honorius III tried to blame Frederick II but public opinion, accurately reflected in the songs of the troubadours, came to a different conclusion. The Norman Guillaume le Clerc wrote in his satire *Le Besant de Dieu* (*c.* 1227): 'We lost this town owing to our stupidity and our sins, on account of the legate who led the Christians ... for it is surely against the law [i.e. canon law] for clerks to command knights; the churchman should recite his Bible and the Psalms and leave the battlefield to the knight.' Still more indignant were the poets of Provence, already embittered by the Albigensian Crusade. Fiercest of them all was Guillem Figueira with his terrible sirventes against Rome. But the Damietta expedition proved to be the Church's final attempt to turn the crusade into an enterprise directed and led by her alone.[83]

11 · THE CRUSADE OF FREDERICK II, 1228–1229

ALREADY the reader will have noticed that in the thirteenth century crusades followed each other in more rapid succession than in the twelfth century and that they have been described here without reference to events in Palestine (for which see below pp. 239ff.). The crusades of the thirteenth century were not in fact brought about by the alarm caused in Christendom by particular events as had been the case with the Second Crusade (the fall of Edessa) and the Third Crusade (the fall of Jerusalem). Instead, leaving purely political motives aside for the moment, they were the result of the permanent state of weakness from which the Holy Land never recovered after the catastrophe of 1187, even though during the Ayubid period it was never exposed to any menace serious enough to jeopardize its very existence. Without some special spark, however, it would hardly have been possible to rouse the great masses that went on crusade in the twelfth century. Instead of the large but quite distinct surges of the twelfth century, there was now a steady stream of crusaders, sometimes no more than a trickle but never quite drying up. A similar stream had existed in the twelfth century; it was from this source that the steadily increasing number of permanent European settlers in the Holy Land had been drawn. In the thirteenth century the immigration of settlers seems to have stopped. Conditions were now too insecure and the competition from the Frankish states in Greece was too strong. There was instead an influx of knights who, every year, came at certain well-defined times in increasing numbers—'seasonal crusaders' they could be called, for their military services were placed at the disposal of the Holy Land for short periods only. The importance of these seasonal crusaders should on no account be underestimated. Apart from the Military Orders who, however, often pursued their own policies indifferent to the interests of the state, they constituted the only reasonably large force whose availability could definitely be counted on. It is here, too, that a change in the contemporary notion of a crusade becomes apparent. The tumultuous *commotio* (mass movement) of the First Crusade gave way to the orderly *passagium*. This term, drawn from the vocabulary of economic life, is an indication of the way in which the twelfth-century crusades developed into a definite seasonal rhythm in the thirteenth century. Typical of this concept of an established rhythm is the statement made by the annalist of St. Médard at Soissons (*c.* 1250). He reported that even before the Children's Crusade animals of the most diverse kinds had set off for the Holy Land at regular ten-year intervals; the departure of animals had always been looked upon as a portent of the approach of the Last Days.

The Italian maritime cities staged two *passagia* a year, the March or Easter voyage and the Autumn voyage. Originally these terms meant no more than the convoys of merchant ships; but these, of course, also offered the best chance of making the pilgrimage. The Easter voyage appears to have been the more popular and the conditions of payment attached to it were more favourable. Whether the Easter date, *ver sacrum*, always had religious associations, as Alphandéry believed, is very much open to doubt, but it is incontestable that pilgrim traffic flourished greatly in the thirteenth century. The financial interest of the cities in this traffic was such that in 1234 Marseilles imposed limits on the monopoly of the Military Orders; from then on the Orders were not allowed to transport more than 6,000 pilgrims a year from Marseilles. In 1233 Venice fixed 8 May as the deadline for the return journey of the Easter voyage and 8 October for the Autumn voyage. The 'season' therefore was very short unless a pilgrim decided to stay for half a year or a full year.[84] The majority of pilgrims, being poor, made the voyage to Outremer under appalling conditions on the lower deck. James of Vitry on the other hand, as a bishop, travelled 'first class'. He rented five cabins for himself, his household and his horses and laid in a three months' supply of wine, meat, and ship's biscuit. But in stormy weather, when the ship lurched in all directions, even the bishop had an uncomfortable time. Nobody dared light a fire, so there was nothing hot to eat, and most of the passengers did not feel like eating anyway. When James disembarked at Acre the voyage from Genoa had lasted about a month.

This change in the nature of the crusades was associated with an altered attitude to heathens. The poets, in particular Wolfram von Eschenbach in his *Willehalm* (*c.* 1220), created the image of the 'noble heathen' as represented by a man like Saladin. In terms of his human qualities and virtues this 'noble heathen' is unquestionably the equal of the Christian knight and it is precisely on account of this that a tragic conflict arises when, in the struggle between Christian and heathen, the knight must take up the sword against an honourable adversary, a man who, like him, had been created by God. It would be too much to speak of tolerance in this context but there was certainly a genuine humanity springing from a courtly culture. A change of this kind in the attitude to heathens presupposed, of course, a more accurate view of Islam as the most important heathen religion. The theory that the Muslims were idol worshippers had been losing currency since the middle of the twelfth century. It was now recognized that, on the contrary, the Muslims were rigorous monotheists and hostile to image worship. From the Christian point of view their error lay not so much in their concept of God as in their attitude to Christ. In 1143 Peter the Venerable, abbot-general of Cluny, had the Koran translated into Latin by the Englishman Robert of Ketton. As a result Muslim doctrine was, for the first time, made available to the Christian world. Peter was also one of the first to prefer peaceful persuasion to the force of arms. He wrote: 'I attack you not with arms, as many of us often do, but with words, not with force but with reason, not with hate but with love. ... I love you; out of love I write to you and with the help of the Scriptures I show you the way to salvation.' Peter still believed that the Muslims, who in terms of numbers represented by far the greater part of the known heathens, made up as much as a third to a half of the total population of the world. But the appearance of the Mongols from 1220 onwards revealed that this estimate was completely false and that beyond the Muslims there were enormous numbers of other heathen peoples. This meant that the proportion of Christians to heathens was altered very much to the disadvantage of the former; and Roger Bacon, in particular, recognized this in his famous *Opus Maius* (c. 1266).[85] Differing conclusions could be drawn from this changed situation: either there would have to be a tremendous increase in the military commitment—a vigorously debated possibility, though a purely theoretical one—or, instead, an unarmed crusade might be tried—an illusion to which only the children of 1212 yielded. One thing, however, was absolutely clear; 'conversion or destruction', the choice offered by Bernard of Clairvaux (letter

457) when writing about the 'crusade' against the Wends (see p. 102), was no longer a choice which made any sense in the East. Thus besides the military aid which was intended to preserve the crusader states there also had to be a greater emphasis on missionary activity. This change in men's knowledge and attitudes created the basis for the intensified missionary activity of the mendicant orders which was to reach deep into Asia. This new appraisal of the situation also made possible an approach that would have been unthinkable in the twelfth century and would have met with bitter resistance from public opinion. Even in the thirteenth century it aroused opposition enough but it could, none the less, be undertaken by a man who was ahead of his time, without, however, being able to detach himself from it completely: Emperor Frederick II (1220–50), the first person to try to bring a crusade to a successful conclusion by using political rather than military means.[86]

At the Fourth Lateran Council Innocent III had completely ignored the crusading vow sworn by Frederick II in 1215; the king's participation would not have fitted in with his conception of a papal crusade. Likewise at first Honorius III also made no attempt to persuade Frederick to fulfil his vow; in any event until 1218 the latter was far too busy with the fight against his rival Otto IV to be able to give any thought to a crusade. Only when this danger had been overcome did Honorius, under some pressure from public opinion, call upon the king to lend active support. This was at about the time of the departure of the first contingent—the Hungarians—on the Damietta Crusade. Without the secular power there could be no crusade and so, because the pope needed the king, he was prepared to make concessions. In 1220 he crowned him emperor and, still more important, resigned himself to allowing Frederick to rule his native kingdom of Sicily as well as the empire. The union of south Italy and the empire under one ruler threatened the very existence of the papacy and Innocent III had tried to prevent it by forcing Frederick to promise to hand over the reins of government in Sicily to his son Henry. But immediately after Innocent's death Frederick had frustrated this plan by having Henry elected as king of Germany, thus ensuring that both realms would be united in the hand of his son. In these circumstances it made little sense for Honorius to hold Frederick to the promise which he had made to Innocent III. At his imperial coronation Frederick renewed his vow to go on crusade. He had already successfully requested the pope to threaten to excommunicate all those who had not fulfilled their vow by the summer of 1219. This was a mistake on Frederick's part for it meant that he had deprived himself of the possibility of choosing a date for his own crusade to suit himself. For this reason his vow became increasingly burdensome to him in the following years. Since the imperial coronation had opened the way to Sicily he now gave first priority to the task of putting an end to the conditions of near anarchy in south Italy. In these years and particularly after his return from crusade he turned the kingdom of Sicily into an efficiently governed, centralized state. Here he built the power base from which he subsequently engaged in his great struggle with the curia. This time it was to be a struggle for political dominance in Italy and not, as in the eleventh century, a contest for primacy between emperor and pope.

At first, however, relations between the new emperor and the curia remained harmonious. Time and again he was granted licence to delay his crusade. H. M. Schaller has shown that his chancery was dominated by a group of churchmen headed by Richard, a Templar who had formerly been papal chamberlain and who now served the emperor in the same capacity. Also influential was Hermann of Salza, Master of the Teutonic Order, and since 1216 a close friend and adviser of the emperor. Both of them tried to act as peace-makers between emperor and pope and they found a sympathetic helper in the curia in the person of Cardinal Thomas of Capua, the Grand Penitentiary. But the efforts of these men could do no more than postpone the threatening conflict.

The failure of the Damietta Crusade in 1221, dealing a severe blow to the pope's prestige, meant that the curia now pressed unremittingly for a new crusade. In July 1225 the final arrangements were made in the Treaty of San Germano. The emperor agreed to pay 1,000 knights for two years and to provide transport for another 2,000. He himself was to go on crusade in August 1227; if he failed to carry out his promise he was to lose an enormous deposit of 100,000 ounces of gold and he would incur the sentence of excommunication to which he had, in advance, expressly given his consent. If the emperor died, his successor in Sicily was to assume his obligations. But in contrast to similar treaties with other rulers in the Treaty of San Germano no allowance was made for the possibility that the emperor might fall ill. Only by accepting these harsh terms could Frederick obtain another two years' delay. It was not, however, a complete victory for the Church. It was to Frederick's advantage that the emperor was once again entrusted with the sole direction of the crusade. The treaty contained no reference to papal financial assistance in the shape of a crusading tax imposed on clerics and laymen. As late as 1223 Frederick had been asking for such a tax, but in fact if the curia made no financial contribution to the crusade it was also unable to exert much influence over the course of events. It ought to be more widely recognized that there were elements of compromise in the Treaty of San Germano.

In November 1225 the emperor acquired a dynastic claim to Jerusalem; he married Isabella, daughter of John of Brienne, king of Jerusalem. At the pope's wish Hermann of Salza had been negotiating this marriage since 1223 but at first Frederick himself had remained very cool on the subject. Now, however, the alliance fitted into his political schemes. John had hoped to be able to rule for the rest of his life but, in the event, he had to resign himself to seeing Frederick assume the royal title immediately after his marriage. Formally Frederick was in the right. John had ruled only as husband of Maria of Montferrat, daughter of Conrad of Montferrat, and then, after her death in 1211, as guardian of their daughter Isabella. His rights were now transferred to Frederick as Isabella's husband. The Frankish barons of Outremer raised no objection; they had higher expectations of the emperor than of John and as yet they knew nothing of Hohenstaufen centralization.

In March 1227 Honorius III died. His successor, Gregory IX (1227-41) was made of sterner stuff; he belonged to the same family as Innocent III. He soon saw that the curia could not tolerate the menacing power of the Hohenstaufen in Italy. But both in Germany and Italy preparations for the crusade were going so well that it was impossible for the pope to intervene. Hermann of Salza had succeeded in persuading Ludwig IV, landgrave of Thuringia, to take the cross together with a large following. In August 1227 an unexpectedly large army mustered at Brindisi and, despite the outbreak of an epidemic, it set sail for Palestine. The emperor and the landgrave followed but they had only been at sea for three days when Ludwig died and Frederick too became seriously ill. To turn back might have the most serious consequences since this eventuality had not been provided for in the treaty of 1225. But even Hermann of Salza advised Frederick to return, so the emperor retired to the spa of Pozzuoli near Naples. Immediately afterwards, on 29 September, Gregory IX denounced him in the most extravagant language and placed him under a sentence of excommunication. Frederick replied with a manifesto which was all the more effective for being a restrained and sober account of the facts. It is clear that, according to the terms of the Treaty of San Germano, Gregory was in the right, but it is equally clear that for him the interruption of the crusade was just a welcome excuse to put the overmighty emperor in his place. The first great power struggle between Frederick II and the curia had begun. From now on both sides waged an incessant propaganda war, attacking each other in fiery manifestos which utilized to the full all the techniques of that art of rhetoric which reached the climax of its development in the thirteenth century. In Palestine meanwhile peace still prevailed. The truce of Damietta (1221) was supposed to last until 1229 and could only be broken by the arrival of a crowned king; in these circumstances the army which had sailed on ahead of Frederick to Palestine did not dare to begin a war. Instead, in the region between Acre and Tyre, the crusaders built Montfort, the castle which was to be the chief stronghold of the Teutonic Order in the Holy Land.

By his sentence of excommunication Gregory IX had, according to canon law, prevented the emperor from using the crusade as an instrument of politics; for all forms of contact, both in material and in spiritual matters, with an excommunicate were prohibited. When Frederick sought a reconciliation, the pope, who was obliged to pardon the penitent sinner, laid down unacceptable conditions—for example, papal supervision of the government of Sicily. If the emperor had given way and had remained in Italy the pope's actions would have seemed to be justified and Frederick would have lost the game almost before it had begun. So he ignored the pope's express command that he should not go on crusade until he had received absolution and announced that he would leave in the summer of 1228. Gregory, however, clearly continued to rely upon the effectiveness of his sentence, for he was utterly astonished when, on 28 June 1228, the emperor embarked at Brindisi and sailed to join his army. It was a move of unparalleled boldness in a game played for high stakes. Frederick left without having succeeded in reaching a peaceful settlement in Lombardy. Still worse was the possibility that the pope might now regard Sicily as an escheated fief of the papacy and might depose him as emperor. But in fact Frederick had very little choice. Only success in the East could secure and enhance his lordship in the West. In all ages, to rule the East had been looked upon as the ultimate achievement of the world-ruler; with this crusade the emperor proudly confronted the Church with the fact that his policies were universal in their range. He was carried high on the waves of those eschatological hopes and promises which were so powerful at the time. It was foretold that the Last Emperor, in a messiah-like role, would win Jerusalem, unite East and West under his universal rule and, as a sign of the advent of perpetual peace, would hang his shield from the branches of the withered tree which would, at that moment, begin to put forth green shoots. Most manuscripts of the *Prophetie de Hannan* of 1219–20 (see above p. 215) had allotted the greatest task, the destruction of Islam, to the Ethiopian negus, but in some texts the negus was replaced by the king of Calabria, i.e. Frederick II. We can safely assume that Frederick, imbued like no one either before or after him with a sense of the dignity of his imperial position, was swayed by ideas like this as well as by all the calculations of *Realpolitik*. By the same token his crusade exposed the papacy to an unprecendented danger. Never before had anyone disputed the exclusive right of the pope to call a crusade. Bernard of Clairvaux had guarded this right jealously (see above p. 97). It meant that in the last resort the pope always possessed the possibility of controlling the crusading movement. But even this right was now threatened by the emperor, an excommunicated man, going on crusade in flagrant disregard of the express prohibition of the pope. It is understandable that Gregory should have done everything in his power to prevent the crusade from succeeding.

After a brief halt at Cyprus while Frederick renewed the feudal overlordship of the empire over the island kingdom and installed imperial garrisons in the castles, he landed at Acre on 7 September 1228, ten years after men had first begun to look for his arrival. None the less he was greeted by an outburst of popular enthusiasm as the man 'by whose hand deliverance was given unto Israel' (I Maccabees 5: 62). But the army had shrunk considerably; moreover it was split into two parties. Frederick could rely on the support of Hermann of Salza and the Teutonic Knights, on the Germans and Sicilians, and finally on the Pisans and Genoese. But ranged against him was the might of the Templars and Hospitallers together with most of the clergy led by Gerold of Valence, the patriarch of Jerusalem (1225–39) and the moving spirit in the opposition to the emperor. But the poet Freidank reflected the popular mood. He lamented the excommunication of Frederick and its effects:

> The cross was given for sin
> To save the most holy sepulchre.
> Now they want to forbid that with the ban
> How then shall a man's soul be nourished?

He also expressed his conviction that he who took the cross in good faith

> Could be sure of the remission of sins
> That is my firm belief.

Frederick was not so rash as to go on crusade without first pre-paring the way diplomatically. The situation was a favourable one for him because the Ayubid brothers, who had united to drive the Franks out of Egypt, had quarrelled more and more since 1221. A power struggle had developed between al-Kamil and al-Mu'azzam. In 1227 al-Kamil, faced by this difficulty and wishing to secure his rear, repeated the offer of 1219 whereby Saladin's conquests would be restored to the emperor. Al-Mu'azzam, of course, would have nothing to do with this offer. His death on 12 November 1227 freed al-Kamil from the danger of a war on two fronts, but by then it was too late to stop the crusade. Immediately after his landing Frederick began negotiations with the sultan, negotiations which the latter prolonged in order to exploit the emperor's difficulties with the ecclesiastical opposition. Frederick's military operations were on a small scale, intended only to exert some occasional pressure in support of the negotiations. The emperor's engaging gaiety—a quality inherited from his Hohen-staufen ancestors—was praised in the Christian sources, but the Muslims were not much impressed by his appearance. They des-cribed him as bald and short-sighted; one of them observed dryly that in the slave market he would not have been worth twenty dirhems. They were impressed, however, by his lively interest in Arab scholarship.

The sultan kept the emperor waiting and forced him to lower his demands considerably and to admit that his imperial prestige would be finished if he had to return home without having achieved some success. Meanwhile rapid negotiations had led to a new partition of the Ayubid empire in the Treaty of Tel-Ajul which was agreed towards the end of 1228. Syria with Damascus was assigned to al-Ashraf, while Palestine fell to al-Kamil. Thus the treaty strengthened the position of Egypt at the expense of the other parts of the Ayubid empire and maintained the over-lordship of al-Kamil. As yet, however, the partition existed only on paper and al-Mu'azzam's son, an-Nasir, would have to be defeated by force of arms if it were to be put into effect. In order to equip himself for the struggle which followed immediately after the conclusion of the treaty, al-Kamil came to terms with Frederick in a peace treaty signed at Jaffa on 18 February

1229. The peace was to last ten years, five months, and forty days;[87] Jerusalem—its fortifications had been dismantled by al-Mu'azzam in 1219—was restored to the Franks together with a few places between Jerusalem and the coast including (certainly) Lydda and Bethlehem and (perhaps, but only according to Christian sources) Nazareth, the lordship of Toron and Sidon. So the Franks gained not only their capital city but also considerable territory in the north. For the rest, the *status quo* was to be upheld, in particular in the case of the castles of the Orders. In Jerusalem itself the Temple area, with the two Islamic shrines of the Dome of the Rock and the mosque of al-Aqsa, was to remain in Muslim hands; they were to have their own administration headed by a qadi. It is not clear whether or not the treaty permitted the rebuilding of the walls of Jerusalem, but there are indications that al-Kamil regarded the cession of Jerusalem as purely temporary and he is therefore unlikely to have allowed it. The emperor's attitude on this question is unknown. In fact Jerusalem remained unfortified until it was lost again to the Muslims in 1244.

The treaty meant that with a stroke of the pen Frederick II had achieved the objective sought for so long: Christian lordship over the Sepulchre of Christ, which all the military efforts of the years since 1187 had failed to attain. More than this it meant that al-Kamil could now concentrate on the ordering of his empire while, for his part, Frederick had immensely enhanced both his reputation in the eyes of the world and his own self-confidence. The efforts made by the curia in the fight against him had been brought to nothing. Both the Christian Church and the orthodox Muslims were angered by the treaty; it was condemned by pope and patriarch. The latter, a fanatical Saracen-hater, was particularly dismayed by the Muslim enclave in the holy city and by the fact that the treaty contained nothing at all about the rights of his church. The area around Jerusalem, where most of the estates of the Church of the Holy Sepulchre had lain, remained Muslim territory. Frederick tried in vain to obtain Gerold's approval of the treaty. On his side the patriarch made a last-minute attempt to prevent the emperor from entering Jerusalem. He sent the archbishop of Caesarea to Jerusalem in order to lay an interdict over the city. This meant the prohibition of all divine services and was the most severe ecclesiastical punishment. The archbishop reached Jerusalem on 19 March, but Frederick had already entered the city on 17 March and had even viewed the Muslim quarter. It is an indication of his excessive self-confidence that, though under sentence of excommunication, he now formed the reckless plan of having mass said in his presence in the Church of the Holy Sepulchre. Hermann of Salza was just able to make him see reason and drop the idea. Since the patriarch was absent and had, in any event, refused—with good legal reasons—to crown Frederick as king of Jerusalem, the emperor placed the crown on his own head in a crown-wearing ceremony at the Church of the Holy Sepulchre on 18 March 1229. The archbishop had arrived one day too late. It was undoubtedly a bold and challenging act but it was in no sense—as has been suggested—a kind of Napoleonic self-coronation. In contrast to the Corsican, Frederick would have welcomed an ecclesiastical coronation. As things were this was impossible, but equally Frederick could not afford to leave Jerusalem without the sacred dignity of the crown, and bad news from Italy made it necessary for him to leave soon. Moreover his dynastic claim to the throne of Jerusalem had been badly in need of strengthening since his wife Isabella had died in childbirth on 8 May 1228—even before Frederick left Italy. Thus although he might choose to call himself king, according to the law of Jerusalem he now ruled only by virtue of being guardian of their son, Conrad IV.

On the coronation day an important imperial manifesto was addressed to all the peoples of the earth, the first to be written in that overpoweringly emotional style that was to be characteristic of the late Hohenstaufen chancery. In it the emperor had himself raised up to a more than earthly position. He stood between God and mankind; in his nearness to God he was like the angels. What he had done, God had done through him. Then he was placed in the context of the tradition of the kingdom of David. We remember the hopes which the crusaders at Damietta had placed in the legendary King David. In medieval thought David was both king and prophet, a prefiguration of Christ to whom he was occasionally likened. 'Thus,' wrote the emperor, 'all those who honour the true faith shall from henceforth know and shall publish it far and wide to the ends of the earth that he who is blessed for all time has visited us, has brought deliverance to his people, and has raised up an horn of salvation for us in the house of his servant David.'

Meanwhile the situation in south Italy had become critical. John of Brienne, still embittered by the loss of his kingdom, had allowed himself to be talked by the pope into invading Sicily at the head of a papal army. There was a distinctly unpleasant flavour about Gregory's actions at this point, for it was still regarded as particularly despicable to infringe the possessions of an absent crusader and this point of view had always been supported by the Church. Frederick's presence in Italy was now

urgently required. So he made sure of the succession of his son
Conrad to the kingdom of Jerusalem—though, in theory, this
would depend upon the year-old boy coming to Acre within the
next twelve months to claim his inheritance—and then he embarked at Acre on 1 May 1229. The people who once had welcomed him so warmly now treated him with unexampled insolence
as he rode down to the harbour; the butchers are said to have
pelted him with entrails. Quite clearly the patriarch's propaganda
had had its effect. But the most powerful lord in Christendom
gave no sign that he had noticed anything amiss. On 10 June he
landed at Brindisi. Not until a month later did the pope even
know that he had left Acre, and by autumn the papal army had
been routed. Gregory IX had lost the first round. He could do
little against a ruler who was victorious in war, who had returned
from Jerusalem surrounded by the aureole of the Last Emperor
who had restored the Holy City to Christendom—a ruler who
moved around the countryside accompanied by an exotically
magnificent court and later by a rare menagerie of wild beasts. In
May 1230 peace was made at San Germano. Superficially it looked
as though the emperor had humbled himself. But although there
was some compensation for the Church in reality he was unquestionably the victor. His rule of Sicily could no longer be
disputed and in the next year he issued the constitutions of Melfi,
re-organizing the kingdom's centralized administration. The sentence of excommunication was lifted and the emperor who, not
long ago, had been called the 'disciple of Muhammad' was once
more the 'beloved son of the Church'. The success of his crusade
was now recognized by the Church. Even before the conclusion of
this peace the emperor had had a pulpit constructed in the cathedral of Bitonto, a town which had just been forced to submit to
him. The relief on this pulpit has been made the subject of a
penetrating analysis by H. M. Schaller who has shown that it
represents the Hohenstaufen Last Emperors from Frederick I to
Conrad IV and thus illustrates a sermon delivered by Nicholas of
Bari in which the emperor was glorified as divine majesty and
elevated to a godlike position. Schaller has rightly emphasized that
the Hohenstaufen conception of the Last Emperor begins with the
coronation manifesto of 18 March 1229 together with Nicholas of
Bari's sermon and the Bitonto pulpit. From now on his supporters
saw the emperor as the long-awaited Messiah and even his most extreme opponents succumbed to this eschatological point of view
when, from 1239 onwards, they described him as the forerunner of
Antichrist. No one doubted that he marked the end of an era.[88]

12 · THE HISTORY OF CYPRUS (1192–1489) AND THE CRUSADER STATES (1192–1244)

As a result of the emperor's determination to incorporate the kingdom of Jerusalem and the island of Cyprus firmly within the Hohenstaufen empire, Frederick II's crusade had momentous consequences for the Holy Land. The Frankish barons were far too conscious of the privileges of their class to allow such a project to go unresisted. Thus the most important episode in the history of the crusader states from 1192 to 1244 is the anti-Ghibelline party's struggle against Hohenstaufen centralization. In the end Frederick was defeated partly because he had underestimated the obstinacy of the barons and partly because he was unable to devote sufficient energy to his Mediterranean plans, particularly after his second excommunication in 1239 when the opening of the last round of his contest with the Roman curia forced him to concentrate his resources in Italy.

The question of Cyprus played an important part in the conflict between the emperor and the Palestinian barons. This then is an appropriate point at which to give a brief survey of the history of the island kingdom until its loss of independence in 1489, before going on to recount the history of the mainland states up until 1244.[89] From the time of its conquest by Richard Coeur de Lion in 1191, Cyprus was of great significance to the crusader states. Once Byzantium had resigned itself to the loss of the island, the possession of Cyprus gave the Franks an unassailable base; not until the days of the Ottoman Empire was Muslim seapower sufficient to make a complete or a lasting conquest of Cyprus possible. The island lies so close to the mainland that from the heights of the pilgrimage centre at Stavrovouni the mountains of Lebanon can be seen across the sea. It served as a supply base, as a port of call for traders and pilgrims, as a springboard for future crusades and as a place of refuge for those who had to flee from the Holy Land. Naturally its secure situation attracted just as many knightly families away from the Christian lordships of the mainland as did Frankish Greece; on the other hand because it was so near the

Frankish barons who kept or recovered their estates as a result of the treaties of 1192 and 1229 treated Cyprus only as a place to retreat to in case of emergency. On the whole they retained their fiefs on the mainland and were available for military operations there. Thus it was that in the following years, through a process of intermarriage and property settlements, the great Palestinian families became firmly established on both sides of the sea.

This process was warmly encouraged by Guy of Lusignan who received the lordship of Cyprus in 1192 in compensation for the loss of his kingdom of Jerusalem (see above p. 145). In his two years' reign he laid the foundations of a new feudal state on the western pattern which was to remain in the hands of his descendants for nearly 300 years. If he was to maintain himself against the native Greek–Cypriot population he had to have vassals. So he freely distributed state property to the knights whom Saladin had driven out of Palestine. Altogether he granted out some 300 knight's fees to the value of 400 bezants a year each and an additional 200 Turcopole fees worth 300 bezants each to non-knightly soldiers who possessed two horses and a coat of mail. By this policy Guy almost completely emptied the state treasury. His brother and successor, Amalric I of Cyprus (1194–1205; king from 1197) believed therefore that his primary duty was to refill the royal coffers. Using a mixture of persuasion and force he made his vassals return a part of their incomes. When he died he had an annual revenue of at least 200,000 bezants. In 1367 the king was to receive 100,000 bezants as the yield from landrents and fiscal rights in the diocese of Limassol alone. The total income of the entire lay nobility in this diocese only equalled the king's and it was this economic preponderance—so different from the situation on the mainland—that established the king's political supremacy. When, in 1197, Amalric took over the throne of Jerusalem (as Amalric II) he made an important decision. Instead of uniting Jerusalem and Cyprus under one crown, as the pope would have liked, he created a purely personal union and thus, by keeping the administrations separate, he prevented Cyprus from being financially milked to the unilateral advantage of Jerusalem. This arrangement was confirmed when the Lusignans recovered the throne of Jerusalem after the Hohenstaufen interlude. But this did not mean that the rulers and knights of Cyprus contributed nothing to the needs of the Holy Land. They took part in the crusades of Henry VI (1197), of the king of Hungary (1217), of John of Brienne at Damietta (1219), and of Louis IX of France

(1249). Within the limits of reasonable political action Cyprus played its part in the defence of the mainland states.

During Amalric's reign the Latin Church in Cyprus was organized (1196). The capital, Nicosia, was made an archbishopric with suffragan sees at Limassol, Famagusta, and Paphos. An unusual feature of the Cypriot Church was that it consisted almost entirely of the upper ranks of the hierarchy. Apart from the cathedral churches there were hardly any parishes; in his analysis of the state of the diocese of Limassol in 1367 Jean Richard found only three, one of which, as well as the cathedral, was in Limassol itself. The parishes, as dependent priories, came directly under the authority of the cathedral church. To celebrate the important religious festivals the Latin population travelled to the cathedrals in the episcopal cities unless there was a house belonging to one of the Mendicant Orders near where they lived or unless, like many of the nobility, they had a chapel of their own. The most important religious houses were the Dominican convent in Nicosia where the kings had their family vault, and the Premonstratensian house, Bellapais. The fourteenth-century ruins of Bellapais still survive as do the thirteenth-century ruins of the cathedral of Sainte Sophie in Nicosia: two of the finest examples of Latin Gothic architecture in Cyprus. As in the Frankish states in Greece the crucial problem of Church politics was the question of the relationship between the Latin and the Greek Orthodox Churches. The chief points of tension were the subordination of the Greek hierarchy to the Latin and the azyme question i.e. the debate as to whether the host should be made of leavened or, according to the Latin custom, unleavened bread. The differences of ritual led to attempts at conversion, but also to persecution, the burning of heretics, expulsion, emigration, and other equally unfortunate developments. In practice the azyme question was never solved; the Greeks remained true to their own rite. As for the first problem, this was settled in theory by Alexander IV's *Constitutio Cypria* of 1260. The Greek bishops kept their episcopal rank but were regarded in canon law as being vicars of the Latin archbishop of Nicosia. They had to swear an oath of fealty to him and were subject to his jurisdiction in matters of faith and discipline. Fierce quarrels had preceded this settlement but it was by no means always observed strictly, nor did it lead to a lasting peace, for besides the tensions between Latins and Greeks there were also bitter internal disputes between the Greek conformists who were prepared to compromise with the Latin Church and the strict Orthodox who were not. As early as 1222 the fourteen Greek bishoprics had been reduced to four and the bishops themselves were not allowed to reside in the diocesan capitals. Thus the Greek bishop of Limassol lived in Lefkara and the bishop of Nicosia in Soli. The possessions of the Greek Church had been badly mauled by the Frankish nobles at the time of the conquest. Even so the bishop of Nicosia had an income of 1,500 florins (9,000 bezants) in 1329. This, of course, was a modest sum compared with the 18,400 bezants which the Latin bishop of Limassol obtained from his much smaller diocese in 1367.

Like Jerusalem, Cyprus suffered from its kings dying early and leaving heirs who were under-age. Amalric's son Hugh I (1205–18) was only ten years old when he came to the throne and his own son and heir Henry I (1218–53) was no more than eight months old. The latter's mother, Alice, daughter of Henry of Champagne, acted as guardian and regent, but the barons appointed relatives from the famous Palestinian family of the Ibelins to serve as administrative *baillis*, first Alice's uncle Philip (1218–27) and then Jean d'Ibelin, the 'Old Lord of Beirut' (1227–8). When Frederick II stayed on the island in 1228 he forced Jean to hand over the young king and the four strong royal castles in the north (Kyrenia, Kantara, Buffavento, and St. Hilarion, called Dieudamour by the Franks). Frederick claimed the *bailliage* for himself and in 1229 farmed it out to his supporters on Cyprus. By doing this without obtaining the consent of the Haute Cour—which was just as important in Nicosia as on the mainland—he offended against the feudal ideas of the time. There are some faint indications that the Cypriot barons had begun by promulgating their own assises, but the law of Jerusalem was soon recognized to be more favourable to them and by 1230 it can be shown to be valid for Cyprus as well. Amalric I's famous *Assise sur la ligece* offered the best way of proceeding against Frederick II because it obliged all the liege-vassals to band together against a feudal lord who confiscated a fief—in this case the *bailliage*—without a judgement of the peers. It should be noted, however, that although the law of Cyprus was in many ways based on the customs of Jerusalem it was not until 1369 that it was completely and officially replaced by the latter. Hardly had Frederick left the island when a revolt broke out against the rule of his *baillis* and Cyprus became caught up in the long drawn out War of the Lombards. However, since this war was fought out chiefly on the mainland it will be described later (see below p. 246) as a part of the history of the Holy Land. In Cyprus the war ended in 1233, ten years earlier than in Palestine, with the capitulation of the imperial fortress of Kyrenia. This marked the end of the Hohenstaufen attempt to seize Cyprus and in 1247 Pope Innocent IV took the island into the protection of the Apostolic See, absolving King Henry I from any oath of allegiance which he may have sworn to the emperor.

The collapse of the Hohenstaufen empire in the eastern Mediterranean put an end to the Oriental plans made by the Master of the Teutonic Order, Hermann of Salza. In 1220 he had bought Count Otto of Henneberg's Palestinian inheritance and thus obtained the important *Seigneurie de Joscelin* (see above p. 129) for the Order. In the Golden Bull of Rimini (1226) he was granted princely rights in Prussia where later the Teutonic Order was to build up a state as a fief of the empire. But at first the bull was no more than an alternative programme, held ready just in case Hermann's Oriental plans should fall through. As the emperor's chief support during his crusade the Order received great privileges from Frederick II, and if the War of the Lombards had not been lost the Teutonic Knights might have achieved a position similar to that of the other Military Orders, with Cyprus, as an imperial fief, playing an important part in their history. In 1230, when it became clear that this was not going to happen, Hermann of Salza obtained from the pope a privilege for the Kulmerland—a privilege parallel to the Golden Bull of Rimini—and then devoted his energies to the realization of the alternative programme of 1226.[90]

In 1246 Henry I of Cyprus succeeded his mother Alice as regent of the kingdom of Jerusalem, taking the title *Seigneur du Royaume de Jérusalem*. Thus, in the absence of the lawful king, responsibility for the government of the mainland kingdom rested once again in the hands of the king of Cyprus. Henry's son and successor, Hugh II (1253-67), the prince for whom St. Thomas Aquinas began to write his important treatise on statecraft, *De regimine principum* (completed by Tolomeo of Lucca), died before he reached adult years. With him the house of Lusignan died out in the direct male line. The next king was his cousin Hugh of Antioch-Lusignan. His mother was a Lusignan and he used her name exclusively in order to emphasize dynastic continuity. As Hugh III of Cyprus (1267-84) he was, like his predecessor, *Seigneur de Jérusalem*. Indeed after the death of the last Hohenstaufen king of Jerusalem, Conradin, in 1268, he became King Hugh I of Jerusalem. His primary concern was for the mainland kingdom which was under severe pressure from the attacks of the Mameluks. In 1272 in order to give it additional support he tried to impose unlimited military service on those Cypriot barons who only had fiefs on the island. This demand was turned down by James of Ibelin who declared proudly that such service had always been purely voluntary and that if there was anyone who had the right to demand it, it was the Ibelins, not the king, for they had led the Cypriot army to the mainland more often than he had. In the next year, as a compromise, it was agreed that four months mainland service might be done. As a result of this limitation Hugh's attempt to defend the kingdom of Jerusalem against the claims of Charles of Anjou failed in 1279 (see below p. 271). Only after Charles's death in 1285 did the kings of Cyprus recover the throne of Jerusalem. In Cyprus itself Hugh III was succeeded by his two sons, John I (1284–5) and the epileptic Henry II (1285–1324). During the latter's reign the last part of the mainland kingdom was lost (1291) and thenceforth the Lusignans ruled Cyprus only, though they continued to be crowned as kings of Jerusalem at a ceremony in Famagusta. As a result of the fall of the Holy Land Henry II suffered much personal misfortune. In 1306 his brother Amalric, the dispossessed lord of Tyre, used his epilepsy as a pretext for seizing power and ruling for four years as a despot with the title *Gouverneur*. Henry was shipped off to Lesser Armenia where he remained for years in the custody of the Armenian king; not until after Amalric's murder in 1310 was he able to return.

Apart from this palace revolution the internal history of Cyprus had been peaceful since 1233. Of course there had been differences of opinion between king and barons; as in Jerusalem the king theoretically was only *primus inter pares* and was subject to the Haute Cour in Nicosia. But for various reasons he was much more powerful than the king of Jerusalem. He was richer than the mainland king for a start. The Cypriot crown fiefs never attained the size of the four great mainland baronies; in 1367 the revenues of his tenants-in-chief varied between 100 and 21,000 bezants but 'ordinary' fiefs of 1,000 to 1,500 bezants were fairly common. Thus at this level the holders of fiefs were two or three times as well-endowed as on the mainland. In addition the important legal principle of collateral succession to the great fiefs in Jerusalem (*le cours des anciens fies est a toz heirs*) did not apply in Cyprus. Thus if the direct male line died out the fief escheated to the crown and there was no *Leihezwang* i.e. the king was not obliged by law to regrant the fief immediately. So he was in a position to build up his landed wealth. The right to mint coin and to exercise jurisdiction over the bourgeoisie remained exclusively royal prerogatives. Thus the barons were clearly subordinate to the king; it is significant, for example, that the notary of the Haute Cour had to render account to the royal *Secrète*. Above all, as a result of the absence of any external threat, the barons held no castles. Only the king and the Military Orders disposed of such fortresses. Thus, as Jean Richard has pointed out, it was impossible for individual barons to rebel. In Cyprus resistance could only take the form of a palace revolution or a rising of the entire nobility. Otherwise state and society in Frankish Cyprus were basically similar to the situation in Jerusalem and for that reason the reader is referred to the description of the kingdom of Jerusalem in chapter eight where attention is drawn to those features which were peculiar to Cyprus, usually as a result of Byzantine influence. The impoverished native Greek population still lived as they had done during the days of Byzantine rule. They were divided into three classes: the *paroikoi* who were tied to the land and had to pay a poll tax and one third of their produce as well as do labour services on two days a week; the *perperiarii* who, though personally free, had to pay an annual tax of fifteen hyperpers (bezants) and one third of their produce; and the *eleutheroi* or *francomati* who held free land and only had to pay one fifth of their produce to the former lord of the land. After the fall of Acre (1291) the economic importance of Cyprus grew as Famagusta took over Acre's role in the Levant trade. The Genoese who had enjoyed a privileged position in Cyprus since 1232 held great economic power and the king was constantly at odds or at war with them. The Venetians did not arrive until after 1291. Sugar, salt (obtained by a process of evaporation), and the famous Cyprus wines and fabrics were the island's most valuable exports. In addition Famagusta was of some importance as a shipbuilding centre.

The later history of Cyprus can only be briefly touched upon. Hugh IV (1324–59) distinguished himself in the war against the Turks. Under his successor, Peter I (1359–69) the Lusignan dynasty reached its high point. Peter undertook successful campaigns of conquest in Cilicia and in 1368 he was elected king of Lesser Armenia though he did not live long enough to take over the reins of government. In fact Lesser Armenia's days were numbered. It was hard pressed by the Mameluks and finally collapsed in 1375. After the death of its last Christian king, Leo VI (1393), Lesser Armenia was joined in permanent union with the crown of Cyprus, but the union existed in name only—the country itself was controlled by the Egyptians until 1516 when it became a part of the Ottoman Empire. When this broke up after the First World War, the Armenian attempts to revive their old Cilician

independence were crushed by the new Turkey in a series of indescribable massacres. Besides his Armenian adventures Peter I
also organized a serious crusade to reconquer the Holy Land; in
this he had the vigorous support of his chancellor, Philip of
Mezières, a figure of some importance in the world of literature.
For years Peter travelled Europe preparing his crusade. The enterprise began well with the capture of Alexandria in 1365 but then
immediately came to a halt because the booty was so immense that
the army had no thoughts of further war, only of getting their
plunder safely away. In 1369 Peter became the victim of a general
revolt of the nobility—the result not, as was thought until
recently, of court intrigue and marriage policy, but of the determined resistance put up by the barons to his somewhat absolutist
tendencies. He had appointed non-noble bourgeois to crown offices
and employed foreign mercenaries who threatened to undermine
the baronial privilege of carrying arms. Taxes which had been
granted for a fixed period he continued to levy after the expiry of
that period. The last straw came when he imprisoned vassals without a judgement of their peers in the Haute Cour. The revolution
which followed destroyed the predominance of the crown in
Cyprus. It was officially decided to make the law of Jerusalem
apply to Cyprus and a baronial committee was commissioned to
search out the best (i.e. the most favourable to the vassals) manu-
script of the *Livre de Jean d'Ibelin*. From now on the Haute Cour
had a voice in the administration of crown lands; from 1369 all
royal charters which concerned the extent or the administration of
the crown estates were 'guaranteed' (i.e. countersigned) by two
members of the Haute Cour. Internal decline set in under Peter's
successor, Peter II (1369–82). In the course of a war with Genoa he
lost control of the port of Famagusta (1373). This soon became a
dependency of the Genoese bank of San Giorgio. Since Famagusta
was the economic centre of the island its recapture now became
the most important objective of royal policy. In the Great Schism
Cyprus remained neutral until 1382, then opted for the pope at
Rome. In 1396 the king changed sides, giving his allegiance to the
pope at Avignon in the vain hope that French pressure on the
Genoese would then force them to relinquish Famagusta. Under
James I (1382–98) and Janus (1398–1432) the kingdom became
steadily weaker. The lower classes profited from this development.
Even Peter I's policies had been partially financed by the fees paid
by villeins to obtain their freedom. The nobles too were forced to
resort to the same expedient in order to be able to pay the royal
tithe which was introduced during the war with Genoa. By the

beginning of the sixteenth century there were only 47,185 *paroikoi* left in contrast to 77,066 *francomati*.

In 1426 the Mameluk sultans took revenge for the attack on Alexandria by overrunning and laying waste the island which was then reduced to the status of a tributary vassal state of the Mameluks. Under John II (1432–58), Charlotte of Lusignan and her consort Louis of Savoy (1458–60), and James II the Bastard (1460–73) who came to power through a revolution, the internal dissensions of Cyprus became increasingly savage. Famagusta was recaptured in 1464 but James II obtained little advantage from it because by marrying Katharina Cornaro, the daughter of a Venetian patrician, he had acknowledged that Cyprus lay within the Venetian sphere of influence. After the death of James III (1473–74) Katharina Cornaro ruled the island until 1489. When she abdicated on 26 February 1489 the Lusignan period came to an end. The standard of St. Mark was hoisted over Famagusta. Until 1571, when it fell to the Turks, Cyprus was a Venetian colony.

We are less well-informed about the internal development of the crusader states on the mainland in the period after 1192 than in the years before that date. Too much archive material has been lost and there was not another chronicler of the stature of William of Tyre. It is true that his chronicle was continued in Old French versions, some of which go up as far as 1277, but these continuations are not in the same historiographical class as their Latin model—and some of them were even written in Europe, not in Outremer. Equally inadequate as histories are the chronicles assembled in the collection known as the *Gestes des Chiprois*. Despite the title some of these chronicles were written on the mainland or, at any rate, by mainlanders. Above all, we lack the finely drawn portraits of the kings which were such an outstanding feature of William's chronicle.[91]

Saladin's truce with Richard Coeur de Lion in 1192 (see above p. 146) had restored the kingdom of 'Jerusalem' but the old capital itself was not returned and its place was taken by Acre. Essentially, the Franks held little more than the littoral, the coastal region from north of Tyre to south of Jaffa. This did not include either Nazareth or Beaufort on the Litani; thus the natural frontier to the east, the Jordan, was lost. Lydda and Ramleh were partitioned between Muslims and Franks. A land connection between Tripoli and the kingdom of Jerusalem no longer existed. Further north Muslim territory around Lattakieh separated Tripoli from Antioch which had managed to hold firm on the line of the Upper

Orontes. Internally the thirteenth century witnessed some shifts
within a nobility which had been decimated by the events of 1187
and by emigration to Greece. Some 'old' families managed to
maintain themselves despite these developments only to die out in
the male line (Arsuf before 1198; Haifa *c.* 1244; Scandelion *c.*
1260). Their places in the higher nobility were taken by other
families, not all of whom came from France—e.g. Walter the
German in Mergecolon, the Flemish family of Termonde in
Adelon, the Spaniard Alvarez *circa* 1250 in Haifa. The Ibelin
family—which was probably of Italian extraction—succeeded in
making itself the undisputed head of the baronage. It controlled
Beirut (from 1197), Arsuf (1206), and the county of Jaffa (1250);
it owned extensive estates in Cyprus and was related by marriage
to all the leading families of Palestine.

After the murder of Conrad of Montferrat, his widow, Isabella,
married Henry of Champagne, count palatine of Troyes. The
count, as the candidate supported by Richard I of England, then
took over the government of the Holy Land. The former king,
Guy of Lusignan, had already been granted Cyprus by way of
compensation. For reasons which are not entirely clear Henry of
Champagne never assumed the title of king, being content to call
himself 'lord of Jerusalem'. A man of considerable diplomatic skill
he saw that his main task, apart from the material reconstruction
of the kingdom, would be to put an end to the terrible feuds
which had originated in the days of Baldwin IV and which had
contributed so much to the fall of Jerusalem. The heirs to these
feuds were the families of Montferrat and Lusignan. Henry relied
much more on the supporters of the murdered Montferrat, including the Genoese, than Richard of England may have foreseen.
He used force to drive the Pisans, who had always been closely
associated with the Lusignans, out of the Holy Land. This caused
a breach with the constable of the kingdom, Amalric of Lusignan.
He too was forced into exile and went to Cyprus where, in 1194,
he succeeded his brother Guy. Henry now thought it advisable to
come to terms with Amalric. He visited Cyprus and arranged marriages between his daughters and Amalric's sons. In return Amalric was remitted the amount still owing from the sum his brother
had agreed to pay for Cyprus, and the Pisans were allowed to
return to the mainland. Henry's plan was a sensible one and, if
carried out, it would have established a strong new dynasty, but in
fact only one of the projected marriages actually took place and
this proved insufficient to ward off the claims of other candidates.
Henry also tried to uphold the rights of the crown in ecclesiastical

matters. In 1194 this led to conflict over the king's right to confirm the election of a patriarch. After beginning by acting in an altogether too heavy-handed way—he had the canons of the Church of the Holy Sepulchre imprisoned—Henry was forced to climb down. On 10 September 1197, shortly after Henry VI's troops, the heralds of a new crusade, had arrived in Palestine, Henry died as the result of a fall from a window. The plans for a new crusade came to a miserable end (see above p. 148); indeed even before Henry of Champagne died Jaffa had fallen.

As his successor the barons elected Amalric of Lusignan who had recently become king of Cyprus. The election was in no sense a free one, untrammelled by the claims of hereditary right, for essentially what the barons were doing was choosing a new husband for Henry's widow, Isabella, who continued to wear the crown. Under pressure from the Germans they opted for the rich Amalric of Lusignan in preference to the native baron, Ralph of Tiberias, who was learned in the law but also poor. Thus a personal union of Jerusalem and Cyprus was established. Amalric's election initiated a period of Hohenstaufen influence in the Levant though Jerusalem, of course, unlike Cyprus, was not an imperial fief. Amalric II (1197–1205) concentrated his attention entirely on the Holy Land. After his coronation, a ceremony which meant that Isabella had been crowned at last, he seems never to have returned to Cyprus. With the help of the German crusaders he was able to recapture Beirut and restore the land connection with Tripoli. The most distinctive feature of his reign was his attempt to restore the old customary law. The task was first assigned to Ralph of Tiberias but he preferred to evade it. Some time later Amalric issued the first code of law for Jerusalem, the *Livre au roi* (see above p. 158), in which a faint glimmer of the strong monarchy of the twelfth century still shines through, revealing Amalric's intention of re-establishing that authority. But already the opposition of the barons was too strong, and when Amalric, without obtaining a judgement from the Haute Cour, declared that Ralph of Tiberias had forfeited his fief, he was met by open resistance. Only with great difficulty was it possible to find a compromise which enabled both sides to save face. The next crusade, the fourth, came to a halt at Constantinople and brought no help to the Holy Land. Time and again, however, it proved possible to renew the truce with the Ayubids. In 1204 Jaffa was recaptured. Until almost the middle of the thirteenth century the kingdom was by and large spared the danger of a decisive Muslim attack thanks, in the early years, to the conciliatory attitude of the sultan, al-Adil, and later, to the civil wars between the Ayubid brothers. The crusader states would never have held out for nearly a century had it not been for these constantly renewed truces (1192–7, 1198–1204, 1204–10, 1211–17, 1221–39, 1241–4, 1255–63, 1272–90). The later Ayubids had little intention of attempting what Saladin had failed to achieve. They resigned themselves to the existence of the crusader states.

On 1 April 1205 Amalric died of a surfeit of fish. Isabella then ruled alone until her death shortly afterwards. Their two sons had not survived their father. Because his other son, Hugh, was the child of a former marriage, with an Ibelin, he could inherit only the crown of Cyprus, not that of Jerusalem. On the mainland the throne returned to a representative of the Montferrat line. From now on the descendants of Isabella from her last three marriages followed one another in the succession to the throne or to the regency. Until 1291 they were kings of Jerusalem. The following family tree illustrates these relationships. It is much simplified, but within this compass it is quite impossible to clarify all its ramifications.

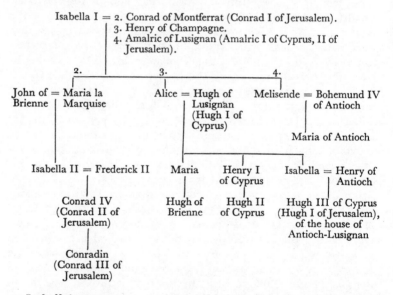

Isabella I = 2. Conrad of Montferrat (Conrad I of Jerusalem).
            3. Henry of Champagne.
            4. Amalric of Lusignan (Amalric I of Cyprus, II of Jerusalem).

Isabella's successor was her child from her second marriage, Maria la Marquise so called because her father was Conrad, the marquis of Montferrat. Jean d'Ibelin, the 'Old Lord of Beirut' and Isabella's half-brother, was appointed *bailli* (regent). With him there begins the long series of thirteenth-century *baillis,* not all of whom can be mentioned here. Like the crown the *bailliage* came to be looked upon as an hereditary dignity. Following the precedent set when the regent for Baldwin V was chosen, the *bailliage* was assumed by the ruler's nearest relative from that branch of the family which was entitled to succeed to the throne; while his nearest relative from the branch which was not so entitled was to be the ruler's guardian. The only exception to this rule occurred when the father himself (as the nearest relative from the branch with the right to succeed) was appointed *bailli* without there being any guardian because in this case, owing to the rule that a father could not be his son's heir, there was no danger that the *bailli* might murder the young ruler in order to seize the throne for himself. If there were several claimants to these offices, it was up to the Haute Cour to decide between them. The *bailli* exercised all the functions of the king and therefore had the crown's revenues at his disposal. But he had to render account to the king when the latter came of age. The barons were at all times on their guard against the possibility of a usurpation and so did not permit the *bailli* to control the royal castles. These were granted to individual noblemen chosen by the Haute Cour. Because the crown vassals were not obliged to swear to the *bailli* the oath of allegiance which they owed the king, the *bailli* was allowed to resume their fiefs for the period of the regency since otherwise he might have been deprived of the service due from them. If the rightful regent lived out of the country he could appoint his own administrative *baillis* to act as his representatives. This was a right of which Frederick II, in particular, made much use.

The regency of Jean d'Ibelin lasted until 1210. Then Maria la Marquise was married to John of Brienne, a man recommended to the barons by the king of France. He was brave and energetic, but by no means a statesman or diplomat of the first rank. His career was remarkable for his continual attempts to obtain one crown after another. His wife died in 1212 leaving him as regent for their daughter Isabella II. Two years later he married Stephanie, daughter of King Leo II of Lesser Armenia. During the Fifth Crusade, the climax of his career, involving war in Syria as well as in Egypt, he tried in vain to wrest control over the crusading army out of the hands of Cardinal-legate Pelagius and to keep Damietta for himself. Outmanoeuvred by Pelagius he then laid claim to succeed to the throne in Cilicia (1220) on the basis of his marriage to Stephanie, but once again in vain. In 1225 he married his daughter Isabella to Frederick II. Again he was outmanoeuvred, this time by the experienced imperial diplomats, with the result that immediately after the marriage he found, much to his astonishment, that he had lost the throne of Jerusalem. He saw no reason to give up, however, and in 1231, six years before his death, he actually succeeded in getting himself crowned as Latin emperor of Constantinople (see above p. 195).

During the whole of this period it was in the north that the most important events took place. Count Raymond III of Tripoli had died soon after the battle of Hattin (1187) and with him the Toulousan dynasty in Tripoli came to an end. As his successor he had designated his godson Raymond of Antioch, the eldest son of the ruling prince of Antioch, Bohemund III (1163–1201). Instead Bohemund installed his younger son, Bohemund (IV), in Tripoli. But in the following years Bohemund began to feel himself increasingly threatened by the 'great power' policy initiated by one of his own vassals, the Roupenian prince of Lesser Armenia, Leo II. The threat was all the more serious since after 1187 Antioch could no longer rely upon support from the kings of Jerusalem. In 1194 Bohemund III was tricked by Leo and taken prisoner, but Leo's attempt to seize Antioch failed in the face of resistance put up by the city commune which was organized to meet this crisis. Then at the request of the Antiochenes Henry of Champagne intervened. He travelled to Lesser Armenia and persuaded Leo to release Bohemund (1194). In return Bohemund renounced Antioch's feudal overlordship over Lesser Armenia. This opened the way for Leo to obtain a royal crown. In 1198 he received it from the hands of the German chancellor and recognized the emperor as his lord. As a symbol of the reconciliation between Antioch and Lesser Armenia Bohemund's son Raymond married Leo's niece Alice; unfortunately he died soon, shortly after a son, Raymond Roupen, had been born to him. His early death left the question of the succession in Antioch wide open with the result that Bohemund III's death in 1201 was followed by a fierce war of succession between Tripoli and Lesser Armenia lasting for fifteen years. Leo II championed the cause of his great-nephew Raymond Roupen who, according to the accepted rules of primogeniture in Antioch was, in fact, the rightful heir. Leo was supported by the higher nobility and by the pope who treated him indulgently on account of the union of the Armenian Church with Rome which had accompanied the coronation of 1198. But Innocent had to observe with disappointment the way in which (on several occasions) Leo first dissolved and then renewed the union according to the requirements of his policy towards Antioch. On the other side stood Bohemund of Tripoli, claiming to be the nearest relative of the last ruling prince and thus stating a principle which was to become increasingly more important in the history of the crusader states. The city commune, in which the anti-Armenian Greeks played a great role, supported Bohemund. At first the count of Tripoli could also rely on the support of the Latin clergy of Antioch but he forfeited this in 1207 when he installed a Greek patriarch who was to remain in office until 1213. Bohemund's intention was to ensure himself of lasting Greek support and now that Constantinople had fallen into Latin hands there was no danger that the installation of a Greek Orthodox patriarch might lead to a revival of Byzantine claims over Antioch. In these circumstances the Latin clergy withdrew their support from Bohemund and then, on a question of taxation, they broke with the commune as well. They were now clearly in the Armenian camp. Bohemund was still able to count on energetic help from Aleppo; like his predecessors he had no qualms about making alliances with Muslims. On several occasions az-Zahir of Aleppo drove Leo out of Antioch, the citadel of which always remained firmly in Bohemund's hands. Only in 1213 did Leo's position begin to improve, when rumours of a new crusade—the preaching of which began with the bull *Quia maior* in 1213—persuaded az-Zahir to associate himself more closely with Sultan al-Adil who favoured Leo's cause. The marriage between Stephanie and John of Brienne ensured that Leo would have the help of Jerusalem. Thus in 1216 he was at last able to take Antioch and instal Raymond Roupen. But the new prince was soon on thoroughly bad terms with the citizens. In 1219 he was ousted by a revolt and Bohemund of Tripoli returned to take over the government of Antioch for good, as Prince Bohemund IV (1219–33).

Leo's frequent interventions in North Syria were paid for in West Cilicia where he suffered losses at the hands of the Seldjuks of Rum. Even so, he was an outstanding ruler. At home he was able to outmanoeuvre the Hethoumians who, as vassals of Byzantium, had for many years fought a fierce struggle against the Roupenians. He did much to promote trade. He reconstructed his kingdom along Frankish lines, to such an extent indeed that under his successor the Assises of Antioch, translated into Armenian by the constable, Sempad, were introduced as the new code of law for the kingdom. When he died in 1219 a struggle for the succession ensued. In the interests of his daughter Isabella, the old king had disinherited Raymond Roupen and though both pressed their claims neither Raymond nor John of Brienne, who championed the right of his wife, Leo's elder daughter Stephanie, were able to make much headway. But in this situation an alliance with Antioch seemed vital so in 1222 the regent, Constantine of Lampron—a member of the Hethoumian dynasty—arranged for Isabella to marry Philip of Antioch, a son of Bohemund IV. But two years later Constantine dropped this plan and then, in 1226, he married Isabella to his own son Hethoum. As Hethoum I (1226–69), this king was able to bury the old feud between the two princely families of Armenia.[92]

One year earlier a new era in the history of the Holy Land had been ushered in by the marriage of Frederick II to John of Brienne's daughter Isabella. Until the death of his wife (1228) Frederick was king of Jerusalem; after that date he was no more than regent for their son Conrad IV (Conrad II of Jerusalem) who had been born on 25 April 1228. The barons refused to recognize him as king so the coronation of 1229 had no validity in constitutional law except perhaps as a retrospective legitimization of Frederick's kingship of 1225–8. Frederick's crusade and the subsequent attempt to incorporate the Holy Land firmly within his empire unleashed a fierce war of resistance. The barons believed that the rights of their order were threatened and they were never prepared to sacrifice their group interests. Clearly they were fighting against an opponent who was equally self-interested, but the account given by the historian Philip of Novare presents only one side of the coin in surrounding the baronial reaction with the aura of a struggle for liberty. Over and above the dynastic interests of the Hohenstaufen it is clear that what the emperor had achieved in the treaty of 1229 held out some promise for positive development—for if the Holy Land needed anything it was strong government. Instead from 1228 to 1243 the War of the Lombards raged in Palestine and reduced the kingdom to a state of 'legalized anarchy' (Runciman). The war was named after Frederick's German and Italian mercenaries—not because they came from Lombardy but because many of them came from south Italy i.e. from the old Byzantine *theme* (province) of Langobardia. Unfortunately we possess only the one-sided accounts written by the anti-imperial party, in particular the memoirs of the famous jurist Philip of Novare which he deliberately entitled *History of the War between Emperor Frederick and Messire Jean d'Ibelin*, in this way elevating the leader of the anti-Ghibellines to an imperial level. The trouble began in Cyprus when the *bailli* on the island, Jean d'Ibelin, handed over the young king to his feudal lord Frederick, but refused to resign either the *bailliage* or the mainland fortress of

Beirut to the emperor. Both of Frederick's demands were illegal
in that they had not been discussed and approved in the courts
of Nicosia and Acre—the course of action recommended by the
'Old Lord of Beirut'. The immediate solution was a compromise
which left Cyprus in the hands of the emperor while the fate of
Beirut was to be decided in the Haute Cour of Acre. But Frederick
did not keep his promise to consult the court and this turned the
Ibelins into obstinate and bitter opponents. Nevertheless the
emperor began well with the success of the treaty with al-Kamil to
his credit. In two places, Jerusalem and Nazareth in Galilee, the
kingdom's territory was extended eastwards. Before returning to
Europe, the emperor farmed the *bailliage* of Cyprus to a consortium of five loyal barons. Understandably enough these men
were determined to recover their costs and so their administration
soon ran into trouble. By June 1230, with the help of reinforcements from the mainland, Jean d'Ibelin had driven them from
the island.

Hardly had Frederick II made his peace with the pope in 1230
when he intervened in the East. In 1231 he sent a squadron of
galleys to Palestine. It was commanded by the imperial marshal,
Richard Filangieri, who was accompanied by his brothers Lothar
and Henry. They did not venture to land on Cyprus but sailed
straight on to Palestine where they took up their headquarters in
Tyre. Leaving Lothar in command here, Richard moved on to
besiege Beirut; his instructions from Frederick were to dispossess
the Ibelins. This had the effect of uniting almost the entire
baronage behind the Ibelins and so once again the kingdom was
split into two warring camps. On one side there were the imperial
troops together with the Teutonic Knights, the Pisans, and the
exiled Cypriot consortium of five. On the other side were the forty-
three most important barons in the Holy Land supported by the
Genoese and the king of Cyprus. The chief centres of Ibelin power
were Beirut and Acre. At Acre a commune made up of the urban
patriciate and city nobility was formed. Determined to resist to
the end, the commune elected Jean d'Ibelin as its mayor in 1232.
As the man most directly threatened he was the moving spirit
behind the rebellion. He was an upright, brave, and cultivated
man. In these circumstances he can hardly be blamed for preferring to defend the privileges of his class rather than submit
to a centralized Hohenstaufen state which, though it might well
have led to a strengthening of the Holy Land, would not necessarily have done so. While Gregory IX attempted to mediate in
the interests of the emperor, the Church in Palestine remained

neutral; so did the north under Bohemund IV and Bohemund V (1233–52) of Antioch-Tripoli. In any case, Antioch, cut off from the other crusader states by the Muslim enclave at Lattakieh, went downhill economically and so declined steadily in influence after the death of Bohemund IV in 1233. For almost thirty years north Syria practically disappears from history. Meanwhile the barons of Jerusalem recognized Richard Filangieri as the lawful representative of the regent but still continued to oppose him vigorously. On 3 May 1232 at Casel Imbert between Tyre and Acre the imperial marshal defeated the Ibelins in battle and then, encouraged by this victory, carried the war to Cyprus. But here he was himself beaten by Jean d'Ibelin on 15 June at Agridi near the castle of Dieudamour. When Kyrenia surrendered in April 1233 the second, and final, liberation of Cyprus by the Ibelins was completed. On the mainland the imperial bureaucracy continued to function but in reality the Holy Land was ruled by the clan of the Ibelins whose far-flung family connections included many of the higher nobility of Europe. During the years 1234–6 Hermann of Salza and the pope tried to arrange a compromise which would have ensured the continuity of the imperial administration. But since they disputed the right of the barons to choose the regent and demanded the dissolution of the commune of Acre—the key to Jean's strong position—their efforts were bound to remain fruitless. In 1236 Jean d'Ibelin died but his brilliant family at once found a new leader in the person of his son Balian. Then in 1239 Balian was in his turn succeeded by his cousin, Philip de Montfort, a relative of Simon de Montfort, the powerful earl of Leicester.

Three years after Jean's death Frederick's treaty with al-Kamil expired. The Muslims at once seized the opportunity to occupy the undefended city of Jerusalem only to be driven out by a group of crusaders led by Theobald IV, count of Champagne and (since 1234) king of Navarre. It was at this time that the only section of the fortifications still standing, the citadel of the Tower of David, was destroyed. The pope had been planning this crusade ever since 1234. At one time he had even considered sending it to Constantinople to help John of Brienne in his war against the Byzantines and Bulgars, but nothing came of this idea. In 1239 the position of the Franks in Palestine was not at all bad. Since 1229 al-Kamil had been occupied with the reconstruction of the Ayubid empire consequent upon the treaty of Tel-Ajul. In addition he had to cope with the Khwarismians. At the end of the twelfth century the shah of Khwarism had created a powerful state out of the ruins of the Seldjuk empire of Iran. With the help of his only superficially Islamicized Kipchak Turks he was, for a short while, overlord of the whole of the Islamic East from his power base in west Turkestan (Khwarism, Transoxania, and Khorassan). Then in 1220 his empire was overthrown by the Mongols and the Khwarismians withdrew westwards. By 1230 they were ruling parts of Armenia and Azerbaijan, serving both as a buffer state against the Mongols and as a threat to the eastern frontiers of the Ayubids and the Seldjuks of Rum. In 1230 a coalition of these two powers defeated the army of Khwarism. They did not foresee that this setback would weaken the shah to such an extent that within a year the rest of his kingdom had been totally destroyed by the Mongols. The gates by which the Mongols would enter the Near East were now open. Soon al-Kamil was at war with the Seldjuks, his former allies. He was defeated and, as a result, had to face a rebellion led by his brother al-Ashraf. Not until al-Ashraf died in 1237 did the civil war come to an end. But al-Kamil himself died a year later and the Ayubid empire collapsed into the turmoil of a civil war between his sons as-Salih Ayub (Damascus) and al-Adil II (Egypt). In 1240 as-Salih took over Egypt. Taking advantage of these convulsions Theobald's crusaders struck southwards in 1239 and recaptured Ascalon. In 1240 another army, led by Richard of Cornwall, arrived in the Holy Land. Because as-Salih, based in Egypt, now found himself in the position of having to try to reconquer his former territories in Syria, he concluded a treaty with Richard in 1241. This confirmed the concessions made by al-Kamil in 1229 and added the hinterland of Sidon, Tiberias, and Eastern Galilee, and the area around Jaffa and Ascalon. Only Samaria and Hebron remained in Muslim hands; in Galilee the Jordan frontier had been restored and the Holy Land had a greater extent than at any time since 1187.[93]

Soon after Richard of Cornwall had gone the War of the Lombards began again. On 25 April 1243 Conrad IV became fifteen years of age and no longer a minor. The barons, their minds attuned to such legal formalities, had waited almost until that time—it marked the end of the emperor's regency—before renewing the war against the imperial adminstrators. In June 1242 at a meeting at Acre they elected Alice of Cyprus, the daughter of Henry of Champagne, as regent, though back in 1229 they had rejected her claims to this office. After her death her indolent son, Henry I of Cyprus, succeeded to the *bailliage* but called himself *Seigneur de Jérusalem*—not king indeed but clearly claiming to be more than just a *bailli*. In reality, however, he was merely a toy in the hands of the Ibelins. They had settled down to besiege Tyre soon after the election of Alice in 1242. Richard Filangieri was captured and Lothar had to surrender the city in order to save his brother's life. The Hohenstaufen take-over bid had finally failed and the more or less complete predominance of the barons in the Holy Land was now assured. It was a clear sign of the weakness of the monarchy that Tyre, the brightest jewel in the crown's estates, was not restored to the king but was granted by the Haute Cour to Philip de Montfort. The commune of Acre was no longer needed and had already—probably in 1241—been dissolved, though the religious fraternities of the city, the seeds out of which the commune had grown, continued to play some part in politics.

The growing tension between as-Salih and his Syrian opponents led to a rapprochement between Damascus and the Franks. The old alliance of 1139 was renewed and in 1243 the Muslims even evacuated their quarter in Jerusalem. But such was the power of thirteenth-century Egypt that the alliance with Damascus no longer possessed its former value. In 1244 the Ayubid rulers declared war on each other. In preparation for this as-Salih had made an alliance with the Khwarismian troops who had been soldiering in Mesopotamia ever since their defeat by the Mongols and who were ready to serve any lord who could pay them. Moving down from the north they swept through the Holy Land and occupied Jerusalem without meeting any resistance worth mentioning. This time Jerusalem had been lost for good. The Khwarismians then joined forces with the Egyptian army and together they inflicted a crushing defeat on the Frankish–Damascene army at Gaza on 17 October 1244. It was the greatest setback since Hattin. Among its results were the re-unification of the Ayubid Empire (1245) and the loss of east Galilee and Ascalon (1247). By 1250 the south had gone; and in the north the Jordan frontier had been lost; from now on the kingdom's eastern border ran through Beaufort and Safed.

THE Khwarismian conquest of Jerusalem, despite the brutal way in which it was carried out, did not make much impression on Europe. In 1245 Innocent IV held a council at Lyons where he had taken refuge from the power of Frederick II. Here he began to preach a new crusade—but with little success. He himself was just as involved as the emperor in the great struggle between the two universal powers. The war of Guelf against Ghibelline was raging in Italy. The disciples of Joachim of Fiore mocked at all attempts to organize a crusade; they relied upon a pseudo-Joachite commentary on Jeremiah according to which Christ himself was opposed to the recapture of Jerusalem. Henry III of England (1216–72) was kept far too busy by his unruly barons to be able to think of going on crusade. France was the only European power that, at that moment, was capable of mounting a crusade and in fact King Louis IX, Saint Louis (1226–70), had anticipated the pope by taking the cross in December 1244. Owing to the silence of the sources it is not clear whether he had been influenced by the news from Jerusalem. The immediate occasion of his decision had been his recovery from a serious illness. Once again, in the person of St. Louis, a great leader of the crusading movement had arisen, a man capable of inspiring enthusiasm, a man who was himself devoted to the pure and unadulterated crusading ideal. From 1245 until his death in 1270 French policy was based on the crusade.[94]

Louis IX was born in 1219 and succeeded to the throne while still a boy. He had the good fortune to have his kingdom ruled by a most vigorous and intelligent regent, his mother, Blanche of Castile. When he came of age in 1234 she married him to Margaret of Provence and continued to exercise a dominating influence over his government. The royal vassals, who had scented an opportunity during the regency, rebelled again and were again put down by Blanche. In 1242 England too was made forcibly aware of the revival of French power. Under St. Louis the south-

ward expansion of France continued unabated. In 1247 the Cape-
tians acquired Provence; in 1249 Toulouse. The stronger north
had triumphed over the more civilized south. At home Louis
proved to be an able, uncompromising, and a just ruler. He
reformed the administration of justice and prohibited the judicial duel. Under him the French economy flourished. The Church
could always count on his support—but not at the expense of the
rights of the crown which he upheld emphatically. He remained
neutral in the great struggle between empire and papacy; both
sides put pressure on him in the hope of gaining his support, but
in vain. He allowed the pope's excommunication of the emperor
to be published in France, but prevented the crusade against the
Hohenstaufen from being preached there. In his eyes Frederick II
was still the emperor and he tried to persuade the pope to be more
moderate. Louis's greatest strength was his character—so highly
praised both by his contemporaries and by posterity. But he was
by no means always the peaceful saint that he was made out to be
by some contemporary hagiographers. Though essentially gentle
and always ready to listen to justified criticism, he was still capable
of fierce outbursts of anger. Despite his delicate health he lived
frugally and ascetically; sometimes his indisputably profound
religious feeling brought him to the brink of ecstasy. The bonds
between him and his mother were unusually close, certainly much
closer than those with his wife, but when it was a question of his
faith or his crusade then even his mother could be overruled. He
was a man who in his daily dealings with his fellow men proved
that power had not corrupted him and that he was as much a man
as a king. In this respect Louis appears very much to advantage
when compared with Frederick II who surrounded himself with a
mystical veil so that he might be raised up to a godlike dignity.
Louis's strength and influence lay in the decisiveness with which
he pursued a moral ideal; only Saladin was his equal here. The
impression he made on men is best illustrated not by the fact
that he was canonized just twenty-seven years after his death but
by the fact that even Voltaire considered the canonization to be
fully justified.

Louis prepared his crusade with great care. The Church had to
bear the chief financial burden in the shape of a crusading
twentieth, but the towns too were heavily taxed. In the fourteenth
century the royal treasury estimated the total cost of the crusade
at 1.3 million *livres tournois*, itemized as follows: on court
expenses 200,000, on the king's ransom 210,000, military expenses
750,000, on ship-building 40,000, on the construction of fortifica-

tions in the Holy Land 120,000, on the ransom of Christian prisoners 1,300. The significance of this treasury estimate becomes clearer in the light of an annual royal income of 1256-9 of about 114,000 *livres*, i.e. the crusade cost about eleven or twelve times the annual budget. It is evident that the Church and the towns had to bear an enormous burden. The arrangements for the transport of the troops were made in treaties concluded with Marseilles—a port which, in formal terms, still belonged to the empire and which Louis hoped to replace by the newly founded port of Aigues-Mortes. The complicated financial arrangements were made by the bankers of Genoa. Louis took the precaution of having large stocks of wine and grain built up in Cyprus. In August 1248 he sailed from Aigues-Mortes while, to the singing of the old crusader hymn *Veni creator spiritus*, the main army embarked in the Old Harbour at Marseilles. Here it was that the expedition was joined by the twenty-five-year-old knight Jean de Joinville. He had been brought up at the civilized court of Count Theobald IV of Champagne and his *Histoire de Saint Louis* is the most vivid as well as the most important account of the crusade, though it should be borne in mind that he did not write it until he was an old man (*c.* 1309) and that historical objectivity is often sacrificed for hagiographical glorification. Particularly one-sided is Joinville's attempt to make the king's brother, Robert of Artois, alone responsible for the failure of the crusade. This, of course, in no way detracts from the work's literary value.

Louis decided to winter in Cyprus while awaiting further reinforcements though the prospects for an immediate attack on Egypt—which was now the only possible target—looked to be good since as-Salih was involved in a war with Aleppo. The army of between 15,000 and 25,000 men which assembled in Cyprus was well organized and included 2,500 knights and 5,000 crossbowmen. They left Cyprus at the end of May and anchored off Damietta on 5 June 1249. The sultan had naturally been kept informed of their approach so the coast was held in force by the Egyptian army. But by using flat-bottomed landing craft the Christians sailed in almost to the beach and then the knights waded the rest of the way. The defenders soon gave way before the onslaught of the dripping wet knights. Although they had as yet lost little the Egyptians decided to withdraw not to Damietta but, for some strange reason, further up the Nile. This led to a panic in Damietta and on 6 June the town was evacuated without there being any resistance offered. In the face of this unexpected success for the crusaders it was as much as the mortally sick sultan could do to restore order in his own army. This then took up position at Mansourah.

Louis decided to spend the summer in Damietta. He wanted to wait for the reinforcements promised by his brother, Alfonso of Poitou. Perhaps he remembered the catastrophe of 1221, when the crusaders had become bogged down in the summer mud of the Nile. In the meantime the war was carried to Syria where Sidon had been lost to the Muslims. In November Louis established an archbishopric at Damietta. Its foundation charter—the only one of its kind to survive from the Latin East—has recently been subjected to a searching analysis by Jean Richard.[95] He has shown that although the Capetian tradition of an expansionist territorial policy had had nothing to do with Louis's decision to take the cross, once out in the East he began to think in these terms. Just as Philip Augustus in his treaty with the Genoese (see above p. 142) had granted them territorial concessions in the Holy Land—which, though he might help to reconquer it, in no way belonged to him—so now even Louis looked upon Damietta as his by right of conquest, though as late as 1218 it had been assigned to the king of Jerusalem. Egypt, as yet unconquered, he regarded in the same light and used its territory to assign revenues of 5,000 bezants to both the archbishop and the chapter. In addition he granted ten fiefs to the archbishop, to be held by knights who were to owe feudal service to Louis and his successors. The charter is a good illustration of the way in which Louis was able to combine ideals with practical politics.

On 20 November 1249 the French army began to march south along the east bank of the Nile towards Cairo, following in the footsteps of the crusaders of 1221, although there had been many who had advised an attack on Alexandria which might have offered better hope of success. The Ayubid empire was in a difficult position because as-Salih died on 22 November. But, with the help of his bodyguard, his favourite wife saved the situation by acting in an unusually vigorous fashion until the heir to the throne, Turanshah, arrived from Mesopotamia. Meanwhile Louis's army advanced very laboriously and not until the end of December did it arrive near Mansourah where, once again, the crusaders found themselves caught in the angle created by the Nile and one of its tributaries. Louis now planned to cross the tributary, then circle around Mansourah and attack from the rear. The river was bridged on 8 February 1250. Then the French advance guard under Robert of Artois made a premature attack on an Egyptian camp, captured it and killed the Egyptian commander-in-chief in his bath. Tempted by this partial success they pressed on to Mansourah and were slaughtered in the narrow streets of the town. When Louis IX with the main army crossed the river he was attacked by the Egyptian forces which had been rapidly reorganized by the new commander, Rukn ad-Din Baibars Bundukdari. The king who, with his golden helmet and German sword, was recognizable from afar, struck fiercely about him. His energy and coolness saved the battle, but the campaign was lost. The losses had been considerable and Louis did not retreat soon enough to Damietta. Not until the end of March did he make up his mind to withdraw and by then it was too late. The troops were weakened by disease and hunger; the Muslims had prevented supplies from getting through to them. The king himself was enfeebled by dysentery and by 6 April when only half-way to Damietta, he saw no other course open to him but to capitulate. He refused to save himself by ship, preferring to be taken prisoner together with his army. Damietta, however, was saved thanks to the intervention of the French queen who, though she had just given birth to a son there, managed, by dint of great efforts, to persuade the Italian merchants to stay; their going would undoubtedly have caused a panic in the town. This meant that the crusaders still held something with which they could bargain with the Egyptians. On 6 May a treaty was concluded; Damietta was exchanged for the person of the king. In addition Louis paid at once the first half of a ransom of 800,000 bezants. On 8 May he left Damietta for Acre. He now had hardly more than 1,400 men left but, ignoring the urgent pleas of his mother who was acting as regent in France and overruling the objections of his own council, Louis decided to stay in the Holy Land. His help was much needed there and, in addition, his army was still in captivity.

Four days before the king's release there had occurred a palace revolution in Cairo which was to have the most far-reaching of consequences. The *coup d'état* had been organized by the Mameluk bodyguard.[96] The Mameluks had always been important as élite troops. They were white Turkish slaves—the word *mamluk* means something that is owned—bought when young and then brought up to be soldiers. Generally they were freed when they were of an age to bear arms. They had no patriotic feeling, only a sense of personal loyalty to their lord. This made them well-suited to being bodyguards but their position as a kind of Pretorian Guard turned them into an arrogant warrior caste, well aware that they were indispensable to their master. So long as the bulk of the

Ayubid army was composed of Kurds, or at least was commanded by them, the Mameluks posed no threat to the state, but as-Salih, thinking in terms of centralization, had brought the Mameluk system to perfection; with the help of this Turkish military machine he had hoped to re-establish the unity of the disintegrating Ayubid empire. The most important troops were the Bahriya Mameluks, named after the island in the Nile where they had their barracks. They made up a fearless cavalry regiment which, though only one thousand in number, controlled the capital city. When as-Salih's successor, Turanshah, seemed to be on the point of saturating the adminstration with men who had come with him from Mesopotamia, the Bahriya Mameluks saw in this a threat to their own position and so they had him murdered on 2 May 1250. This brought the period of Ayubid rule in Egypt to an end. Aibek then became the first Mameluk sultan. The Kurdish regime was replaced by a Turkish military oligarchy. An-Nasir of Aleppo now became the leader of the Ayubid legitimists in Syria which, in contrast with the economically strong Egypt, was the centre of Islamic culture in the Arabic-speaking world. War between Mameluks and Ayubids followed and it was not until April 1253 that some agreement was reached. The Ayubids kept Syria and north Palestine while the Mameluks held Egypt and south Palestine. The next development was the outbreak of fierce fighting within the Bahriya regiment itself. This lasted until 1254 and was only half settled by the emigration of a part of the regiment; up until 1260 these Mameluks in exile in Syria formed a militant group which threatened the security of Egypt.

Saint Louis profited from these quarrels. Both Ayubids and Mameluks bid for his support. He saw clearly enough that the future lay with Egypt and in 1252 made a treaty with the Mameluks as a result of which his army was liberated and he was released from payment of the second instalment of his ransom. But, from a military point of view, the Franco–Egyptian alliance came to nothing. The Ayubids were not so easily defeated. For the four years that he was in Palestine, from 1250 to 1254, Saint Louis ruled the Holy Land. There was no one, neither baron nor Master, who could challenge his authority. During these years the *bailliage* of the kings of Cyprus and of their representatives, the Ibelins, was purely nominal. With great prudence Louis rebuilt the fortifications of Jaffa, Acre, Caesarea, and Sidon. He tried to settle the family feuds in Antioch and had no hesitation in exiling the marshal of the Templars who, without his knowledge, had come to terms with the Ayubids. He became the patron of the school of painting at Acre and once more a masterpiece was produced there—the superb Paris Arsenal Bible for which Byzantine manuscripts, possibly purchased by Louis himself from the permanently bankrupt Emperor Baldwin II of Constantinople, served as models. During the winter of 1250/1 Joinville was inspired by the king's sermon-like conversation to write his *Credo*, in which the most important articles of the Christian faith were elucidated. This work, decorated with miniatures, was designed to be read and shown to the dying, as a comfort to them and to protect them from the temptations of the devil.

In the spring of 1254 the king came to realize that he could stay no longer in the Holy Land. His mother had died towards the end of 1252 and his brothers, though they took her place as regent, were but poor substitutes. On 24 April 1254 Saint Louis, the last crusader-king, left the Holy Land. He had sought to win glory for God but he had also won it for himself. Such was the moral prestige which still accrued to a king who went on crusade that Louis became the arbiter of Europe and the 'uncrowned emperor'—especially since Frederick II had died in 1250 and the empire was now in a state of disintegration.

Before leaving the Holy Land, Louis IX entered into discussions with the Mongols in the hope that in them the Franks might find a powerful ally against the Muslims.[97] And in fact the Mongols were the only people in the second half of the thirteenth century who were capable of destroying Islam, though in this event the Christians would have had to face the very real danger that they would be their allies' next victims. A vital consideration in the plans which were eagerly discussed at the curia and in Europe generally until about 1300, was the fact that the Mongols, though the vast majority of them were neither Christians nor Muslims, had been influenced by Nestorians. These were Christians who, in the fifth century, had been declared to be heretics for emphasizing the human rather than the divine aspect of Christ's nature. They had then withdrawn to Central Asia and their descendants had now won some influence over the Mongol Great Khans and their wives. Some Mongol tribes indeed were solidly Nestorian. For this reason it was hoped that the Mongols were more likely to be converted to Christianity than to Islam; in that event it was believed that it would not be too difficult to deal with the Nestorian heresy. As early as 1245–7 Innocent IV had sent a Franciscan friar, John of

Pian del Carpine, to the East in order to convert the Great Khan of the Mongols. The latter had replied by demanding the submission of the pope. Equally unsuccessful was another attempt at conversion, the mission (1249-52) of Andrew of Longjumeau, a Dominican dispatched from Cyprus by Louis IX. What the Christians had failed to grasp was that the Great Khans were indifferent in religious matters and treated the unorthodox Muslims and Buddhists hardly less well than they treated the Nestorians. These attempts do, however, reveal just how much the Mongols had become the decisive factor in the politics of the Near East. The attitude of the individual powers to the Mongol problem increasingly became the measure by which they themselves were judged by other powers.

Neither before nor since has there been anything in history to compare with the empire of the Mongols.[98] It was astounding both for its immense size and for the explosive speed with which it grew. It was precisely this extremely rapid expansion which led the Muslims into the initial mistake of underestimating the Mongol peril, particularly during the period when the Khwarismian empire still lay between them and the Mongols. The Mongols were a nomadic people divided into several tribes. Like the Turks they originated from the infertile steppe regions between Lake Baikal and the Altai Mountains. They first appeared in the light of history in the tenth century when they pushed southwards, driving before them the Khitai who went on to establish the empire of the Liao in North China. This empire was destroyed *circa* 1125, whereupon the Liao withdrew westwards and built up the empire of the Kara Khitai east of the Jaxartes. After this first contact with the culture of China the Mongols sank back again into the chaos of tribal warfare. Their meteoric rise began shortly after 1200. Within a decade one of their leaders, Temujin, had made himself lord over all the Mongol tribes. In 1206 a tribal assembly acclaimed him as Great Khan of the Mongols with the (linguistically unexplained) title of Genghis Khan. From now on the great hordes of the Mongols were prepared to act as one political unit; they believed that it was their divine mission to unite the world under Mongol lordship—'one sun in the sky, one lord on earth'. Within a few years Genghis Khan had organized his empire. He had the customs of the Mongols collected and written down in a law-book, the Yasa, in which regulations of draconian severity protected private property. The army was organized in groups of ten and multiples of ten; a group of 10,000 formed a unit which could operate independently. Its strength lay partly in the audacious, death-defying courage of the Mongols, but chiefly in the army's extraordinary mobility which enabled the Mongol horsemen to attack their enemy before he had time to organize his defences properly. The army was held together by iron discipline. During the years of conquest it was increasingly reinforced by Turkish units. The Mongols made war in the most brutal fashion. They ruthlessly harnessed their subjects to the transportation of immense quantities of siege materials. Unless they had surrendered in advance, the citizens of a captured town were nearly all massacred. The best that men capable of bearing arms could hope for was to be used by the Mongols at later sieges, driven on in front of the army to act as 'arrow-fodder'. The women and children were enslaved; only craftsmen and engineers, who could be of use to the conquerors, could count on being spared. Thus the nomadic Mongols destroyed the economic and cultural life of Central Asia which was based on an old urban civilization, and drove a permanent wedge between Persian Iran and the Arab world. But in the Far East, attracted by the superior Chinese civilization, they completely accepted Chinese customs.

When Genghis Khan had completed his work of reform he set about satisfying the land hunger of his nomadic steppe tribesmen. In 1211–12 he attacked north China; its subjugation was completed when Peking fell in 1215. Then in 1219/20 he destroyed the eastern part of the Khwarismian empire in Transoxania and Khorassan. The rapid collapse of these two empires which had previously been thought of as unconquerable, established the reputation of the Mongols and created a state of panic in the minds of their prospective victims. They drove the once-powerful Shah of Khwarism helplessly before them until in desperation he sought protection south of the Indus, though only shortly before this he had himself threatened to extinguish the Abbasid caliphate. The unfortunate neighbours of the Mongols were left only 'the choice between voluntary submission—which generally meant annihilation—and a resistance which they believed was hopeless' (Cahen). From 1220 to 1223 the conquerors devastated Azerbaijan, south Russia, and the territories around the middle Volga; then they withdrew for a while. Genghis Khan died in 1227 but his sons, under the Great Khan Ogodai, continued the expansion. In 1230–3 Iran and the rest of the Khwarismian empire fell; this opened the way to the Middle East. In 1231–4 Korea was captured. South Russia followed in 1237–9; here the Mongols founded the Tatar lordship of the 'Golden Horde' which was to endure for centuries. In 1240 they swept westwards through the Ukraine and Poland and destroyed a German army at Liegnitz in 1241. Only Ogodai's death in 1241 saved Europe from their on-slaught; they turned back for home, moving eastwards through the Balkans. In 1243 they made Anatolia into a Mongol protectorate. During the rest of this decade internal dissensions temporarily pre-vented further conquests, but with the accession of Mongka Khan (1251-9) the expansion, both to the east and to the west, was renewed and accelerated. In the east, with the help of his brother Kubilai Khan (himself Great Khan 1260-94), Mongka Khan con-quered south China; here his brother, the founder of the Yuan dynasty, developed the brilliant, purely Chinese court culture which was to be described by the Venetian Marco Polo who lived there for twenty years. By about 1280 the whole of China had sub-mitted to the Mongols; Cambodia and Tonkin were reduced to the status of dependent protectorates. In the west, Iran and Mesopotamia were thoroughly subjugated during this period. It was now possible to travel from Kiev or Baghdad to Peking with-out once crossing a frontier. But the Great Khan became in-creasingly involved in Chinese politics. As a result the western parts of the empire, Iran, Transoxania, and Russia, were left more and more to their own devices.

From the Holy Land Louis IX sent a second embassy to the court of Mongka Khan at Karakorum. This time political rather than religious considerations were uppermost; an alliance was sought. The envoy, the Flemish Franciscan William of Rubruck, returned after his long mission (1253-6) convinced that the Latins were theologically superior to all other believers and that it would probably be fairly easy to convert the East. But Mongka Khan would agree to an alliance only if Louis became his vassal and on these terms agreement was impossible. By the time William returned home in 1256, Mongka's brother Hulagu had already begun the conquest of the Islamic lands in the west. In 1255, with about 120,000 men, he had entered the Middle East. In 1256 he annihilated the Persian Assassins at Alamut. On 10 February 1258 the Mongols took Baghdad by storm and smothered the last Abba-sid caliph in a carpet. In this way the orthodox Sunnites lost their spiritual head and the Shi'ites could breathe again. Between 1258 and 1260 Hulagu subjugated Upper Mesopotamia. The Christians in the Holy Land, though they saw in him the enemy of the Mame-luks, awaited his coming with mixed feelings. In 1259 and 1260 he captured Damascus and Aleppo and then sent a section of his army under Kitbuqa south towards Egypt. But in September 1260 at Ain Jalud in Galilee Kitbuqa was met by the Mameluk army under Sultan Qutuz and his general Baibars. After a fierce fight the Mongols were defeated. It was one of the decisive moments in history; the legend of the invincibility of the Mongols was destroyed, their expansion to the west towards North Africa was halted for good, the continued existence of Islam was ensured and the Mameluk suzerainty over Syria and Palestine established. Refugees from Mesopotamia and Syria ensured that from now on Cairo would be the cultural centre of the Arabic-speaking Islamic world. At Ain Jalud the first cracks in the structure of the great Mongol empire had been revealed; fighting on the Mameluk side there were some Mongol troops sent from the Golden Horde which had for some time been at loggerheads with Hulagu's Mongols. Hulagu (d. 1265) contented himself with Iran where he founded the empire of the Il-Khans (princes of the land) and beat off the attacks of the Mameluks. In religious matters he and his immediate successors tended towards Buddhism and they continued to co-operate closely with the Great Khan. But after Kubilai Khan's death in 1294 the system broke down. Quite simply the empire had grown too big—it took six months for a man travelling from the empire's western frontier to reach its capital at Karakorum. The eastern part of the empire became thoroughly Buddhist while in 1295 the Il-Khans were converted to Islam—the final blow to all the hopes which, since 1245, the Christians had placed in the Mongols.

14 · THE CRUSADER STATES, 1254–1291

IN 1254, the year that Saint Louis left Palestine, Conrad IV, the Hohenstaufen king of Jerusalem, died in Italy. His son Conradin was then two years old and clearly no more likely to travel to the East and to rule the kingdom of Jerusalem in person than his father had been. Despite this—or perhaps because of this—the barons, assembled at Acre, recognized him as the rightful king of Jerusalem (Conrad III 1254–68). The succession made no difference whatever to the realities of power. The *baillis*, subordinate to the Haute Cour, continued to rule the country; there was probably no form of government which would have suited the barons better. Clearly there was no special loyalty to the Hohenstaufen dynasty in this adherence to Conradin although a certain respect for the law may possibly have played a part. Only the nobility ever had a vote in the Haute Cour but Prawer's researches have shown that from *circa* 1240 onwards its meetings were attended by the Masters of the Military Orders, by the heads of the privileged Italian settlements and by the principals of the urban confraternities. In theory they did no more than accept the decisions of the nobility but in fact they must have been able to influence the outcome of the discussions since they represented those sections of the Frankish community which controlled the army and the economy. Behind a procedural veil there were concealed the beginnings of a development in the direction of a parliamentary state, though in Jerusalem of course, this development was soon cut short. But the transition from the monarchical rule of a king to a genuine system of representative government—the transition which, in England, was to be carried through to completion—had at least begun.

Initially the kingdom's foreign policy was directed towards maintaining intact the old system of constantly renewed truces which was familiar from the Ayubid period.[99] Before his departure Louis IX had arranged such a truce for two and a half years with Damascus, though he himself was inclined to prefer Egypt. A year later (1255) the Franks in fact concluded a ten years' truce with the

Egyptians. Internally the little kingdom was plagued by fierce quarrels; after Louis IX's departure a strong government was badly missed. In 1256 the first big colonial war in the Levant broke out between Venice and Genoa.[100] The bone of contention was the monastery of St. Sabas standing on the hill of Montjoie which separated the Venetian and Genoese quarters in Acre. Both cities claimed the monastery. One day, while the lawyers were still arguing, the Genoese occupied first the hill and then the Venetian quarter. Only with difficulty were the Venetians able to drive them out again. Philip de Montfort seized the chance to expel the Venetians from his new lordship of Tyre where they had held a third of the town ever since the treaty of 1123 (see above p. 80). Although the Venetians already had their hands full with the trouble at Acre they could not possibly reconcile themselves to the loss of Tyre, their most important settlement in the Holy Land. When it came to the election of a *bailli* in 1258 the Venetians and Genoese inevitably supported opposing candidates; the feudal nobility were now involved in the quarrel and what had once been a local conflict broadened out into the War of Saint Sabas. The whole land was up in arms. On one side were the Venetians, supported by the Pisans, the Provençals, the Ibelins, the Templars, and the Teutonic Knights; on the other were the Genoese together with Philip de Montfort, the Hospitallers, and the Catalan merchants. Most of the fighting was done by the Italians and by the fleets which were sent out by their home ports. There were fierce battles in Acre and many houses were destroyed by stone projectiles. The sources give the number of dead as 20,000, though this is clearly an exaggeration. In 1258 the Genoese fleet suffered a severe defeat in a battle off Acre while Philip de Montfort's simultaneous attempt to seize the city itself was beaten back. This meant that in practice the Venetians had won the war. As symbols of their triumph the Venetians were supposed to have taken two pillars from St. Sabas and erected them in the Piazzetta of San Marco in Venice. This, at any rate, was the official Venetian version of how these *Pilastri d'Acre*, still standing today, came to be there. But in fact they are identical down to the last detail and even to the stonemason's mark with pillars which archaeologists from Dumbarton Oaks have recently excavated in Constantinople; they are part of the Venetian booty of 1204.

After 1258 the scale of military operations diminished somewhat though with each *passagium* the conflict automatically flared up again i.e. twice a year when the Italian fleets came to Outremer. In 1261 a temporary peace was patched up. The Genoese kept an establishment in Tyre but were barred from Acre which was to remain the resort of the Venetians and Pisans. The Genoese took their revenge by signing the Treaty of Nymphaeum (1261) with the Greeks, thus threatening the Venetian monopoly of trade within Byzantium (see above p. 196). The Byzantine Empire now became the main theatre of war but sea battles continued to be fought off the Syrian coast until 1270 when at last St. Louis was able to bring about a genuine peace. The Genoese were allowed to return to their quarter in Acre though it was now lying in ruins; in 1277 the Venetians went back to Tyre. But Pisa would have no part in the peace and so the war between the Tuscan and Ligurian republics raged on until 1288. In Palestine the continuing state of civil war revealed that neither the royal *bailli* nor the urban aristocracy exercised any real authority in the towns; here the Italian communes were the effective rulers, particularly in Acre which had become a kind of Venetian dependency. In terms of power only the Military Orders who owned castle-like town houses and controlled sections of the town walls could in any way compare with the Italians.

One reason for the diminishing scale of military activity in the War of Saint Sabas after 1260 was the growing urgency of the Mongol problem. The North took an emphatically pro-Mongol line—indeed it had very little choice. As early as 1243 the Mongols had established a protectorate over the Anatolian state of the Rum Seldjuks and from that time the Armenians of Cilicia had also looked for support from the new lords. In 1254 King Hethoum I thought it wise to go to Karakorum himself to make a firm alliance with Mongka Khan. Mongka granted concessions to the Armenian Church in the Mongol Empire and appointed Hethoum as a kind of consultant for Christian affairs. In return Hethoum promised to take part in Hulagu's Middle Eastern campaign. From Hethoum's point of view this alliance was obviously sensible. To resist the Mongols was impossible and anyway it was in fact the Mongols who had released the Lesser Armenians from the pressure of their arch-enemies, the Seldjuks of Anatolia. In addition there was always the hope that the Nestorian influence would in the end convert the Mongols to Christianity, especially since Mongka's principal wife was a Nestorian. A late thirteenth-century Armenian historian greeted Hulagu and his wife (another Nestorian) with the old imperial acclamation as a new Constantine and a new Helena, as the champions of Christendom. For his part, Hethoum always remained true to the alliance, first with the Mongols and then with the Il-Khan. In 1254, the year that Hethoum went to Karakorum, the ancient quarrel between Lesser Armenia and Antioch was finally ended. Ever since 1224 when the Hethoumian regent of Armenia had ousted the country's legitimate ruler, a member of the princely house of Antioch (see above p. 246), relations between the two states had been difficult. But now Bohemund VI of Antioch-Tripoli (1252–75) married Sibylla, Hethoum's daughter, and whether or not this was the occasion for Bohemund to become Hethoum's vassal for Antioch, there can be no doubt that Antioch was swept completely into the orbit of Armenian politics. From now on Antioch was in practice ruled by the king of Lesser Armenia while the prince of Antioch resided exclusively in Tripoli. There is further evidence for the rapid way in which the two states were merging in the fact that during this period Lesser Armenia took over the law code of Antioch. Thus Antioch too was incorporated into the Armenian–Mongol alliance, an alliance which was at first clearly advantageous to both sides. The Armenians helped the Mongols at the siege of Aleppo and then the Antiochenes joined their army before the walls of Damascus. After the capture of the city its famous Great Mosque was, to the dismay of the Muslims, turned into a Christian church. As a reward for his help Hethoum was allowed to extend his territory in the direction of Anatolia at the expense of the Seldjuks and in the southeast at the expense of Aleppo. The protective shadow of the Mongols enabled Bohemund to recapture the Muslim coastal enclave at Lattakieh and thus to re-establish the land connection between Tripoli and Antioch that had been broken since 1187. In return Bohemund had to put up with the presence of a Mongol resident in Antioch and also, since the Mongols were well aware of the importance of the Greek element in the population of the city, he had to instal a Greek patriarch. As a result he was excommunicated by the pope.

The Franks in the south were unsure how to react to the Mongol advance; here Egypt seemed both nearer and more menacing than the Mongols. But whatever might happen they were far too afraid of the Mongols to risk provoking them. In 1260 they painted a sombre picture of the Mongol danger in an urgent though ineffective appeal which they sent to Charles of Anjou. Meanwhile the Mameluk sultan, Qutuz, had already made up his mind to counter-attack. He sought an alliance with the Franks and, under his pressure, they were at first inclined to agree to this suggestion, but finally they took the advice of the Master of the Teutonic Order and opted for neutrality. They allowed Qutuz free passage through Palestine but would not give him any military support.

The Master of the Teutonic Order may have taken the line he did out of consideration for the policies of Lesser Armenia. Relations between the different Military Orders were just as bad as were all relations between evenly matched powers in the Holy Land. The Hospitallers and the Templars had long pursued opposing policies. This had first become apparent in 1168 when the Hospitallers had supported Almaric I's expansionist schemes in Egypt while the Templars had held back. Later the Hospitallers supported Conrad of Montferrat's party so the Templars went over to the Lusignan camp. In their opposition to Frederick II the two Orders were, for once, united, but even here the Hospitallers were noticeably less enthusiastic than the Templars. Then during the last stages of the War of the Lombards the Hospitallers moved towards the imperial side with the result that the old rivalry reasserted itself—almost to the point of open war. In 1243 the Templars and the barons made an alliance with Damascus while the Hospitallers had been inclined to look towards Egypt. On the other hand since the collapse of Hohenstaufen power in the Holy Land the Teutonic Order had concentrated its interests in Cilician Lesser Armenia rather than in Palestine. The kings of Lesser Armenia, as vassals of the emperor, had endowed them richly and it may have been concern for their possessions there that persuaded the Master to advise against military action against the Mongols. After 1243 the kingdom of Jerusalem became smaller and weaker, but the Templars and the Hospitallers grew more and more powerful. While the Italians controlled the towns, the Military Orders dominated as much of the countryside as was still in Christian hands. They held the great castles, particularly north of Tripoli, where the power of the Hospitallers was concentrated at Marqab and Krak des Chevaliers, and where the Templars held Chastel Blanc and Tortosa. But the situation was no different in the south. Here the Templars held Safed and Athlit (Château Pèlerin) and the Hospitallers Belvoir. Only the Military Orders were able to recruit European knights who were prepared to fight for long periods in the Holy Land. Thus they controlled the only effective fighting force. In addition, thanks to the innumerable gifts of land which they had received in Western Europe, they were immensely rich and their far-flung network of establishments enabled them to carry out important financial transactions; naturally they found themselves cast in the role of bankers. But between themselves relations were no better after 1243 than they had been before. A never-ending series of clashes sometimes flared up into open war—as in the War of Saint Sabas (1259)—with a regrettable loss of

human life as the result. The pope was unable to find any satisfactory solution to their differences; in the West he relied upon the
goodwill of both Orders and could not afford to alienate either of
them.

As the nobles of the Holy Land became increasingly impoverished they were forced to relinquish their castles and lordships to the Orders. The fate of the lord of Marqab in the twelfth
century (see above p. 159) was shared by the lord of Sidon in the
thirteenth. From 1254 to 1260 he sold a considerable part of his
estates to the Orders; finally, after the Mongols had devastated
Sidon in 1260, he lost the whole of his remaining fief to the Templars. Bit by bit the lord of Arsuf, a member of the once so powerful Ibelin family, had to sell his lordship to the Hospitallers until
by 1261 it had completely gone, just four years before the Mameluks
moved in and occupied it. Bloodthirsty feuds between the nobles
were common. The authority of the state was more or less non-
existent. It became increasingly difficult for the barons to find
wives who were not related too closely to them. The European
nobles were not much inclined to marry off their daughters into
such uncertain territory so the pope was more and more forced to
grant dispensations to permit marriages within the prohibited de-
grees. After the departure of Saint Louis the kingdom of Jerusalem
disintegrated rapidly. Ironically enough it was at this time, in 1265,
on the eve of the great Mameluk offensive, that Jean d'Ibelin,
count of Jaffa, undertook his codification of the law—a codification which gives no hint of the disintegration but instead builds
up a picture of an aristocracy which, if greedy for power, was also
powerful. And this at a time when the count of Jaffa was himself
deep in debt! In reality the kingdom had fallen apart into a number of warring groups of which only two, the Italian communes
and the Military Orders, were relatively (i.e. in comparison with
the barons) powerful. Thus the chief characteristic of this period
in the history of the crusader states was the absence of any consistent and purposeful policy.

In 1264, four years after the battle at Ain Jalud, there occurred
a remarkable development in the constitutional history of the
kingdom. Two men presented themselves to the Haute Cour as
candidates for the then vacant *bailliage*: Hugh of Antioch-
Lusignan and Hugh of Brienne (see the genealogy on p. 242).
According to the custom which had hitherto prevailed, Hugh of
Brienne ought to have been successful. Both men were descendants
of Queen Alice of Cyprus, Isabella I's daughter by her third marriage, and as such had a hereditary claim to the *bailliage*, but

Brienne was the son of Alice's eldest daughter, whereas Antioch-Lusignan was the son of her younger daughter. After days of debate, however, the Antioch–Lusignan claim was upheld by the Haute Cour on the grounds that the decisive factor was degree of kinship to the last holder of the office—and that had been Lusignan's mother, Isabella. This decision, for which there had been a precedent in the Antioch succession dispute of 1201 (see above p. 245), was to be of importance in the later history of Cyprus. The reality behind the decision was probably the fact that Hugh of Antioch–Lusignan was already *bailli* of Cyprus and might succeed to the throne there, that he was, in other words, a man who counted for more than Hugh of Brienne. Indeed the new *bailli* turned out to be a vigorous leader who took his office seriously and who divided his time fairly between Cyprus and Acre—even after 1267, the year in which he became king of Cyprus. For a while it looked as though Hugh might succeed in restoring the authority of the crown. He managed to obtain the support of the Military Orders; he won over Philip of Tyre by ceding that city to him; and by marrying one of the Ibelins he was able at least to neutralize them. But in the end his work was brought to nothing by the grandiose, expansionist schemes which Charles of Anjou pursued from Italy.

The mainland kingdom desperately needed a strong regent, indeed to save the country he would have to have been much stronger than Hugh. For in the meantime there had been more changes in the political situation in the Mameluk Empire. Sultan Qutuz had been murdered shortly after the Battle of Ain Jalud and one of the conspirators, Rukn ad-Din Baibars Bunduqdari (1260–77) had taken his place.[101] Baibars was the greatest statesman ever to emerge from the Bahriya regiment. The only man in any way comparable with him is Saladin. It is true that the blood of two murders—that of Turanshah in 1250 and that of Qutuz in 1260—stained his path to power, but that does not alter the fact that he was an extraordinarily gifted and able ruler. If, in contrast to Saladin, there was no moral ideal which he was seeking to achieve and which might have carried him still higher, he compensated for this by possessing a fine sense of strategy. He was the only Mameluk to try to build an Egyptian navy, though even he could not entirely free himself from the ways of thought engrained in a people who fought on horseback—he never saw that it was only the Italian domination of the eastern Mediterranean that enabled the Franks to resist the Mameluks for as long as they did. He was unable to comprehend the kind of strength that was possessed by all sea-powers in contrast to purely continental powers. After his whole fleet had been lost in an attempt to make a landing on Cyprus in 1270, he wrote a letter to the king of Cyprus in which all the pride of the nomadic mounted warrior was reflected: 'Your horses are ships, but our ships are horses.' He could never forgive the Franks for the alliance which north Syria had made with the Mongols— though he was, as it happens, a great admirer and imitator of Mongol legislation. He was determined to ensure that even the Franks of the south who had remained neutral would pay for that alliance. His declared intention was to drive the Franks into the sea once and for all. This would have the additional advantage of diverting the trade of Syria into Egyptian ports. His great advance was prepared thoroughly. First he brought the Syrian hinterland, especially Aleppo and the Transjordan, firmly under his control. Everywhere he ensured that the castles were carefully repaired and put into a state of readiness. He took particular trouble to see that he obtained news quickly—for this enabled him to react with un-expected speed. He made use of pigeon post on an hitherto un-precedented scale and he insisted on being informed of every piece of news as soon as it was received, even if he was undressed at the time.

While still engaged in subduing the last Ayubids, Baibars began to threaten Antioch. In 1263 he sacked Nazareth and destroyed its famous church of the Virgin. He appeared unexpectedly before the walls of Acre, supposedly acting as Genoa's ally in the War of Saint Sabas. Then in January 1265 he launched the big offensive which was to be pressed forward until 1271. First he captured Caesarea and thus cut off Jaffa from the rest of the kingdom. Then, further to the north, he occupied Haifa, Toron, and Arsuf. Acre itself was saved only by the prompt intervention of the *bailli*, Hugh. In this campaign Baibars used the scorched earth policy which his succes-sors were to continue. The ports were completely destroyed in order to prevent them being used by the Franks as assembly points or beach-heads. In 1266 he attacked on all fronts simultaneously. His first concern was to wreak vengeance on the Armenians now that their Mongol overlord Hulagu (d. 1265) was dead. He sacked the Armenian capital. Soon afterwards King Hethoum I abdicated in favour of his son Leo III (1269–89) and retired to a monastery. By making a new alliance with the Mongols Leo was able to win a breathing space for a few years. In 1270 Baibars turned against the Syrian Assassins, always the foci of a special kind of unrest, and destroyed them. In the south, Baibars's 1266 campaign had been aimed principally at Safed and when it fell the whole of Galilee was effectively his. Two years later, in 1268, Jaffa capitulated after a siege of just one day; a few weeks later the new line of defence running through the Litani river and the castle of Beaufort, the line built up by the Franks after the fall of Safed, was breached. Shortly afterwards the sultan suddenly appeared before Antioch. The city soon surrendered and its inhabitants had to pay dearly for the Frankish alliance with the Mongols; Antioch was turned into a bloodbath. The rest of north Syria yielded without a fight. Antioch had been the first Syrian city to fall into Christian hands (in 1098) and they had held it without interruption for 170 years. Its fall was a portent of approaching disaster.

Baibars's victorious campaign made an impression in Europe. That tireless crusader, Saint Louis, took the cross again in 1267, possibly under the influence of Dominican missionaries, but the nobility of France was not so enthusiastic. Even Joinville emphatically refused to follow the king. Louis's brother, Charles of Anjou, who had been enfeoffed by the pope with Sicily in 1265, manipulated the crusade for his own ends. When, in 1270, the king at last departed, he sailed not to Egypt but to Tunis, whose sultan he hoped to convert, but Charles of Anjou, the man behind the diversion, looked upon it as just a part of his own grandiose Mediterranean plans. Nothing came of the enterprise. His strength gone, Louis died in the camp outside Tunis on 25 August 1270. On 1 November Charles of Anjou brought the campaign to an end after the sultan had agreed to allow him the same rights in North Africa as those which the Norman kings of Sicily had once possessed.[102] Only one latecomer, Prince Edward of England, having arrived too late in Tunis, sailed on to Acre where he landed in 1271, just in time to learn that Baibars had broken through Tripoli's line of defence by capturing Chastel Blanc, Krak des Chevaliers, and Akkar, the great castles of the Military Orders. Edward remained in the Holy Land until September 1272. His only successes were in mediating between the king of Cyprus and his knights (see above p. 236) and in arranging an eleven years' truce with Baibars.

With Prince Edward in the Holy Land was the archdeacon of Liège who, in 1271, was elected pope as Gregory X (d. 1276). He made tremendous efforts to organize a crusade but met with nothing except disappointments. From 1272 to 1274 he called for reports and plans for a new crusade and four of these are still extant. In them we have clear evidence for contemporary criticism of the crusading movement, criticism which was directed chiefly at the trade in indulgences and at the misuse of crusading taxes. The critics regretted the decline of the belief in the crusade's spiritual merit. Their plans for reform included ideas like giving more

weight to the crusade in eastern Europe against the Slavs or setting up a kind of standing army of crusaders. But recommenda-
tions such as these could do little to combat the general lack of
enthusiasm. The council which Gregory X held at Lyons in 1274
could do nothing to help the crusading cause and almost its only
achievement was to bring about a short-lived union of the churches
which was made a practical possibility by the fact that the Greeks
were worried by Charles of Anjou's plans for expansion.[103]

Meanwhile the shadow of Charles of Anjou had reached out over
the kingdom of Jerusalem. In 1268 young Conradin had tried to
recapture Sicily for the Hohenstaufen. But he had been defeated in
battle at Tagliacozzo and then executed, on Charles's orders, at
Naples on 29 October 1268. This marked the formal end of Hohenstaufen rule in Palestine. Acre celebrated the news with a firework
display and with festive illuminations. The crown, which the pope
had declared to be forfeit earlier, on 5 April 1268, now passed to
Hugh III of Cyprus from the house of Antioch–Lusignan, as King
Hugh I of Jerusalem (1268–84), though his right was disputed in
the Haute Cour at Acre by Maria of Antioch (see the genealogy on
p. 242). She was the grand-daughter of Isabella I by her fourth
marriage and she argued that after the death of Queen Alice of
Cyprus the regency should have gone, not to Alice's son Henry,
but to her sister Melisende, the mother of Maria of Antioch. Perhaps Maria was not entirely in the wrong, but to recognize the
justice of her claim would have meant admitting that a mistake had
been made in 1264 when Hugh had been chosen as regent and
thus recognized as heir presumptive. It was, in fact, precisely the
1264 decision laying down that the determining factor should be
degree of kinship with the last holder of the office which favoured
Hugh now, for he was of the direct line of Alice whereas Maria
belonged to a collateral branch. Thus Maria was outvoted. She did
not, however, resign her claim. She issued a formal protest on the
occasion of Hugh's coronation in 1269 and then, in 1277, sold her
right to Charles of Anjou. He at once sent a detachment of troops
to Acre together with Roger of San Severino to act as his *bailli*. As
though Baibars had not created problems enough, the Franks
managed to make things infinitely worse for themselves by indulg-
ing in the luxury of two kings. Acre, Sidon, and the Templars
opted for Charles of Anjou while Tyre and Beirut continued to
recognize Hugh I. Hugh had made himself somewhat unpopular
with his few remaining vassals, particularly by demanding—unsuccessfully—to be made guardian of the young Bohemund VII of
Tripoli (1275–87) after the death of Bohemund VI in 1275. In

1279 Hugh gave up his attempt to rule the mainland and, grumbling about the unruly men of Acre, retired to Cyprus.

In 1277, the year that Charles of Anjou became king, Baibars died in Damascus. The state of truce with the Franks in his last years had permitted him to concentrate on fighting the Mongols, the Armenians (in 1275), the Nubians, and the Seldjuks of Anatolia. During the seventeen years of his reign he undertook thirty-eight campaigns, travelled about 25,000 miles and personally fought in fifteen battles. He banished the double threat to the Islamic Middle East which was posed by the Franks and the Mongols. He fought nine times against the Mongols, five times against the Armenians, three times against the Assassins of Syria. Most of all, he had defeated the Franks twenty-one times. They had lost all the strong points which they had held in the interior of the country. All that was now left to them was the coastline from Athlit (Castle of the Pilgrims), south of Mount Carmel, to Lattakieh in the north. Baibars's death vouchsafed them another short breathing space since it took his successor, Qalawun (d. 1290) some three years to establish himself in power. The government of Roger of San Severino lasted until 1282; it might have achieved some success if the country had been united but, as it was, Roger had no choice but to make a ten years' truce with Qalawun. His example was followed by Bohemund VII of Tripoli who from 1277 to 1282 was at war with the Templars and with rebel vassals in Jebail whom he finally punished by burying them up to their necks in the earth and leaving them to starve.

In March 1282 the Sicilian Vespers brought down the government of Charles of Anjou and Charles himself was driven out of Sicily. Acre and Sidon, however, continued to recognize him as king until his death in 1285. Then Henry II of Cyprus, the son of Hugh I (d. 1284) was able, as Henry I of Jerusalem, to reassert his family's claim to the mainland kingdom. But it was no longer possible to talk of an ordered royal administration. Each man had to look after himself. Already some vassals had been forced to make separate treaties with Baibars, without obtaining the king's permission, for example at Beirut in 1272. This development continued under Sultan Qalawun. The Lady of Tyre, for example, had to make very great concessions in order to obtain a ten years' truce in 1285. She had to promise to stay neutral if war broke out between Franks and Mameluks, to build no new fortifications and to share the whole lordship with the sultan: administration and justice outside the city of Tyre were to be their common responsibility and they were each to take half the profits. In the same year

Marqab, the chief fortress of the Hospitallers, was captured although it had always been regarded as impregnable. Qalawun no longer took any notice of truces. A year later, in 1286, Henry I was crowned king of Jerusalem in Tyre and for the last time the royal court at Acre was the scene of splendid festivities. For two weeks the coronation was celebrated in the Great Hall of the Master of the Hospitallers. Scenes from the story of King Arthur and the Round Table, Lancelot and Tristan, and many other knightly romances were enacted. But there was nothing that could stop the Mameluks now. In 1287 Lattakieh fell; in 1289 Tripoli. In Tripoli after the death of Bohemund VII in 1287 the ruling dynasty had been ousted and a commune under the Genoese Bartolomeo Embriaco had been formed. Genoa itself, however, championed the claim of Bohemund's sister Lucia, and in 1288, when it became known that Bartolomeo wanted to be count himself, she managed to win the support of the commune. So Lucia was recognized as countess and in return she confirmed the rights of Genoa and the commune. This strengthening of Genoa's position was not at all to the liking of the Venetians and in 1289 they urged Qalawun to attack Tripoli. The last attempt to build up an alliance against the Mameluks was made by the Mongol Il-Khan Arghun (1284–91). Reading the situation correctly he did not bother to look for support from the Palestinian Franks but went directly to the West. From 1285 to 1289 his envoys toured Europe; the Il-Khan's letters were read in Rome, Paris, and London. But all the European powers were busy with their own affairs and the envoys met with nothing except empty promises and polite excuses.[104]

In 1290 Qalawun moved against Acre. Then his sudden death looked as though it might save the Franks but next spring his son, al-Ashraf Khalil, returned to Acre with an enormous army and 100 siege engines. With its 20,000 or more inhabitants, forty churches, and its double line of walls, Acre was an imposing monument to Frankish rule in the Holy Land. The Franks mustered all available troops in the city. The Military Orders summoned knights from Europe and there was a company of English soldiers under a Swiss commander, Otto of Grandson. At last the true extent of the danger had been realized and differences were forgotten in the will to resist—but it was too late. On 6 April the siege began with a non-stop barrage from the mangonels and catapults and with an incessant rain of arrows. On 4 May King Henry arrived from Cyprus bringing reinforcements, but on 15 May the outer wall was breached. Three days later the Muslims began a general assault along the entire length of the wall. They took a tower known as the Accursed Tower by storm and then forced their way into the city. Everybody now tried to escape by ship and there were, of course, far too few available. At the quayside there were terrifying scenes of panic. Among the more prominent defenders to escape were King Henry, his brother Amalric, and Otto of Grandson; the patriarch, Nicholas of Hanape, was drowned while trying to get away. By evening it was all over. The population was decimated. The Dominicans, with the old hymn *Veni Creator Spiritus* on their lips, were cut down in their own church. Only the Templars, in their city castle, held out for any length of time, but on 28 May their fortress was undermined and came crashing down.

The rest of Palestine yielded without a struggle. Tyre capitulated on 19 May; Sidon at the end of June although the Castle of the Sea there held out until 14 July. Beirut followed on 31 July and the two Templar fortresses, Tortosa and the Castle of the Pilgrims, were evacuated on 3 and 14 August. Deliberately and carefully the Mameluks devastated the whole coast in order to ensure that the Franks could never return. The political victory of the Mameluks was won at the cost of the destruction of the ancient Syrio–Palestinian city civilization. In 1333 Jacob of Verona wandered sadly through the deserted ruins of the coastal cities. Only the ruins of palaces survived to tell of former splendour. The city walls had collapsed and within their perimeters there was no one except a few Saracens living in the most primitive conditions. The fine Gothic doorway of the church of Saint Andrew in Acre, once the headquarters of the commune, had been transported to Cairo where it has stood from 1293 until the present day as part of the sepulchre of the victorious sultan, al-Ashraf Khalil.

The days of Frankish lordship in the Holy Land were past. Only Peter Embriaco, lord of Jebail, though under Mameluk surveillance, held on to his domain until 1298, possibly because he could count on the traditional support of the Maronites of the Lebanese mountains, whose resistance the Mameluks were unable to break until after 1300. In 1303 the Templars evacuated their last base, the waterless island of Ruad off the coast near Tortosa. But if the Holy Land was lost, it was not forgotten. When an Italian, Martoni, visited Cyprus in 1394 he noticed that when the noble ladies went out of doors they wore long black garments which revealed only their eyes. When he asked for an explanation of this custom, he was told that it was a token of mourning for the loss of the city of Acre in 1291.

15 · THE AFTERMATH:
CONSEQUENCES AND PERSPECTIVES

THE Templar base on the island of Ruad was useful only for as
long as it was planned to return to the Holy Land. The fact that
they held on to it until 1303 shows that they did have such hopes.
It was as inconceivable to them as to the rest of their contemporaries that the littoral should be in any but Christian hands and
there was no lack of schemes for injecting new life into the crusading movement.[105] One contemporary, Thaddeus of Naples, wrote
an account of the catastrophe of 1291 with precisely this in mind.
Even earlier, Fidenzio of Padua, in his *Liber recuperationis Terrae Sanctae*, had recommended that Egypt should be blockaded
from the sea. On the other hand, the famous Majorcan missionary,
Raymond Lull (1235–1316), an almost terrifyingly prolific writer,
put less emphasis, in his *Liber de Fine*, on purely crusading
activity. For him the best way to recover the Holy Land was by
peaceful missionary work aimed at converting all the Muslims to
Christianity; war played only a supporting role in his plans. He
argued vigorously that an education in foreign languages was
essential for missionaries and in fact the Council of Vienne (1311)
did decree that chairs of Greek, Arabic, Hebrew, and Syriac should
be established in the universities. Nothing much came of this
decree but it did at least give the first impulse to oriental studies in
Europe. Pierre Dubois, an adviser to Philip IV of France (1283–
1314), submitted a memorandum to the king in which he un-
folded a scheme for the political union of Europe under French
hegemony as the necessary prelude to a crusade. He envisaged the
empire as an hereditary monarchy held by a French dynasty; the
papacy was to be permanently based at Avignon; disputes were to
be brought before an international commission of three clerics
and three laymen and economic sanctions were to be used against
states which refused to accept their judgements. Money for a new
crusade was to come from the resources of the Military Orders.
Philip IV seized on this last point and, in co-operation with the
pope at Avignon, he suppressed the Templars (1307–12). They

were accused of heresy and as a result many of them were burned at the stake; but these accusations were nothing more than an excuse for laying hands on the immense wealth of the Templars. James of Molay, the last Master of the Templars, died at the stake in Paris in 1314 after he had withdrawn the confessions he had made under torture. Then in 1321 Marino Sanudo the Elder, in his *Secreta fidelium crucis*, returned to the idea of a blockade of Egypt as a method of forcing Islam to its knees. These publicists were just the forerunners in a literary field which flourished greatly during the fourteenth century. It was an age when plans for reviving the crusades were discussed with enormous enthusiasm and in great detail; but all these plans were basically unrealistic. A French hereditary monarchy in the empire was as unthinkable as the participation of the Italians in a blockade of the Levant. The discussion, in fact, merely served to demonstrate that the problem was insoluble.

On the occasions when talk was accompanied by action, the field of operation was generally further north than it had been previously. Europe was worried by the rise of the Ottoman Empire, emerging rapidly and powerfully out of the ruins of the Seldjuk state in Anatolia. From the time of Sultan Bayezit I (1389–1402) the Ottomans paid a good deal of attention to naval development and for this reason Anatolia became a much more serious threat than Egypt to the Christian island-states in the Aegean. The Mameluks still lacked an effective fleet. In 1344 a Holy League made up of Venice, the Hospitallers, and Cyprus captured the Anatolian port of Smyrna which had not yet been incorporated within the Ottoman Empire. Smyrna remained in Christian hands until 1402. The Turkish counter-measures came to nothing in 1345 because a small army under Humbert II, Dauphin of Vienne, went to the aid of the Christians in Smyrna. Humbert assumed the grandiloquent title of 'Captain-General of the Crusade against the Turks and Infidels' but actually he was a weak and rather melancholy man who in 1347 retired into a Dominican house. Peter I of Cyprus launched another, more genuine crusade against Egypt in 1365, but it ended unsuccessfully (see above p. 238). Count Amadeus of Savoy had hoped to join this crusade but his departure was too long delayed and so when he finally left, in 1366, he preferred to help his kinsman, the Byzantine emperor. On his behalf he captured the Gallipoli peninsula but by 1367 the Turks had reoccupied it. An expedition which Duke Louis II of Bourbon, following in the footsteps of Saint Louis, led to Tunis in 1390 also failed to achieve any lasting success. In 1395 King Sigismund of Hungary appealed for help against the Ottomans. Duke Philip the Bold of Burgundy responded and he took with him many French and German magnates. Reinforced by contingents from England, Spain, and Italy and supported by a fleet from Genoa, Venice, and the Hospitallers, Sigismund left Buda in 1396 and advanced down the Danube. On 25 September his army was overwhelmingly defeated at Nicopolis. The catastrophe made a great impression on the West. Philip of Mezières, who had helped to prepare the crusade of 1365, took up his pen again to write his *Epistre lamentable et consolatoire*. In this he returned to his favourite plan of founding one united order of knights to combat the Turks. But he had no illusions about the fact that he was preaching to a world which was tired of this subject. In 1444 a second attempt to help the Hungarians in their valiant struggle against the Turks came to a disastrous end at Varna on the Black Sea. Soon afterwards, in 1453, Constantinople, for more than 1,000 years the capital of the East Roman Empire, fell to the Turks. Pius II called once more for a crusade against the Ottomans but after his death in 1464 nothing more was heard of his project.

If a balance sheet of these centuries of armed combat between Christendom and Islam were drawn up, what would it look like? Would the loss in human lives on both sides be outweighed by progress or by new insights in other fields? Had both sides come to understand one another better and, as a consequence, to respect each other? Had they drawn closer together? Once these questions would have received thoroughly positive answers. In 1808 the Institut de France proposed the following title for a prize essay competition: 'What was the influence of the crusades on the political freedom of the European peoples, on their civilization, their culture, their trade, and industry?' The question awoke a rich response. But in recent times it has become increasingly clear that the cross-fertilization of the two cultures in fact took place, independently of the crusades, in Sicily and above all in Spain.[106] It would, of course, be absurd to say that the crusades had no consequences. The Europeans' ideas of geography had undergone a tremendous transformation, particularly after travellers like Marco Polo and missionaries like John of Monte Corvino and Odoric of Pordenone had penetrated deep into furthest China. The mission to China, though on far too small a scale to achieve any far-reaching result, was itself a consequence of the crusades. Missionary zeal produced a more intensive study of the Islamic languages. Words of Arabic origin—damask, muslin, arsenal, sugar, syrup, lemon, admiral, almanack, alchemy—found their way into Europe through Spain and Italy rather than as a result of the crusades, but Palestinian placenames, sanctified by their biblical associations, were introduced into France and the Turks borrowed many words from the language spoken by Italian seamen. The ancient East–West trade in relics developed considerably as a result of the crusades. In siege warfare and in the technique of castle building the crusader states seem to have witnessed a two-way process of influence; the same is probably true of military tactics though this has not yet been fully investigated. For poets the crusades provided a limitless treasury of chivalrous and romantic subjects; when Emperor Charles IV visited the king of France in Paris he was entertained by a brilliant pageant of knightly scenes from the First Crusade. In the Canterbury Tales Chaucer portrayed the knight as a man who had fought the heathen in Prussia, Lithuania, and in the Mediterranean lands, taking part in Peter I's 1365 crusade against Alexandria. Shakespeare made Henry IV (Part I, Act I, Scene I) decide to go on crusade in order to cleanse himself from his share in the guilt for Richard II's death; if, in the eyes of the Elizabethan public this was dramatically effective, the crusade must still have been something to be taken seriously. The theme of Jerusalem was used by the sixteenth-century Italian poet Torquato Tasso. In Germany in the eighteenth century the still potent figure of Saladin inspired Lessing to write *Nathan der Weise*. In the nineteenth century Sir Walter Scott was happy to use the crusades as a background for his novels of knightly adventure. But this is more or less the end of the story.

It was at one time customary to attribute the rise of the important Levant trade to the influence of the crusades. Between 1922 and 1935 the great Belgian scholar Henri Pirenne developed the thesis that it was not the Germanic invasions which brought down the Roman Empire and its culture but rather the seventh-century Muslim expansion which closed the Mediterranean and destroyed the flourishing Gallo-Syrian trade of the Merovingian period. The great merit of Pirenne's work was that it put an end to the habit of looking at events only in Germanic or Roman terms, but more recent research has shown that the Gallo–Syrian trade was less important than Pirenne thought, that the Arabs hardly possessed the means to close down sea-routes, and finally that there was a very respectable Levant trade in the Carolingian period as well. The commercial consequences of the crusades were thus limited to, at most, an increase in the volume of trade, though in fact some of this increase went through the ports of Egypt.[107]

No process of cultural osmosis took place in the crusader states; basically this was the result of their isolation. In matters of dress, food, and other external forms the Franks adopted whatever the climate and the environment might seem to require; possibly they also took over the pointed arch from the Islamic architecture of the region. But this was all at a superficial level. Hardly one of the Frankish ruling class learned Arabic, and the institutions of political and economic life were only based on Muslim models if the hard facts of the environment made this unavoidable. In Acre at the end of the thirteenth century knowledge of Islam as a religion was still utterly rudimentary whereas at Toledo the Koran had already been translated into Latin. Arab scholars were given no opportunity to work in the crusader states—in contrast to the court of the Norman kings of Sicily, where, for example, Idrisi, the greatest Arab geographer of the Middle Ages, was to be found. The Franks never came into contact with the true centres of Arab culture: Aleppo, Damascus, and Baghdad.

On the other hand the crusades had no profound influence on the Islamic world either. They helped to bring about the migration of the centre of the Arab speaking part of Islam from Baghdad to Cairo, but this process owed much more to Mongol pressure than to Christian. Apart from stimulating a revival (not a further development) of the old theories of the *jihad*, the holy war, the Frankish newcomers made little impact on the Islamic philosophers and theologians who, for one thing, found it very difficult to understand the nature of a crusade. The Arab concept of *hurub as-salibiyya* (wars of the cross) did not appear until the Ottoman period and even then it was in all probability a Christian formulation. In Muslim eyes the crusaders were 'Franks'—a group defined by race rather than by religion. Once the crusades were over Islamic doctrine could again emphasize the spiritual value of a pilgrimage to the Holy Places in Jerusalem. There was nothing new about this, but, for the historian, the rediscovery of its spiritual value is a welcome piece of evidence to show that the Jerusalem motif lies at the heart of the crusading ideal. Thus far at least, albeit unconsciously, the Muslims had appreciated the nature of a crusade. Doubtless the expansion of Sunnite orthodoxy was accelerated by the crusades, but here too other influences were more important and Persia always remained as a stronghold of the Shi'ites. Equally the crusades helped to create a certain amount of unity in the Islamic world—but only a certain amount. The Islamic East, and even the caliph himself, was only faintly interested in these quarrels on the furthest edge of the world of Islam. Essentially it was only the Muslims directly affected by the crusades who responded to the Christian challenge. On the other hand it is clear that the crusades did lead to an unwelcome hardening of the Muslim attitude to Christians. In the thirteenth and fourteenth centuries the Maronites of Lebanon, who as late as 1461 were still waiting longingly and vainly for the return of the Franks, and the Christians of Lesser Armenia had to suffer a good deal of persecution at the hands of the Muslims.[108] Their position was very different from that of the Christian *dhimmis* of earlier centuries who had paid a levy and in return had enjoyed the status of a protected minority. In Egypt mass conversions to Islam were no longer rare. Literature in the Syriac language, once the *lingua franca* of the non-Greek-speaking East, came to an end with the writings of Bar Hebraeus (d. 1286); and already he had been compelled to have his works translated into Arabic in order to reach a wider public. Today Syriac is spoken only in a few isolated parts of Lebanon. On the whole it is clear that the consequences of the crusades for both Western Christendom and Islam must be judged to be either insignificant or possibly harmful.

The crusades, however, never threatened more than the edges of the Islamic world; the damage they did to Byzantium was considerably more serious. The empire's dependence upon its capital city, Constantinople, made it peculiarly vulnerable, and from the time of the Second Crusade onwards it was again and again confronted with the prospect of extinction at the hands of the crusaders. Yet despite the sufferings endured as a result of this threat, it proved impossible to avert the catastrophe of 1204. Apparently without qualms the crusaders destroyed an empire which was the most civilized ever to emerge from the Medieval West—we may speak of the East Roman Empire and of Eastern Christendom but essentially Byzantium was a product of the Western–Christian culture, though of its Greek and not its Latin part. It was, moreover, an empire which for centuries had protected Latin civilization from the advance of Islam. It is, of course, true that the empire was restored in 1261, but it was only a shadow of its former self and never fully recovered from the pitiless destruction of 1204. Once Islam had gathered its strength the end of Byzantium was now inevitable. One theme that runs throughout the historical studies of Sir Steven Runciman is that of the irreparable breach between the Christians of the East and the Christians of the West which was made by the crusaders. Only as a result of the crusades did the schism of 1054 become a bitter reality. In view of the old dispute over the leadership of Christendom between Rome and

Constantinople it is obviously doubtful if, even without the crusades, things could have developed in an essentially different direction. If these two cultural worlds came into prolonged contact—it did not matter how—then a struggle between them was the most likely result. And in the long run, as mere distance became less of a barrier and the world became a smaller place, such contact was inevitable. But if the historian simply observes and registers what *did* happen, then he cannot deny that the crusades only served to widen the gulf between the two Christian camps.

Leaving aside this question of the consequences of the crusades —a question posed in terms of profit and loss and therefore somewhat naive—it is tempting to try to come to some general conclusion about the crusading movement. But it soon becomes abundantly clear that this is practically impossible. Only from the standpoint of the Christian faith can the movement be justified and a fervently devout Christian can still, if he so wishes, see it in its essentially positive aspects: as a kind of collective penance, as the triumphant unfolding of the Christian faith, as 'the testing of the faith in history' (Waas). The materialist on the other hand can emphasize the underlying economic factors. The sociologist can interpret the crusades as a safety valve for the increasing pressure of population in Western Europe and thus basically as a demographic phenomenon. The enlightened sceptic is likely to shake his head over the lunacy of spending two hundred years in fighting over what was, in the final analysis, only an empty hole in a rock. The romantic may be drawn to what he imagines is an exotic oriental world; or he may well admire the indisputable courage of the knights. The humane man will have to lament the butchery that was done at Jerusalem in 1099, at Constantinople in 1204, at Antioch in 1268. So each one will see the crusades filtered through the material of his own mind, indeed filtered two or three times since no single person would belong to one and only one of the above categories. Each of them has seen a part of the truth, but none can understand the whole. None the less most people, after examining the course and consequences of the crusades in as dispassionate way as is possible, are likely to feel that the disadvantages outweighed the advantages and that, seen from a modern standpoint—not from the medieval standpoint which it is hardly possible to recreate—the cost in terms of human life was out of all proportion to the goal that was sought.

But did the crusades have a genuine, clearly discernible goal? If there was such a goal it can only be discovered by keeping the crusades themselves distinct from their forerunners and descendants. It is obviously true that a movement as profound as the crusades could not have come to an abrupt end the moment Acre had been captured in 1291. No contemporary felt that anything like this had happened. The struggle between Christians and Muslims continued well into the seventeenth and eighteenth centuries. It has been argued, above all by A. S. Atiya in a series of studies which are thorough and well worth reading, that the fourteenth-century and, to some extent, also the fifteenth-century wars against Islam should properly be regarded as crusades. The next stage in the struggle, lasting until the Battle of Lepanto in 1571, when the Mediterranean was freed from the threat that it would be as much dominated by the Ottoman Turks as it previously had been by the Italians, he would then characterize as the period of the 'counter-crusade'. But in fact the Turkish expansion continued after 1571; in 1683 the Ottoman army stood at the gates of Vienna just as it had done in 1529. If we are looking for the point in time which marked the end of the crusades then the Battle of Lepanto is no better than 1291 or the capture of Constantinople and the end of the East Roman Empire in 1453.

Although in recent times scholars have not been inclined to accept 1291 as the end of the crusading period, they have naturally recognized that the date does at least mark some kind of turning point. But there is no unanimity as to what term should be used for the wars of the fourteenth and early fifteenth centuries. There is some justification for calling them crusades, but in other ways the word is a misleading one and the confusion is not diminished by calling the next period the age of the counter-crusade. For in that case how should we describe the gradual dismembering of the Ottoman Empire by the European powers in the period from 1571 to the 1830 War of Greek Independence or even to the Russo–Turkish War of 1877/8? Were these wars a kind of 'anti-counter-crusade'? Or should this later period be excluded from the alternating succession of crusade and counter-crusade only because no significant use was made of the terminology and ideology of crusade or *jihad* (holy war)? For, after all, it is clear that as early as the fourteenth century the crusading ideal was being used partly as a cloak to cover enterprises which were really intended to achieve quite different ends. Of course, if the decisive criteria are the use of the appropriate terminology and the presence of the correct external characteristics of a crusade as laid down by canon law, then these were indeed crusades. But in that case so were the thirteenth-century wars against the Albigensians and, in the same period, the political struggle of the papacy against the Hohenstaufen—who were perfectly orthodox Christians. Yet no one can deny that these wars were very far removed from the original crusades. It is perfectly true that the rise of the Ottoman Empire— the last of the great empires to be raised up by the amazing political creativity of the Turkish peoples—and this empire's fierce *Drang nach Westen* were, among other things, a reaction to two hundred years of Christian attacks on Islam. On the other hand it is equally clear that the so-called 'late crusades' after 1291 were generally part of a purely defensive reaction to this Ottoman advance which, by 1365, had resulted in the Balkan city of Adrianople being made the residence of the Ottoman sultan. This can be seen as early as 1344, for the expedition of that year was directed against Smyrna, an Anatolian city. It is significant that this 'late crusading movement' came to a temporary halt after the 1396 Nicopolis Crusade i.e. when the Ottomans themselves stopped their westward advance because they had their hands full with the defence of their eastern frontier against the second Mongol Empire under Timur the Lame who annihilated an Ottoman army near Ankara in 1402. Not until the Turks resumed their westward advance was there a new 'crusade', the Crusade of Varna (1444).

All these late medieval wars had one element in common: they were fought to protect Europe. A crusade in the true sense of the word, however, is not just a war which is called for by the pope and in which an oath is demanded and indulgences and worldly privileges are granted. It is also a war which is aimed at acquiring or preserving Christian dominion over the Sepulchre of Our Lord in Jerusalem i.e. a clear-cut objective which can be geographically pinned down to a particular region.[109] At first glance this definition seems to exclude the expeditions against Egypt, but they were in fact merely means to an end and the end was the conquest or defence of Jerusalem. The crusades were not intended, like the wars against the heathen in the Carolingian period and in the tenth century, to beat off an invasion; nor were they meant, like the 'crusades' against the Slavs, to achieve a forcible extension of the Christian community. The almost unbelievably obstinate simplicity of the believer's heart meant that these wars, the crusades, were directed again and again to the same goal: Jerusalem. This simplicity of thought, feeling, and action must not be overlooked. It is one of the things which did—and still do—most to make the crusade attractive. Of course it is impossible to deny that the crusading movement underwent many transformations before Acre was lost. The author of this book is the last man to want to overlook the worldly or the commercial aspects of the crusades. The crusades became ensnared in European politics; they were dragged into the struggle of the two universal powers; in the eyes of merchants from Italy, south France, and Catalonia they served as the starting point for far-reaching commercial policies which were judged in purely rational terms. They could satisfy the longing for adventure or the land hunger of the French nobility; they could serve as the basis of a vigorous missionary activity reaching deep into Asia. But always in the background of emotion there was Jerusalem—it was to defend Jerusalem or to reconquer it that the crusader states had been established—and along with Jerusalem went the whole *Terra Sancta*, the Holy Land. And it is this that distinguishes *the* crusades from all other, superficially similar undertakings. Before 1095 the war against the heathen had not been concerned with Jerusalem; after 1291 Jerusalem was only involved once, in 1365, for the way there did not go through Gallipoli, Nicopolis, or Varna, but only through the Levant or Egypt. Naturally when the real aim was to fight the Ottomans, Jerusalem was still useful as a bait, but it was now nothing more than a hollow slogan masking an entirely different political conception. Nor was there any real similarity between the crusades and the Islamic holy war (*al-Jihad*) which, along with the Islamic creed, regular prayer, dues paid to the state, the great fast at Ramadan and the pilgrimage to Mecca, was the 'sixth pillar' of Islamic theology. The idea behind the holy war is that all non-Muslims should be fought against until the whole world is subject to Allah. Right from the start a conception on this grand scale was foreign to the crusader's view of the world and in the course of time it became even further removed as it became increasingly clear how few Christians there were in the world and how many non-Christians. Moreover any such conception would have been contradictory to the Christian theory of the just war.

The thesis put forward here is by no means shared by all modern scholars; on the contrary, the present tendency is for the crusades to be defined more and more broadly. Doubtless the late 'crusades' should be covered in every full-length modern history of the crusades if only to show how the movement tailed off, but the point of view which sees them as genuine crusades is neither free from ambiguity nor immune from contradiction. It cannot be disputed that from the standpoint of world history the crusades are a part of the great conflict between East and West which, in historically knowable times, began with the conflict between Greece and Persia and still goes on today. The wars of Rome against the Huns and

Parthians, the breathtaking expansion of Islam in the seventh and eighth centuries, the wars on the eastern frontiers of Byzantium, the expulsion of the Magyars from Germany, of the Saracens from France and Italy in the tenth and eleventh centuries, the Spanish *Reconquista* only completed in 1492, the crusades, the wars against the Turks, the colonial expansion of France and England in Africa and the Near East (and in South and South-East Asia as well), the undermining of the Chinese Empire by European cunning and power, the early hostility of Japan to the Europeans, the nationalist movement in the Arab peoples after the Second World War, the conflict between communism and democracy, long since transformed into a power struggle between Russia and America—all of it belongs to this world-historical conflict between East and West which, from a European point of view, is the main theme of political history. The last pages in the history of this conflict are not yet written; the shadow of China has already been cast over Russia and America while they have carried their own rivalry into the entirely new dimension of space. But within the broader perspective of world history it still seems possible to distinguish the crusades from, on the one hand, the defensive struggle against Islamic expansion which preceded them and the defence against the Ottomans which came after; from, on the other hand, the Spanish *Reconquista* and the wars on the eastern frontiers of Byzantium. As we have shown, historians of the crusades still disagree with one another. But until an unambiguous, lucid, and generally accepted definition of the term 'crusade' has been found, the debate is only too likely to go round in circles without coming to any satisfactory conclusion. Even though the difficulty of trying to comprehend so complex a problem within the limits of a brief definition cannot be ignored, it has seemed worthwhile to attempt to state one point of view in as clear-cut a way as possible in the hope that thereby the debate will be further stimulated.

As late as 1940 the *bula de la cruzada* was still being used in Spain simply in order to finance church services. Yet who would want to call this a crusade?[110] But we will get nowhere if we remain in the realm of 'ifs' and 'buts', if we spend too long on cautious glances at peripheral aspects of the crusades—movements which may be undeniably important in their own right and which undoubtedly require further research, but which are, none the less, peripheral to the problem of the crusades. The Gordian knot must be cut. Only if those who disagree with the definition given here are prepared to state their own view equally unambiguously can there be any hope of meeting somewhere in the middle. But as things are at present enormous amounts of time and energy are being expended on research into the crusades without there being any agreement as to just what the crusades were. This state of affairs is surely indefensible.

BIBLIOGRAPHY

THE notes are primarily intended to refer the reader to the literature on the subject; only occasionally are they concerned with matters of controversy. The titles listed there represent only a selection from the literature which was used in the preparation of this book; they do not represent a critical survey of all the authorities. They were chosen with an eye to referring the reader to the most important recent literature where he can easily find for himself both a discussion of problems of detail and a guide to the rest of the literature. Thus the bibliography here is limited to the most important general works which, in consequence, are normally omitted from the notes.

COLLECTIONS OF SOURCES: *Recueil des Historiens des Croisades* (1841–1906; abbreviated as *RHC*) divided into the following classes: *Historiens Occidentaux* (*Hoc.*), 5 vols.; *Historiens Orientaux* (*Hor.*), 5 vols.; *Historiens Grecs*, 2 vols.; *Documents Arméniens* (*Arm.*), 2 vols.; *Lois*, 2 vols. *Archives de l'Orient Latin*, 2 vols. (1881–4). Supplementing this is the *Revue de l'Orient latin*, 12 vols. (1893–1911). *Corpus scriptorum historiae Byzantinae*, 50 vols. (1828–97). As a guide to this there is **G. Moravcsik**, *Byzantinoturcica*, vol. 1 (2nd edn. 1958). **J. P. Migne**, *Patrologiae cursus completus, Series Latina*, 217 vols. (1844–64). In addition there are the great national collections: 'Monumenta Germaniae Historica' (abbreviated as MGH), 'Recueil des Historiens des Gaules et de la France', 'Rerum Britannicarum scriptores medii aevi,' 'Rerum Italicarum scriptores', which are cited in every historical bibliography.

SOURCES: In general the Western and Byzantine sources each deal with one particular period and for this reason they can be referred to in the notes to the appropriate chapter. But of special importance for the first century of the crusades is the *Historia rerum in partibus transmarinis gestarum* of Archbishop William of Tyre (d. 1186), ed. *RHC Hoc.* 1 with a supplement (XIX, 12) ed. **R. B. C. Huygens**, in *Latomus*, 21 (1962), 811ff. A new edition of William of Tyre is being prepared by R. B. C. Huygens and H. E. Mayer. The present state of publication of oriental sources means that the great Arabic universal chronicles of the thirteenth century are indispensable, above all **Ibn Al-Athir** (d. 1234), *al-Kāmil fi t-ta'rih* (*Sum of World History*), ed. C. J. Tornberg, 14 vols. (1851–76); extracts with French translation in *RHC Hor.* 1 and 2. Then **Abu'l Feda** (d. 1331). *Muhtsar ta'rih al-bašar* (*World History*) ed. J. J. Reiske as *Annales Muslemici*, 5 vols. (1789–94); extracts with French translation *RHC Hor.* 1. As for the rest, there is an excellent introduction to the Arab chronicles in **C. Cahen**, *La Syrie du Nord* (1940), 33–93, and for the thirteenth century in **H. L. Gottschalk**, *Al-Malik al-Kāmil von Egypten und seine Zeit* (1958), 6–19. Cf. also *Historians of the Middle East*, ed. **B. Lewis** and **P. M. Holt** (1962) and **J. Sauvaget**, *Introduction à l'Histoire de l'Orient musulman: élements de bibliographie*, 2nd edn., ed. C. Cahen (1961). On all points of detail see **C. Brockelmann**, *Geschichte der arabischen Literatur*, 2nd edn., 2 vols. (1943–9); Supplement: 3 vols. (1937–42). **G. Graf**, *Geschichte der christlichen arabischen Literatur*, 5 vols. (1944–53). Among the important Syriac universal chronicles are: **Michael the Syrian** (d. 1199), *Chronique*, ed. with French translation by J. Chabot, 4 vols. (1899–1924) and the *Chronography of Gregory Abu l-Farağ, commonly known as Bar Hebraeus* (d. 1286), ed. W. Budge, 2 vols. (1932). Armenian universal chronicles: **Vartan the Great** (to 1269), extracts with French translation in *RHC Arm.* 1; in addition there is *La Flor des Estoires de la Terre d'Orient* (ed. *RHC Arm.* 2), by **Hethoum of Corycus** (d. after 1308) which was written in Latin and French for Western readers. On the Syriac and Armenian chronicles cf. also **A. Lüders**, *Die Kreuzzüge im Urteil syrischer und armenischer Quellen* (1964).

CHARTERS: Most important are the papal charters, listed together with a summary of their contents in **Ph. Jaffé**, *Regesta pontificum Romanorum* (as far as 1198), 2nd edn., 2 vols. (1885–8); **A. Potthast**, *Regesta pontificum Romanorum* (1198–1304), 2 vols. (1874–5), as well as the registers of the thirteenth-century papal chancery edited by the Ecole française de Rome and supplemented by **P. Pressutti**, *Regesta Honorii papae III*, 2 vols. (1888–95). For the register of Innocent III see below note 70. Byzantium: *Regesten der Kaiserurkunden des Oströmischen Reiches*, ed. **F. Dölger**, in 5 parts covering 565–1453 (1924–65). In contrast the charters of the Western emperors and kings are of little value. An important Italian collection is: **G. L. F. Tafel** and **G. M. Thomas**, *Urkunden zur älteren Handels- und Staatsgeschichte der Republik Venedig mit besonderer Berücksichtigung auf Byzanz und die Levante*, 3 vols. (1856–7). The charters of the Holy Land itself are listed in **R. Röhricht**, *Regesta regni Hierosolymitani* (1893), together with the *Additamentum* (1904).

MODERN WORKS: **L. Boehm**, 'Gesta Dei per Francos—oder Gesta Francorum? Die Kreuzzüge als historiographisches Problem', *Saeculum*, 8 (1957), 43ff. (historiographcial). **H. E. Mayer**, *Bibliographie zur Geschichte der Kreuzzüge* (1960; 2nd, unaltered edn. 1965), supplemented by **H. E. Mayer**, 'Literaturbericht über die Geschichte der Kreuzzüge' (1958–67), *Historische Zeitschrift*, Sonderheft 3 (1969). **A. S. Atiya**, *The Crusade, Historiography and Bibliography* (1962). **P. Alphandéry**, *La Chrétienté et l'idée de Croisade*, ed. A. Dupront, 2 vols. (1954–9). **J. A. Brundage**, *Medieval Canon Law and the Crusader* (1969). **M. Villey**, *La Croisade. Essai sur la formation d'une théorie juridique* (1942). *A History of the Crusades*, ed. **K. M. Setton**, 2 vols. so far (1955–62; reprinted 1969); 3 further vols. are planned and vol. 3 is now in the press. **S. Runciman**, *A History of the Crusades*, 3 vols. (1951–4). **A. Waas**, *Geschichte der Kreuzzüge*, 2 vols. (1956). **R. Grousset**,

Histoire des Croisades, 3 vols. (1934–6). **P. Rousset,** *Histoire des Croisades* (1957). Much emphasis is placed on the world-historical aspect (East–West question) in **A. S. Atiya,** *Crusade, Commerce and Culture* (1962). **L. Bréhier,** *L'Église et les Croisades* (5th edn. 1928). **B. Kugler,** *Geschichte der Kreuzzüge* (2nd edn. 1891; an excellent account despite both its age and the emotional style in which it is written). **F. W. Wentzlaff-Eggebert,** *Kreuzzugsdichtung des Mittelalters* (1960). For a Marxist point of view see **W. Spiewok,** 'Die Bedeutung des Kreuzzugerlebnisses für die Entwicklung der feudalhöfischen Ideologie und die Ausformung der mittelalterlichen deutschen Literatur', *Weimarer Beiträge* 9/10 (1963/4), 669ff. Cf. also the important works cited in note 58, *especially* **J. Prawer.** *Histoire du royaume latin de Jérusalem*, Vols. 1 & 2 (1969–70), *The Cambridge Medieval History*, vol. 4: *The Byzantine Empire*, Parts I and II (1966–7). **G. Ostrogorsky,** *History of the Byzantine State* (2nd edn. 1968). **A. A. Vasiliev,** *History of the Byzantine Empire*, 2nd edn., 2 vols. (Reprinted 1961). **H. G. Beck,** *Kirche und theologische Literatur im Byzantinischen Reich* (1959). **W. Norden,** *Das Papsttum und Byzanz* (1903). **C. Brockelmann,** *History of the Islamic Peoples* (1949). **B. Spuler,** *Geschichte der islamischen Länder*, 2 vols (Handbuch der Orientalistik, 6, 1952–3). *The Encyclopedia of Islam*, 4 vols. and supplement (1908–38). A new edition of this is being prepared. **R. Roolvink** and others, *Historical Atlas of the Muslim People* (1957). **E. De Zambaur,** *Manuel de généalogie et de chronologie pour l'histoire de l'Islam* (1927). **S. Lane Poole,** *The Mohammadan Dynasties* (2nd edn. 1925). **N. Daniel,** *Islam and the West. The Making of an Image* (1960). **R. W. Southern,** *Western Views of Islam in the Middle Ages* (1962). **E. Sivan,** *L'Islam et la croisade. Idéologie et propagande dans les réactions musulmanes aux croisades* (1968).

NOTES

1. S. Runciman, *The Eastern Schism* (1955).

2. B. Lewis, 'The Ismā'īlites and the Assassins', in *A History of the Crusades*, ed. K. M. Setton, 1 (1955), 99ff.; M. G. Hodgson, *The Order of the Assassins* (1955).

3. C. Cahen, 'La première pénétration turque en Asie Mineure', *Byzantion*, 18 (1946–8), 5ff.; Cahen, 'En quoi la conquête turque appellait-elle la croisade?', *Bulletin de la Faculté des Lettres de Strasbourg*, 29 (1950), 118ff. There is an expanded, English version of this article: Cahen, 'An Introduction to the First Crusade', *Past and Present*, 6 (1954), 6ff.

3a. But see the different interpretation by M. F. Hendy, 'Byzantium 1081–1204: an Economic Reappraisal', *Transactions of the Royal Historical Society*, 5th series vol. 20 (1970).

4. W. Holtzmann, 'Studien zur Orientpolitik des Reformpapsttums und zur Entstehung des ersten Kreuzzuges', *Historische Vierteljahresschrift*, 22 (1924–5), 167ff.; Holtzmann, 'Die Unionsverhandlungen zwischen Kaiser Alexios I und Papst Urban II im Jahre 1089', *Byzantinische Zeitschrift*, 28 (1928), 38ff.; D. C. Munro, 'Did the Emperor Alexios I ask for Aid at the Council of Piacenza 1095?', *American Historical Review*, 27 (1922), 731ff.; P. Charanis, 'Byzantium, the West and the Origin of the First Crusade', *Byzantion*, 19 (1949), 17ff.

5. Works of general importance for this chapter are: C. Erdmann, *Die Entstehung des Kreuzzugsgedankens* (1935), particularly valuable for the idea of Holy War; Alphandéry, vol. 1 (see above p. 288); P. Rousset, *Les origines et les caractère de la première croisade* (1945).

6. D. C. Munro, 'The Speech of Pope Urban II at Clermont', *American Historical Review*, 11 (1906), 231ff. In contrast to the opinion expressed here and on the following pages, H. E. J. Cowdrey, 'Pope Urban II's Preaching of the First Crusade', *History*, 55 (1970), 177ff., believes that precisely because Jerusalem was so potent a slogan, Urban was likely to have made it both the object of the war and the goal of the march—and to have done this right from the very beginning of his plans for the crusade. By showing how frequently the word Jerusalem crops up in sources (charters and local chronicles from Anjou) which are outside the usual run of sources for the crusade, Cowdrey is able to build up a very impressive argument. I would like to make a point of drawing attention to Cowdrey's work because it undoubtedly runs counter to my own views. It is, however, also necessary to look at the consequences of Cowdrey's hypothesis and ask oneself whether or not the pope really had any interest in talking about Jerusalem and in directing the crusade to it. Would he have

given priority to the capture of Jerusalem or to the liberation of the Church
in the East? Once in Christian hands Jerusalem might all too easily become
a rival to Rome for, as the Anonymous of York put it, the centre of Christendom was not Rome, but Jerusalem. On the other hand, with the liberation of
the eastern Churches the pope could hope to achieve a union of the Churches
and the overall primacy of Rome. If the pope consciously intended the crusade
to capture Jerusalem rather than free the Church in the East, then he was
setting up a new rival to Rome (i.e. Jerusalem) instead of eliminating an old
one (Constantinople). Yet despite these doubts I would have no hesitation in
accepting Cowdrey's hypothesis if it were possible to show that in 1095 men
talked exclusively of Jerusalem rather than of Jerusalem in the context of the
eastern Churches. But neither in the second canon of the Council of Clermont
nor in Urban's letter to the Flemings was this the case—and these are the
only two sources which date from 1095. Certainly Cowdrey's use of the *Frag-
mentum historiae Andegavensis* of February 1096 adds significantly to our
sources for the First Crusade, but even here, as in the second canon of the
Council of Clermont, Jerusalem is mentioned only in association with other
things, i.e. that people should go there to subdue the race of the heathen
who had seized that city and all the land of the Christians up as far as
Constantinople. So here too, if I interpret this passage correctly, we have a
reference to the liberation of the Christian church in Asia Minor. And there
is another piece of evidence which should, perhaps, be considered at this
point, a papal letter (JL.5703) written in May 1098. By that time the crusading
army had come to a halt outside Antioch, yet in this letter the pope, who,
according to Cowdrey, placed Jerusalem at the heart of his notion of the
crusade, wrote not one word about Jerusalem but instead declared that the
task of the moment was to fight the Turks in Asia and the Moors in Europe
(*in Asia Turcos, in Europa Mauros*). Cowdrey can neither find a source from
the time immediately after the Council of Clermont which refers exclusively to
Jerusalem, nor can he really show that a single one of the sources he uses
(apart, of course, from the pope's own letters) was influenced more by Urban
than by popular opinion. Cowdrey merely suspects that it was so. None the
less I find his work somewhat disquieting for it is certainly true that things
might have gone the way which he suggests, and, if this were so, then very
considerable revisions might have to be made in the interpretations of the
papacy's eastern policy in the eleventh century.

7. S. Mähl, 'Jerusalem in mittelalterlicher Sicht', *Die Welt als Geschichte*,
22 (1962), 11ff.; R. Konrad, 'Das himmlische und das irdische Jerusalem im
mittelalterlichen Denken', in *Speculum historiale* (Festschrift Spörl), (1965).

8. B. Kötting, *Peregrinatio religiosa. Die Wallfahrten der Antike und das
Pilgerwesen der alten Kirche* (1950); H. Leclercq, 'Pèlerinages aux Lieux
Saints', *Dictionnaire d'Archéologie chrétienne et de Liturgie*, 14 (1939), 65ff.

9. R. H. W. Regout, *La doctrine de la guerre juste de St. Augustin à nos jours*
(1934); Erdmann (above n.5).

10. C. Erdmann, 'Die Aufrufe Gerberts und Sergius IV. für das Hl. Land',
Quellen und Forschungen aus italienischen Archiven und Bibliotheken, 23
(1931-2), 1ff.; A. Gieysztor, 'The Genesis of the Crusades. The Encyclica of
Sergius IV', *Medievalia et Humanistica*, 5 (1948), 3ff.; 6 (1950), 3ff.

11. M. Defourneaux, *Les Français en Espagne aux XIe et XIIe siècles* (1949).

12. G. Duby, *La société aux XIe et XIIe siècles dans la région mâconnaise*

(1953). D. Herlihy, 'The Agrarian Revolution in Southern France and Italy', *Speculum*, 33 (1958), 23ff.

13. A. Gottlob, *Kreuzablass und Almosenablass* (1906); N. Paulus, *Geschichte des Ablasses im Mittelalter*, 3 vols. (1922–3); B. Poschmann, *Der Ablass im Lichte der Bussgeschichte* (1948); C. Vogel, 'Le pèlerinage pénitentiel', in *Pellegrinaggi e culto dei santi in Europa fino alla Ia crociata* (Convegni del Centro di Studi sulla spiritualità medioevale, 4, 1963), 34ff. In this chapter I have argued along lines similar to those which Vogel follows, i.e. that indulgences were proclaimed despite the fact that the Council of Clermont gave no authority for doing this, and that it was only later that the canonists provided a theoretical framework to support this, theologically speaking, still unjustifiable practice. In a sense J. A. Brundage, *Medieval Canon Law and the Crusader* (1969), 145ff., propounds yet more radical views when he argues that all 'crusading indulgences' right up until the Council of Lyons (1245)—including therefore even the indulgence issued at the Fourth Lateran Council (1215)—were unclearly formulated. Thus he claims that the popes never proclaimed true indulgences until after the great scholastic theologians of the thirteenth century had worked out the doctrine of the Treasury of Merits. It seems that Brundage wishes to interpret all earlier indulgences as simply remissions of penance or commutations. In this case the episcopal power of the keys would undoubtedly be sufficiently authoritative. Although I do not share this view—a view which exonerates the twelfth-century Church—I would like to draw attention to it here as the opinion of one of the leading experts.

14. General bibliography for chapter three. Principal sources: *Anonymi Gesta Francorum et aliorum Hierosolymitanorum*, ed. R. Hill (1962); Fulcher of Chartres, *Historia Hierosolymitana*, ed. H. Hagenmeyer (1913), English translation by F. R. Ryan (ed. H. Fink), *A History of the Expedition to Jerusalem* (1969); Albert of Aix, *Historia Hierosolymitana*, RHC Hoc. 4; Raymond of Aguilers, *Historia Francorum qui ceperunt Iherusalem*, RHC Hoc. 3; new edition, *Le 'Liber' de Raymond d'Aguilers*, ed. J. H. and L. L. Hill (Documents relatifs à l'histoire des croisades, 9, 1969), English translation by J. H. and L. L. Hill (1968); Radulph of Caen, *Gesta Tancredi*, RHC Hoc. 3; Anna Comnena, *Alexiad*, ed. B. Lēib, 3 vols. (1937–45, with a French translation), English translation by E. R. A. Sewter (1969); Matthew of Edessa, *Chronique avec la continuation de Grégoire le Prêtre*, French translation by E. Dulaurier, in *Bibliothèque historique arménienne*, I (1858); S. D. Goitein, 'Contemporary Letters on the Capture of Jerusalem by the Crusaders', *Journal of Jewish Studies*, 3 (1952), 162ff. Secondary works: Mayer, *Bibliographie*, nos. 1902–2007; F. Chalandon, *Histoire de la première croisade* (1925); H. von Sybel, *Geschichte des ersten Kreuzzuges*, (2nd edn. 1881; important on account of a critical evaluation of the sources which long remained authoritative); Rousset (see above n. 5); H. E. Mayer, 'Zur Beurteilung Adhémars von Le Puy', *Deutsches Archiv*, 16 (1960), 547ff. and including a summary of the debate between Hill and Brundage—on this see also J. Richard, *Journal des Savants*, 1960 (1961), 49ff.; J. C. Andressohn, *The Ancestry and Life of Godfrey de Bouillon* (1947); G. H. Hagspiel, *Die Führerpersönlichkeit im Kreuzzug* (1963; needs to be used with caution); by contrast, G. Waeger, *Gottfried von Bouillon in der Historiographie* (1969) is an excellent study; P. Gindler, *Graf Balduin I von Edessa* (1901); R. B. Yewdale, *Bohemund I Prince of Antioch* (1924; reprinted 1970); see also the fine article by D. Girgensohn, 'Boemondo I', *Dizionario biografico degli Italiani*, 11 (1969), 117ff; R. L. Nicholson, *Tan-*

cred, A Study of His Career and Work (1940); C. W. David, *Robert Curthose Duke of Normandy* (1920); J. H. and L. L. Hill, *Raymond IV Count of Toulouse* (1962); J. A. Brundage, 'An Errant Crusader: Stephen of Blois', *Traditio,* 16 (1960), 380ff.; P. Rousset, 'Étienne de Blois, croisé fuyard et martyr', Geneva, N.S. 11 (1963), 183ff.; F. Chalandon, *Les Comnène. Etudes sur l'Empire byzantin aux XIe et XIIe siècles,* i: *Essai sur le règne d'Alexis Ier Comnène* (1900); L. Dasberg, *Untersuchungen über die Entwertung des Judenstatus im 11. Jh.* (1965); better is H. Liebeschütz, 'The Crusading Movement in its Bearing on the Christian Attitude towards Jewry', *Journal of Jewish Studies,* 10 (1959), 97ff.

15. The privileges are very clearly summarized in the canons of the Lateran Council of 1123 where they are all attributed to Urban; cf. Mansi, *Sacrorum Conciliorum nova et amplissima collectio,* 21, 284. On the canonistic doctrine at the end of the twelfth century see J. A. Brundage, 'The Crusade of Richard I. Two Canonical Quaestiones', *Speculum,* 38 (1963), 443ff. On the crusader's vow see A. Noth, *Heiliger Krieg und Heiliger Kampf in Islam und Christentum* (1966). He emphatically denies the existence of any such binding vow before the departure of the First Crusade. But on this point Brundage's opinion, based on a deeper knowledge of the sources, is to be preferred. See J. A. Brundage, 'The Army of the First Crusade and the Crusade Vow', *Medieval Studies,* 33 (1971), 334ff.; also Brundage, 'The Votive Obligation of the Crusader: The Development of a Canonistic Doctrine, *Traditio,* 24 (1968), 77ff., and Brundage, 'A Note on the Attestation of Crusaders' Vows', *The Catholic Historical Review,* 52 (1966), 234ff., and Brundage, 'Cruce Signari: The Rite for Taking the Cross in England', *Traditio,* 22 (1966), 289ff. On the position of the crusader's wife in canon law see Brundage, 'The Crusader's Wife', *Studia Gratiana,* 12 (1967), 425ff., and 'The Crusader's Wife Revisited', ibid., 14 (1968), 241ff.

16. H. Hagenmeyer, *Le vrai et le faux sur Pierre l'Hermite* (1883); F. Duncalf, 'The Peasants' Crusade', *American Historical Review,* 26 (1920/21), 440ff.

17. It is possible that Raymond believed that there were threats to the hereditary rights of his descendants in Provence and Toulouse, but on this point further research is needed.

18. J. Richard, 'Quelques textes sur les premiers temps de l'église latine de Jérusalem', *Mélanges Clovis Brunel,* 2 (1955), 421.

19. According to Anna Comnena the fight took place on Maundy Thursday but on this point modern Byzantinists accept the date given by Albert of Aix; cf. Dölger, *Regesten der Kaiserurkunden des Oströmischen Reiches,* no. 1196. Following the Byzantine custom Alexius adopted several of the leaders of the crusade in order to demonstrate their dependent position; cf. F. L. Ganshof, 'Recherche sur le lien juridique qui unissait les chefs de la première croisade à l'Empereur byzantin', *Mélanges P. E. Martin* (1961), 49ff.

20. Bohemund's 'house chronicle', the *Gesta Francorum,* tells of a secret arrangement whereby Bohemund was to receive Antioch but this is a later interpolation (inserted *c.* 1105 or even after 1108) designed to give support to Bohemund's claim to Antioch; cf. A. C. Krey, 'A Neglected Passage in the Gesta', in *The Crusades and other Essays presented to D. C. Munro* (1928), 57ff., and recently questioned by R. Hill, *Gesta Francorum,* 12f., n.2.

21. Cf. L. A. M. Sumberg 'The "Tafurs" and the First Crusade', *Mediaeval Studies,* 21 (1959), 224ff.

22. S. Runciman, 'The Holy Lance found at Antioch', *Analecta Bollandiana*, 68 (1950), 197ff.

23. This has often been seen as a clerical attempt to establish a kind of theocracy in the Crusader States; cf. J. Hansen, *Das Problem eines Kirchenstaates in Jerusalem* (1928). Emphatically, and rightly, critical of this view is J. G. Rowe, 'Paschal II and the Latin Orient', *Speculum*, 32 (1957), 471ff. On Arnulf of Rohes cf. R. Foreville, 'Un chef de la première croisade: Arnoul Malecouronne', *Bulletin philol. et hist. du Comité des travaux hist. et scientif.* 1953-4 (1955), 377ff.

24. This is not intended to imply that religious motives played no part in Godfrey's decision; merely that they were inseparably linked with political considerations. At that date the title of advocate carried with it well-defined rights to authority over Church lands.

25. Mayer, *Bibliographie*, nos. 170–275; R. Blanchard, *Asie occidentale (Géographie universelle*, 7, 1929); R. Thoumin, *Géographie humaine de la Syrie centrale* (1936); R. Dussaud, *Topographie historique de la Syrie antique et médiévale* (1927); F. M. Abel, *Géographie de la Palestine*, 2 vols. (2nd edn., 1933–8); G. Dalman, *Arbeit und Sitte in Palästina*, 7 vols. (1928–39); meteorological measurements for 1928–33 are given in the *Zeitschrift des Deutschen Palästina-Vereins*, 52–5 (1929–32), and 57 (1934); I. Schattner, *The Lower Jordan Valley* (1962).

26. General bibliography for chapter four. Principal sources: Albert of Aix (until 1120), Fulcher of Chartres (until 1127), Anna Comnena (until 1118), Matthew of Edessa, and Gregory the Priest (until 1162)—for all of these see above n. 14; Walter the Chancellor, *Bella Antiochena* (1115–22), ed. H. Hagenmeyer (1896); William of Tyre (from 1127), see above p. 287; John Cinnamus, *Epitome rerum gestarum*, ed. A. Meineke (1836); R. Le Tourneau, *Damas de 1075 à 1154. Traduction annotée d'un fragment de l'Histoire de Damas d'Ibn al-Qālanisī* (1952). Secondary works: A. Wollf, *König Balduin I. von Jerusalem* (1884) and the biographies listed in note 14; R. L. Nicholson, *Joscelin I Prince of Edessa* (1954); A. Herzog, *Die Frau auf den Fürstenthronen der Kreuzfahrerstaaten* (1919); F. Chalandon, *Les Comnène*, 2: *Jean II Comnène et Manuel Ier Comnène* (1912); Mayer, *Bibliographie*, nos. 3937–41.

27. It is generally accepted that the text of the letter in William of Tyre X, 4 is not genuine. Nevertheless it is hardly possible to deny the existence of a letter with contents very similar to this.

28. Ekkehard of Aura, *Hierosolymita*, RHC. Hoc. 5. S. Runciman, 'The Crusades of 1101', *Jahrbuch der österreichisch-byzantinischen Gesellschaft*, 1 (1951), 3ff.

28a. On this war see J. G. Rowe, 'Paschal II, Bohemund of Antioch and the Byzantine Empire', *Bulletin of the John Rylands Library*, 49 (1966), 165ff. and Kindlimann (below n.38).

29. In truth the constitutional position was even more complicated than this; see J. Richard, *Comté de Tripoli* (1945), 26–43.

30. J. G. Rowe, 'The Papacy and the Ecclesiastical Province of Tyre', *Bulletin of the John Rylands Library*, 43 (1960), 160ff.

31. Possibly this was intended as some kind of compensation for the fact that, at roughly the same time (*JL.* 7314 of 29 May 1128), the pope rejected the renewed claims of Patriarch Stephen to Jaffa etc. and gave a decision in favour

of the king—in practice at least, although the actual words of the decision were
rather obscure. But it is not permissible to use JL. 7314 as evidence that
Jerusalem was feudally subordinate to the Church—as historians were at one
time inclined to do.

32. Marquis d'Albon, *Cartulaire général de l'Ordre du Temple* (1913; until
1150); M. Dessubré, *Bibliographie de l'Ordre des Templiers* (1928); H. Neu,
Bibliographie des Templer-Ordens 1927–1965 (1965); G. Schnürer, *Die ur-
sprüngliche Templerregel* (1903). There is no good modern history of the
Templars. Older works are listed in Mayer, *Bibliographie*, nos. 1433–8, 1621–
3, 3561–621. See also Bernard of Clairvaux, *De laude novae militiae*, in Migne,
Patrologia Latina 182, 921ff.; J. Delaville Le Roulx, *Cartulaire général de
l'Ordre des Hospitaliers de St. Jean de Jérusalem*, 4 vols. (1884–1906); Delaville
Le Roulx, *Les Hospitaliers en Terre Sainte et à Chypre* (1904); J. Riley-Smith,
The Knights of St. John in Jerusalem and Cyprus (1967); E. J. King, *The Rules,
Statutes and Customs of the Hospitallers* (1934); Mayer, *Bibliographie*, nos.
54–5, 108–17, 1414–32, 1618–20, 3478–560.

32a. On the succession to Baldwin II cf. R. Hiestand, 'Zwei unbekannte Dip-
lome der lateinischen Könige von Jerusalem aus Lucca,' *Quellen und Forschungen aus italienischen Archiven und Bibliotheken*, 50 (1970), 25ff., and
H. E. Mayer, 'Studies in the History of Queen Melisende', *Dumbarton Oaks
Papers*, 26 (1972).

33. It is not possible to date the revolt precisely; see William of Tyre XIV,
15–17, but cf. J. Richard, *Royaume latin de Jérusalem* (1953), 90 and J. Prawer
in *Le Moyen Age*, 65 (1959), 51 n.3. On this revolt and that of Count Hugh of
Jaffa in particular see the study by Mayer (n. 32a above).

34. C. Cahen, 'Le premier cycle de la croisade (Antioche—Jérusalem—Chétifs)',
Le Moyen Age, 63 (1957), 311ff.

35. General bibliography for chapter five. Sources: Odo of Deuil, *De Pro-
fectione Ludovici VII in Orientem*, ed. with an English translation by V. G.
Berry (1948); Suger of St. Denis, *Vie de Louis le Gros* (including his *Histoire
du roi Louis VII*) ed. A. Molinier (1887); Suger's correspondence is in his
Oeuvres complètes, ed. A. Lecoy de la Marche (1867); Otto of Freising,
Chronica sive Historia de duabus civitatibus, ed. A. Hofmeister, MGH, Scrip-
tores rerum Germanicarum (2nd edn. 1912), English translation by C. C.
Mierow (1928); id., *Gesta Friderici*, ed. G. Waitz and B. von Simson (3rd edn.
1912), English translation by C. C. Mierow (1953); Wibald of Stablo, *Epistolae*,
ed. Ph. Jaffé, *Bibliotheca rerum Germanicarum* 1 (1864); Bernard of Clairvaux,
Epistolae, in Migne, *Patrologia Latina*, 182. In addition see above n.26 for
William of Tyre, John Cinnamus, Ibn al-Qālanisī and Gregory the Priest.
Secondary works: Mayer, *Bibliographie*, nos. 2015–61; B. Kugler, *Studien zur
Geschichte des zweiten Kreuzzuges* (1866; supplemented by Mayer, *Bibliographie*, nos. 2017–18); G. Constable, 'The Second Crusade as Seen by Con-
temporaries', *Traditio*, 9 (1953), 213ff.; H. Gleber, *Papst Eugen III.* (1936);
E. Delaruelle, 'L'idée de croisade chez St. Bernard,' *Mélanges de St. Bernard*
(1953), 53ff.; E. Willems, 'Cîteaux et la seconde croisade', *Revue d'Histoire
ecclésiastique*, 49 (1954), 116ff.; E. Vacandard, *Vie de St. Bernard*, vol. 2 (4th
edn. 1910); P. Rassow, 'Die Kanzlei St. Bernhards von Clairvaux', *Studien und
Mitteilungen zur Geschichte des Benediktinerordens*, 34 (1913), 243ff.; W. v.
Bernhardi, *Konrad III.* (1883); P. Lamma, *Comneni e Staufer*, 2 vols. (1955–7);

F. Chalandon, *Comnène*, vol. 2 (see n.26); id., *Histoire de la domination normande en Italie et en Sicile*, vol. 2 (1907).

36. The best survey of the polemical literature is contained in E. Caspar, 'Die Kreuzzugsbullen Eugens III', *Neues Archiv*, 45 (1924), 285ff., together with a text of the March bull.

37. L. Grill, 'Die Kreuzzugsepistel St. Bernhards *Ad peregrinantes Jerusalem*', *Studien und Mitteilungen zur Geschichte des Benediktinerordens*, 67 (1956), 237ff. On the crusade against the Wends cf. Mayer, *Bibliographie*, nos. 2058–61 and the collection of essays by H. Beumann, *Heidenmission und Kreuzzugsgedanke in der deutschen Ostpolitik des Mittelalters* (1963; also useful for later developments in the Slav regions).

38. W. M. Daly, 'Christian Fraternity, the Crusaders and the Security of Constantinople', *Mediaeval Studies*, 22 (1960), 59ff. S. Kindlimann, *Die Eroberung von Konstantinopel als politische Forderung des Westens im Hochmittelalter* (1969).

39. On the following see Lamma (above n.35); P. Rassow, *Honor imperii. Die neue Politik Friedrich Barbarossas* (1940); K. Heilig, 'Ostrom und das deutsche Reich um die Mitte des 12. Jh.', in Th. Mayer, C. Erdmann and K. J. Heilig, *Kaisertum und Herzogsgewalt im Zeitalter Friedrichs I* (1944), 159ff.

40. Osbernus, *De expugnatione Lyxbonensi*, ed. with an English translation by C. W. David (1933); F. Kurth, 'Der Anteil niederdeutscher Kreuzfahrer an den Kämpfen der Portugiesen gegen die Mauren', *Mitteilungen des Instituts für österreichische Geschichtsforschung*, Ergänzungsband, 8 (1911), 133ff.

41. Gerhoh of Reichersberg, *De Investigatione Antichristi*, MGH, Libelli de lite, 3, 374ff., 380ff.; *Annales Herbipolenses*, MGH, Scriptores, 16, 3; Bernard of Clairvaux, *De Consideratione II*, 1, in Migne, *Patrologia Latina* 182, 741.

42. General bibliography for chapter six. Sources: William of Tyre (to 1184; above p. 287); *Anonymi Chronicon Terrae Sanctae* (for 1187), ed. H. Prutz, *Quellenbeiträge zur Geschichte der Kreuzzüge* (1876); in addition there are the sources for the Third Crusade referred to below in n.40; John Cinnamus (up to 1176), Ibn al-Qālanisī (until 1154), see above n.26; Nicetas Choniates, *Historia*, ed. I. Bekker (1835; up to 1206). On the Arabic sources see H. A. R. Gibb, 'The Arabic Sources for the Life of Saladin', *Speculum*, 25 (1950), 58ff.; the article by Gibb on two unedited fragments from 'Imad ad-Dīn al-Iṣfahānī, *al-barq aš-ša 'mi* (the most important source on Saladin) in the *Wiener Zeitschrift für die Kunde des Morgenlandes*, 52 (1953–5), 93ff.; J. Kraemer, *Der Sturz des Königreichs Jerusalem* (1952), an analysis of the *Al-fath al-qussi* of 'Imad ad-Dīn. For the main secondary works on the crusader states see below n.58; also R. C. Smail, 'Latin Syria and the West 1149–1187', *Transactions of the Royal Historical Society*, 5th series, 19 (1969), 1ff. On the civil war of 1152 and the events which led up to it see Mayer (above n.32a); H. E. Mayer, 'Kaiserrecht und Heiliges Land', *Aus Reichsgeschichte und Nordischer Geschichte* (1972) will deal with the interventions of European rulers in the Latin Kingdom, especially with the spectacular embassy of Patriarch Heraclius (see above p. 135f.), and will advance the hypothesis that the patriarch was, in fact, attempting to overthrow the ruling dynasty of Jerusalem and may have based his attempt on a political theory which allowed European rulers, especially the Emperor, a right to intervene in Outremer; Chalandon and Herzog (above n.26); C. M. Brand, *Byzantium Confronts the West 1180–1204* (1968). See also the article on Nur al-Din in the *Encyclopedia of Islam*. On the

Islamic anti-Frankish propaganda the basic work is E. Sivan, *L'Islam et la croisade. Idéologie et propagande dans les réactions musulmanes aux croisades* (1968), together with the preparatory articles by Sivan in: *Studia Islamica*, 27 (1967); *Revue de l'histoire des religions*, 172 (1967), and *Revue des études islamiques*, 1967 (1968).

43. G. Schlumberger, *Renaud de Châtillon*, 2nd edn. (1923).

44. G. Schlumberger, *Campagnes du roi Amaury de Jérusalem en Egypte* (1906); G. Wiet, *L'Egypte arabe de la conquête arabe à la conquête ottomane* (Paris, no date); S. D. Goitein, 'From the Mediterranean to India', *Speculum*, 29 (1954), 181ff.

45. Article on Saladin, *Enzyklopädie des Islam*; article on Ayyubids, *Encyclopedia of Islam*, new edition. Cf. also the new interpretation of Saladin in Prawer, *Histoire* (below n.58) 1, 540ff. Prawer too does not believe that the expulsion of the Franks was the be-all and end-all of Saladin's policies (see above p. 127) right from the moment that he seized power in Cairo (1169). But when he began to intervene more and more in Syrian affairs from 1174 onwards, he recognized that the idea of a holy war against the Franks had great value as a unifying force within the Islamic world and so he exploited it for his own purposes. None the less for Saladin too the destruction of the Frankish states became increasingly important, for once in Syria he inherited the traditions of Nur ed-Din. A. Helbig, *Al-Qāḍī al-Fāḍil* (1908); S. Lane-Poole, *Saladin and the Fall of the Kingdom of Jerusalem* (1898); H. A. R. Gibb, 'The Achievement of Saladin', *Bulletin of the John Rylands Library* 35 (1952), 44ff.

46. J. L. La Monte, 'To what extent was the Byzantine Empire the Suzerain of the Latin Crusading States?', *Byzantion*, 7 (1932), 253ff.

47. B. Lewis, 'The Sources for the History of the Syrian Assassins', *Speculum*, 27 (1952), 475ff.; Lewis, 'Kamal al-Din's Biography of Rashid al-Din Sinan', *Arabica*, 13 (1966), 225ff.; Lewis, *The Assassins. A Radical Sect in Islam* (1967); C. E. Nowell, 'The Old Man of the Mountain', *Speculum*, 22 (1947), 497ff.; F. M. Chambers, 'The Troubadours and the Assassins', *Modern Language Notes*, 64 (1949), 245ff.

48. On the following cf. M. W. Baldwin, *Raymond III of Tripolis and the Fall of Jerusalem* (1936); A. C. Krey, 'William of Tyre', *Speculum*, 16 (1941), 149ff.; F. Groh, *Der Zusammenbruch des Reiches Jerusalem* (1909); L. Usseglio, *I marchesi di Monferrato in Italia ed in Oriente durante i secoli XII e XIII*, 2 vols. (1926). On the battle of Hattin cf. the articles by J. Prawer, *Israel Exploration Quarterly*, 14 (1964) and P. Herde, *Römische Quartalschrift für Altertumskunde und Kirchengeschichte*, 61 (1966).

49. General bibliography for chapter seven. Sources: Nicetas Choniates and the Arabic sources referred to in n.42; *Quellen zur Geschichte des Kreuzzuges Kaiser Friedrichs I.*, ed. A. Chroust, MGH, Scriptores rerum Germanicarum N.S. 5 (1928; containing above all the 'Ansbert' and the *Historia peregrinorum*); Ambroise, *L'Estoire de la Guerre Sainte*, ed. G. Paris (1897) with a translation into modern French; *Das Itinerarium peregrinorum*, ed. H. E. Mayer (1962; the 1864 edition by W. Stubbs is based on a later version of the chronicle); *Die lateinische Fortsetzung Wilhelms v. Tyrus*, ed. M. Salloch (1934); Ernoul, see below n.91; Roger of Hoveden, *Chronica*, vol. 3, ed. W. Stubbs (1870; since 1953 this has been recognized as the work of a participant in the crusade); Rigord, *Oeuvres*, vol. 1, ed. H. F. Delaborde (1882). Secondary works; Mayer, *Bibliographie*, nos. 2066–118; P. Zerbi, *Papato, impero e 'Res*

publica christiana' dal 1187 al 1198 (1955); G. Kleemann, *Papst Gregor VIII.* (1912); P. Munz, *Frederick Barbarossa* (1969); K. Jordan, *Friedrich Barbarossa, Kaiser des christlichen Abendlandes* (2nd edn. 1967); H. Heimpel, 'Friedrich I.', in *Neue Deutsche Biographie*, 5 (1961), 459ff.; A. Cartellieri, *Philipp II. August, König von Frankreich*, vols. 1 and 2 (1900–6); K. Norgate, *Richard the Lion Heart* (1924); H. Fichtenau, 'Akkon, Zypern und das Lösegeld für Richard Löwenherz', *Archiv für österreichische Geschichte*, 125 (1966), 11ff.; Y. Congar, 'Henry de Marcy, abbé de Clairvaux, cardinal-évêque d'Albano et légat pontifical', *Studia Anselmiana*, 43 (1958), 1ff.; Lamma, above n.35; Saladin above n.45; Conrad of Montferrat, above n.48; Henry of Champagne, below n.91.

50. It is significant that Henry II of England forestalled every attempt by his sons to go on crusade in his place, even though this would have rid him of them, at least temporarily.

51. F. A. Cazel, 'The Tax of 1185 in Aid of the Holy Land', *Speculum*, 30 (1955), 385ff.

52. Brand (above n.42); S. O. Riezler, 'Der Kreuzzug Kaiser Friedrichs I.', *Forschungen zur deutschen Geschichte*, 10 (1870), 1ff.; K. Fischer, *Geschichte des Kreuzzuges Kaiser Friedrichs I.* (1870). On the German–Byzantine conflict 1189/90 cf. K. Zimmert, *Byzantinische Zeitschrift*, 12 (1903), 42ff.; 11 (1902), 303ff.; C. Cahen, 'Selğukides, Turcomans et Allemands au temps de la troisième croisade', *Wiener Zeitschrift für die Kunde des Morgenlandes*, 56 (1960), 21ff.; P. Scheffer-Boichorst, *Das Grab Barbarossas*, in *Gesammelte Schriften*, 2 (1905), 154ff.

53. M. Tumler, *Der Deutsche Orden im Werden, Wachsen und Wirken bis 1400* (1955); K. Forstreuter, *Der Deutsche Orden am Mittelmeer* (1967); W. Hubatsch, 'Montfort und die Bildung des Deutschordensstaates im Hl. Lande', *Göttinger Nachrichten*, phil.-hist. Klasse (1966), no. 5; M. L. Favreau, *Studien zur Frühgeschichte des Deutschen Ordens* (unpublished Ph.D. thesis Kiel 1972; to be published) takes issue with the older views and adds significantly to our knowledge of the German Hospital in Jerusalem in the 12th century and of the early Palestinian history of the Teutonic Knights; E. Strehlke, *Tabulae ordinis Theutonici* (1869); H. Prutz, *Die Besitzungen des Deutschen Ordens im Hl. Lande* (1877); Mayer, *Bibliographie*, nos. 57, 118–20, 1439–50, 3622–47.

54. R. Röhricht, 'Die Belagerung von 'Akkā', *Forschungen zur deutschen Geschichte*, 16 (1876), 483ff.

55. Peter of Blois, *De Hierosolymitana peregrinatione acceleranda*, in Migne, *Patrologia Latina*, 207, 1057ff.; *Passio Reginaldi*, ibid., 957ff.; Ralph Niger, *De re militari et triplici via peregrinationis Jerosolimitanae*, ed. G. B. Flahiff, *Medieval Studies*, 9 (1947), 179ff.

56. H. Grundmann, *Neue Forschungen über Joachim v. Fiore*, (1950), 48ff.; Grundmann, 'Joachim v. Fiore und Rainer v. Ponza', *Deutsches Archiv*, 16 (1960), 499ff.

57. H. Toeche, *Kaiser Heinrich VI.* (1867); E. Traub, *Der Kreuzzugsplan Kaiser Heinrichs VI.* (1910); W. Leonhardt, *Der Kreuzzugsplan Kaiser Heinrichs VI.* (1913), but on this see also Dölger, *Regesten der Kaiserurkunden des Oströmischen Reiches*, no. 1619.

58. Of great value for this chapter are the works by Prawer, Richard, Cahen, and La Monte cited in the following notes. Particularly important for the

kingdom of Jerusalem in general are: J. Prawer, *Histoire du royaume latin de Jérusalem*, vols. 1 and 2 (1969 and 1970); J. Richard, *Le royaume latin de Jérusalem*, (1953); R. Röhricht, *Geschichte des Königreichs Jerusalem* (1898); D. C. Munro, *The Kingdom of the Crusaders* (Reprint 1966); J. L. La Monte, *Feudal Monarchy in the Latin Kingdom of Jerusalem* (1932); A. Ben-Ami, *Social Change in a Hostile Environment. The Crusaders' Kingdom of Jerusalem* (1969) is unhelpful; J. Prawer and M. Benvenisti, *Atlas of Israel* IX/10 (1970); C. du Cange, *Les familles d'Outremer*, ed. E. G. Rey (1869; genealogies); Cahen, *Féodalité* (below, n. 106). For reasons of space this chapter concentrates on the kingdom of Jerusalem. On the other crusader states see: C. Cahen, *La Syrie du Nord à l'époque des croisades et la principauté franque d'Antioche* (1940) and J. Richard, *Le comté de Tripoli sous la dynastie toulousaine* (1945). J. Richard, *Documents chypriotes* (below, n.89) is particularly informative on the subject of Cyprus.

59. On the history of the settlement see J. Prawer, 'The Assise de Teneure and the Assise de Vente. A Study of Landed Property in the Latin Kingdom', *Economic History Review*, 2nd Series, 4 (1951), 77ff.; Prawer, 'The Settlement of the Latins in Jerusalem', *Speculum*, 27 (1952), 490ff.; Prawer, 'Colonization Activities in the Latin Kingdom of Jerusalem', *Revue belge de philologie et d'histoire*, 29 (1951), 1063ff.; R. B. C. Huygens, 'Un nouveau texte du traité "De constructione castri Saphet"', *Studi medievali*, 3rd Series, 6 (1965), 355ff.; J. Prawer, 'Jewish Resettlement in Crusader Jerusalem', *Ariel. A Review of the Arts and Sciences in Israel*, no. 19 (1967), 60ff.

60. On the king and nobility see J. Prawer, 'Les premiers temps de la féodalité dans le royaume latin de Jérusalem', *Tijdschrift voor rechtsgeschiedenis*, 22 (1954), 401ff.; Prawer, 'La noblesse et le régime féodal du royaume latin de Jérusalem', *Le Moyen Age*, 65 (1959), 41ff., English translation in F. L. Cheyette, *Lordship and Community in Medieval Europe* (1968), 156ff.; Prawer, 'Étude sur le droit des Assises de Jérusalem: droit de confiscation et droit d'exhérédation', *Revue historique de droit français et étranger*, 4th Series, 39 (1961), 520ff.; 40 (1962) 29ff. On the feudal geography see Röhricht, 'Studien zur mittelalterlichen Geographie und Topographie Syriens', *Zeitschrift des Deutschen Palästinavereins*, 10 (1887), 195ff., and the much more penetrating articles by G. Beyer in the same journal (Mayer, *Bibliographie*, nos. 3012, 3019, 3028, 3057, 3062, 4402); index by O. H. Schmidt, ibid., 86 (1970), 117ff.; on the nobility see also Riley-Smith, below n.66.

61. The Assises of the Haute Cour: *RHC, Lois* 1; M. Grandclaude, *Étude critique sur les livres des Assises de Jérusalem* (1923).

62. J. Richard, 'Le statut de femme dans l'Orient latin', *Recueils de la Société Jean Bodin*, 12 (1962), 377ff.

63. R. C. Smail, *Crusading Warfare* (1956); P. Deschamps, *Les châteaux des croisés en Terre Sainte*, 2 vols., 2 albums (1934–9).

64. W. Hotzelt, *Kirchengeschichte Palästinas im Zeitalter der Kreuzzüge* (1940); R. Hiestand is preparing the Regesta of the papal charters for the Holy Land (Oriens pontificius); cf. his *Vorarbeiten zum Oriens pontificius I* (1972). While it is true that the Investiture Contest was not an issue in Palestine (see above p. 169), it is equally true that at a turning point in the struggle the opposition against the Emperor Henry V who had imprisoned the pope in 1111 was first voiced in the Latin Kingdom by the papal legate Kuno of Praeneste, who excommunicated the Emperor at a time when the Roman

curia was still totally inactive; cf. R. Hiestand, 'Legat, Kaiser und Basileus', *Aus Reichsgeschichte und Nordischer Geschichte* (1972); he is also preparing a detailed study of the papal legates in the Holy Land. C. H. Kohler, 'Un rituel et un bréviaire du St. Sépulcre de Jérusalem', in *Mélanges pour servir à l'histoire de l'Orient latin et des croisades* (1906), 286ff.; H. E. Mayer, 'Das Pontifikale von Tyrus und die Krönung der lateinischen Könige von Jerusalem', *Dumbarton Oaks Papers*, 21 (1967), 141ff.; Runciman (above n.1); P. Kawerau, *Die jakobitische Kirche im Zeitalter der syrischen Renaissance* (2nd edn. 1960); R. W. Crawford, 'William of Tyre and the Maronites', *Speculum*, 30 (1955), 222ff.; K. S. Salibi, 'The Maronite Church in the Middle Ages and its Union with Rome', *Oriens Christianus*, 42 (1958), 92ff.; cf. also below n.108. On the 'Easter Fire miracle' see A. S. Tritton, 'The Easter Fire at Jerusalem', *Journal of the Royal Asiatic Society* (1963), 249ff.

65. The Assises des Bourgeois: *RHC, Lois* 2; J. Prawer, 'Étude préliminaire sur les sources et la composition du "Livre des Assises" des Bourgeois', *Revue historique de droit français et étranger*, 4th Series, 32 (1954), 198ff., 358ff.

66. J. L. La Monte, 'The Communal Movement in Syria in the Thirteenth Century', *Haskins Anniversary Essays*, ed. C. Taylor (1929), 117ff.; J. Prawer, 'Estates, Communities and the Constitution of the Latin Kingdom', *Proceedings of the Israel Academy of Sciences and Humanities*, II, no. 6 (1966), reprinted in F. L. Cheyette, *Lordship and Community in Medieval Europe* (1968), 376ff.; H. E. Mayer, 'On the Beginnings of the Communal Movement in the Holy Land: The Commune of Tyre', *Traditio*, 24 (1968), 443ff.; H. E. Mayer, 'Zwei Kommunen in Akkon?', *Deutsches Archiv*, 26 (1971); J. Riley-Smith, 'The *Assise sur la ligece* and the Commune of Acre', *Traditio*, 27 (1971), 179ff.; id., 'A Note on Confraternities in the Latin Kingdom of Jerusalem', *Bulletin of the Institute of Historical Research*, 44 (1971), 301ff.

67. W. Heyd, *Histoire du commerce du Levant au moyen âge*, 2 vols. (1885-6); A. Schaube, *Handelsgeschichte der romanischen Völker des Mittelmeergebietes bis zum Ende der Kreuzzüge* (1906); E. Bach, *La cité de Gênes au XIIe siècle* (1955); H. E. Mayer, *Marseilles Levantehandel und ein akkonensisches Fälscheratelier des 13. Jahrhunderts* (1972); C. Cahen, 'Orient latin et commerce du Levant', *Bulletin de la Faculté des Lettres de Strasbourg*, 29 (1950-1), 328ff.; J. Richard, 'Sur un passage du "Pèlerinage du Charlemagne": Le marché de Jérusalem', *Revue belge de philologie et d'histoire*, 43 (1965), 552ff.; C. Cahen, 'A propos des coutumes du marché d'Acre', *Revue historique de droit français et étranger*, 4th Series, 41 (1963), 287ff.; Cahen, 'L'alun avant Phocée', *Revue d'Histoire économique et sociale*, 41 (1963), 433ff.; cf. also, and in particular with regard to the Italian settlements, Mayer, *Bibliographie*, nos. 2489, 2498-9, 4278-97, 4302, 4473-511; S. Y. Labib, *Handelsgeschichte Ägyptens im Spätmittelalter* (1965); G. Wiet, 'Les marchands d'épices sous les sultans mamlouks', *Cahiers d'histoire égyptienne*, 7 (1955), 81ff.

67a. E. Sivan, 'Réfugiés syro-palestiniens au temps des croisades', *Revue des études islamiques*, 1967 (1968), 135ff.

68. J. Prawer, 'Étude de quelques problèmes agraires et sociaux d'une seigneurie croisée au XIIIe siècle', *Byzantion*, 22 (1952), 5ff.; 23 (1953) 143ff.; C. Cahen, 'Le régime rural syrien au temps de la domination franque', *Bulletin de la Faculté des Lettres de Strasbourg*, 29 (1950-1), 286ff.; J. Richard, 'Le casal de Psimolofo et la vie rurale en Chypre au XIVe siècle', *Mélanges d'Archéologie et d'Histoire*, 59 (1947), 121ff. On the *rais*, especially on the distinction between town and village *rais*, as well as on other lower officials

see the very fine paper by J. Riley-Smith, 'Some Lesser Officials in Latin Syria', *English Historical Review*, 87 (1972), p. 1ff.

69. C. Enlart, *Les monuments des croisés dans le royaume de Jérusalem*, 2 vols., 2 albums (1925–8); M. Barash, 'The Nazareth Capitals', *Eretz-Israel*, 7 (1964), 125ff.; Z. Goldmann, 'The Hospice of the Knights of St. John in Akko', *Archaeology*, 19, no. 3 (1966), 182ff.; G. Schlumberger, *Numismatique de l'Orient latin* (1878); Schlumberger, *Sigillographie de l'Orient latin* (1943); H. Buchthal, *Miniature Painting in the Latin Kingdom of Jerusalem* (1957); K. Weitzmann, 'Thirteenth Century Crusader Icons on Mount Sinai', *The Art Bulletin*, 45 (1963), 179ff.; Weitzmann, 'Icon Painting in the Crusader Kingdom', *Dumbarton Oakes Papers*, 20 (1966), 49ff.; *Chanson des Chétifs*, see above n. 34; R. B. C. Huygens, *Latijn in 'Outremer'. Een Blik op de Latijnse letterkunde der Kruisvaarderstaten in het Nabije OOsten* (1964); J. Richard, 'La Fauconnerie de Jean de Francières et ses sources', *Le Moyen Age*, 67 (1963), 893ff.

70. General bibliography for the Fourth Crusade. Sources: Innocent III, *Epistolae*, in Migne, *Patrologia Latina*, 214–217; Geoffrey of Villehardouin, *La conquête de Constantinople*, ed. E. Faral, 2 vols. (1938–9), English translation by M. R. B. Shaw (1963); Robert de Clari, *La conquête de Constantinople*, ed. P. Lauer (1924). Gunther of Pairis, *De expugnatione Constantinopolitana*, ed. P. Riant (1875); Nicetas, above n. 42. Secondary works: There is no monograph on the Fourth Crusade which fully satisfies the requirements of modern scholarship (though see below n. 71, particularly Frolow, and also Daly, above n. 38). On questions of detail see the works cited by Mayer, *Bibliographie*, nos. 2119–59; F. Kempf, *Papsttum und Kaisertum bei Innozenz III.* (1954); H. Roscher, *Papst Innozenz III. und die Kreuzzüge* (1969); A. Luchaire, *Innocent III. La Question d'Orient* (1907); H. Kretschmayr, *Geschichte von Venedig*, 2 vols. (1905–20); E. Winkelmann, *König Philipp v. Schwaben* (1873); Boniface of Montferrat, above n.48; E. H. McNeal, 'Fulk of Neuilly and the Tournament of Ecry', *Speculum*, 28 (1953), 371ff.; D. E. Queller, 'L'évolution du rôle de l'ambassadeur: les pleins pouvoirs et le traité de 1201 entre les croisés et les Vénitiens', *Le Moyen Age*, 67 (1961), 479ff.

71. The best summary of the nineteenth-century debate is E. Gerland, 'Der vierte Kreuzzug und seine Probleme', *Neue Jahrbücher für das klassische Altertum*, 13 (1904), 505ff. Since then the most important contributions have been H. Gregoire, 'The Question of the Diversion of the Fourth Crusade. An Old Controversy solved by a Latin Adverb', *Byzantion*, 15 (1940/1), 158ff.; J. Folda, 'The Fourth Crusade. Some Reconsiderations', *Byzantinoslavica*, 26 (1967), 277ff.; Brand (above n.42); A. Frolow, *Recherches zur la déviation de la IVe croisade vers Constantinople* (1955). The pope is held responsible for the diversion by M. A. Zaborov in *Vizantiiskii vremennik*, N.S. 5 (1952), 152ff. and by S. de Mundo Ló, *Cruzados en Bizancio. La cuarta cruzada a la luz de las fuentes latinas y orientales* (1957). The most recent studies of the Venetian share in what happened are: R. Cessi, 'Venezia e la quarta crociata', *Archivio veneto*, 81 (1951), 1ff.; Cessi, 'L'eredità di Enrico Dandolo', *Archivio veneto*, 91 (1960), 1ff. A summary of recent discussion: D. E. Queller and S. J. Stratton, 'A Century of Controversy on the Fourth Crusade', *Studies in Medieval and Renaissance History*, 6 (1969), 233ff.

72. J. Ebersolt, *Orient et Occident*, 2 (1929), 19ff.

73. Latin Empire. Sources: Villehardouin (until 1207) and Robert de Clari (until 1216), above n. 70; Henry of Valenciennes, *Histoire de l'Empereur Henri*

de Constantinople, ed. J. Longnon (1948); Georgios Akropolites, *Opera*, vol. 1, ed. A. Heisenberg (1903); A. Heisenberg, 'Neue Quellen zur Geschichte des lateinischen Kaisertums und der Kirchenunion', *Sitzungsberichte der Bayerischen Akademie der Wissenschaften*, 1922–3. Secondary works: J. Longnon, *L'Empire latin de Constantinople et la principauté de Morée* (1949); E. Gerland, *Geschichte des lateinischen Kaiserreiches von Konstantinopel*, 1 (1905); K. Hopf, *Geschichte Griechenlands von Beginn des Mittelalters bis auf die neuere Zeit*, 2 vols. (1867–8). In addition there are the important articles by R. L. Wolff in *Traditio*, 2 (1944); 6, (1948); *Speculum*, 23 (1948); 27, (1952); 29, (1954); *Dumbarton Oaks Papers*, 8 (1954); P. E. Schramm (and R. Elze), *Herrschaftszeichen und Staatssymbolik*, 3 (1956) 837ff.; J. Deér in *Byzantinische Zeitschrift* 54 (1961), 306ff, places more emphasis on the Byzantine influence on the coronation of the Latin emperors; W. Norden (above p. 289); L. Santifaller, *Beiträge zur Geschichte des lateinischen Patriarchats von Konstantinopel und der venezianischen Urkunde* (1938); E. A. R. Brown, 'The Cistercians in the Latin Empire of Constantinople and Greece', *Traditio*, 14 (1958), 63ff.; R. Clair, 'Les filles d'Hautecombe dans l'Empire latin de Constantinople', *Analecta sacri ordinis Cisterciensis*, 17 (1961), 261ff.; F. Thiriet, *La Romanie vénitienne au moyen âge* (1959); Mayer, *Bibliographie*, nos. 2771–88, 3873–85 (Church history).

74. K. Hopf, *Chroniques gréco-romanes inédites ou peu connues* (1873); *Chronicle of Morea* (editions in several languages, see Mayer, *Bibliographie*, no. 1215); there is an English translation by H. E. Lurier, *Crusaders as Conquerors* (1963); *Les Assises de Romanie*, ed. G. Recoura (1930); on their sources, application and diffusion see D. Jacoby, *La féodalité en Grèce médiévale* (1971); Longnon, above n.73; E. Dade, *Versuche zur Wiedererrichtung der lateinischen Herrschaft in Konstantinopel 1261–1310* (1937); D. J. Geanakoplos, *Emperor Michael Palaeologus and the West* (1959); Mayer, *Bibliographie*, nos. 2789–814

75. A. Rubio i Lluch, *Diplomatari de l'Orient Català* (1947); R. J. Loenertz, 'Athènes et Néopatras. Regestes et documents pour servir à l'histoire (ecclésiastique) des duchés catalans', *Archivum Fratrum Praedicatorum*, 25 (1955), 100ff.; 28 (1958), 5ff.; Ramon Muntaner, *Cronica*, ed. A. de Bofarull y Broca, 2 vols. (1860–6), English translation by Lady Goodenough (1920); Georgios Pachymeres, *De Michaele et Andronico Palaeologis libri XIII*, ed. I. Bekker, 2 vols. (1835); R. I. Burns, 'The Catalan Company and the European Powers 1305–1311', *Speculum*, 29 (1954), 751ff.; K. M. Setton, *Catalan Domination of Athens 1311–1388* (1948); Mayer, *Bibliographie*, nos. 2247–65, 2824–42.

76. H. Pissard, *La guerre sainte en pays chrétien* (1912); P. Belperron, *La croisade contre les Albigeois et l'union de Languedoc à la France* (1942).

77. There is no satisfactory modern monograph. For the older works see Mayer, *Bibliographie*, nos. 2160–6. Still valuable is Alphandéry (above p. 288), 2, 115ff.; G. Miccoli, 'La crociata dei fanciulli del 1212', *Studi medievali*, 3rd Series, 2 (1961), 407ff.

78. General bibliography for chapter ten. Sources: James of Vitry, *Lettres*, ed. R. B. C. Huygens (1960); *Historia Orientalis*, ed. J. Bongars, *Gesta Dei per Francos* (1611), 1047ff.; *Die Schriften des Kölner Domscholasters ....* *Oliverus*, ed. H. Hoogeweg (1894); R. Röhricht, below n. 82. The collection of charters known as the 'Collection Courtois' has now been shown to be a forgery; cf. R. H. Bautier, *Comptes-rendus des séances de l'Académie des Inscriptions et Belles-Lettres* (1956), 382ff. Secondary works: H. L. Gottschalk,

Al-Malik al-Kāmil von Egypten und seine Zeit (1958); R. Röhricht, *Studien zur Geschichte des fünften Kreuzzuges* (1891); H. Hoogeweg, 'Der Kreuzzug von Damiette', *Mitteilungen des Instituts für österreichische Geschichtsforschung*, 8 (1887), 188ff.; 9 (1888) 249ff.; Mayer, *Bibliographie*, nos. 2171–80 J. Clausen, *Papst Honorius III.* (1895); J. P. Donovan, *Pelagius and the Fifth Crusade* (1950); on John of Brienne see below n.91.

79. F. Kempf, 'Das Rommersdorfer Briefbuch des 13. Jh.', *Mitteilungen des österreichischen Instituts für Geschichtsforschung*, Ergänzungsband, 12 (1933), 502ff.

80. The decree is printed in Mansi, *Sacrorum conciliorum nova et amplissima collectio*, 22, 1058ff. On the crusading taxes see Mayer, *Bibliographie*, nos. 4575–81 and A. Gottlob, *Die päpstlichen Kreuzzugssteuern des 13. Jahrhunderts* (1892).

81. G. Golubovich, *Biblioteca bio-bibliografica della Terra Santa e dell' Oriente francescano*, 1 (1906), 1ff.; M. Roncaglia, 'San Francesco d'Assisi in Oriente', *Studi francescani*, 50 (1953), 97ff.; G. Basetti-Sani, *Mohammed et St. François* (1959); C. Dawson, *The Mongol Mission* (1955; texts); A. van den Wyngaert, *Sinica franciscana*, 1 (1929; texts); G. Soranzo, *Il papato, l'Europa cristiana e i Tartari* (1930); P. Pelliot, 'Les Mongols et la papauté', *Revue de l'Orient chrétien*, 23 (1922–3), 3ff.; 24 (1924), 225ff.; 28 (1931–2), 3ff.; J. Richard, 'La papauté et les missions catholiques en Orient au moyen âge', *Mélanges d'Archaéologie et d'Histoire*, 58 (1941–6), 248ff.; B. Altaner, *Die Dominikanermissionen des 13. Jahrhunderts* (1924).

82. On the prophecies: R. Röhricht, *Quinti belli sacri scriptores minores* (1879); 203ff.; *Liber Clementis*: James of Vitry, *Lettres* (see n.78), 152ff.; *Relatio de Davide* and texts concerning Prester John, ibid., 141ff. and F. Zarncke, 'Der Priester Johannes', *Abhandlungen der philol.-hist. Klasse der Sächsischen Gesellschaft der Wissenschaften*, 7 (1879), 827ff.; 8 (1883), 1ff.; V. Slessarev, *Prester John. The Letter and the Legend* (1959). The best summary of research is J. Richard, 'L'Extrême-Orient légendaire au moyen âge. Roi David et Prêtre Jean', *Annales d'Ethiopie*, 2 (1957), 225ff. Especially important is P. Pelliot, 'Mélanges sur l'époque des croisades', *Mémoires de l'Académie des Inscriptions et Belles-Lettres*, 44 (1960), 73ff.

83. From this point on the—in any event somewhat dubious—numbering of the crusades lacks all consistency. Many scholars do not count the Damietta crusade at all and, for them, Frederick II's crusade of 1228/9 is the fifth and Saint Louis's first crusade (1248–50) the sixth. Others count the Damietta crusade, but not Frederick II's. Still others count the Damietta crusade as the fifth, Frederick II's as the sixth, and Saint Louis's as the seventh.

84. On the *passagium*, Alphandéry (above p. 288), 2, 131ff. Schaube (above n.67), 195ff., 201ff.

85. For the Christian picture of the heathen: F. W. Wentzlaff-Eggebert (above p. 289), 247ff. For knowledge of Islam: Southern and Daniel (above p. 289), especially Daniel, 309ff. (on the question of idolatry); U. Monneret de Villard, *Lo studio dell' Islam in Europa nel XII e nel XIII secolo* (1944). Translations of the Koran: M.-Th. d'Alverny, 'Deux traductions latines du Coran au moyen âge', *Archives d'histoire doctrinale et littéraire du moyen âge*, 16 (1947–8), 69ff.; J. Kritzeck, *Peter the Venerable and Islam* (1964); P. Herde, 'Christians and Saracens at the Time of the Crusades. Some Comments of Contemporary Medieval Canonists', *Studia Gratiana*, 12 (1967), 359ff.

86. There are no special sources for Frederick II's crusade; but see below n.91. List of charters: Böhmer–Ficker–Winkelmann, *Regesta imperii* V, 5 vols. (1881–1901). The most important manifestos and documents are in: MGH, Constitutiones, 2 (1896). There are important papal letters in: MGH, Epist. saec. XIII, 3 vols. (1883–94). Main secondary works: H. Grundmann, in B. Gebhardt, *Handbuch der deutschen Geschichte*, *1* (9th edn. 1970), 446ff., with full references to the specialist literature; H. M. Schaller, *Kaiser Friedrich II.*, *Verwandler der Welt* (1964); E. Kantorowicz, *Kaiser Friedrich II.*, 2 vols. (1927–31); R. Röhricht, 'Die Kreuzfahrt Kaiser Friedrichs II., in *Beiträge zur Geschichte der Kreuzzüge*, 1 (1874) 1ff.; E. Kestner, *Der Kreuzzug Friedrichs II.*, (1873); on the coronation of 1229 in Jerusalem cf. Mayer (above n.64); Gottschalk, *Al-Kāmil* (above n.78), 152ff.; H. Heimpel, 'Hermann von Salza', in *Der Mensch in seiner Gegenwart* (1954), 87ff.; W. Jacobs, *Patriarch Gerold von Jerusalem* (1905); E. Sivan, 'Le caractère sacré de Jérusalem dans l'Islam aux XIIe–XIIIe siècles', *Studia Islamica*, 27 (1967), 149ff. On the question of Cyprus see below n.91.

87. The apparently peculiar lengths of time arranged for truces are the results of the difference between the Christian and Muslim year.

88. F. Kampers, *Die deutsche Kaiseridee in Prophetie und Sage* (1896), 73ff.; H. M. Schaller, 'Das Relief an der Kanzel der Kathedrale von Bitonto: ein Denkmal der Kaiseridee Friedrichs II.', *Archiv für Kulturgeschichte*, 45 (1963), 295ff. The controversy over Frederick II's 'self-coronation' between A. Brackmann and E. Kantorowicz (*Historische Zeitschrift*, 140, (1929), 534ff.; 141 (1930), 457ff.) was not very fruitful.

89. General bibliography for Cyprus. Sources: L. de Mas-Latrie, *Documents nouveaux servant de preuves à l'histoire de l'île de Chypre sous le règne des princes de la maison de Lusignan* (1882); J. L. La Monte, 'A Register of the Cartulary of the Cathedral of Santa Sophia of Nicosia', *Byzantion*, 5 (1929–30), 439ff.; J. Richard, *Documents chypriotes des Archives du Vatican* (1962); *Les Gestes des Chiprois*, ed. G. Raynaud (1887), also in *RHC Arm*. 2, 651ff.; Leontios Machairas, *Recital Concerning the Sweet Land of Cyprus entitled 'Chronicle'*, ed. R. M. Dawkins, 2 vols. (1932); *Chroniques de Chypre d'Amadi et de Strambaldi*, ed. R. de Mas-Latrie, 2 vols. (1891–3); Florio Bustron, *Chronique de l'île de Chypre*, ed. R. de Mas-Latrie (1886); Francesco Balducci Pegolotti, *La pratica della mercatura*, ed. A. Evans (1936). Secondary works: G. Hill, *A History of Cyprus*, vols. 2 and 3 (1948); L. de Mas-Latrie, *Histoire de l'île de Chypre sous le règne des princes de la maison de Lusignan*, 3 vols. (1852–61; vols. 2 and 3 print source material); on the capture of Alexandria in 1365 see Mayer, *Bibliographie*, nos. 2275–80; J. Richard, 'La révolution de 1369 dans le royaume de Chypre', *Bibliothèque de l'École des Chartes*, 110 (1952) 108ff.; L. de Mas-Latrie, 'Histoire des archevêques latins de l'île de Chypre', *Archives de l'Orient latin*, 2a (1884), 207ff.; J. Richard, 'Le royaume de Chypre et le Grand Schisme', *Comptes-rendus des séances de l'Académie des Inscriptions et Belles-Lettres*, 1965 (1966), 498ff.; C. Enlart, *L'art gothique et de la Renaissance en Chypre*, 2 vols. (1899); Mayer, *Bibliographie*, nos. 2900–20, 3901–12.

90. W. Hubatsch, 'Der Deutsche Orden und die Reichslehnschaft über Cypern', *Nachrichten der Akademie der Wissenschaften in Göttingen* (1955), 245ff.

91. Crusader states 1192–1247. Sources. P. Richter, 'Beiträge zur Historiographie in den Kreuzfahrerstaaten', *Mitteilungen des Instituts für öster-*

reichische Geschichtsforschung, 13 (1892), 255ff.; 15 (1894), 561ff. French translations and continuations of William of Tyre: *Estoire d'Eracles, RHC Hoc.* 2 and *Chronique d'Ernoul et de Bernard le Trésorier*, ed. L. de Mas-Latrie (1871); *Gestes de Chiprois* (above n. 89). Among these the memoirs of Philip of Novara are particularly important and there is a separate edition by C. Kohler (1913) and an English translation by J. L. La Monte and M. J. Hubert, *The Wars of Frederick II against the Ibelins in Syria and Cyprus* (1936). A. Sanchez Candeira, 'Las cruzadas en la historiografía española de la epoca. Traduccion castellana de una redacción desconocida de los "Annales de Tierra Santa" ', *Hispania*, 20 (1960), 325ff.; *Documents relatifs à la successibilité au trône et à la régence, RHC, Lois*, 2, 397ff. On the Arabic sources see Gottschalk above n.78 and also H. W. Duda, *Die Seltschukengeschichte des Ibn Bibi* (1959; contains 1192–1280 in German). Secondary works: above n. 58; A. Herzog, above n.26; H. Bettin, *Heinrich II. von Champagne, seine Kreuzfahrt und Wirksamkeit im Hl. Lande* (1910); L. Böhm, *Johann von Brienne, König von Jerusalem, Kaiser von Konstantinopel* (1938); J. M. Buckley, 'The Problematical Octogenarianism of John of Brienne', *Speculum*, 32 (1957), 315ff.; J. L. La Monte, 'John d'Ibelin, The Old Lord of Beirut', *Byzantion*, 12 (1937), 417ff.; H. Müller, *Der Longobardenkrieg auf Zypern* (1890).

92. Lesser Armenia. Sources: *RHC Arm.* 1 and 2; S. Der Nersessian, 'The Armenian Chronicle of the Constable Smpad or of the "Royal Historian" ', *Dumbarton Oaks Papers*, 13 (1959), 141ff.; cf. also n.98; V. Langlois, *Le trésor des chartes d'Arménie* (1863). Secondary works: article on Arminya, *Encyclopedia of Islam*, new edition; L. M. Alishan, *Léon le Magnifique* (1888); Alishan, *Sissouan ou l'Arméno-Cilicie* (1899); F. Tournebize, *Histoire politique et religieuse de l'Arménie* (1910); W. H. Rüdt-Collenberg, *The Rupenids, Hethumids, and Lusignans. The Structure of the Armeno-Cilician Dynasties* (1963).

93. R. Röhricht, 'Die Kreuzzüge der Grafen Theobald von Navarra und Richard von Cornwallis nach dem Hl. Lande'. *Forschungen zur deutschen Geschichte*, 26 (1886), 67ff.

94. Saint Louis's Crusade. Sources: Jean de Joinville, *Histoire de St. Louis* ed. N. de Wailly (1874), English translation by M. R. B. Shaw (1963); *Continuation de Guillaume de Tyr dite du manuscrit de Rothelin, RHC. Hoc.* 2, 483ff.; L. T. Belgrano, *Documenti inediti riguardanti le due crociate di S. Ludovico IX Re di Francia* (1859); L. J. Friedman, *Text and Iconography for Joinville's Credo* (1958). Secondary works: There is no specialist modern monograph on Louis's first crusade. E. Delaruelle, L'idée de croisade chez St. Louis', *Bulletin de littérature ecclésiastique*, 61 (1960), 241ff.; H. Wallon, *St. Louis et son temps*, 1 (1875); E. Berger, *St. Louis et Innocent IV* (1893); A. Schaube, 'Die Wechselbriefe König Ludwigs d. Hl.', *Jahrbücher für Nationalökonomie und Statistik*, 70 (1898), 603ff., 730ff.

95. J. Richard, 'La fondation d'une église latine en Orient: Damiette', *Bibliothèque de l'École des Chartes*, 120 (1962), 39ff.

96. H. L. Gottschalk, 'Die ägyptische Sultanin Sagarrat ad-Dur in Geschichte und Dichtung', *Wiener Zeitschrift für die Kunde des Morgenlandes*, 61 (1967), 41ff.; Article on Bahriyyah, *Encyclopedia of Islam*, new edition; D. Ayalon, 'Studies on the Structure of the Mamluk Army', *Bulletin of the School of Oriental and African Studies*, 15 (1953), 203ff.; 448ff.; 16 (1954) 57ff.; Ayalon, 'Le régiment Bahriya dans l'armée mamelouke', *Revue des études islamiques* (1951), 133ff.

97. Texts in Van den Wyngaert (above n.81), vol. 1; Simon de Saint-Quentin, *Histoire des Tartares*, publ. par J. Richard (1965); A. Dondaine, 'Ricoldiana, Notes sur les oeuvres de Ricoldo da Montecroce', *Archivum Fratrum Praedicatorum*, 37 (1967), 119ff.; P. Pelliot (above n.81); on the Nestorians cf. F. Nau, 'L'expansion nestorienne en Asie', *Annales du Musée Guimet*, 40 (1913), 193ff.

98. Mongols. Sources: *Die geheime Geschichte der Mongolen* (German translation by E. Haenisch, 2nd edn. 1948); P. Pelliot and L. Hambis, *Histoire des campagnes de Gengis Khan*, vol. 1 (1951). On Mongol-Armenian relations: Kirakos of Gantzag, *Histoire*, French translation by M. F. Brosset, *Deux historiens arméniens*, 1 (1870); R. P. Blake and R. N. Frye, *History of the Nations of the Archers (the Mongols) by Grigor of Akanc'* (1954). Secondary works: articles on Čingiz-Khan and Čingizids in *Encyclopedia of Islam*, new edition; Pelliot (above n.81); W. Barthold, *Zwölf Vorlesungen über die Geschichte der Türken Mittelasiens* (Reprint 1962); B. Spuler, *Geschichte der islamischen Länder. Die Mongolenzeit* (1953); Spuler, *Die Mongolen in Iran. Politik, Verwaltung und Kultur der Ilchanzeit* (1939); *The Cambridge History of Iran*, vol. 5, *The Saljuk and Mongol Periods* (1968). Especially important is the chapter by I. P. Petruschevsky on the agricultural, social, and economic developments, all the more so since Petruschevsky's fundamental work in Russian on Iranian agriculture in the fourteenth and fifteenth centuries (1960) has not yet been translated into any language except Persian. This chapter seems to throw very clearly into relief the unfortunate consequences of the Mongol invasions for the old urban civilization of Central Asia. However, B. Lewis, 'The Mongols, the Turks and the Muslim Polity', *Transaction of the Royal Historical Society*, 5th Series, 18 (1968), 49ff. cautions against overestimating the extent of Mongol destruction.

99. Sources and general secondary works for this chapter as above notes 58, 66 (Prawer), and 91. In addition, R. Röhricht, 'Études sur les derniers temps du royaume de Jérusalem', *Archives de l'Orient latin*, 1 (1881), 617ff.; 2a (1884), 365ff.; Röhricht, 'Der Untergang des Königreiches Jerusalem', *Mitteilungen des Instituts für österreichische Geschichtsforschung*, 15 (1894), 1ff.

100. *Annali Genovesi*, ed. C. Imperiale di Sant'Angelo, 4 (1926), 30–69; Martino da Canale, 'Cronaca Veneta', *Archivio storico italiano*, 8 (1845), 452–630; G. Caro, *Genua und die Mächte am Mittelmeer*, 2 vols. (1895–1899); R. M. Harrison and N. Firatli, 'Excavations at Saraçhane in Istanbul', *Dumbarton Oaks Papers*, 19 (1965), 231ff.

101. M. E. Quatremère, *Histoire des sultans mamlouks de l'Egypte*, 2 vols. in 4 parts (1837–42); Ibn 'Abd Az-Zāhir, *Baybars I of Egypt*, ed. F. S. Sadeque (1956); *Encyclopedia of Islam*, new edition, article on Baybars I.

102. R. Sternfeld, *Ludwigs d. Hl. Kreuzzug nach Tunis und die Politik Karls I. von Sizilien* (1896). On Charles: Mayer, *Bibliographie*, nos. 2533–42. On the crusade of Prince Edward see B. Beebe, *Edward I and the Crusades* (unpublished Ph.D. thesis St. Andrews 1970).

103. L. Gatto, *Il pontificato di Gregorio X* (1959). V. Laurent, 'La croisade et la question d'Orient sous le pontificat de Grégoire X', *Revue historique du Sud-Est européen* 22 (1945) 105ff. P. A. Throop, *Criticism of the Crusade. A Study of Public Opinion and Crusade Propaganda* (1940).

104. A. Mostaert and F. W. Cleaves, *Les lettres des 1289 et 1305 des ilkhan Argun et Öljeitü à Philippe le Bel* (1962); E. A. W. Budge, *Monks of Kûbláí Khân, Emperor of China, or the History of Rabban Sawmâ* (1928); Pelliot

(above n.81); D. Sinor, 'Les relations entre les Mongols et l'Europe jusqu'à la mort d'Arghoun et de Bela IV', *Cahiers d'Histoire mondiale*, 3 (1956), 39ff.; Mayer, *Bibliographie*, nos. 2226–37.

105. A. S. Atiya, *The Crusade in the Later Middle Ages* (1938); Atiya, *Crusade, Commerce and Culture* (1962); Mayer, *Bibliographie*, no. 2238–46, 2266–358.

106. For the old point of view cf. J. L. La Monte, 'The Significance of the Crusaders' States', *Byzantion*, 15 (1940/41), 300ff. Recent research: C. Cahen, articles on Crusades and Dhimma, *Encyclopedia of Islam*, new edition; Cahen, 'La féodalité et les institutions politiques de l'Orient latin', *Accademia nazionale dei Lincei. Fondazione A. Volta. Atti dei convegni*, 12 (1957), 167ff.; Cahen, *Autour des croisades. Points de vue d'Orient et d'Occident* (forthcoming); J. Richard, 'La vogue d'Orient dans la littérature occidentale du moyen âge', *Mélanges René Crozet*, 1 (1966), 557ff.; P. Jonin, 'Le climat de croisade des chansons de geste', *Cahiers de civilisation médiévale*, 7 (1964), 279ff.

107. H. Pirenne, *Mahomet et Charlemagne* (2nd edn. 1937); A. Riising, 'The Fate of Henry Pirenne's Thesis on the Consequences of Islamic Expansion', *Classica et Mediaevalia*, 13 (1952), 87ff.

108. M. Perlmann, 'Notes on Anti-Christian Propaganda in the Mamluk Empire', *Bulletin of the School of Oriental and African Studies*, 10 (1940–2), 843ff.; K. S. Salibi, 'The Maronites of Lebanon under Frankish and Mamluk Rule', *Arabica* 4 (1957), 288ff.; E. Sivan, 'Notes sur la situation des chrétiens à l'époque ayyubide', *Revue de l'histoire des religions*, 172 (1967), 117ff., confirms the accepted view that the change in the once essentially tolerant attitude of Islam to the Christian and other non-Muslim minorities came about during the years 1258–60 when the Christians of the East were clearly backing the Mongols. He does find isolated examples of the persecution of Christians from as early as 1219, but the central authorities never took an active part in these incidents; they either tolerated or suppressed the Muslim activists.

109. There is a different emphasis in the lucid definition of a crusade given by C. Cahen (incidentally this is the only noteworthy attempt at a definition known to me): a war intended to defend or liberate one's fellow-believers. If on this point I would dissent from the opinion of this outstanding French scholar it is chiefly because it is precisely he who has shown that in 1095 the Christians of the East neither needed protection nor wished to be liberated.

110. J. Goñi Gaztambide, *Historia de la bula de la cruzada en España* (1958); article on Croisade (bulle de la) in *Dictionnaire de Droit canonique*, vol. 4 (1949), 780ff.

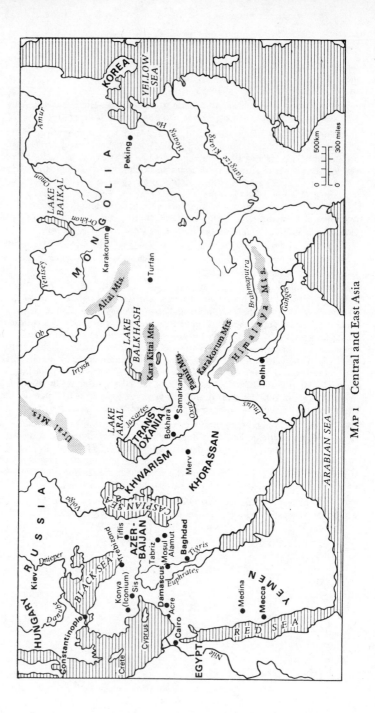

MAP 1   Central and East Asia

MAP 2 Southern Syria and Palestine

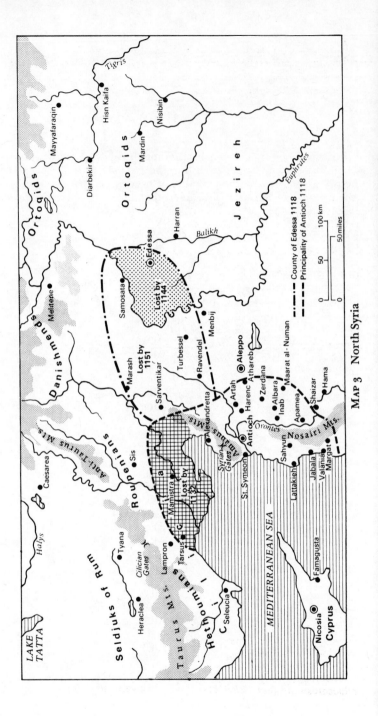

MAP 3   North Syria

INDEX

This index comprises personal names and place names as well as selected subjects. In the alphabetical listing the Arabic article *al* has not been taken into account. For a plurality of persons bearing the same name the listings are in hierarchical order, the clergy taking precedence over the laity.

Anti-Taurus Mountains, 51f.
apostasy, 156
appointments, ecclesiastical, 114, 129, 155
Apulia, 72, 79, 84, 90, 166
al-Aqsa (*Templum Salomonis*), mosque in Jerusalem, 60, 82, 126, 132, 228
Aqsonqor il-Bursuqi, ruler of Mosul, 76, 83f.
Aquinas see Saint Thomas
Aquitaine, French duchy, 69f., 90, 135.—Aquitanians, 70
Arabia, 124, 175.—Arabic language, 149, 154, 180, 275, 279f. —Arabs, 5, 16, 94, 154, 278
Aragon, 2, 66, 199f., 202
Arcadia (Peloponnese), 199
arch, pointed, 180, 279
archers, 151.—English a., 144
Archipelago, duchy, 192, 197
architecture, 180
archontes, 198
Argun, Il-Khan of Iran, 273
aristocracy, high, 133, 156f.; see also nobility
Armenia, 52, 249; see also Cilicia, Lesser Armenia.—Armenian language, 245.—Armenians, 52f., 90, 94, 117, 154, 159, 264f., 269, 272
army, Frankish, 116, 131, 161, 164.—knight's fee, 232.—turcopole fee, 232.—seasonal crusaders, 219; see also mercenaries, tactics.—Mongol army, 258f.— Muslim army, 111, 124, 126, 131; see also *iqta*.
Arnold of Toroga, Master of the Templars, 135
Arnold of Brescia, preacher, 98
Arnulf of Rohes, patriarch of Jerusalem, 47, 61f., 66, 77, 166
Arnulf, bishop of Marturano, 61
Arqa, Syrian town, 59, 62
Arrabit, knightly family, 178
Arsenal Bible, 181, 257
Arsuf, Palestinian lordship and

town, 74, 240, 267, 269.—battle of A., 144
Artah, Antiochene bishopric and town, 66, 121
Artois, French county, 253f.
Ascalon, Palestinian bishopric, county, crown demesne, town, 60–2, 74f., 77, 80, 87, 93, 115, 119f., 129, 132, 145f., 151f., 249f.; see also Jaffa-Ascalon, double county
al-Ashraf, Ayubid ruler in Mesopotamia, 210f., 215, 217, 227, 249
al-Ashraf Khalil, Mameluk sultan of Egypt, 273f.
Asia, 30, 75, 154, 214, 216, 222, 257, 259, 284f.
Asia Minor, 6f., 9, 14, 44, 48f., 53, 102–5, 138, 192, 194f., 200
Asov (Russia), 196
Assassins, Persian, 5, 260.—Syrian A. 5, 114, 125, 145f., 160, 269, 272; see also Ismailites, Nizarites
Assise de l'an et jour, 64, 150
Assise de Bilbeis, 164
Assise du coup apparent, 150
Assise sur la ligece, 119, 156, 234
Assises of Antioch, 162, 245, 265.— A. des Bourgeois, 170.—Cypriot A., 234.—A. de Jérusalem, 158. —A. de Romanie, 193, 197, 200; see also law, legislation
Assisi (Italy), 214
Asturia-Leon, Spanish kingdom, 2
Aswan, Egyptian town, 215
Athens, duchy and town, 194, 197, 199f.
Athlit see Castle of the Pilgrims
Atsiz, Turcoman chief, 6
Attalia (Anatolia), 105
Attica (Greece), 194
auditor, royal, 162
Austin canons, 166, 209
Austria, 69, 106, 143, 146, 209
Auvergne, French county, 135, 152
Auxerre, French county, 194
Avignon (France), 238, 275
Ayub, Saladin's father, 123